Institutional Roots of India's Security Policy

Institutional Roots of India's Security Policy

Edited by

MILAN VAISHNAV

OXFORD
UNIVERSITY PRESS

OXFORD
UNIVERSITY PRESS

Great Clarendon Street, Oxford, OX2 6DP,
United Kingdom

Oxford University Press is a department of the University of Oxford.
It furthers the University's objective of excellence in research, scholarship,
and education by publishing worldwide. Oxford is a registered trade mark of
Oxford University Press in the UK and in certain other countries

Published in the United States of America by Oxford University Press
198 Madison Avenue, New York, NY 10016, United States of America

British Library Cataloguing in Publication Data

Data available

Library of Congress Control Number: 2023951792

ISBN 978–0–19–889461–2

DOI: 10.1093/oso/9780198894612.001.0001

Acknowledgements

Any project of a collaborative nature necessarily depends on the goodwill and assistance of a great many friends and colleagues. This volume is no different.

I would like to begin by expressing my gratitude to our wonderful chapter authors and fellow collaborators. Despite the difficulties of the pandemic and the limits on travel and in-person meetings, they managed to produce unique insights that will shed light on the institutional roots of India's security policy for decades to come. I would like to thank each and every one of them for their dedication, flexibility, and patience. I am especially grateful to my friend and colleague, Rudra Chaudhuri, who helped conceptualize this volume and make it a reality. I would also like to acknowledge the generous support of my employer, the Carnegie Endowment for International Peace, which provided seed funding to make this project a reality.

In March 2021, in the middle of the pandemic, we held a virtual authors' workshop organized by Carnegie India. I am grateful to Rahul Bhatia, Rudra Chaudhuri, Shibani Mehta, Raghuveer Nidumolu, and Shreyas Shende for logistical support in arranging this workshop. For the workshop, we were fortunate to recruit a stellar group of discussants who helped review and ultimately improve the chapters in this volume. I owe special thanks to Christopher Clary, Walter Ladwig III, Amitabh (Tony) Mathur, Rajesh Rajagopalan, and Joshua White. Contributors also benefited from input and comments from several other workshop participants, including Tanvi Madan, Anit Mukherjee, and Constantino Xavier.

I also owe special thanks to Cooper Hewell, a former Carnegie colleague, who lent his considerable editorial talents to getting all of the chapters in shape for submission. I express my gratitude to Caroline Duckworth, Aislinn Familetti, and Caroline Mallory for their help in editing and formatting the chapters and to Caroline and Navroz Singh for additional research assistance. Kathryn Hockman, Randi Kimble,

Emeizmi Mandagi, and Rachel Osnos helped us stay on top of the logistics of the project.

When I approached Oxford University Press about this volume in early 2021, they were extremely enthusiastic from the start. Thanks, above all, to Barun Sarkar and Sohini Ghosh for shepherding this volume through the editorial and peer-review processes. Thanks also to Amrita Brahmo, Barbara Ball, and Praveena A. for valuable production assistance. I acknowledge the helpful comments of several peer reviewers, both at the book proposal and manuscript submission stages.

This volume was a team effort in the best sense of the phrase, and I remain grateful to all who had a hand in bringing it to life.

Milan Vaishnav
November 2023

Contents

Figures

Tables

Abbreviations

AMRAAM	Advanced Medium-Range Air-to-Air Missile
ADA	Aeronautical Development Agency
AddlSP	Additional Superintendent of Police
AJT	Advanced Jet Trainer
ANO	Anti-Naxalite Operations
APF	Armed Police Force
AR	Assam Rifles
ARC	Aviation Research Centre
ASCON	Army Static Switched Communications Network
B. Tech	Bachelor of Technology
BADP	Border Area Development Programme
BGFs	Border Guarding Forces
BOPs	Border Outposts
BPRD	Bureau of Police Research and Development
BSF	Border Security Forces
CAG	Comptroller and Auditor General
CAPFs	Central Armed Police Forces
CBI	Central Bureau of Investigation
CCTNS	Crime and Criminal Tracking Networks
CDO	Central Design Office
CENWOSTO	Central Workshop and Stores
CIA	Central Intelligence Agency (United States)
C-i-C	Commanders-in-chief
CISF	Central Industrial Security Force
CLS	Controller of Logistical Support
CoBRA	Commando Battalion for Resolute Action
COIN	Counterinsurgency operations
COL	Chief of Logistics
COM	Chief of Material
COS	Chief of Staff
CPI	Communist Party of India
Cr.P.C.	Criminal Procedure Code
CRPF	Central Reserve Police Force
CVC	Central Vigilance Commission
CWP&A	Controller Warship Production and Acquisition
DGRR	Directorate General of the Rashtriya Rifles

DIG	Deputy Inspector General
DNC	Directorate of Naval Construction
DOI	Directorate of Indigenization
DRDO	Defence Research and Development Organization
DSPE	Delhi Special Police Establishment
DTE	Directorate
DySP	Deputy Superintendent of Police
ECOs	Emergency Commissioned Officers
EEZ	Exclusive Economic Zone
EME	Corps of Electronics and Mechanical Engineers
FIR	First Information Report
FOC-in-C	Flag Officer Commanding-in-Chief
FOGA	Flag Officer Goa Area
FONA	Flag Officer Naval Area
FOSM	Flag Officer Submarines
FY	Fiscal Year
GD	General Duty cadre
GoM	Group of Ministers
HADR	Humanitarian Assistance and Disaster Relief
HAL	Hindustan Aeronautics Limited
HQ DGAR	Headquarters Directorate General of Assam Rifles
HR	Human Resources
HUMINT	Human Intelligence Capabilities
IAF	Indian Air Force
IAS	Indian Administrative Service
IB	Intelligence Bureau
IBGs	Integrated Battle Groups
ICG	Indian Coast Guard
ICG	Intelligence Coordination Group
IGAR North	Nagaland Assam Rifles Sector
IGAR South	Manipur Assam Rifles Sector
IGAR East	Assam/Mizoram/Tripura Assam Rifles Sector
IGP	Inspector General of Police
IPC	Indian Penal Code
IPS	Indian Police Service
ISI	Inter-Services Intelligence (Pakistan)
ISRO	Indian Space Research Organisation
ITBP	Indo-Tibetan Border Police
JCOs	Junior Commissioned Officers
JD	Joint Director
JIC	Joint Intelligence Committee
KRC	Kargil Review Committee
LAC	Line of Actual Control

LIA	Lead Intelligence Agency
LoC	Line of Control
LTTE	Liberation Tigers of Tamil Eelam (Sri Lanka)
MARL	Minimum Acceptable Risk Level
MEA	Ministry of External Affairs
MHA	Ministry of Home Affairs
MNF	Mizo National Front
MoD	Ministry of Defence
MPF	Modernization of State Police Forces
NCRB	National Crime Records Bureau
NDA	National Defence Academy
NE	Non-Empanelled
NFFU	Non-Functional Financial Upgradation
NHQ	Indian Naval Headquarters
NIA	National Investigation Agency
NIIO	Naval Innovation and Indigenization Organization
NSA	National Security Advisor
NSCS	National Security Council Secretariat
NSG	National Security Guard
NTRO	National Technical Research Organization
OROP	One Rank, One Pension
ORs	Other Ranks
OSINT	Open-Source Intelligence
OTA	Officers Training Academy
PAF	Pakistani Air Force
PC Act	Prevention of Corruption Act
PLA	People's Liberation Army (China)
PP&R	Policy Planning and Research Division
PPR	Police-to-Population Ratio
PSYWAR	Psychological Warfare Division
R&AW	Research and Analysis Wing
RAF	Rapid Action Force
RAF	Royal Air Force
RAS	Research Analysis Service
RR	Rashtriya Rifles
SLL	Special and Local Laws
SLOCs	Sea Lines of Communication
SP	Superintendent of Police
SPE	Special Police Establishment
SRP	State Reserve Police
SSB	Sashastra Seema Bal
SSB	Service Selection Board
SSC	Staff Selection Commission

TBA	Tactical Battle Area
TCG	Technical Coordination Group
TECHNIT	Technical Intelligence Division
TS	Time Scale
UAPA	Unlawful Activities Prevention Act
UPA	United Progressive Alliance
UPSC	Union Public Service Commission
WESEE	Weapons and Electronics Systems Engineering Establishment
WESO	Weapons and Electronics Systems Organization

Contributors

Atul Bhardwaj is a former Indian Navy officer. He is the author of *India–American Relations (1942–62): Rooted in International Liberal Order* (Routledge, 2021). He is a columnist on strategic affairs at *Economic and Political Weekly* and an Adjunct Fellow, Institute of Chinese Studies, New Delhi. He is a graduate of the National Defence Academy, Pune, and holds a PhD in History and MA in War Studies from King's College, London.

Rahul Bhatia is an Analyst with Eurasia Group. He focuses on political, economic, and foreign policy developments in India and its neighboring countries. He was previously a Research Analyst at Carnegie India where his research focused on India's foreign and security policies, with a particular emphasis on India's military modernization and defense innovation. Rahul holds a Master's degree in Security Policy Studies from the Elliott School for International Affairs at the George Washington University.

Rudra Chaudhuri is the Director of Carnegie India. His research focuses on the diplomatic history of South Asia, contemporary security issues, and the important role of emerging technologies and digital public infrastructure in diplomacy, statecraft, and development. He and his team at Carnegie India chair and convene the Global Technology Summit, co-hosted with the Ministry of External Affairs, Government of India. He is the author of *Forged in Crisis: India and the United States Since 1947* (published in the United Kingdom by Hurst in 2013 and in the United States and South Asia by Oxford University Press and Harper Collins, respectively, in 2014). He is the editor of *War and Peace in Contemporary India* (published in the United Kingdom by Routledge in 2022). His research has been published in scholarly journals such as *The International History Review*, *Diplomacy & Statecraft*, the *Journal of Strategic Studies*, *International Affairs*, *RUSI Journal*, *India Review*, and *Defense Studies*, along with other academic and policy-focused journals.

Anirudh Deshpande is Professor in the Department of History at Delhi University. He has authored numerous books and volumes, including *Hope and Despair: Mutiny, Rebellion and Death in India, 1946* (Primus Books, 2016); *The Practice of History: Essays in Search of a New Past* (Akaar Books, 2020); and *The Rise and Fall of a Brown Water Navy: Sarkhel Kanhoji Angre and Maratha Seapower on the Arabian Sea in the 17th and 18th Centuries* (Akaar Books, 2021), among numerous others. His latest book in Hindi is called *Aitihasik Nausainik Vidroh 1946 Aur Bharatiya Jan Andolan* (Aakar Books, 2022). He is writing a volume on the Kashmir War of 1947–8 for the Indian

Ministry of Defence and has authored numerous research papers, articles, reviews, and international encyclopaedia entries. He also writes fiction in English and Hindi.

Jabin T. Jacob is Associate Professor in the Department of International Relations and Governance Studies, and Director of the Centre of Excellence for Himalayan Studies, Shiv Nadar Institution of Eminence, Delhi National Capital Region. He was formerly Fellow and Assistant Director at the Institute of Chinese Studies, Delhi. As part of his research, he has travelled in many of India's border states and visited parts of the country's disputed borders with China and Pakistan. He is also a PhD supervisor at the Naval War College, Goa. Jacob's latest publications included two co-edited special issues for the *China Report* on the Communist Party of China's 100th anniversary (February and August 2022) and a co-edited volume titled, *China's Search for 'National Rejuvenation': Domestic and Foreign Policies under Xi.*

Vineet Kapoor is a scholar working on access to justice, human rights, and evidence-based police reforms. He is also a practising police officer belonging to the Indian Police Service and has served in various capacities in India and also in United Nations Peacekeeping missions. He holds a PhD in Human Rights from Tata Institute of Social Sciences Mumbai and has been a Visiting Professor of Practice on Global Security and Justice at University of Virginia, a Visiting Scholar on Human Rights and Access to Justice at London School of Economics, a British Chevening Human Rights Fellow at the University of Essex, and contributor to the Doctrine Development group at the United Nations Department for Peacekeeping Operations. His research interests include human rights; Sustainable Development Goal 16; organizational socialization; training and police cultures; access to justice for women, children, and disadvantaged groups; community policing; conflict management; and peacekeeping.

Akshay Mangla is Associate Professor of International Business at Saïd Business School at the University of Oxford. His research examines the institutions and politics of inclusive development, with a focus on bureaucracy, public services, local governance, and state–society relations. He is the author of the book, *Making Bureaucracy Work: Norms, Education and Public Service Delivery in Rural India* (Cambridge University Press, 2022). His research has been supported by the Jameel Poverty Action Lab (J-PAL), the World Bank, the Research England Global Challenges Research Fund, the American Institute for Indian Studies, and the NSEP David L. Boren Fellowship. Prior to joining Oxford, he was an Assistant Professor at Harvard Business School. He holds a PhD in Political Science from the Massachusetts Institute of Technology, an MSc in Management Research from the University of Oxford, and a BS in Finance and BA in Philosophy from the University of Pennsylvania.

Shibani Mehta is a Senior Research Analyst with the Security Studies Program at Carnegie India. Her research focuses on India's security and foreign policies. A postgraduate from the S. Rajaratnam School of International Studies, Singapore, she writes widely on India's relationship with China, and has a keen interest in understanding policy decision-making and the role of institutions in diplomacy.

Raghuveer Nidumolu is a PhD student in Government at Cornell University, studying political theory. Previously, he worked as a programme coordinator and researcher at Carnegie India in its Security Studies Program. Prior to joining Cornell, he obtained an MA in International Relations from the University of Chicago, and an MA in Liberal Studies from Ashoka University.

Srinath Raghavan is Professor of International Relations and History at Ashoka University. He is also a Non-resident Senior Fellow at Carnegie India. He is the author of several books, including *The Most Dangerous Place: A History of the United States in South Asia* (2018); *India's War: The Making of Modern South Asia, 1939–1945* (2016); *1971: A Global History of the Creation of Bangladesh* (2013); and *War and Peace in Modern India: A Strategic History of the Nehru Years* (2010). He co-authored, with Sunil Khilnani, *NonAlignment 2.0: A Foreign Strategic Policy for India in the Twentieth Century* (2013). He has edited *Imperialism, Nationalism, Democracy: The Collected Essays of Sarvepalli Gopal* (2013), and co-edited *The Oxford Handbook of Indian Foreign Policy* (2015). He is the recipient of the K. Subrahmanyam Award for Strategic Studies (2011) and the Infosys Prize for Social Sciences (2015). Srinath received a PhD in War Studies from King's College London.

Ayesha Ray is Professor of Political Science at King's College, Pennsylvania, US. She has a PhD in Political Science from The University of Texas at Austin, and MPhil and MA degrees in International Relations from the School of International Studies, Jawaharlal Nehru University (JNU), Delhi. Her research focuses on security, defence, war, and conflict in South Asia. She is the author of *The Soldier and the State in India: Nuclear Weapons, Counterinsurgency, and the Transformation of Indian Civil–Military Relations*; and *Culture, Context, and Capability: American and Indian Counterinsurgency Approaches*. She has also authored several book chapters and peer-reviewed articles. She has been Visiting Fellow at the Institute for Defense Studies and Analyses (IDSA), Delhi, and The Institute of Advanced Studies, JNU, Delhi; and invited guest speaker at venues that include Defense Studies Staff College, Wellington, India; USI, Delhi; Carleton University, Canada; Defense Intelligence Agency, US; and New York University, US.

Shreyas Shende is researcher working on South Asian security, political economy, and intelligence studies. Previously, he worked as a research assistant in the Security Studies program and as the executive assistant to the Director at Carnegie India. He obtained an MA in International Relations from the University of Chicago, and a BA in Political Science and International Relations from Ashoka University.

Paul Staniland is Professor of Political Science at the University of Chicago and a nonresident scholar in the South Asia Program at the Carnegie Endowment for International Peace. He is also the faculty chair of the Committee on International Relations MA programme. His research focuses on political violence and international security in South Asia. His first book, *Networks of Rebellion: Explaining Insurgent Cohesion and Collapse*, was published by Cornell University Press in 2014.

His second book, *Ordering Violence: Explaining Armed Group–State Relations from Conflict to Cooperation*, was published by Cornell in 2021. He received the 2022 Karl Deutsch Award for contributions to the study of International Relations and Peace Research from the International Studies Association.

Praveen Swami is a New Delhi-based journalist, who writes on regional security and intelligence issues. His most recent work is an edited volume, together with Manoj Joshi and Nishtha Gautam, on Indian national security. He is the author of *India, Pakistan and the Secret Jihad: The Covert War in Jammu and Kashmir*; *The Kargil War*; and chapters in several edited volumes. He has written for *Contemporary South Asia*, and the *CTC Sentinel* of the Combating Terrorism Centre.

Milan Vaishnav is a Senior Fellow and Director of the South Asia Program at the Carnegie Endowment for International Peace. His primary research focus is the political economy of India, and he examines issues such as corruption and governance, state capacity, distributive politics, and electoral behaviour. He also conducts research on the Indian diaspora. He is the author of *When Crime Pays: Money and Muscle in Indian Politics* (Yale University Press, 2017) and co-editor (with Devesh Kapur) of *Costs of Democracy: Political Finance in India* (Oxford University Press, 2018) and (with Pratap Bhanu Mehta and Devesh Kapur) of *Rethinking Public Institutions in India* (Oxofrd University Press, 2017). His work has been published in scholarly journals such as *American Journal of Political Science*, *Asian Survey*, *Governance*, *India Review*, *Journal of Democracy*, *Perspectives on Politics*, *PS: Political Science and Politics*, and *Studies in Indian Politics*.

Navneet Rajan Wasan is a retired Indian Police Service Officer of 1980 Batch, with experience working in the Indian Central Bureau of Investigation (CBI), National Investigation Agency (NIA), and in the State Police of Andhra Pradesh. He superannuated as Director General, Bureau of Police Research and Development (BPR&D). He has supervised the investigation and prosecution of multiple cases of corruption, fraud, cyber-crimes, and terrorism-related cases. He has led several noteworthy cases, including the Harshad Mehta Bank Scam and the 2013 Hyderabad, Patna, and Bodhgaya attacks. He specialized in conducting investigation in overseas jurisdiction and headed the National Central Bureau (Interpol) India. He holds an MA and MPhil degree in International Relations from Jawaharlal Nehru University; Post Graduate Diploma in Management from the Management Development Institute, Gurgaon, and LLB from the University of Delhi.

1

Institutions and the Future of
Indian National Security

Milan Vaishnav

Introduction

It is hard to conceive of a global or transnational issue being debated today by world leaders and key international organizations for which India is not considered an important—even vital—player. From terrorism and nuclear proliferation to climate change and pandemics, India has emerged as an essential protagonist on the global stage.

In 2023, India surpassed China as the world's most populous country. This demographic weight, when coupled with the country's economic dynamism following economic liberalization in 1991 and the subsequent emergence of a muscular nationalism, has encouraged a greater ambition in world affairs.[1]

India has long been considered a balancing power and a key global 'swing state'.[2] But its current leadership envisions a world in which India behaves as a 'leading' power.[3] For decades, Indian foreign policy towards Asia was guided by the 'Look East' policy—an effort to diversify the country's economic and strategic linkages with the nations of South East Asia. Today, India espouses an 'Act East' policy—a rhetorical shift clarifying its goal to develop trade and security ties with countries in the region.[4] Of late, India has also embraced the Quadrilateral Security Dialogue, or Quad, where fellow democracies Australia, India, Japan, and the United States coordinate policy to maintain a 'free and open Indo-Pacific'. India was initially reluctant to engage with the Quad out of fear that its participation in the grouping, broadly perceived to be 'anti-China',

Milan Vaishnav, *Institutions and the Future of Indian National Security* In: *Institutional Roots of India's Security Policy*. Edited by: Milan Vaishnav, Oxford University Press. © Oxford University Press 2024.
DOI: 10.1093/oso/9780198894612.003.0001

could exacerbate tensions with its north-eastern neighbour. Recent Chinese aggression along the disputed China–India border, as well as China's expansionist activities in the Indian Ocean region, have jettisoned such concerns.[5]

India's renewed enthusiasm for global engagement is, no doubt, also a function of the dangerous neighbourhood in which it finds itself. In addition to tensions with China, India's decades-long rivalry with Pakistan continues unabated. The persistence of cross-border terrorism—emanating from safe havens located in Pakistan-controlled territory—led to the most serious escalation in bilateral tensions in years when a suicide bomber killed 40 Indian paramilitary soldiers in Indian-administered Kashmir in early 2019. India retaliated with a bombing raid on sovereign Pakistani territory before both sides de-escalated, but future terror attacks on Indian soil are a virtual certainty. Regional tensions are further heightened by the dominance of the Taliban in Afghanistan and the chaotic exit of US and coalition forces from the country in August 2021. Intelligence assessments suggest that several terrorist groups, including ISIS and al-Qaeda, have found some degree of safe harbour in Taliban-controlled Afghanistan. New Delhi fears that Pakistan-based militants and global jihadists, having achieved their desired outcome in Afghanistan, will turn their gaze eastward towards India.

Of course, questions of India's security policy cannot be reduced to worries abroad. At home, matters of internal security remain a pressing concern. Over the last few decades, India has faced three significant insurgencies—in Jammu and Kashmir, the north-east, and in the so-called 'red corridor', also referred to as the Naxalite belt. Both government and independent data suggest that anti-state violence is now well below its peak; in all three locations, conflict-related fatalities have declined precipitously.[6]

However, while the flames of insurgency may have been tamped down, their embers continue to smoulder. In Jammu and Kashmir, heightened security following the central government's nullification of the state's constitutional semi-autonomy in August 2019 has facilitated a prolonged lockdown, severely constricting daily life and ordinary economic activity. Despite this government intervention, insurgents continue to target civilians. These attacks, part of a vicious cycle of government clampdowns and violent terrorist reprisals, could be harbingers of further conflict in the state.[7] Similarly, the insurgencies in the north-east and across eastern India are down but not necessarily out. An April 2021 Naxalite attack that claimed the lives of 22 elite paramilitary soldiers in the state of Chhattisgarh is a deadly reminder of the significant insurgency threat, even as its numbers have dwindled and geographic spread has narrowed.[8] Left-wing extremism may no longer pose an existential threat to the Indian state, but it retains the capacity to inflict deadly violence and undermine governance in areas where guerrillas find safe haven.[9] At the time of writing, internal conflict has wracked the northeastern state of Manipur, reviving once-buried fears of civil war in India's remote frontier.

The shape of internal violence, too, is morphing. As the scholar Paul Staniland argues, riots and insurgent attacks have decreased in frequency just as bouts of localized mob and vigilante violence have ticked upwards.[10] These emerging violent manifestations are, in contrast to the tools wielded by insurgents, often conducted by the state or its affiliates as opposed to entities trying to overthrow it. Thus, not only is India concerned with anti-state violence, but it can also be complicit in violence against groups or individuals perceived to be out of step with the ruling dispensation.

Against this backdrop of domestic and external pressures, the capacity shortcomings of India's security and foreign-policy institutions appear stark. Many agencies are plagued by endemic personnel vacancies, which sap their ability to fulfill their mandates and hamper efforts to retain and recruit talent. This is not to say, however, that the size of the Indian security sector has declined or even plateaued. India's paramilitary forces, for instance, have mushroomed in size over the past few decades. Central Armed Police Force units have doubled in size—a fact rarely raised in contemporary discussions on India's internal security.[11] Yet even these burgeoning organizations suffer from a shortfall of adequately skilled, trained, and equipped personnel.

Even if each and every vacancy were filled, however, it is unlikely that this alone would resolve the capacity constraints needed to address India's mounting security challenges. Many of India's security institutions were developed in response to external shocks, such as India's disastrous 1962 war with China. Six decades later, questions linger as to whether the institutional mandates of yesteryear have the dexterity to adapt to the Indian state's current security objectives.

Furthermore, as new institutions have been established, few legacy ones have been decommissioned. Uncertainty about mandates, institutional division of labour, and policy coordination have often resulted in rivalries between organizations working in the same domain. The rise of paramilitary forces, for instance, has bred not only rivalries among different units but also tensions with the armed services.

The goal of this volume is to unpack and interrogate capacity gaps in India's security institutions. In recent times, there have been innumerable examinations of India's foreign and security policies, exploring issues from foreign-policy doctrine to nuclear posture and civil–military relations. Nearly all of them have lamented the severe capacity constraints India's institutions face on a day-to-day basis. For instance, a recent report issued by leading public-policy intellectuals decries the fact that India's police forces—whose primary task of guaranteeing public order is a core function of sovereign states—are organizationally top heavy and notoriously resistant to structural reforms that could improve their ability to meet citizens' needs.[12] Another review of India's national security architecture bemoans the 'pervasive shortage of manpower trained in national security matters', especially in new, cutting-edge domains such as cyber security, counterterrorism, and geospatial intelligence.[13]

Despite such lamentations, there is very little scholarly work on the administrative and operational capacity of India's security institutions.[14] This lacuna persists in spite of the fact that myriad inadequacies related to both procedure and personnel continue to hamper the Indian state's ability to perform one of its most essential functions: protecting Indians from security threats at home and abroad. This volume aims to remedy that gap.

Origins of the Volume

The origins of this book can be traced back to *Public Institutions in India: Performance and Design*, a seminal 2005 collection edited by scholars Devesh Kapur and Pratap Bhanu Mehta.[15] That volume was one of the first studies to grapple with the design, performance, and adaptability of India's principal governing institutions. Rather than focusing on the set of policy or doctrinal choices these institutions make as a matter of course, Kapur and Mehta convened a group of scholar-practitioners to evaluate how well public institutions—such as the Supreme Court, the Reserve Bank of India, and the civil services—function as organizational entities. Instead of taking these institutions' capacity to execute policies as a given, this work shed light on the ways in which internal capacity (or lack thereof) stymied policy execution.

A decade later, Kapur and Mehta—joined by the editor of this volume—sought to re-examine the capacity dimension of India's core federal institutions in light of the dramatic political, economic, and social changes India experienced during the 2000s and early 2010s. During the intervening period, economic growth boomed (and then busted), the political party system was upended, and social churn—from urbanization to demographic change—gathered pace. This assessment, *Rethinking Public Institutions in India*, was published in 2017. It largely confirmed the findings of the earlier volume while focusing attention on previously unanalysed institutions.[16]

While the approach of these twin volumes was novel, it was also decidedly quiet on matters of security. With the exception of one chapter on the police in the original 2005 volume and a chapter on accountability agencies (such as the Central Bureau of Investigation, or CBI) in the newer volume, questions of security were excluded. This was a concerted choice made by the editors to keep their examination focused and relatively narrow in scope.

With the passage of time, this gap in our understanding of India's security architecture has become ever more pronounced. After all, India' security matrix is no less deserving of the attention of serious scholarship than its civilian counterparts. This volume, therefore, is an attempt to address this shortcoming at a time when India's security agencies are being asked to take on more responsibilities than ever before.

While many of India's security institutions have gained public trust and forged a reputation for operational excellence, nearly all face governance challenges that—if left unaddressed—could undermine their long-term effectiveness. These challenges vary, but even a cursory glance at news headlines lays bare their centrality to guaranteeing India's ability to safeguard its territory at home and secure its objectives abroad.

If, as the saying goes, personnel is policy, then India's security institutions leave much to be desired. According to government data, the Indian

Army lacks nearly 7,500 officer-rank personnel out of 50,000 sanctioned positions. In percentage terms, a similar shortfall bedevils the Indian Navy; a smaller, but still substantial, share of Indian Air Force (IAF) officer positions sit vacant.[17] Roughly one-fifth of police positions across the country lie empty, with especially severe gaps in large, populous states such as Uttar Pradesh and West Bengal, which also face numerous security challenges.[18]

The paucity of basic capacity in infrastructure, too, plagues the ability of troops to protect India's high-altitude border with China as the two countries tussle along the Line of Actual Control (LAC). For long, substandard roads, the absence of mobile connectivity, and the dearth of supporting civic amenities have hamstrung Indian government efforts to deploy and sustain forces in the region.[19] These infrastructure challenges extend to high-value assets as well. As India contemplates the prospects of waging a two-front war against both China and Pakistan, defence analysts question whether the IAF's shrinking fleet has the capacity to do so. As Sushant Singh writes, the IAF currently possesses 30 squadrons of fighter jets at a time when top officials in the services state that the force requires a bare minimum of 42 squadrons to sustain a two-front conflict.[20]

One could easily chalk up shortfalls in human and physical capital to resource shortages. After all, India remains an extremely poor country and a recent slowdown in economic growth, compounded by the COVID-19 pandemic, has strained the country's fiscal coffers. There is much truth to this argument, but non-material factors play a contributing role as well. For instance, in most states, civilian police continue to suffer from pervasive political interference as elected authorities in state capitals prioritize political point-scoring over law enforcement and community policing.[21] This creates a recruitment challenge as potential officers interested in serving the public realize that, in order to survive in the force, they must take orders from elected representatives rather than respond to the needs of local residents. The absence of any semblance of work–life balance and limited prospects for upward advancement for most rank-and-file officers only compound matters.[22]

On the defence front, incessant red tape and bureaucratic procedure have long hampered military procurement. The License Raj era may have been ushered out with market-friendly reforms in the early 1990s, but defence contracting in India retains the hallmarks of India's labyrinthine bureaucracy. As one assessment notes, amendments to India's contracting procedures are notified more quickly than the Ministry of Defence can execute arms contracts.[23] India's Army Chief of Staff is on record lamenting that the rules and regulations governing defence acquisition have more in common with the Industrial Age than today's era of big data and rapid technological advancement.[24]

India's intelligence agencies continue to be a black box, even to many in the upper echelons of government. The paucity of officers with specialized expertise (from language to technology to finance) has been a constant source of anxiety for the country's intelligence chiefs. But little is known about the true nature of the agencies' capacity challenges due to the lack of scrutiny they face from both the public and Parliament. While clandestine operations must be, by definition, kept secret, some have argued that opacity has allowed the intelligence community to function without any modicum of oversight and accountability—thwarting the national interest.[25] Such concerns reached a crescendo with the explosive allegations levelled by the Canadian government that Indian intelligence agents assassinated a Canadian Sikh separatist leader on Canadian soil in the summer of 2023.

Coverage of the Book

The ultimate aim of this volume is to introduce the institutions responsible for maintaining and upholding India's internal and external security policy. There is no obvious or commonly accepted set of institutions that merit inclusion in a volume like this. Therefore, we concede that a degree of subjectivity exists in deciding which institutions to cover and which to exclude from our analyses. However, the selection of institutions in these pages is premised on a framework in which we classify security institutions under four headings.

The first category is the armed forces, represented here by the three major service branches: the Indian Army, Navy, and Air Force. The second category covers the intelligence apparatus, represented here by India's two leading intelligence agencies—the Research and Analysis Wing (R&AW) and the Intelligence Bureau (IB). The third category comprises institutions responsible for internal and border security. These include the Central Paramilitary Forces (such as the Central Reserve Police Force, or CRPF); counter-insurgency forces like the Assam Rifles and Rashtriya Rifles; and border-guarding forces including the Indo-Tibetan Border Police (ITBP), the Sashastra Seema Bal (SSB), and the Border Security Force (BSF). The fourth and final category can be considered a subset of police and investigative agencies focused on internal security. It includes the civilian police, the National Investigation Agency (NIA), and the Central Bureau of Investigation (CBI).

The aim of each chapter is to explain to the reader the role of a given institution in the maintenance of India's security. Each analysis focuses on four common issues: (1) raison d'état, or the institution's core objectives and the environment in which it operates; (2) organizational structure; (3) personnel issues; and (4) performance and reform.

Each chapter begins with a clear statement of the agency's core objectives in addition to the history and context necessary to explain how and why it was established. Since the volume is focused on the organizational foundation of institutions, each chapter describes the agency's internal structure. All of the agencies under study here have been given certain powers that are exercised through the organization's internal procedures and protocols. Our aim is to provide a detailed understanding of how the organization works in the day-to-day exercise of its powers.

All institutions are ultimately comprised of individuals, so chapters devote significant attention to how institutions recruit and manage talent—exploring both the method of entry as well as what happens to individuals once they have been selected into service. Where relevant, chapters also discuss the state of internal and external accountability mechanisms (for instance, to the public, Parliament, or an executive ministry). Finally, each chapter discusses the key vectors for institutional reform. In many instances, there are emerging policy, legal, or institutional issues that are hotly debated and which are central to ongoing reform efforts.

Key Themes

Any book of this breadth and depth will contain numerous cross-cutting themes, complicating efforts to extract a targeted list of key takeaways. Be that as it may, this section attempts to shed light on five particularly important themes from these chapters. While these in no way do justice to the granularity of the analyses in this collection, they do suggest several areas deserving of sustained policy attention.

Personnel Shortcomings

The Indian state is regularly pilloried for being too large and too invasive. While this is certainly true in procedural terms, it misrepresents the personnel realities of most state organs, which are plagued by endemic vacancies. The security domain is no exception to this rule.

As Anirudh Deshpande points out in his chapter on the Border Security Force (Chapter 8), effective personnel management has been a constant challenge for the BSF. The force's increased responsibilities—coupled with difficult working conditions and a constantly evolving operational environment—have led to serious attrition in its ranks. Many BSF personnel have chosen to resign their commissions or have opted for early retirement, further increasing burdens on recruitment. Unfortunately, the force has not consistently attained its recruiting targets, leading to a double-digit vacancy rate that has adversely impacted its operational effectiveness.

India's premier investigative agencies—the CBI and NIA—have not fared much better in this regard. As N.R. Wasan notes in Chapter 11, a paucity of trained personnel has severely limited the CBI's performance. To address these vacancies, which are most acute at senior levels but present across the organizational chart, the agency has taken to recruiting officers from the Central Armed Police Forces. While this may be an obvious short-term fix, it has led to deeper problems as these officers are neither trained nor equipped to handle the country's most complex investigations. The situation facing the NIA is scarcely different, harming both agencies' reputation for integrity and competence.

Perhaps no institution in India has earned a reputation for being starved of human and financial resources more than the police. Vacancies in state police forces, briefly described earlier and further analysed by Vineet Kapoor and Akshay Mangla in Chapter 10, confirm the general impression that the police resemble a moth-eaten institution. Vacancies are rife up and down the hierarchy, and state-based quotas for historically disadvantaged communities are regularly unmet. Difficult working conditions, irregular working hours and days off, and shortages in personnel ranging from forensic specialists to patrol cops exacerbate the police's well-documented travails with corruption, abuse, and political meddling.

As far as India's security institutions are concerned, human resource difficulties do not stop with recruitment alone. They also pertain to weaknesses in training, professional development, internal mobility, and job satisfaction. For instance, in Chapter 5, Praveen Swami argues that the lack of competent instructors compounded by consistent resource shortages has prevented the IB's new training facility in New Delhi from turning out enough recruits to cover organic attrition. In extreme instances, dissatisfaction and poor morale can be fatal. Deshpande notes that, between 2015 and 2018, more than 120 BSF jawans committed suicide while on the job. Career stagnation, rising stress levels, and declining motivation have been cited as contributing factors to a growing number of mental-health challenges in the ranks.

Institutional Rivalries

Another common theme across the institutions under study is the development of institutional rivalries. As the complexity of India's security challenges have grown, so too have the number and mandates of India's security institutions. As one might expect, this has led to institutional rivalries that have undermined the effectiveness of the state's security apparatus.

For instance, many military experts have raised questions about the viability of large, expensive aircraft carriers in modern warfare. However, Atul Bhardwaj's examination of the Indian Navy in Chapter 2 highlights the fact that the navy is leery to revisit the centrality of carriers given its inter-service rivalry with the IAF. As the author argues, a carrier-less navy would end the service's monopoly on marine aviation, potentially shifting greater budgetary resources to the IAF. In a world of scarce resources and debates about the trade-offs between 'guns and butter', such competition quickly becomes zero-sum.

Ayesha Ray's chapter on the Indian Army (Chapter 1) also notes that inter-service rivalries have damaged even the best-laid plans for 'jointness' and collaboration across services. Rahul Bhatia and Shibani Mehta's examination of the IAF in Chapter 3 echoes this sentiment, noting that inter-service rivalry—along with tensions between senior officials and the lack of joint institutional structures—has resulted in the IAF and the Indian Army working at cross-purposes, not least during the tense days of the 1999 Kargil War with Pakistan. Civilian leaders at the Ministry of Defence, Ray notes, are also implicated in this disjointedness insofar as they are wary of yielding powers to the uniformed services.

Inter-service rivalries are not limited to the armed forces; on the contrary, they are widespread in the internal security domain. In Chapter 9, Raghuveer Nidumolu and Srinath Raghavan detail the tensions that have arisen between the counter-insurgency-oriented Rashtriya Rifles and other security and border forces. The authors recall that during the Kargil War, the BSF refused to serve under the Rashtriya Rifles because doing so would make it subordinate to a peer security/paramilitary organization—even though the Rashtriya Rifles are a modified infantry formation of the Indian Army, rather than an organ of the Ministry of Home Affairs (MHA). When policymakers raised the prospect of creating a force dedicated to countering militancy in Jammu and Kashmir, the MHA questioned whether such a force was required, given the endemic nature of the conflict in that border state.

Irrespective of the domain in question, it is rarely clear where one agency's remit begins and another's ends. Thus, agencies with overlapping mandates are incentivized to protect their perceived turf from their government peers. In the case of the intelligence and investigative agencies, Praveen Swami writes in Chapter 5 that the amorphous domestic security role of the IB has meant that it too often competes, rather than collaborates, with the NIA on high-profile counterterrorism cases. These divisions not only poison the working relationship between these agencies, but they also filter down to the police forces they partner with on the ground.

Critical Junctures

It is remarkable how many of India's leading security institutions were either borne of, or greatly upended by, India's humiliating defeat at the hands of the Chinese in the Sino-Indian War of 1962. The war served as a critical juncture, motivating India's political leadership to prioritize investments in the security establishment. However, the response to exogenous forces was hurried and lacked strategic planning. As a result, many of the decisions made six decades ago have created path-dependent realities that do not align with current policy objectives.

In Chapter 8, Deshpande notes how the establishment of the BSF was a direct consequence of inadequate border policing laid bare by the Sino-Indian War and subsequent border crises between 1962 and 1965. When the Pakistanis began making incursions into Indian territory in early 1965, both state police and CRPF soldiers failed to repel their advances. The government eventually deployed the army, which managed to stabilize the situation, but policymakers quickly realized the need for a dedicated border security force.

Similarly, in Chapter 7, Jabin Jacob explains that both the ITBP and the SSB trace their roots to the same period: the ITBP was set up days after the 1962 conflict commenced, while the SSB was founded the following year. While they were initially created as paramilitary units to protect the border with China, both agencies have experienced a degree of mission creep over time. As Jacob notes, the ITBP was conceptualized as a hybrid organization combining guerilla warfare capabilities with reconnaissance and intelligence collection. However, necessity has forced it to support civilian administrations in conflict-prone areas, expanding its narrow writ of border protection to include domestic conflict management. By the late 1970s, it had morphed into a traditional border protection outfit. The SSB's mandate, meanwhile, has also evolved. In 2001, the SSB transitioned its focus to India's mountainous borders with Bhutan and Nepal.

The 1962 and 1965 conflicts also inspired the government to stand up the R&AW as India's principal external intelligence agency, argue Shreyas Shende Rudra Chaudhuri in Chapter 4. While the IB was a veteran organization with deep colonial roots, the war with China exposed many of its capacity gaps—as Swami notes in Chapter 5—leading officials to press for new investments in its analytical and intelligence-gathering capacity.

Questions about Legal Status

The legal and constitutional bases of many Indian security institutions remain open questions—which is especially surprising given their longevity. Uncertainty about an institution's legal foundation not only raises questions about the legality of their actions, but also makes accountability and norm-setting more challenging.

The CBI provides a stunning example of this. As Wasan explains in Chapter 11, the British colonial government created the Special Police Establishment in 1941 as a centralized anti-corruption body. In 1946, this organization mutated into the Delhi Special Police Establishment (DSPE) and was given statutory status. Given the expansion of corruption and subsequent increase in anti-corruption investigations in the 1950s and 1960s, the government established the CBI via executive order in 1963, subsuming the erstwhile DSPE as one of its subordinate components. However, the CBI itself was never given formal legal authorization, despite repeated urgings from Parliament. This narrative became an outright farce when the Gauhati High Court ruled the original 1963 resolution setting up the CBI unconstitutional. According to the court, the CBI was not part of the DSPE under the DSPE Act—a ruling the central government challenged. The Supreme Court stayed the high court judgment, allowing the CBI to continue its operations, but the matter is still pending—leaving the body's legal basis in a semi-permanent state of purgatory.

The R&AW, Shende and Chaudhuri remind us, also has no explicit constitutional authorization. In fact, the protagonists responsible for establishing the agency worked assiduously to ensure that the body remain free from oversight and external scrutiny. As a result, virtually nothing is known about the operations of the R&AW, even among those in Parliament and the judiciary. In the authors' words, there is simply no 'institutional bridge' between the agency and the general public. Like its external counterpart, the IB too functions in the shadows. The agency, writes Swami, also has no clear legal authorization—a deficiency he believes is largely responsible for its uncontrolled use by the political executive.

Absence of Oversight

As the previous discussion makes clear, the absence of legal authorization inhibits accountability and transparency in the security sector. But the lack of external oversight is a more common malady. Staniland notes in his discussion of India's central paramilitary forces (Chapter 6) that these forces come under the MHA, a notoriously difficult central ministry to penetrate. As the author notes, many of the ministry's operating domains are kept under wraps and successive central governments and ministry functionaries have endeavored to keep it that way. This strategy gives the government in power wide latitude in planning and conducting counter-insurgency operations, border management, and the repression (and/or cooptation) of local actors. Although the MHA's budget has grown significantly in recent years, it still pales in comparison to the defence budget. Staniland posits that this disparity has allowed the MHA to operate with far less scrutiny.

Wasan is even more pointed in his discussion of oversight over the CBI (Chapter 11). He writes that, as far as the CBI is concerned, '[e]xternal accountability via the power of superintendence—whether exercised by the CVC [Central Vigilance Commission] or by the central government—remains nothing more than an academic exercise of periodical review'. While the judiciary can, and sometimes does, hold the CBI accountable for abusing its authorities, the judiciary's own capacity shortfalls—delays, backlogs, and personnel shortages—seriously limit its ability to rein in the agency.

Not all attempts to exercise oversight have failed, however. Shende and Chaudhuri (Chapter 4) note that the establishment of the National Security Advisor (NSA) position during Prime Minister's Atal Behari Vajpayee government in late 1998 brought a modicum of political oversight to the otherwise direct, two-way line the R&AW maintained with the Prime Minister's Office. The head of the R&AW was now required to report to the Prime Minister through the NSA, whose hand was further bolstered by the establishment of the National Security Council Secretariat (NSCS). Suffice it to say, however, that the external intelligence agency has limited checks on its authority beyond the Prime Minister's Office.

Roadmap

What follows is a series of 11 institutional 'analytic narratives' on India's most central security institutions. Contributors have relied on quantitative data, qualitative research (including interviews and archival work), and their own expertise to provide an accurate picture of the institutional foundations of India's security policy.

The remainder of the book proceeds in four parts. Part I examines the three branches of the armed services—namely, the Indian Army, Navy, and Air Force. Part II delves into the principal intelligence agencies, the R&AW and the IB. Part III looks at the domain of internal and border security, with chapters on the central paramilitary, counter-insurgency, and border security forces. Part IV explores the Indian police and key investigative agencies.

Acknowledgements

The author is grateful to Caroline Duckworth, Aislinn Familetti, Kathryn Hockman, and Caroline Mallory for their help in preparing this chapter. Rudra Chaudhuri contributed his valuable ideas to developing many of the themes outlined here. Cooper Hewell provided excellent editorial assistance. All errors are the author's own.

Notes

1. Alyssa Ayres, *Our Time Has Come: How India is Making Its Place in the World* (New York: Oxford University Press, 2018).
2. Richard Fontaine and Daniel M. Kliman, "International Order and Global Swing States," *The Washington Quarterly* 36, no. 1 (January 2013): 93–109.
3. Ashley J. Tellis, "India as a Leading Power," Carnegie Endowment for International Peace Paper, April 4, 2016, https://carnegieendowment.org/files/CP_268_Tellis_India_final1.pdf.
4. Chietigj Bajpaee, "Dephasing India's Look East/Act East Policy," *Contemporary Southeast Asia* 39, no. 2 (August 2017): 348–72.
5. Tanvi Madan, "India is Not Sitting on the Geopolitical Fence," *War on the Rocks* (blog), October 27, 2021, https://warontherocks.com/2021/10/india-is-not-sitting-on-the-geopolitical-fence/.
6. Paul Staniland, "Political Violence in South Asia: The Triumph of the State?," Carnegie Endowment for International Peace, September 3, 2020, https://carnegieendowment.org/2020/09/03/political-violence-in-south-asia-triumph-of-state-pub-82641.

7. Rahul Pandita, "Kashmir's New Insurgency," *OPEN* (October 22, 2021), https://openthemagazine.com/feature/kashmirs-new-insurgency/.

8. Yashovardhan Azad, "Maoism Remains India's Biggest Internal Security Threat," *Hindustan Times*, April 6, 2021, https://www.hindustantimes.com/opinion/maoism-remains-india-s-biggest-internal-security-threat-101617719120339.html.

9. Niranjan Sahoo, "Half a Century of India's Maoist Insurgency: An Appraisal of State Response," Observer Research Foundation Occasional Paper 198, June 2019, https://www.orfonline.org/research/half-a-century-of-indias-maoist-insurgency-an-appraisal-of-state-response-51933/#_ednref108.

10. Staniland, "Political Violence in South Asia."

11. For instance, Kapur notes that, between 2006 and 2014, the personnel increase in the Ministry of Home Affairs (largely on account of CAPFs) was more than six times the net personnel increase across the entirety of the central government. See Devesh Kapur, "The Worrying Rise of Militarisation in India's Central Armed Police Forces," *ThePrint*, November 29, 2017, https://theprint.in/opinion/worrying-rise-militarisation-indias-central-armed-police-forces/19132/.

12. Yamini Aiyar et al., *India's Path to Power: Strategy in a World Adrift* (New Delhi: Centre for Policy Research, 2021).

13. P.S. Raghavan, "The Evolution of India's National Security Architecture," *Journal of Defence Studies* 13, no. 3 (July–September 2019): 33–52.

14. A notable exception is Amit Ahuja and Devesh Kapur, eds., *Internal Security in India: Violence, Order, and the State* (New York: Oxford University Press, 2023).

15. Devesh Kapur and Pratap Bhanu Mehta, eds., *Public Institutions in India: Performance and Design* (New Delhi: Oxford University Press, 2005).

16. Devesh Kapur, Pratap Bhanu Mehta, and Milan Vaishnav, eds., *Rethinking Public Institutions in India* (New Delhi: Oxford University Press, 2017).

17. "78,291 Jobs Available in the Indian Armed Forces; 9,427 Officer Ranks Vacant," *Business Today*, July 1, 2019, https://www.businesstoday.in/jobs/story/78291-jobs-available-indian-armed-forces-9427-officer-ranks-vacant-212457-2019-07-01.

18. Bureau of Police Research and Development, Ministry of Home Affairs, Government of India, *Data on Police Organisations* (New Delhi: Government of India, 2021).

19. Vikram Sharma, "Poor Infrastructure, Not the Enemy, Hampered Indian Army's Movement on LAC," *New Indian Express*, September 10, 2017, https://www.newindianexpress.com/thesundaystandard/2017/sep/10/poor-infrastructure-not-the-enemy-hampered-indian-armys-movement-on-lac-1654736.html.

20. Sushant Singh, "Can India Transcend its Two-Front Challenge?," *War on the Rocks* (blog), September 14, 2020, https://warontherocks.com/2020/09/can-india-transcend-its-two-front-challenge/.

21. Beatrice Jauregui, *Provisional Authority: Police, Order, and Security in India* (Chicago: University of Chicago Press, 2016).

22. Common Cause and Centre for the Study of Developing Societies, *Status of Policing in India Report, Volume 1, 2020–2021* (New Delhi: Common Cause and Lokniti-CSDS, 2021).

23. Angad Singh, "Indian Defence Procurement: Righting the Ship," Observer Research Foundation Issue Brief 43, February 2021, https://www.orfonline.org/wp-content/uploads/2021/02/ORF_IssueBrief_443_DefenceProcurement.pdf.

24. "Army Chief on Transformation Imperatives for Indian Army in Coming Decades," *Bharat Shakti,* August 3, 2021, https://bharatshakti.in/army-chief-on-transformation-imperatives-for-indian-army-in-coming-decades/.

25. "Spooky Change: Intelligence Agencies Need Parliamentary Oversight. Let That Be the Post-Pegasus Consensus," *Times of India*, July 25, 2021, https://timesofindia.indiatimes.com/blogs/toi-editorials/spooky-change-intelligence-agencies-need-parliamentary-oversight-let-that-be-the-post-pegasus-consensus/.

PART I

ARMED FORCES

Part I of this volume provides an overview of the history of the three main branches of the Indian armed forces—the army, navy, and air force, reviewing how their roles have evolved over time and to what extent their structures and training programmes have adapted to changing circumstances. It also reflects on the capacity of their fiscal and human resources to meet the demands of the twenty-first century.

2

The Indian Army

Ayesha Ray

The Indian Army is the largest component of the Indian armed services and, in manpower terms, the second largest standing army in the world. The Indian Army has colonial roots, dating back to the consolidation of the British East India Company's position in India in the late eighteenth century. Since India's independence in 1947, however, the Indian Army has evolved into a modern fighting force and a fierce defender of India's territorial integrity and sovereignty.

This chapter interrogates the capacity of the Indian Army to fulfil its core objectives as India's premier land-based military service. It begins with an overview of the army's core objectives, which have evolved over time in line with advances in military doctrine and developments on India's periphery. The army's objectives can be categorized into three domains: external security, internal security, and nuclear policy. The next section looks at innovations within the army over the past seven decades, particularly those pertaining to its organizational structure. The army prides itself on continuous training and skill development, and this chapter also evaluates its success in this regard. An important element of this army's upgradation has involved a debate about the role of women, an understudied subject that this chapter delves into. Finally, it closes with reflections on the human and financial resource challenges the army faces as it navigates a complex domestic and external environment in the twenty-first century.

Ayesha Ray, *The Indian Army* In: *Institutional Roots of India's Security Policy.* Edited by: Milan Vaishnav, Oxford University Press. © Oxford University Press 2024. DOI: 10.1093/oso/9780198894612.003.0002

Raison d'Etat and Objectives

The Indian Army's rationale and objectives can be gleaned from institutional changes in pre- and post-independence India, the evolution of its military doctrines, internal security challenges and 'aid to civil power', and the advent of nuclear weapons.[1]

The Indian Army's creation and development as an institution of defence in post-independence India stems from several legislative and administrative changes introduced in the 1900s. As part of the British imperial army, Indian soldiers had been heavily involved in expeditionary missions ranging from British Malaya, Burma, and Singapore to Afghanistan, Iran, and Iraq. More than a million Indian troops fought in both the First and Second World Wars. Modernization and Indianization of the army—when the officer cadre was opened to Indians—lasted from 1918 to 1939.

In 1921, a committee chaired by Lord Esher recommended placing the Indian armed forces directly under the control of the British government.[2] Then in 1928, at the All Parties Conference chaired by Motilal Nehru, the Indian National Congress made the following recommendations in what came to be known as the Nehru Report:

> The Governor-General-in-Council would appoint a Committee of Defence consisting of the Prime Minister, the Minister of Defence, the Minister of Foreign Affairs, the Commander-in-Chief, the Commander of the Air Forces, the Commander of the Naval Forces, the Chief of the General Staff, and two other experts. The Prime Minister would serve as the Chairman of the committee; and there would be a permanent staff including a secretary attached to this committee. The functions of this committee shall be to advise the government and the various departments concerned with questions of defence and upon general questions of policy.[3]

The Nehru Report was significant in defining future conversations on higher defence organization in post-independence India. From the 1930s, a process of Indianization sought to replace British officers with Indian officials. The Second World War introduced the recruitment of emergency commissioned officers (ECOs), who were both British and British-Indian.[4]

After India gained independence, Lord Ismay, Chief of Staff to Winston Churchill and Secretary to the Defence Committee of the British Cabinet, proposed a set of recommendations that laid the foundation for the Indian Army's institutional edifice. Several political and military committees were created. On the political side, the Defence Committee of the Cabinet was established at the highest level, followed by the Defence Minister's Committee. On the military side, the Chiefs of Staff Committee was created to supervise smaller committees such as the Joint Planning Committee and Joint Training Committee. The Defence Minister acted as the principal link between the Cabinet and the three service chiefs. The Defence Minister was supported by a secretariat led by the Defence Secretary, which was responsible for executing military policies regarding finance, supply, and administration.[5]

The Army Act of 1950 codified the laws that apply to the Indian Army. It is 'an act to consolidate and amend the law relating to the government of the Indian army'.[6] This statute contained the central rules and regulations that governed the conduct of the Indian Army during war and peacetime. It was replaced by the Army Rules of 1954. Then in 1993, further amendments were added to revise the legacy Indian Army Act of 1911, a holdover from British military law. In 1955, the Commanders-in-Chief were renamed as the Chief of the Army Staff, the Chief of the Naval Staff, and the Chief of the Air Staff.[7]

In 1999, the 169th Report of the Law Commission of India recommended the establishment of a special tribunal for the Indian Army, Navy, and Air Force. The objective was to consider disciplinary matters and emerging disputes from the services. The Armed Forces Tribunal Act of 2007 created the Armed Forces Tribunal, its primary role defined as the 'adjudication or trial of disputes and complaints with respect to commission, appointments, enrolments, and conditions of service in respect of persons subject to the Army Act 1950, the Navy Act 1950, and the Air Force Act 1950'.[8] It was an important step towards creating a separate institution with powers to adjudicate over all military matters.

The Indian Army's military doctrines developed in consonance with operational and structural changes in the army. These changes, while incremental, were influenced by key developments and critical moments that embraced different strategies in approaching external wars and internal threats. Overall, there has been a shift from defensive to offensive operations. When India gained independence, Prime Minister Jawaharlal Nehru steered nation-building efforts towards social and economic development. Defence was given little priority. Indian military doctrine was not terribly sophisticated and there seemed to be little political will to focus on improving the nation's military capabilities. Therefore, Indian military doctrine until the 1980s was mostly defensive in nature. Perhaps the watershed moment for a break in defensive postures came in the 1980s, when the Indian Army re-evaluated the strategic use of nuclear weapons. Even though India's nuclear policy at the time did not lay out a cogent framework for offensive postures, India's intention to pursue the development of nuclear weapons to match Pakistan's growing military capabilities gave senior military officers a moment to pause and rethink strategy.

However, military doctrine did not develop only in the context of Pakistan. It was driven by both external and internal considerations. As discussed in this chapter, the army's core doctrinal objectives are a response to India's external security environment, its internal challenges, and the presence of nuclear weapons. At times these doctrines have overlapped; at other times, they have been in fundamental variance. Doctrinal development was also accompanied by significant institutional changes.

The Ministry of Defence (MoD) outlines the Indian Army's basic warfighting doctrine in Chapter Two, Section II of the Headquarters Integrated Defence Staff's *Joint Doctrine of the Indian Armed Forces*, which refers to the 'Nature and Character of Conflict/War'.[9] Military activities concentrate on four levels of war: political or grand strategic, military strategic, operational, and tactical. Military strategy is exclusively tied to national security and issues pertaining to national interest. In other words, the purpose of warfare is largely to defend the sovereignty and territorial integrity of India. The planning is executed by the Service Headquarters and the Headquarters Integrated Defence Staff. At the operational level, campaigns are planned by the Command Headquarters/Corps. The operational level integrates military strategy with battlefield tactics to deliver a range of options (land, air, maritime, and cyberspace) to achieve successful outcomes. At the tactical level, warfighting is designed to achieve operational objectives in which land, air, maritime, logistics, and special forces are deployed to achieve success in battle. On conflict and war, the doctrine specifically states:

> India has moved to a proactive and pragmatic philosophy to counter various conflict situations. The response to terror provocations could be in the form of 'surgical strikes' and these would be subsumed in the sub-conventional portion of the spectrum of armed conflict. The possibility of sub-conventional escalating to a conventional level would be dependent on multiple influences, principally: politically determined conflict aims; strategic conjuncture; operational circumstance; international pressures and military readiness. Conflict will be determined or prevented through a process of credible deterrence, coercive diplomacy, and conclusively by punitive destruction, disruption, and constraint in a nuclear environment across the spectrum of conflict. Therefore, undertaking 'integrated theater battle' with an operationally adaptable force, to ensure decisive victory in a network centric environment across the entire spectrum of conflict in varied geographical domains, will be the guiding philosophy for evolution of force application and warfighting strategies.[10]

Much of the Indian Army's military doctrine is embedded in this document. While it is poorly phrased with several inconsistencies, certain components are emphasized. A combination of deterrence and coercion guide overall operational plans:

> Coercion and deterrence will communicate to potential adversaries the consequences of their anticipated action or inaction. Deterrence and coercion strategies will only succeed if an opponent understands that the threats or incentives are credible. Effective deterrence and coercion strategies comprise four principles—credibility, communication, comprehension, and capability.[11]

Further, while the actual use of battlefield tactics rests on destruction, disruption, and constraint, the exact methods used to achieve these goals remain unclear. Indeed, if this is the case, a discussion of external security, internal threats, and nuclear policy will demonstrate that India's military doctrines during crises or wartime do not consistently align with these principles. The principles reflect an intent but not a perfect outcome—however desirable.

Most problematic of the four principles is perhaps the one on credibility and capability. It is not exactly clear whether the Indian Army has established the purported credibility or sophisticated capability with any of its existing external adversaries needed to maintain effective deterrence. The lack of clarity is an outcome of different factors, each of which appear as major themes in this chapter: tensions in civil–military approaches; the absence of political directions; the poorly equipped state of the Indian Army; and serious gaps in communication between the army and the MoD, which senior defence officials, former soldiers, and civilian leaders have all observed.

External Security

Among India's central adversaries on the subcontinent, China and Pakistan remain the most visible. Since independence, India has fought one war with China and four with Pakistan, in addition to a series of limited border engagements. Over time, India has tried to develop approaches better suited to fighting the enemy. Perhaps the starkest change in its approach to both Pakistan and China is a preference for combining defensive and offensive military approaches. This fundamental shift in warfare occurred alongside the development of nuclear weapons for strategic use, in combination with sub-conventional warfare with Pakistan. Therefore, even if the Indian Army had intended to maintain defensive postures, the nuclearization of the subcontinent from the late 1990s—accompanied by several crises—influenced its current preferences towards offensive options.

The debate surrounding the Cold Start doctrine offers an illustrative example. After the December 2001 attack on the Indian Parliament and the ensuing stand-off between India and Pakistan (known as Operation Parakram), the Indian Army produced a new limited war doctrine called Cold Start. To plug the holes in India's conventional military doctrine and to meet Pakistan's provocation, Cold Start was created to develop the capability to launch a retaliatory conventional strike against Pakistan while keeping the conflict below the nuclear threshold. The doctrine demanded 'a reorganization of the Indian army's offensive power away from three large strike corps into eight smaller division-sized integrated battle groups (IBGs) that combined mechanized infantry, artillery, and armor' with the ability to launch multiple strikes into Pakistan along several different centres of attack.[12] Cold Start was the culmination of Operation Brasstacks, a military exercise in the late 1980s led by General Krishnaswamy Sundarji, who first tried to test some of the same principles in a possible war with Pakistan.

Some scholars have suggested that 2019 marked 'a new security order', with a more assertive India that was less averse to taking risks. Much of this commentary came in the aftermath of India's 2019 Balakot air strike against Pakistan, after more than 40 paramilitary personnel were killed in a terrorist attack in Pulwama, Kashmir, orchestrated by the Jaish-e-Mohammed. While conflicting claims over the actual course of events are shrouded in murky evidence, India's approach to Pakistan had decidedly changed. Between 2002 and 2016, New Delhi had been fairly restrained in its approach to war with Pakistan, and diplomacy and economic engagement had worked. The Balakot operation indicated that punishment was privileged over restraint.[13] It demonstrated that the government of Prime Minister Narendra Modi and the more hawkish officers in the army were willing to adopt a muscular approach—even risking escalation—to deter future attacks orchestrated by Pakistan.

On the threat from China, the newly created Mountain Strike Corps of the Indian Army (XVII Corps) under the Eastern Command, located in Panagarh, West Bengal, promises a fundamentally new approach to deterring Chinese influence along the Line of Actual Control (LAC). After the 1962 war in which India suffered a humiliating defeat by China, the LAC served as a de facto border in the eastern, central, and western sectors. However, both sides disagreed over the exact cartographical boundaries. Subsequently, China often tested Indian defences by increasing troop levels, enforcements, and subtly encroaching into parts of Indian territory.[14] In October 2019, more than 5,000 soldiers from the Indian Army were part of a large-scale military exercise in the eastern Indian state of Arunachal Pradesh. The soldiers came from the 59 Infantry Division of the XVII Corps and included armoured regiments, battle tanks, and infantry combat vehicles. To achieve precision in wartime scenarios with China, the formations were converted into integrated battle groups meant to perform offensive operations with the support of artillery firepower.[15]

The Mountain Strike Corps currently has only one division, with another division to be based in Pathankot. However, this second division has not been completed due to a lack of resources and funding.[16] While an artillery brigade was added to the existing division during the 2020 confrontation with China in the Galwan River valley, it may still be a few years until the Strike Corps is fully operational. Some believe the newly created Mountain Strike Corps has changed the battle landscape with China in fundamental ways by acting as a much-needed deterrent to Chinese aggression. Clearly, the creation of this strike corps and the objectives it seeks to meet reflect the shift from a defensive military posture to an offensive one. It is also an important step in preparing the Indian Army for the gruelling standards of mountain warfare. The 2020 India–China crisis in Ladakh and the contradictory messaging from New Delhi did, however, seriously undermine this vision.

Discussions on the creation of joint theatre commands brought further urgency to building improved and efficient military doctrines that can in the future integrate operational readiness and wartime functions of the Indian Army, Navy, and Air Force. The impetus for the creation of India's theatre commands is incentivized to manage threats from both Pakistan and China. India has 17 military commands in addition to the Strategic Forces Command and the Andaman and Nicobar Command. The army and navy argue that these 19 commands do not always work in tandem towards mutually shared goals. Since speed and flexibility are central to the success of modern warfare, only two commanders—one for each joint command theatre, instead of the present 19—may provide a more optimal solution.[17]

Internal Security

In civil affairs, the Indian Army historically has maintained a deeply important role in internal security operations. A variety of subnational threats in the form of insurgent, rebel, and guerilla groups falls within the Indian military's jurisdiction. It has a robust record in counter-insurgency missions in Nagaland, Mizoram, Assam, Manipur, and Jammu and Kashmir—the latter of which has proven to be the most challenging. Anti-Naxalite operations in Chattisgarh, Telengana, and Madhya Pradesh are mostly conducted by Indian paramilitary forces receiving some assistance and training from the army.

The 2006 *Doctrine for Sub-Conventional Operations* outlines India's core counter-insurgency principles, though challenges remain in the Indian Army's operational capacity and its unclear boundaries with police functions. Internal security doctrines mostly reflect defensive postures. While the Indian Army's doctrine on sub-conventional operations appears to have taken several pages out of the United States' counter-insurgency playbook, it operates in a fundamentally different context. The US military's role in counter-insurgency has been external, fighting in countries outside its territory with the objective of state-building. The Indian Army's counter-insurgency operations are internal, managing threats inside Indian territory while developing approaches to eliminate or reduce the probability of these threats with an emphasis on state preservation.[18] Here, the army's record of success is mixed—successful operations coexist alongside serious institutional and operational weaknesses.

The Indian Army's performance maintaining law and order in Jammu and Kashmir has consistently revealed that kinetic options are an ineffective way to fight militant groups. This ineffectiveness has become considerably acute against the backdrop of a series of events: an uptick in militancy, defection in police ranks, failure to prevent militant attacks, and the growing radicalization of a Kashmiri population that views the army as an aggressor.

In 1990, the Rashtriya Rifles, a specialized counter-insurgency force, was created to break the momentum of the 1989–90 insurgency in Kashmir. While the Rashtriya Rifles draws from infantry battalions, its goal was never to secure a permanent presence in Jammu and Kashmir. Over time, problems with unit cohesion and the lack of coordination with paramilitaries like the Border Security Force (BSF) and the Central Reserve Police Force (CRPF) only entrenched the army deeper with disastrous consequences. Though large in presence, the poorly trained force has been routinely chastised for its unprofessionalism towards local Kashmiris, offering, at best, an ill-conceived approach to internal security or, at worst, a broken system. While obvious problems were

always present, these failures became further amplified from 2016 onwards when the army found itself cornered without alternative courses
of action. Statements from senior military officials outlined failures while
proposing a reduction in military presence. Their concerns were, and remain, largely ignored by India's political leadership, which seems intent
on stretching the army thin by using it unwisely in both conventional and
unconventional operations.

As the army and police exercise little legitimacy among local
Kashmiris—given their dark record of human rights violations—
the army's organizational approach and methods in internal security, especially in Jammu and Kashmir, require a serious overhaul.
Organizationally, separating police and military functions is vital. While
the Rashtriya Rifles works under the aegis of the MoD, the Central Armed
Police Forces (or CAPFs, such as the CRPF, the BSF, and the Indo-Tibetan
Border Police) are supervised by the Ministry of Home Affairs. CAPFs
often display weak policing, unprofessionalism, and poor training, consequently jeopardizing missions. In the north-eastern states of Assam,
Manipur, and Nagaland, for instance, local police have been found col-
luding with insurgents.[19] Recently, Kashmir's Deputy Superintendent of
Police, Davinder Singh, was arrested because of his alleged links to Hizbul
Mujahideen terrorists. Without a clear separation in police and military
roles, the performance, image, and morale of the army in Kashmir will
continue to suffer.

Nuclear Policy

India's nuclear policy has seen remarkable, though incremental, shifts in
operational, doctrinal, and strategic objectives since India's decision to
develop nuclear energy for peaceful purposes and its first nuclear test in
1974. The preference for nuclear weapons was gradually embraced in the
1980s in response to Pakistan's and China's nuclear policies. The impetus
came not just from India's civilian leadership but from many senior officials in the Indian military.[20] The 1998 nuclear tests gave India the global
recognition it had long aspired.[21]

India's nuclear doctrine was crafted around the principles of no first
use and credible minimum deterrence. There is little ambiguity that
India's desire for nuclear capability was a direct response to threats from

Pakistan and China. Aligning India's nuclear doctrine to match its institutional structures and command and control operations became a top priority for New Delhi, although it took several years. By the early 2000s, India had developed a concise nuclear doctrine and outlined the basic principles of its nuclear policy. This doctrine maintained that India's nuclear posture was built around credible minimum deterrence, no first use, retaliatory attacks only to be authorized by civilian political leadership, non-use of nuclear weapons against non–nuclear weapon states, the option to retaliate with nuclear weapons to a biological or chemical attack, continued controls on the export of nuclear- and missile-related materials and technology, and nuclear disarmament.[22] But how has the nuclearization of South Asia affected the Indian Army? Information on this topic is mostly classified and not easily available to the public. Yet some aspects of nuclear policy that could affect the army are still worth exploring.

First, the 1999 Kargil crisis revealed that limited conventional conflict remains possible even in the shadow of nuclear weapons. It also showed that nuclear weapons do not provide deterrence in all scenarios.[23] This means that the army must prepare for a situation in which a conventional war could potentially escalate to the nuclear level. While this scenario is unlikely, as nuclear weapons are firmly under civilian political control, it still requires careful thought, planning, and an assessment of all possible contingencies. Currently, there is no evidence to indicate that India's political leadership has prepared for such a scenario or even discussed plans with any of the three services on how to execute strategy if such a situation were to arise.

Second, the potential for conflict between civilian leadership and the military over the control of nuclear weapons—and specifically which service would exercise greater authority—remains real. Even though the military has been largely kept out of decision-making on nuclear policy, retired generals in the army are lending significant weight to such issues in seminars and security forums. With delivery of nuclear weapons largely resting with the air force, the military could see turf wars intensify between its three services over the allocation of resources.

Third, there appears to be little knowledge available on the command-and-control infrastructure of the Indian Army. As Lauren J. Borja and M.V. Ramana wrote in 2020, in 2008, the army displayed considerable interest in developing underground tunnels for troop shelter, ammunitions storage, and command centres. It also ordered a digital communications network from Tata Power SED and BEL that could connect deployed troops to battalion headquarters. However, some plans failed to materialize due to delays in the 'fielding of various components'.[24]

Since the 2000s, several operational questions have emerged around India's doctrinal posture and nuclear capability. Indian nuclear security experts and practitioners have been debating whether India's nuclear arsenal aligns with its capabilities. A subject inspiring both debate and caution is whether Indian nuclear doctrine has abandoned its strict adherence to the no-first-use principle and may, in fact, be in the process of embracing counterforce targeting. While no such formal declaration has been made by India's political leadership, public statements by senior military and civilian officials indicate that such changes may not be completely off limits. According to Shivshankar Menon, there is a potential grey zone where nuclear weapons could be used first against another state with nuclear capacity: 'Circumstances are conceivable in which India might find it useful to strike first, for instance, against a nuclear-weapon state that had declared that it would certainly use its weapons, and if India were certain that adversary's launch was imminent'.[25] This debate on pre-emption compels a reconsideration of whether the strategies that India has held close for almost 15 years could possibly shift from countervalue targeting to counterforce targeting. Menon suggests that India's nuclear doctrine is not etched in stone, which, if true, offers unanswered questions in the context of India's future conflicts with Pakistan and China. Concerned critics observe that Pakistan has never taken India's no-first-use pledge seriously and a 'perceived shift to counterforce could prompt Pakistan to upgrade its numbers of delivery systems, dramatically'.[26] Similarly, political scientists Christopher Clary and Vipin Narang caution that the risk of first-strike instability may force India to consider circumstances under which it would renege on its no-first-use declaration.[27]

These concerns are accurate in their assessment of an ambiguous doctrine's destabilizing effects and the pressure from certain sections of the military to favour counterforce postures. Yet even if these changes are to be considered, they do not imply that India is even able to successfully execute such operations. In fact, the absence of evidence that India is developing requisite capabilities to execute a pre-emptive strategy may be a better indicator of how Indian policymakers intend to take this conversation forward. Political scientist Rajesh Rajagopalan has argued that India's ballistic missile programme is over two decades old, making it hard to reasonably assume that the programme is connected, in any way, to a changing nuclear doctrine.[28] Further, a first-use strategy would require India to have a larger nuclear arsenal, precipitating a dangerous arms race with Pakistan.[29] Whatever the case, these debates carry significant implications for the Indian Army's role in nuclear command and control.

Institutional Innovation and Defence Reorganization

Stephen Cohen and Sunil Dasgupta, two notable experts on Indian civil–military relations, have argued that since the turn of the century the Indian Army has tried 'to build on a range of capabilities that define modernization for most professional armies: mobility and precision ordnance, electronic warfare, communications, and personal equipment used by soldiers especially in the context of counterinsurgency.'[30] The authors outline changes in the Indian Army's modernization that occurred in the context of wars and insurgency while there was an urgent need to rethink the army's role. According to them, 'the changes that occurred have mainly expanded force size, added new weapons, and created new agencies, commands, and positions; but they have not tackled the difficult tasks of retrenchment, coordination, and strategic balance.'[31]

A problem that continues to afflict Indian defence modernization is that, despite the existence of external and internal security threats, there is a failure to develop institutions of higher defence in a timely manner. In the words of journalist B.G. Verghese,

> the larger and far more important issue to be addressed is the dismaying exhibition of deep systemic and structural rot for which successive governments across parties must take responsibility. Indecision, drift, and factionalism not just on defence issues have become the hallmarks of governance and politics.[32]

Two possible reasons may explain why this innovation has been so slow: the first is inter-service rivalry, popularly understood as turf wars between the army, navy, and air force. Here, the air force does not want the army to become too powerful. The second reason is bureaucratic politics—the MoD wants to exercise strict control over the three services.[33]

The Indian Army is organized into combat and support arms. These include the armoured corps, artillery, army air defence, army aviation corps, corps of engineers, signals corps, mechanized infantry, infantry, army medical corps, ordnance corps, corps of electronics and mechanical engineers (EME), and other sub-groups like the military police. Here, it is important to underline that some roles within the army are more important than others and power is unequally distributed between various divisions. For example, as an institution with a rich history in conventional warfare focused on defending the nation's borders from incursions by both Pakistan and China, much of the onus within the army has fallen on combat arms like the infantry. Yet the infantry is currently faced with the challenging task of restructuring its divisions to perform more effectively in battle. This issue takes on greater salience with the invention of new doctrines like Cold Start. Ashley J. Tellis of the Carnegie Endowment for International Peace has argued that in the event of a quick rapid attack on Pakistani forces, the Indian Army can mobilize approximately 24 divisions. Yet not all of the Indian Army's divisions would be available because of their dispersed geographies.[34] In such a situation, the lethality and mobility of its infantry forces would count more than the numerical superiority. But achieving this carries trade-offs and requires significant capital investment in combination with different operational competencies. Further, such a step carries its fair share of risks. If the attempt to build smaller and more sophisticated forces fails, India's external security may be greatly diminished in the short term. Tellis points to this as an explanation for the army's decision to stay with the status quo—that is, maintaining and improving an incrementally expanding, infantry-dominant force. This, too, requires significant resources. 'Although the Indian Army has world-class competencies in high altitude and jungle warfare and is capable of both effective special operations and large-scale infantry operations,' Tellis writes,

> it urgently needs to upgrade everything from its individual and crew-served weapons to its artillery, air defence, and aviation systems to be

able to fight effectively at night, in adverse weather, and in an increasingly dense electronic and cyber warfare environment.[35]

Support arms such as the ordnance corps, signals, and EME play important roles in supporting the infantry in insurgency affected states like Jammu and Kashmir. The signals corps, for example, has developed technologies like troposcatter communications to help mechanized infantry formations adapt quickly to changing tactical environments. They enable quickly deployable mobile systems to provide cross-linkages and integration with the communication networks in tactical zones. A separate system, called the Army Static Switched Communications Network (or ASCON), was created to integrate the telecommunications infrastructure with tactical communication networks.[36]

Other service organizations within the army face challenges similar to the infantry in rebuilding reserves that lack critical resources. For instance, the Indian Army's artillery regiments were, for many decades, woefully short of equipment. The Field Artillery Rationalisation Plan, proposed in the aftermath of the 1999 Kargil conflict, is aimed at acquiring around 3,000 pieces of 155-millimetre weaponry—including tracked self-propelled artillery, truck-mounted gun systems, towed artillery pieces, and wheeled self-propelled guns—over two decades. The modernization plan picked up speed only in the last few years with the induction of the M777 ultra-lightweight howitzers and the indigenously built Dhanush guns.[37] All of these issues point to some broad conclusions about how the slow pace of institutional change is affecting the army's organization and defence capabilities.

First, in the absence of clear functions and streamlined processes, there is an increased likelihood of friction in civil–military relations over the conduct of wars. Second, institutional changes must match development in strategic doctrines to meet external and internal security threats in a timely manner. Third, unless systemic issues are addressed, the lack of coordination will continue to affect civil–military functions in both peace and wartime. Harsh Pant of New Delhi's Observer Research Foundation notes that

> altering the institutional design of existing bureaucracies to enable joint civil-military deliberation over the granular aspects of defence

policies—pertaining to force structures and employment, jointness, promotion policies, doctrine and education—enhances civilian control. Such institutional redesigning should be accompanied by encouraging the growth of civilian expertise.[38]

The inadequate allocation of funds to the army is also the focus of ongoing scrutiny related to defence modernization and reform. In 2019, a report by the Parliamentary Standing Committee on Defence criticized the Indian government, stating that 'the government does not meet the requirement of funds for increasing threat perceptions and modernization to face a two-front war'.[39] The report observed that allocations under the capital budget for 2018–19 had fallen far short of projections made by the MoD, underscoring a failure to meet the ministry's liabilities. For the army, the committee noted an allocation of about 153.86 trillion rupees against a projection of nearly 196.39 trillion rupees during 2018–19.[40] The Comptroller and Auditor General's (CAG) reports are also particularly damning. CAG reports indicate little to no improvement in the availability of India's war wastage reserve ammunition for tanks and artillery, which is at a critical level. In addition, one article reports that according to the CAG report, availability of 55 per cent types of ammunitions was below the Minimum Acceptable Risk Level (MARL). MARL is the requirement of ammunition for 20 days. The CAG also reported that 40 per cent of ammunitions were at a critical level with stocks that would last only 10 days.[41]

Training and Performance

Commissioned officers in the Indian Army are recruited through the Union Public Service Commission (UPSC), which holds entrance examinations for the National Defence Academy (NDA) and the Naval Academy twice a year. Having completed the UPSC written exam, eligible candidates undergo Service Selection Board (SSB) interviews for over five days. Successful candidates join the NDA after a medical test. Upon completion of the initial NDA course, they are sent to their respective service academy for pre-commissioned training.[42] The NDA offers training to permanent commissioned officers, while the Officers

Training Academy (OTA) in Chennai offers training to short-service commissioned officers. The Service Selection Board recruits junior commissioned officers (JCOs) and other ranks (ORs) into the officers' cadre through three different ways: entry into the Army Cadet College, the special commissioned officers scheme, and the permanent commission special list.[43] Army recruitment is done through zonal recruiting offices, two Gorkha recruiting depots, one independent recruiting office, and 59 army recruiting offices, in addition to 48 regimental centres that carry out recruitment through rallies in their respective areas of jurisdiction.[44] JCOs and ORs are recruited through an online application system.[45]

It must be noted that from the late nineteenth century, the martial race theory—a highly racist set of principles that privileged some ethnicities over others—set the context for how classes and castes in India were evaluated for recruitment into the Indian Army. Some ethnic groups were considered stronger, and many Jat, Sikh, Gorkha, and Pathan fighters were recruited to the Bengal army after the Indian Rebellion of 1857.[46] The policy was actively pursued by both British and Indian officers leading to inconsistencies and contradictions, not to mention inequality, in the Indian Army's recruitment process.[47] This effectively relegated other regiments in status. For instance, during the early 1900s under the British Raj, the Bengal army acquired a special status while the Bombay and Madras armies were downgraded. Punjab became the most sought-after province for recruitment.[48]

The entry standards for officers and ORs in the Indian Army also offer sharp disparities when compared to officers in the Indian Administrative Service (IAS) and Indian Police Service (IPS). For example, one retired army officer has argued that

> an IAS officer becomes a deputy secretary after five years of service; an IPS officer becomes an SSP, the equivalent rank, after nine years of service, while the equivalent rank in the Army—that of lieutenant colonel—is reached after 13 years of service.[49]

And as IAS and IPS officers rise in the ranks, the gap in seniority with their army peers widens dramatically. Promotions beyond the rank of lieutenant colonel are done through selections via a board. For IAS and IPS officers, the promotion ladder is relatively straightforward, with few hurdles and no interim exams. This has caused much consternation within the army.

In this context, a recent initiative reviewing the performance and training of Indian soldiers is focused on cadre restructuring. It includes the following measures:

> Direct Entry in IMA for officers is to be stopped—NDA entry only to provide Regular Officers; Short Service / OTA entry to be increased—only 25% to be subsequently given Permanent Commission; Lt. Col to Col promotions to be increased from current 35–38% to about 55–60%; Col. to Brigadier promotions to be reduced from current 35–38% to about 25–30%; Brigadiers to be automatically promoted to the ranks of Maj Gen after 2–3 years but both ranks to be placed in same Pay Level 14; Brigadier ranks to be worn while commanding Brigades, serving in Tri-Service organizations, on deputation postings and foreign assignments; Time Scale (TS) Col. for Non Empanelled (NE) Lt Cols in 23 yrs and TS Brig for NE Cols one year before their retirement; Staff Stream to start from Col onwards; about 20% reduction of officers in Delhi, including four ADGs—only Cols and above to be posted to Army HQ in Delhi; most of Sub Area HQ to be abolished and responsibilities transferred to Corps HQ.[50]

The army frequently conducts routine military exercises with several of India's international defence partners to enhance its training regimens. For instance, in September 2018, US and Indian soldiers completed a two-week training exercise at Chaubattia Military Station. Designed to share tactical and technical understanding between the two forces, the training integrated soldiers from both the US Army's 7th Infantry Division and the Indian Army's 99th Mountain Brigade into a single unit for a command post and field training exercise.[51] In 2019, all three of India's services participated together for the first time in a training exercise, *Tiger Triumph*, with US forces.[52]

Despite domestic setbacks to attempts to modernize India's arsenal, the Indian Army maintains a modern repository of weaponry, much of which has been imported from its primary defence partners—the United States and Russia. The army inducted US M777 howitzers in 2019. With a range of 24–30 kilometres, they can provide accurate artillery fire support in mountainous terrain. Outdated INSAS rifles will soon be replaced by US-built SIG716s, which have a more powerful cartridge.[53] The army will also receive a new batch of Israeli light machine guns for use by soldiers in front-line positions. More recently, in April 2021, the Indian Army issued a request for information for 350 amphibious light tanks with state-of-the-art mobility and protection systems that can operate in varied terrains and high-altitude areas. Currently, the army mostly uses medium tanks of the T-72/T-90 variety and BMP-2 infantry combat vehicles. But thanks to their mobility and adaptability in difficult terrains, reconnaissance, and airborne or amphibious operations, light tanks are in high demand.[54] As Lieutenant General (ret.) H.S. Panag proposes, lessons from India's recent war with China point to the pressing need for a multi-purpose combat platform for its mechanized forces.[55]

Women in the Armed Forces

Central to the Indian Army's performance is a rather underexamined subject—the roles assigned to female officers in combat. The army's prevalent culture is quite patriarchal. Most arguments in favour of opening combat arms to women are frowned upon or resisted by senior male officers. These officers argue that contact battle is too dangerous for women, the probability of being captured is too high, and unit cohesion is too precious, even though data from the experience of Western female combat soldiers disprove such claims. This remains the subject of polemical debate, after the Supreme Court in 2020 extended permanent commissions to women officers in the army, effectively positioning them to take on commanding roles. According to the BBC,

> the ruling means that all women officers will now be on par with men when it comes to promotions, ranks, benefits and pensions. The Supreme Court rejected the government's plea to overturn the Delhi high court's order on the same matter.[56]

While this is a significant step towards gender integration, full equality will elude the army until women are accepted and allowed into combat arms.

This issue first gained traction in early 2016, when India announced that women would be allowed to occupy combat roles in all sections of the three services. However, it was unclear whether India's political leadership was committed to making it happen. Out of 1.3 million personnel across India's armed forces, only 2.5 per cent are female—1,436 in the army, 1,331 in the air force, and 532 in the navy. Female pilots and navigators are confined to non-combat roles, serving in transport and helicopter units. India began recruiting women to non-combat positions in the armed forces in 1992—mostly as administrators, intelligence officials, doctors, nurses, or dentists in the Army Medical Corps. In February 2016, President Pranab Mukherjee made an official statement approving the induction of women as short-service commissioned officers and fighter pilots in the Indian Air Force.[57] In June 2017, then Chief of Army Staff Bipin Rawat, echoed similar sentiments about including women in the armed forces.

However, these announcements came with a caveat. Women's inclusion in the armed forces would only begin with the induction of women in the military police corps. Military police perform a variety of functions. They police cantonments, army establishments, prevent breaches of rules and regulations by soldiers, and maintain the movement of soldiers as well as logistics during peace and wartime. But this has left many unanswered questions, none of which have been clarified by the government or the MoD. For instance, will the induction of women in the military police corps be used as an experiment to evaluate female performance in combat? Or will the induction of women in the military corps be a necessary step to establish their permanent presence in combat arms? And what is the proposed timeline for implementing the programme?

Within the three services, the demand for women in combat roles is weighed according to different standards and requirements. The air force has been the most receptive to recruiting women. The navy has been the most resistant. Women in the Indian Air Force were slated to fly warplanes beginning in June 2017 on a three-year experimental basis. India's first female combat aircraft pilots were assigned to a Sukhoi-30 squadron in October 2017. In March 2016, the Ministry of Home Affairs reserved spaces for women in the paramilitary CAPFs, giving them a certain advantage in combat roles. Among the five CAPFs, the CRPF, the Central Industrial Security Force, the BSF, and the Sashastra Seema Bal allow women to apply as direct-entry officers. New rules also allow women to apply as direct-entry officers in the Indo-Tibetan Border Police Force (ITBP), the only paramilitary unit that did not allow women to join in supervisory combat roles. By opening these posts in ITBP to women, all existing restrictions have been lifted. Women are expected to be commissioned as assistant commandants after undergoing a year of training.[58]

Human and Financial Resources

The Indian Army faces substantial problems related to manpower, salaries, promotions, and management of personnel. In 2009, army headquarters suggested a new policy on promotions that effectively gave the infantry and artillery arms a disproportionate edge in number over other services. According to historian Srinath Raghavan, 'The infantry garnered 441 of the 734 new vacancies and the artillery registered a 53 per cent increase over two phases while almost all other branches saw a steep drop in the vacancies allotted to them.'[59] Raghavan suggests following the recommendations of the Ajay Vikram Singh Committee, which proposed increasing the admission of short-service commissioned officers to reduce the number of permanent commissioned officers contending for senior ranks.[60] In 2018, top military commanders met to advance several proposals. These included 'making Short Service Officers entry scheme more popular, streamlining the intake pattern, employment of women officers and grant of Honorary ranks to Junior Commissioned Officers and Non-Commissioned Officers'.[61]

In recent years, the issue of salaries and pensions has become front and centre for many serving and retired military officers. More than half of India's defence spending—58 per cent—goes to pay and pensions, but it still seems unable to maintain parity within and between ranks. In its 2015 report, the 7th Central Pay Commission recommended a 23.55 per cent increase in the pay and pensions of government employees.[62] The report also stated that army personnel deserve additional pay and benefits, including free rations and tax concessions. It noted that Indian defence service officers' salaries are 29 per cent higher than their administrative counterparts in the Indian Civil Service.[63] Yet there seem to be anomalies in India's defence budgeting. A.K. Saxena, Controller General of Defence Accounts, lamented the 'wasteful expenditure and lack of transparency' that is affecting defence budgets.[64] Sceptics argue that with the increase in manpower, the huge expenditure dedicated to pay and pensions comes at the cost of defence modernization.[65]

On the issue of salaries, the One Rank, One Pension (OROP) policy announced by the Modi government in September 2015 has come under heavy scrutiny. The basic rationale for OROP is that 'uniform pension be paid to defence personnel who retire at the same rank with the same length of service, regardless of their date of retirement'.[66] The intent was 'to bridge the gap between the rates of pension of current and past pensioners at periodic levels'. However, OROP has run into several legal hurdles, given certain anomalies identified by retired defence personnel. Ex-servicemen have argued that the main discrepancies in the policy relate to the date of implementation, the way pensions are calculated, and the decision to revise pensions annually instead of at five-year intervals.[67] Ex-servicemen have protested the non-implementation of OROP and even filed a case at the Supreme Court. Yet, again, the question comes down to what percentage of India's defence budget should be allocated to salaries. This creates a fundamental conflict between salaries and defence modernization. For example, in 2017, 67 per cent of the defence budget was spent on salaries for serving and retired personnel; only 33 per cent was spent on new hardware or equipment. Some argue for a healthier ratio by increasing the outlay for capital expenditure.[68]

Occupational stress among soldiers in the army remains quite high. A new study by Sakshi Sharma in the *IIMB Management Review* notes that, according to

> figures presented by the Defence Minister A K Antony to the Lok Sabha on March 6, 2013, a total of 368 defence personnel committed suicide from 2010 to 2012, out of which 310 soldiers belong to the Indian army alone; in 2010, 115 cases were reported as compared to 102 in 2011 and 93 in 2012. In addition, the Indian army was reported to be facing a shortage of 26,433 personnel below officer rank.[69]

The study of 415 soldiers in the army concluded that 'ineffective leadership style, unsupportive colleagues, indifferent organizational attitude, inadequate training, inadequate awareness about profession, workload and job pressure, lack of control at work, role ambiguity and role conflict' were the primary factors exacerbating occupational stress in the army.[70]

In May 2020, the Indian Army advanced a proposal called Tour of Duty to allow civilians, including young working professionals, to join the force for a three-year tenure as officers or as ORs in a variety of roles—even as front-line combatants in key forward locations—without any restrictions. It is unclear what this scheme will accomplish, although some sources argue that it could financially benefit the army by saving large sums on gratuity, severance packages, leave encashment, and pensions. However, it remains to be seen whether this will improve the financial resources of the army or adversely impact the quality and training of the forces.[71]

The Indian Army is also reviewing the selection process for elite special forces and airborne battalions. The intention is to expand the scope of their functions to multiple theatres. A centralized, training-based selection process of volunteers at the Special Forces Training School at Nahan in Himachal Pradesh may be the result. The current training and selection process, called probation, is conducted by different units of the Parachute Regiment. The army has proposed that volunteers for the special forces and the Parachute Regiment be given a two-month notice before the selection process begins, after which they will undergo a week-long preparatory orientation. Once orientation is complete, the first phase of training will include a four-week selection and screening process at the Special Forces Training School. After this screening, a board of officers will assign them to either the Parachute Regiment or a special forces battalion. Once assigned to a battalion, volunteers will undergo phase two of their probation, including three months of training in basic skills. In the final phase, the selected group will go through phase three of their training, which will include a four-week basic parachute course at the Parachute Training School in Agra.[72] If implemented, this process—a critical investment in improving a highly skilled force—may enhance the performance of the Indian Army.

Conclusion

Over the decades, the Indian Army has evolved as a professional fighting force under direct civilian control. While several challenges and gaps remain, the Indian Army's military objectives—as operationalized in

its doctrines, training, performance, and institutional reorganization—
promise room for continued improvement.

Notes

1. In addition to defending the country from external and internal threats, the Indian Army aids civil authorities in the maintenance of law and order, essential services, and disaster relief. For more on such instances, see: https://indianarmy. nic.in/Site/FormTemplete/frmTempSimple.aspx?MnId=rnd1UkME4UbZwE4 WjGKB5A==&ParentID=9SFI6UortWL5GObPAj6rpA==.

2. Srinath Raghavan, *India's War: The Making of Modern South Asia 1939–1945* (New Delhi: Penguin, 2016), 36.

3. Lt. Col. Gautam Sharma, *Nationalization of the Indian Army 1885–1947* (New Delhi: Allied Publishers, 1996), 101–02.

4. "India 1930–1947," British Military History Online Archives, https://www.british militaryhistory.co.uk/documents-india-1930-1947/.

5. For more on the early history of these organizational changes, see, Ayesha Ray, *The Soldier and the State in India: Nuclear Weapons, Counterinsurgency, and the Transformation of Indian Civil–Military Relations* (New Delhi: SAGE 2013), 29-32; S.K. Sinha, "Higher Defense Organization in India," *USI Papers*, no. 7 (1980).

6. The Army Act, 1950, Act No. 46 of 1950, 20 May 1950, Ministry of Defense, Government of India, https://mod.gov.in/dod/sites/default/files/TheArmyAct1 950.pdf.

7. "Organizational Set-Up and Functions," Official Website of the Indian Army, http://indianarmy.nic.in.

8. Armed Forces Tribunal, National Informatics Center, Government of India, http://aftdelhi.nic.in/act/AFT_Act_2007.pdf.

9. Ministry of Defense (MoD), "Spectrum of Conflict," in Joint Doctrine of Indian Armed Forces, Headquarters Integrated Defense Staff, 12–13.

10. MoD, "Spectrum of Conflict," 14.

11. MoD, "Spectrum of Conflict," 15.

12. Walter Ladwig, "A Cold Start to Hot Wars? The Indian Army's New Limited War Doctrine," *International Security* 32, no. 3 (Winter 2007/2008): 164.

13. Paul Staniland, "India's New Security Order," *War on the Rocks*, December 17, 2019, https://warontherocks.com/2019/12/indias-new-security-order/.

14. Taylor M. Fravel, "Why Are China and India Skirmishing at Their Border? Here's 4 Things to Know," *The Washington Post*, June 2, 2020, https://www.washingtonp ost.com/politics/2020/06/02/why-are-china-india-skirmishing-their-border-heres-4-things-know/.

15. Saurav Jha, "With 'Him Vijay' and Mountain Strike Corps, India Can Alter the Way China Border Is Managed," *ThePrint*, October 9, 2019, https://theprint.in/

opinion/with-him-vijay-mountain-strike-corps-india-can-alter-the-way-china-border-is-managed/303071/.

16. Sushant Singh, "Explained: What Happened to the Mountain Strike Corps?" *The Indian Express*, June 19, 2020, https://indianexpress.com/article/explained/explained-what-happened-to-the-mountain-strike-corps-6465221/.

17. Pravin Sawhney, "The Time for India to Have Joint Theater Commands Has Not Come," *The Wire*, July 22, 2018, https://thewire.in/security/the-time-for-india-to-have-joint-theatre-commands-has-not-come (accessed August 16, 2023).

18. For a comparison between American and Indian counterinsurgency approaches, see Ayesha Ray, *Culture, Context, and Capability: American and Indian Counterinsurgency Approaches* (New Delhi: Institute for Defense Studies and Analyses (IDSA), 2016).

19. Bibhu Prasad Routray, "India's Internal Lives: Counterinsurgency Role of Central Police Forces," *Small Wars and Insurgencies*, 24, no. 4 (2013): 657.

20. See Ayesha Ray, *The Soldier and State in India: Nuclear Weapons, Counterinsurgency, and the Transformation of Indian Civil–Military Relations* (New Delhi: SAGE, 2013), in which the author traces the exact historical and political moments in the debate on the use of nuclear weapons for strategic use and the key players involved.

21. For more on the causes of why states build nuclear weapons, and more specifically why India has built nuclear weapons, see, George Perkovich, *India's Nuclear Bomb: The Impact on Global Proliferation* (Berkley: University of California Press 1999); Ashley Tellis, *India's Emerging Nuclear Posture: Between Recessed Deterrent and Ready Arsenal* (Washington, DC: RAND 2001); Scott Sagan, *Inside Nuclear South Asia* (Stanford: Stanford Security Studies, 2009); andRaj Chengappa, *Weapons of Peace* (Delhi: Harper Collins 2000).

22. Draft of India's Nuclear Doctrine; Harsh V. Pant, "India and the Global Nuclear Order: A Quiet Assimilation," in *Indian Foreign Policy: An Overview* (Manchester: Manchester University Press, 2016), 217; Harsh V. Pant, "India's Nuclear Doctrine and Command Structure: Implications for India and the World," *Comparative Strategy* 24, no. 3 (July 2005): 277–93.

23. Gurmeet Kanwal, "India's Nuclear Doctrine and Policy," *Strategic Analysis* 24, no. 11 (February 2001): 1951–1972.

24. As quoted in Lauren J. Borja and M.V. Ramana, "Command and Control of India's Nuclear Arsenal," *Journal for Peace and Nuclear Disarmament* 3, no. 1 (2020): 9.

25. Shivshankar Menon, *Choices: Inside the Making of India's Foreign Policy* (Washington, DC: Brookings Institution Press, 2016): 110.

26. Shashank Joshi, "India's Nuclear Doctrine Should No Longer Be Taken for Granted," The Lowy Institute, March 22, 2017.

27. Christopher Clary and Vipin Narang, "India's Counterforce Temptations: Strategic Dilemmas, Doctrine, and Capabilities," *International Security* 43, no. 3 (Winter 2018/19): 7–52.

28. Rajesh Rajagopalan, "India's Nuclear Strategy: A Shift to Counterforce?" *ORF*, March 30, 2017, https://www.orfonline.org/expert-speak/india-nuclear-strat egy-shift-counterforce/.

29. Rajagopalan, "India's Nuclear Strategy."

30. Stephen Cohen and Sunil Dasgupta, "Army Modernization," in *Arming Without Aiming: India's Military Modernization*, ed. Stephen P. Cohen and Sunil Dasgupta (Washington, DC: Brookings Institution Press, 2010): 53.

31. Cohen and Dasgupta, "Army Modernization," 69.

32. B.G. Verghese, "Is India's Defense Establishment Rotting?" *Rediff*, April 5, 2012 https://www.rediff.com/news/slide-show/slide-show-1-is-indias-defence-establ ishment-rotting/20120405.htm.

33. Author's interview with Anit Mukherjee, Visiting Research Fellow, IDSA, New Delhi, July 2, 2012. For a more detailed and excellent exposition on defence re- forms, inter-service rivalry, see Anit Mukherjee, *The Absent Dialogue: Politicians, Bureaucrats, and the Military in India* (New Delhi: Oxford University Press, 2019).

34. Ashley J. Tellis, "India: Capable but Constrained," Strategic Studies Institute Report, US Army War College, 2020, 134.

35. Tellis, "India," 134.

36. The Indian Army, https://www.indianarmy.nic.in/Site/FormTemplete/frmTem p2PMR7C.aspx?MnId=fmKvW8J62Rsxv3FgA5pBiA==&ParentID=U3ij/ viLr0X2i5K7oOLmAQ==&flag=8CKP966uzg96kLov0aWdfQ==

37. Amrita Nayak Dutta, "How Army's Artillery Modernization Plan, Stuck in a Rut after Bofors, Is Picking up Pace," *ThePrint*, November 28, 202, https://theprint.in/ defence/how-armys-artillery-modernisation-plan-stuck-in-a-rut-after-bofors- is-picking-up-pace/553053/.

38. As quoted in Anit Mukherjee, *The Absent Dialogue: Politicians, Bureaucrats, and the Military in India* (New Delhi: Oxford University Press, 2019), 273.

39. Shaurya Karanbir Gurung, 'Parliamentary Standing Committee Criticizes Government for Inadequate Allocation of Funds to Army,' *The Economic Times*, January 8, 2019, https://economictimes.indiatimes.com/news/defence/parlia mentary-standing-committee-criticises-govt-for-inadequate-allocation-of- funds-to-army/articleshow/67427334.cms.

40. Gurung, "Allocation of Funds to Army."

41. Shaurya Karanbir Gurung, "No Improvement in Army's Availability of Ammunition," *Economic Times*, July 14, 2018. https://economictimes.indiati mes.com/news/defence/no-improvement-in-armys-availability-of-ammunit ion-cag/articleshow/59705766.cms?from=mdr; also see, Brendan Cole, "India's Military Might: Country Only Has 10 Days' Worth of Ammunition, Most Army Weapons Now Considered Vintage," *Newsweek* (March 4, 2019).

42. Government of India (GoI), *Ministry of Defense Report 2017–2018*, 114.

43. GoI, Ministry of Defense Report 2017–2018, 116.

44. GoI, Ministry of Defense Report 2017–2018, 117.

45. GoI, Ministry of Defense Report 2017–2018, 117.

46. Stephen Cohen, "The Untouchable Soldier: Caste, Politics, and the Indian Army," in *The South Asia Papers: A Critical Anthology of Writings by Stephen Philip Cohen*, ed. Stephen Cohen (Washington, DC: Brookings Institution Press, 2016), 88.

47. For an extensive discussion on this, see Kaushik Roy, "Race and Recruitment in the Indian Army: 1880–1918," *Modern Asian Studies* 47, no. 4 (July 2013): 1310–1347.

48. Amar Farooqui, "Divide and Rule? Race, Military Recruitment and Society in Late Nineteenth Century Colonial India," *Social Scientist* 43, no. 3–4 (2015), 54.

49. Lt. Col. D.K. Havanoor, "Make Army an Attractive Career Option," *New Indian Express*, August 29, 2018, https://www.newindianexpress.com/opinions/2018/aug/29/make-army-an-attractive-career-option-1864222.html.

50. Lt. General Prakash Katoch, "Cadre Restructuring in Indian Army," *Indian Defense Review*, November 16, 2019, http://www.indiandefencereview.com/news/cadre-restructuring-in-indian-army/.

51. Staff Sgt. Samuel Northrup, "US and Indian Armies Complete Exercise Yudh Abhyas," *US Army*, October 1, 2018, https://www.army.mil/article/211871/u_s_and_indian_armies_complete_exercise_yudh_abhyas_18.

52. Gina Harkins, "US Military Makes Bold Statement in First-of-Its-Kind Exercise with India," *Military News*, December 1, 2019, https://www.military.com/daily-news/2019/12/01/us-military-makes-bold-statement-first-its-kind-exercise-india.html.

53. "Indian Army is Buying New, More Powerful US Rifles," *Business Standard*, February 16, 2019, https://www.business-standard.com/article/defence/indian-army-is-buying-new-more-powerful-us-rifles-all-you-need-to-know-119021400977_1.html.

54. Lt. General H.S. Panag, "Light Tanks Served Well in '62. But Ladakh Needs a Stryker-Like Multipurpose Combat Platform," *ThePrint*, April 29, 2021, https://theprint.in/opinion/light-tanks-served-well-in-62-but-ladakh-needs-a-stryker-like-multipurpose-combat-platform/647939/.

55. Panag, "Light Tanks Served Well in '62."

56. "India Supreme Court Makes Landmark Ruling on Women in Army," *BBC News*, February 17, 2020, https://www.bbc.com/news/world-asia-india-51528141.

57. "Indian Armed Forces to Open All Combat Roles to Women," *Al Jazeera*, February 25, 2016, https://www.aljazeera.com/news/2016/2/25/indian-armed-forces-to-open-all-combat-roles-to-women.

58. "Paramilitary Forces to Get Woman Officers," *The Hindu*, March 14, 2016, https://www.thehindu.com/news/national/paramilitary-forces-to-get-woman-officers/article8349184.ece.

59. Srinath Raghavan, "The Battle within the Indian Army for Promotions," *NDTV*, May 5, 2015, https://www.ndtv.com/opinion/the-battle-within-indian-army-for-promotions-760514.

60. Raghavan, "The Battle Within Indian Army for Protections."

61. "Indian Army to Reorient HR Policy Considering Societal Changes," *The Economic Times*, July 11, 2018, https://economictimes.indiatimes.com/news/ defence/indian-army-to-re-orient-hr-policy-considering-societal-changes/arti cleshow/58329270.cms.

62. "Six Charts Tell You All You Need to Know about the Pay Commission Recommendations," *Scroll.in*, November 15, 2020, https://scroll.in/article/770 540/six-charts-tell-you-all-you-need-to-know-about-the-pay-commission-reco mmendations.

63. Mayank Jain, "Two Charts Show How Much Indian Soldiers Are Paid vs Their British and US Counterparts," *Scroll.in*, November 25, 2015, https://scroll.in/arti cle/771184/two-charts-show-how-much-indian-soldiers-are-paid-vs-their-brit ain-and-us-counterparts.

64. Dinesh Narayanan, "How Pay, Pensions, and Sloth Eat Up India's Defense Funds," *Economic Times*, July 11, 2018, https://economictimes.indiatimes.com/news/ defence/how-pay-pensions-and-sloth-eat-up-indias-defence-funds/articles how/52843465.cms?from=mdr.

65. Abhay Kumar Singh, "Military Manpower Cost in India and the United States: A Comparative Analysis," *IDSA Special Feature*, May 29, 2020, https://idsa.in/spe cialfeature/military-manpower-cost-in-india-aksingh.

66. "One Rank, One Pension (OROP) to the Defense Forces Personnel," Department of Ex-Servicemen, Ministry of Defense, Government of India, http://desw.gov. in/orop

67. Dinakar Peri, "Protesting Veterans Meet Rajnath," *The Hindu*, July 4, 2019, https://www.thehindu.com/news/national/orop-protesting-veterans-meet-rajn ath/article28286838.ece.

68. "Editorial: A Large Chunk of India's Defense Budget Goes Toward Staff Salaries, Not Equipment," *Hindustan Times*, May 3, 2018, https://www.hindustantimes. com/editorials/a-large-chunk-of-india-s-defence-budget-goes-towards-staff- salaries-not-equipment/story-zuIYniuudWxWCGOmqZvDGK.html.

69. Sakshi Sharma, "Occupational Stress in the Armed Forces: An Indian Army Perspective," *IIMB Management Review* 27, Issue 3 (September 2015): 185–95.

70. Sharma, "Occupational Stress in the Armed Forces."

71. "Indian Army Considers Allowing Young Professionals to Join Force for the 3- Year Tenure: A Look at Military Conscription Laws around the World," *Firstpost*, May 14, 2020, https://www.firstpost.com/india/indian-army-considers-allow ing-young-professionals-to-join-force-for-3-year-tenure-a-look-at-military- conscription-laws-around-the-world-8368111.html.

72. Amrita Nayak Dutta, "Army Plans to Expand Roles for Elite Special and Airborne Forces Known for Surgical Strikes," *ThePrint*, June 10, 2020, https://theprint.in/ defence/army-plans-to-expand-roles-for-elite-special-and-airborne-forces- known-for-surgical-strikes/438995/.

3

The Indian Navy

Atul Bhardwaj

Introduction

The Indian Navy is India's primary instrument for projecting maritime power in the Indian Ocean region and its extended neighbourhood. Since its inception, the navy has been an indispensable tool of Indian foreign policy and an integral part of the nation's grand strategy. Although it does not set the domestic security agenda, it often acts as the lodestar when it comes to establishing India's international security priorities.

Originally part of the multilateral naval force led by the British Royal Navy, the Indian Navy was nonetheless a crucial factor in burgeoning Indo-Soviet ties during the 1960s. As an integral part of India's non-aligned policy, even in the heyday of its association with the former Soviet Union, the navy's relationship with the West flourished.

In the aftermath of the Cold War, as India drew closer to the United States, the navy once again played a critical role in forging strategic bonds between two large democracies. Based on a mutual need to address the looming threat from China, the Indian Navy altered its priorities, force planning, and operational doctrines to achieve greater interoperability with the US Navy and other friendly navies.

This chapter traces the evolution of the Indian Navy's roles and missions through the prism of its experiences with three major sea powers: Britain, the Soviet Union, and the United States. The chapter also looks at debates within the navy over what strategy will best prepare it to address the present security scenario, as well as reviewing the

Atul Bhardwaj, *The Indian Navy* In: *Institutional Roots of India's Security Policy.* Edited by: Milan Vaishnav, Oxford University Press. © Oxford University Press 2024. DOI: 10.1093/oso/9780198894612.003.0003 navy's attempts at indigenization. The final section examines personnel, promotion polices, organizational structure, and how the Indian Navy has upgraded its training and recruitment structures to keep pace with technological changes.

Raison d'Etat and History

According to the Indian Maritime Doctrine, the Indian Navy's full range of operations include four distinct roles: military, diplomatic, constabulary, and benign.

The essence of the Indian Navy is its military character. Capable of projecting offensive power both on and from the sea, the navy's primary area of operations extend 'at a minimum within the Bay of Bengal and Arabian Sea and at a maximum from Cape of Good Hope to the South China Sea through the straits of Malacca'.[1] As both an offensive and defensive force, its role is to deter any adverse naval actions against India through its conventional assets as well as India's sea-based nuclear second-strike capability. As part of its military role, it also safeguards sea lines of communications (SLOCs) by providing protective cover to Indian shipping in coastal waters and on the high seas. The navy's current mission-based deployments involve positioning mission-ready ships and aircraft along critical SLOCs and chokepoints.

The Indian Navy's diplomatic role is to favourably shape the maritime environment in the furtherance of national security and economic objectives. It performs goodwill visits to friendly countries and undertakes regular exercises with allied navies.

The Indian Navy is also an essential component of the country's coastal defence architecture. Its defensive—or constabulary—mission balances coastal and offshore security with more irregular operations, such as anti-piracy, anti-trafficking, and counterterrorism missions.

Finally, the navy's so-called benign role—thus named because it does not involve violence—primarily involves responding to humanitarian crises, called Humanitarian Assistance and Disaster Relief (HADR). It also plays a role in facilitating the growth of India's blue economy, which currently contributes about 4 per cent of the country's gross domestic product.[2]

Many naval experts feel that the dominant elite in India is beset with a continental mindset that has prevented India from reaching its maritime potential. As former Chief of the Naval Staff Arun Prakash has said,

> A lack of political resolve and diplomatic lassitude have been contributory factors, [but] it is the absence of an over-arching vision which conceptualizes the [Indian Ocean region] in a 50–75 year perspective that has led to the neglect of maritime issues critical to India's vital interests.[3]

Over the years, the navy presented its case for a blue-water fleet many times to key government leaders, highlighting maritime history, conventional sea-power concepts, the size of India's coastline, and the need to provide HADR in the Indian Ocean region as reasons to invest in naval power. However, none of these rationales had much impact. As a trio of US Naval War College professors have argued,

> It may be difficult to sustain a navy over the long haul, both politically and fiscally, if its primary mission falls towards the peacetime end of the spectrum and its benefits to the nation are indirect and tough to quantify. Waiting for tsunamis is not an idea that can sustain a forward maritime strategy.[4]

That predicament changed in the twenty-first century with the stupendous rise of Chinese naval power. The Indian Navy now has a clear and present adversary, which is beginning to force the government to consider the navy's needs with greater alacrity. It now unhesitatingly asserts that the Indian Navy is 'a force instrument as opposed to merely a protective tool concerned with regulatory and custodial duties'.[5]

The threat posed by China has also compelled the Indian Navy to end its isolation and reimagine how it can act in concert with the other three members of the Quadrilateral Security Dialogue (or Quad): Japan, Australia, and the United States. According to the former Chief of the Naval Staff, Admiral Karambir Singh, the four Quad navies have evolved to a 'high degree of interoperability' and can come together in an 'almost plug and play mechanism'.[6]

One legacy of India's evolving defence relationships is that the Indian Navy still uses an eclectic mix of Soviet and Western equipment.

A sweeping plan to modernize the Indian Navy is focused on enhancing the precision accuracy of its weapons systems, improving its ship and air-borne reconnaissance capabilities, streamlining its logistics operations, and enhancing the skill set of its personnel.

The Four Schools

The Indian Navy's association with three major sea powers has been the defining feature of its intellectual as well as material growth. The navy's first mentor was Britain—by then, an exhausted sea power—which introduced it to the idea of command of the oceans and fed India's blue-water ambitions with aircraft carriers. Its second mentor was Russia (and earlier, the Soviet Union)—predominantly a continental power—which taught it sea denial and gave it nuclear submarines. But both Britain and Russia were declining powers. The United States, India's third mentor, is currently helping transform the Indian Navy into a network-centric force capable of operating in a complex, multilateral environment. As the United States valiantly defends its status as the world's pre-eminent sea power by building diverse alliances and partnerships, it is urging the Indian Navy to direct its efforts against a powerful mutual adversary: China.

Scholar Iskander Rehman identifies four schools of thought that have shaped the Indian naval mind since independence: the Indian Continentalist School, the Raj Pan-Oceanic (or British) School, the Soviet School, and the Monrovian School. The Monrovian School, which draws its strength from the United States' Monroe Doctrine (which emphasizes the central of 'spheres of influence'), forms the basis of India's desire to control marine activity in its maritime neighbourhood and prevent competing powers from intruding.[7] It could also be called the American School, as it is closely linked to the Indian Navy's relationship with the US Navy following the collapse of the Soviet Union. The Monrovian School is more pragmatic than the British School and more audacious than the Soviet School. According to Rehman, 'The Raj Pan-Oceanic vision is that of a future overwhelmingly self-confident power in the Indian Ocean, whose primacy is uncontested. The Monrovian school, on the other hand, envisions a navy geared towards the possibility of an external threat.'[8]

The inward-looking Indian Continentalist School focused primarily on protecting the country's land borders. It envisaged a minimalist navy that did not operate beyond India's exclusive economic zone (EEZ). This school believed that since India's strategic objectives do not demand an expeditionary naval force, naval development should not be an overriding priority. As the Indo-Pacific and Indian Ocean have become more prominent in global geopolitics, this school has been rendered essentially defunct.

The Raj Pan-Oceanic School, inspired by the British Royal Navy, dominated naval planning from independence till the late 1960s. At the end of the war, three factors determined the scope and speed of India's naval development: demobilization, mutiny, and the Partition-induced pain of sharing its meagre naval resources with Pakistan. These three pain points propelled the Indian Navy to think afresh and almost start from scratch.

The Indian Naval Headquarters (NHQ) released its first plan for the Royal Indian Navy in 1948.[9] The ambitious vision imagined an Indian blue-water fleet.[10] But it was guided by the needs of a vanishing empire, and appeared unrealistic for a post-colonial infant nation plagued by constant food shortages.[11] The reason Britain advanced its grand vision for the post-colonial navy was the sterling expenditures it had sunk into India and the use of India's armed forces—£1,160 million by July 1947.[12] The British government leveraged its maritime expertise and sold surplus warships produced during the Second World War to retain British influence as well as reduce its debt burden.

It was natural for young Indian naval officers and strategists to buy into the British vision because history had taught them that India's future was tied to the oceans. They were also in awe of the Royal Navy that had transformed a small island nation into a colossal global power. According to historian Greg Kennedy, 'The dominions and colonies of the Empire regarded the Royal Navy as "the embodiment of martial aspect of Imperial defence"'.[13]

In the British retreat, Indian navalists saw an opportunity to fill the vacuum. As historian Martin Wainwright notes, 'Although the two regimes markedly differed ... the attitudes of their members towards South Asian security were remarkably similar.'[14]

Sardar K.M. Panikkar and Keshav Vaidya were two early proponents of the British School. They advocated for a navy that would defend not only India's coast but its distant oceanic frontiers.[15] Panikkar's book, *The*

Future of South East Asia, focused on building a security architecture in the Indian Ocean region akin to the idea of the old Indian Empire, which functioned as a common defence area through the creation of a commonwealth entity—including Pakistan and Myanmar—that was tethered to Britain. Panikkar's security concert also included 'countries of "Further India"—Thailand, Indo-China, the Netherlands, East Indies, Malaya and Singapore.'[16]

In 1943, a British member of parliament, George Schuster, wrote two articles in *The Spectator* titled 'India's World Role'. In the first article, he lamented the loss of British legitimacy in managing the stability of the Indian Ocean region. He reiterated the urgent need to create a 'sufficient lawful power' for the peaceful management of the 'key-area of the East, the broad belt of land and sea between Aden and Singapore.'[17] In his second article, he critiqued Panikkar's idea of a regional security concert, saying it was not feasible because the three competing nationalities— India, Pakistan, and Burma—could not be tied into an 'organic relationship' in which defence was the only common thread. The British were not willing to pass the leadership baton to India.

In 1947, a 32-year-old Indian officer, future Admiral A.K. Chatterji, served as Director of Naval Plans and Intelligence at NHQ. As one of the authors of the audacious first plan, he foresaw an Indian Navy that would one day be as powerful as the Royal Navy. Chatterji, who went on to define the contours of the future navy in the 1960s, remained a steadfast believer in the Indian Navy's potential to be a moderating force in the region. In 1966, he penned an article in *The Hindu* entitled 'Sea Power and India', advocating the expansion of the Indian Navy.[18]

Britain's retreat from east of Suez in 1968 motivated the formation of a study group in 1969 that redefined the strategic situation from the Indian Navy's perspective.[19] The study group's report was lambasted by adherents of the Indian Continentalist School, who labelled it 'notorious' and neo-colonialist in its outlook. In a scathing critique, Major General D.K. Palit stated that

> unlike the other services the imperial tradition in the navy overlapped by a good many years into the era beyond 1947 so that the Royal Navy mentorship of the IN [Indian Navy] continued as guiding influence

until very recently. The result is that the navy's attitudes and approaches to maritime strategy are sometimes conditioned by the grandiose, world power outlook of the British Navy rather than by the more realistic aspirations of an economically backward, newly independent, status quo nation like India.[20]

As the reality of India's financial picture sharpened, the Navy's leadership was forced to tweak their original plan.[21] in 1957, Admiral R.D. Katari—the first Chief of the Naval Staff—complained that the government's budgetary allocations were just enough 'to keep the service just ticking over and its morale just above the demoralization level'.[22] The cash-strapped Indian government could do little to assuage the navy's feelings. Yet the navy's budget allocations saw a steady upward climb from 1951 to 1964. The naval budget increased from 4 per cent (of the overall defence budget) in 1950–51 to 9 per cent in 1956–57, reaching 12 per cent in 1959–60. But after the Sino-Indian War of 1962, allocations plummeted to 4 per cent in 1964–65. These jumps in the allocations were certainly due to the lingering British influence on the IN under the commonwealth umbrella.[23]

During this first decade after independence, the foundations for a formidable surface fleet were laid. The Indian Navy worked in a multilateral environment alongside Pakistanis and Sri Lankans, participating in joint exercises under the aegis of the Royal Navy's squadron based at Trincomalee. After the closure of the Royal Navy's Sri Lankan base in 1958, these exercises shifted to Kochi before subsequently petering out.[24]

Freedom from Colonial Legacy

Until 1965, Britain was India's main supplier of naval platforms and weapon systems. But by the mid-1960s, non-aligned countries began seeking military help from the Soviet Union too.[25] Both the Americans and the British refused to supply the Indian Navy with submarines, leaving India with no choice but to procure them from the Soviets. This opened fresh avenues for the financially challenged Indian economy to meet its naval needs. The Soviets offered equipment on long-term credit—initially 10 years, later extended to 17—with payments beginning in June following the year of delivery. This offer, according to Finance Ministry calculations, worked out to a mere 1.8 per cent annual interest rate.[26]

Thus began the Indian Navy's so-called Soviet School era. According to Rehman, the new, Soviet-influenced sea strategy was conservative and defensive. It defined the Indian Navy's reach and range in terms of controlling chokepoints and focused on defending areas in its vicinity. The success of the strategy was evident in India's brilliant and innovative use of its resources against Pakistan in the 1971 War through which Bangladesh (formerly East Pakistan) achieved its independence.

Over the next two decades, the Indian Navy's blue-water dreams were partially realized. The government approved the ambitious 1972–74 defence plan, paving the way for Soviet acquisitions, indigenous vessel construction, and the induction of corvettes and Sea King antisubmarine helicopters from Britain. In 1975, the central government convened the Second Apex Group to revise the 1974–79 defence plan and align its physical and financial targets. Says Vice Admiral (ret.) Gm Hiranandani,

> For the first time after independence, defence planning was viewed in the wider perspective of the national economy in an attempt to mesh the Defence Five Year Plan with the national Five Year Plan. The Second Apex group accepted most of the Navy's projections. This Committee recommended enhanced allocation of funds to support core naval schemes.[27]

By 1987, 70 per cent of India's warships were supplied by the Soviets.[28] But despite the overwhelming presence of Soviet equipment, the Soviet Union's overall influence on the Indian Navy was limited, and its relationship remained largely transactional and tactical. The Indian Navy continued to rely on naval knowledge produced in the West—the US Naval Institute's *Proceedings* magazine and the Royal Navy's *Naval Review* were among the most popular professional publications in the Indian Navy. As British sea power declined, the US Navy assumed its place as the Indian Navy's intellectual mentor.

From Commonwealth to Quad

If the British School prescribed utopian dreams of sea power and the Soviet School introduced an element of realism and focus, the new American School has spurred India to take on a new, asymmetrically powerful threat: China.

In the mid-1990s, the Indian Navy forged a new relationship with the United States, hinging on shared strategic and security concerns related to growing Chinese aggression and assertiveness in the South China Sea and the Indian Ocean. According to Admiral K.B. Singh, the Indian Navy believes in 'developing the idea of collective military competence to tackle regional challenges'.[29]

Although the Indo-US Framework for Maritime Security Cooperation was not signed until 2006, the two countries' naval relationship goes back more than three decades. The first joint naval exercises, called Malabar, began in 1992.[30] The Malabar initiative has matured since then; in 2020, Australia participated in this exercise as well. In 2004, the two navies worked together as a team in post-tsunami relief operations in the Indian Ocean. Two years earlier, the Indian Navy provided protection to US ships in the Indian Ocean. Joint anti-piracy operations in the Arabian Sea also strengthened the bonds of friendship.

The two navies are now engaged in developing interoperable doctrines and technology-driven networks.[31] In 2007, India purchased the INS *Jalashwa*, a US-built Trenton-class amphibious ship. The biggest addition to the Indian Navy's weapons list is the P8I maritime reconnaissance aircraft, which has opened fresh avenues for joint antisubmarine operations. The United States is selling India two dozen multi-role MH-60R Seahawk maritime helicopters armed with Hellfire missiles, capable of antisubmarine warfare. Underwater maritime patrol and reconnaissance is another potential area for positive engagement between the two navies, as unmanned underwater vehicles will almost certainly dominate the naval space in the coming decades. India's procurement priorities are shifting to keep pace; the Indian Navy is buying 10 tactical MQ-9 Reaper drones from US defence corporation General Atomics.

India is also seeking technological expertise from the United States to help realize its dreams of building an indigenous aircraft carrier. The two navies have set up a Joint Working Group on Aircraft Carrier Technology

Cooperation to exchange information under the ambit of the India–US Defence Technology and Trade Initiative.

In October 2020, the United States and India signed four foundational defence agreements: the General Security of Military Information Agreement, the Logistics Support Agreement, the Communications and Information Security Memorandum of Agreement, and the Basic Exchange and Cooperation Agreement for Geospatial Intelligence. These agreements have removed existing roadblocks, opening avenues for closer cooperation between the two navies and new institutional mechanisms for interaction between the Indian Navy and the US Indo-Pacific Command.

Specifically, India and the United States see myriad opportunities to collaborate on maritime domain awareness, search and rescue, non-combatant evacuation operations, coastal security, and HADR operations. Besides politically non-sensitive relations, the navies are also focused on information sharing. India's National Command Control Communications and Intelligence Network and naval fusion Information Management and Analysis Centre collaborate with the US intelligence community.

The United States and India differ in their interpretation of the United Nations Convention on the Law of the Sea regarding military activities in exclusive economic zones (EEZs). New Delhi demands prior notification for innocent passage and prior consent for military exercises or manoeuvres in its EEZ. China's position on these two aspects is roughly the same as India's. On the other hand, Washington considers these as 'excessive maritime claims'. The US Navy has carried out Freedom of Navigation patrols (FNOPs), contradicting India's position, and these instances are reflected in its annual FNOPs reports. This is perhaps one reason why the Indian Navy has not been a part of US FNOPs in the South China Sea. Despite these differences, however, India and the United States are both committed to an open, inclusive, and rules-based international order.

The Indian Navy sees the US Navy as its best hope to realize its power-projection ambitions. For India, the long-term benefits of a relationships with the US Navy include access to the US military–industrial complex and opportunities to kickstart its indigenous warship-building programme.

Unlike in the 1970s, the Indian Navy does not intend to make the Indian Ocean a 'zone of peace'. Hoping to contest China's dominant position, New Delhi is keen to invite like-minded navies into the region. In April 2021, India, along with other members of the Quad, participated for the first time in France's La Pérouse naval exercise in the Bay of Bengal. The possibility of a "Quad +" framework has also taken root, with Germany, the European Union, and the United Kingdom eager to define their Indo-Pacific tilt.[32]

The Call of Mahan

The Indian Navy's unflinching faith in sea power has made it an ardent fan of Alfred Thayer Mahan, the influential American naval strategist whose writings on sea power helped define it.[33] A storied American politician, Henry L. Stimson, once remarked of the US Navy that it 'frequently seemed to retire from the realm of logic into a dim religious world in which Neptune was God, [Alfred Thayer] Mahan his prophet, and the US Navy the only true church'.[34] But Indian navalists often ignore the fact that India's quest to be a sea power is constrained more by its poor economy than by its continental security needs or lack of maritime consciousness.

As China's People's Liberation Army (PLA) Navy inches closer to par with the US Navy's tonnage and firepower, India's maritime strategists are once again debating whether sea control or sea denial is the best strategy to confront the Chinese navy. In India, the concept of sea control is usually tied to aircraft carriers; sea denial is about nuclear submarines. Even the concept of a 'balanced fleet', composed of aircraft carriers as well as submarines, remains moored to the idea that sea denial is a subset of sea control. As Australian Rear Admiral (ret.) James Goldbrick and Indian Rear Admiral (ret.) Sudarshan Y. Shrikhande argue, ' "strategies of denial" would in fact be part of a multidimensional fight to compete for sea control' and a "balanced force" is vital' to deter the conflict from escalating.[35]

One option for denying the PLA Navy use of the sea, which is both pragmatic and frugal, is based on using submarines. According to Abhijit Singh's analysis, 'Such a plan would impose fewer burdens on Indian naval force structures, setting goals that would be more practically achievable.' But Singh draws an important distinction between the strategy during war as opposed to peacetime. He argues that, in peacetime, power projection is exclusive to aircraft carriers because submarines are too provocative. 'In peacetime,' he writes, 'sea control is more "attitude" than "strategy" and the use of offensive sea denial assets (such as submarines) isn't an available option.'

The aircraft carrier does play an important role in power projection during peacetime. However, the question is how many times the INS *Vikrant* or *Viraat* have actually played that role for India? Rumours that US aircraft were headed to the Indian Ocean to support India during the India–China War of 1962 and against India in 1971 caused a massive furore in the Indian as well as international media. How many times did the news that Indian carriers were in contested waters have similar impact? If India could not achieve power projection through carriers when the Indian Ocean region was relatively peaceful, it is difficult to imagine greater success when the world's most powerful navies are jostling for space in Indian Ocean waters.

The Indian Navy is not designed to take on a sea power capable of commanding the oceans. Defying the US Navy was—and still is—considered unimaginable in Indian naval circles. However, when it comes to confronting China, there is no dearth of audacity. What is needed is a critical examination of the validity of India's sea-control strategy and the relevance of aircraft carriers in confronting a 350-ship Chinese navy. Indian aircraft carriers have a poor record of success in battle. In the 1962 conflict with China, the aircraft carrier, acquired in 1961, played no role; in the 1965 war with Pakistan, the carrier was kept out of harm's way; and in the 1971 war, INS *Vikrant* was chased by a Pakistani submarine right up to Vishakhapatnam. To imagine that one or two aircraft carriers can serve as effective platforms against a massive navy is overly ambitious, if not preposterous.

India's carrier battle group can only operate as a part of a bilateral (with the United States) or multilateral (with Quad countries) force. Military strategist Thomas Barnett predicted in 2001 that India would emerge as a regional power only in conjunction with the US Navy and not in opposition to it.[36] That association will come at a price. As former US Assistant

Secretary of State for European and Eurasian Affairs A. Wess Mitchell suggests,

> Making the most of the US-Indian relationship to thwart China's advance is not a one-way street; it will also require India to continue taking on greater burden and risks than it became accustomed to in the Cold War and its immediate aftermath.[37]

Another reason for the Indian Navy's enduring faith in aircraft carriers is its interservice rivalry with the Indian Air Force (IAF). A carrier-less force would end the navy's monopoly on marine aviation. This rivalry is likely to grow as efforts to evolve joint theatre commands pick up momentum in the Indian armed forces. The antagonism was on display during recent India–US exercises in the Indian Ocean. For instance, the Press Information Bureau's media release highlighted the IAF's participation and omitted the navy's role in an exercise with the USS *Ronald Reagan* carrier strike group during its transit through the Indian Ocean region in June 2021.[38] The press release stated: 'IAF has extensive experience in maritime operations in [the Indian Ocean region]. This has been consolidated over the years by the conduct of exercises from countries island territories.'[39]

India's first maritime theatre command is being erected at Karwar, on the country's west coast. It will exercise full operational control over extant Western and Eastern naval fleets, maritime strike fighter jets, and transport aircraft from both the air force and the navy, two amphibious infantry brigades, and other assets under the Andaman and Nicobar Joint Command. With IAF assets placed under a naval commander, the navy may reconsider the need for an aircraft carrier in the future. Furthermore, the need for fourth-generation autonomous fighting vehicles and swarm warfare will be even more reason for the Indian Navy to not invest in platforms that are likely to lose relevance before 2150. The former Chief of Defence Staff General Bipin Rawat wanted the navy's limited defence budget to be used on cruise missiles and submarines,[40] rather than a third proposed carrier, the INS *Vishal*—which is estimated to cost between $6 and $8 billion and to take at least 10 years to build.[41]

The Indian Navy presently operates two aircraft carriers: INS *Vikrant* and INS *Vikramaditya*. According to the serving Chief of Naval Staff

Admiral Hari Kumar, the Navy intends to commission Cochin Shipyard for another 40,000 ton Vikrant class carrier. The small short-range carrier, capable of operating only 25 aircraft, is considered inadequate for a serious power projection role. [42] Furtehr, land-based aircraft are not adequate to achieve India's geopolitical objectives that extend beyond 1,000 kilometres from the coastline. Such geopolitical compulsions make sea-based aviation a necessity. But to achieve such range of operations, the Indian Navy needs a carrier that is 65,000 tons with optimal combat capability. [43]

What advocates of sea control ignore is that India is merely an aspirational sea power. India has adequate warships to guard its coastline and blue-water capabilities, but that does not make it a potent sea power.

According to military historian Geoffrey Till, there is more to sea power than warships. The military assets that constitute sea power may be deployed from land or air. Non-military, industrial elements—like merchant shipping, fishing, marine insurance, and shipbuilding or repair—also contribute to sea power. [44] Leverage over ocean-bound trade during times of both peace and war is one of the most important elements of sea power. [45]

India has limited ability to harness non-military sea power, including its shipping fleet, shipbuilding industry, and modern ports. It also has almost no presence in the global marine service industry, the invisible force that underwrites sea-borne commerce. Indian naval power can guard the SLOCs in the Indian Ocean, but the country has little influence over the rhythms of international trade and commerce. It is this mismatch that makes the Indian Navy's Mahanian aspirations appear ambitious under the present circumstances.

Indigizenation

Like sea control, indigizenation—moving from being a buyer's navy to a builder's navy—is also an article of faith in the Indian Navy. Although the navy has made greater strides towards indigizenation than India's other military services, it still has a long way to go.

According to Vice Admiral G.M. Hiranandani, 'Mr. Krishna Menon's contribution to naval self-reliance was as monumental as Admiral

Mountbatten's contribution.'[46] Menon was instrumental in acquiring the Mazagon Dock shipyard in Mumbai (now Mazagon Dock Limited) and the Garden Reach shipyard in Kolkata (now Garden Reach Shipbuilders and Engineers Limited, or GRSE)—both important hubs of India's shipbuilding efforts. Admiral Chatterji, who became the Chief of Naval Staff in 1966, continued Menon's efforts. He spearheaded a naval dockyard expansion scheme, starting construction on a new dockyard in Visakhapatnam as the Indian Navy began acquiring Soviet ships and submarines.

The Directorate of Naval Construction (DNC), formed in 1954, moved on from designing tugs and other small crafts to designing warships. In 1964, the DNC became the Central Design Office (CDO).[47] Since the 1970s, the CDO—in conjunction with Mazagon Dock Limited, GRSE, and Goa Shipyard Limited—have delivered ships ranging from frigates to survey vessels. Indigenously built ships include *Leander*-class frigates, *Sandhayak*-class survey vessels, *Godavari*-class frigates, *Brahmaputra*-class frigates, *Delhi*-class destroyers, LST (L), and *Khukri*-class missile corvettes.

As the Indian Navy gained proficiency in designing and constructing hulls and propulsion machinery, a significant portion of the weaponry and sensor systems continued to be sourced from international markets. To reduce this dependence, the Weapons & Electronics Systems Organization (WESO), was created in 1978 and tasked with systems integration on board *Godavari*-class frigates.[48]

In 1985, WESO was renamed the Weapons & Electronics Systems Engineering Establishment (WESEE). It moved beyond systems integration to designing and developing command-and-control systems and software. It also began devising a data-link system between ships and aircraft known as Project Skylark.[49] Using a very low-frequency transmission facility commissioned at Tamil Nadu in 1990, this system aids communications between ships and submarines at sea. The facility is essential for command and control of nuclear weapons on board a submerged nuclear submarine.

Twenty-first century challenges have added further impetus for self-reliance in defence production. Naval warfare has been disrupted by technologies of the fourth industrial revolution. Commodore (ret.) Sujeet Samaddar sorts the technologies that will dramatically change naval warfare into four baskets: (1) technology that drives information, (2) advanced, man-made materials, (3) autonomous vehicles, and (4) transformational energy generation and storage systems.[50]

The Indian Navy has renewed its focus on improving its force levels through indigization and harnessing disruptive technologies through innovation. The navy set up the Naval Innovation and Indigenization Organization (NIIO) in 2020. Its nodal agency is the Directorate of Indigenization (DOI), established in 2006. Within the NIIO, the technology development acceleration cell works on studying disruptive technologies and how they can be inducted into naval platforms.

The Indian Navy also closely collaborates with the Defence Research and Development Organization (DRDO). The two bodies hold regular meetings to review critical technologies being pursued. These collaborative efforts have made a significant impact, including the *Arihant*-class submarines, the Brahms supersonic cruise missile, and the Barak 8 medium-range surface-to-air missile.

The navy has also collaborated with the Indian Space Research Organization (ISRO). Their work together resulted in Rukmani, a multi-band communication-cum-surveillance satellite dedicated to naval needs. Since 2013, the satellite has played a crucial role in enhancing the navy's maritime domain awareness, allowing ships to exchange positional information and communicate on a real-time basis across the Indian Ocean.[51] According to retired Vice Admiral Satish Soni,

> Exploitation of space, capabilities to network at sea to achieve battle space transparency, unarmed combat, specialised munitions and cyber warfare are the core areas [India] must focus on. Setting up an [Advanced Technology Project] type structure to facilitate assimilation and integration of advanced technologies for building modern aircraft carriers is recommended.[52]

In order to indigenously develop technologies that will determine its future capabilities and capacities, the Indian Navy will have to forgo some of its older platforms. If the navy continues to expend its limited budget on platforms that are fast becoming obsolete, India's dreams of becoming a bigger sea power will remain elusive.

Tumultuous Times

The Indian Navy was a largely uncontroversial force until the end of the Cold War. In 1990, fissures in the top echelons emerged into the public domain.

At the heart of the controversy was then Rear Admiral (later Chief of Naval Staff) Vishnu Bhagwat. He was slated to command the Western Fleet but was denied the position by Admiral J.G. Nadkarni, who was Chief of Naval Staff at the time. Seeing his high-profile career go up in flames, Bhagwat sought redress before the courts. He won his case and was eventually appointed Fleet Commander in 1991. In 1996, he became Chief of Naval Staff. He was unceremoniously removed by the Vajpayee government in 1998, on charges that he had talked to the press about India's secret nuclear submarine programme without authorization. Bhagwat claimed that what he had revealed was already out in the open. The government undermined the position of the naval chief by refusing to accept his recommendation that Vice Admiral Harinder Singh not be appointed as his deputy. This assertion of civilian supremacy over India's armed forces generated considerable debate over civil–military relations in the country.

The controversy over Bhagwat was an extension of the friction between the British and Soviet Schools that had been brewing since the 1970s. Bhagwat was considered to be an ardent supporter of the Soviet School. He was inspired by US Admiral Hyman G. Rickover, the so-called father of the nuclear navy. Bhagwat saw nuclear submarines as the backbone of the Indian Navy and was instrumental in pushing to lease INS *Chakra I*, a nuclear submarine, from the Soviet Union in the 1990s. To Bhagwat, the Indian Navy's association with the Soviets was not a problem. However, adherents of the British School saw India's reliance on Soviet equipment as a burden imposed by Indian's foreign policy of non-alignment and were keen to move closer to the West. The disintegration of the Soviet Union in 1991 disrupted India's supply of spare Soviet equipment, pushing devotees of the British School—which was fast metamorphosizing into the American School—to advocate for a bold course alteration. Bhagwat was likely the lone voice trying to protect the Indian Navy's legacy relations with the Russians.

After the Bhagwat incident, the navy and its chiefs remained in the news. Admiral Sushil Kumar, who replaced Bhagwat as Chief of Naval Staff, was named by the Central Bureau of Investigation in a first information report on alleged corruption regarding the purchase of Barak 1 missile systems.[53] Admiral Arun Prakash, who served as Chief of Naval Staff from 2004 to 2006, was also enmeshed in scandal during the naval war-room leak and the Scorpene deal scam. And one of the worst episodes in the Indian Navy's history occurred in 2014, when in a span of seven months it suffered 10 adverse incidents—including a series of fatal submarine accidents—that challenged its operational ethos as well as its maintenance standards.[54] In the wake of these accidents, Admiral D.K. Joshi took moral responsibility and resigned as the Chief of Naval Staff.

Ever since that tumultuous phase, the Indian Navy has been cruising along at a steady pace and increasing its engagement in the Indo-Pacific with other democracies. Unlike in the 1970s, today's navy enjoys a broad consensus regarding its growing collaboration and interoperability with the US Navy. During the heyday of its relations with the Soviet Union, they had no common enemy to build around. Today, however, the Indian Navy's force-level planning is based on its strategic and ideological links with the US Navy, and the two are united in viewing China as the common threat.

Organization

The Indian Navy has three commands: one each in Mumbai, Visakhapatnam, and Kochi. The Andaman and Nicobar Command is a tri-service command, but the commander-in-chief billet is reserved for the navy.

In 1985, Naval Headquarters (NHQ) undertook its first major review to streamline the navy's command-and-control structure. The review committee proposed reducing the number of operational control authorities from three to two and tasking the Southern Naval Command, based in Kochi, with all naval training activities. The Flag Officer Commanding-in-Chief (FOC-in-C) Western Naval Command was given the jurisdiction of the western seaboard and the Arabian Sea. The FOC-in-C Eastern Naval Command was made responsible for the eastern seaboard and the Bay of Bengal. Another major decision taken by the review committee was to put the Flag Officer Goa Area (FOGA) in charge of the Naval Air Arm as the Flag Officer Naval Aviation (FONA), making them responsible directly to NHQ for all aviation matters. However, the operational deployment of all air assets remains with the FOC-in-Cs of the Western and Eastern Naval Commands. The committee also created the position of Flag Officer Submarines (FOSM) to manage the Submarine Arm. Further major changes included redesignating the Chief of Logistics (COL) as Controller of Logistic Support (CLS) and making the Chief of Material (COM) the single point of accountability for maintenance and logistics.

In 1990, Vice Admiral K.A.S.Z. Raju led a committee to again review the navy's command structure. Though the committee made far-reaching recommendations, none were implemented. In 1994, another committee, headed by Vice Admiral Madhvendra Singh, was formed to look into reorganizing NHQ and the command headquarters. His major recommendations included reducing the workload of the Vice Chief of Naval Staff by having fewer directorates report to him and upgrading the CLS and Controller Warship Production & Acquisition (CWP&A) to be principal staff officers.[55]

FOC-in-Cs of the Eastern and Western Commands enjoy operational autonomy. They are assisted by a senior vice admiral who serves as chief of staff (COS). In the Southern Command, the COS is a rear admiral. The two most crucial appointments in the operational commands are fleet commanders, with the rank of rear admiral, who report to their respective FOC-in-Cs.

Training

The nature of naval platforms and operations demand highly skilled manpower. The Indian Navy is divided into four main branches: Executive, Engineering, Electrical, and Logistics. The Air and Submarine Arms are both part of the Executive branch, as are divers and the marine commandos. Other supporting arms include naval architects (ship designers), naval armament inspectors, education, meteorology, air traffic control, and the judiciary.

The command of a ship is the sole reserve of Executive branch officers. Naval aviators must complete their mandatory sea-time to be eligible for command at sea. Similarly, submariners also may get an opportunity to command surface units after they complete their mandatory service with their own arm. All officers get promoted to the rank of commander after completing 14 years of service. However, they are further divided into two categories based on their performance: 'wet list' and 'dry list'. Only wet-listed officers are eligible for command or second-in-command appointments on board a ship. Dry-listed officers generally man the shore billets. This listing system is, by and large, considered fair; officers must consistently perform well both at sea and in their training courses to be included on the wet list.

According to the current system, officer candidates are selected to join the Indian Naval Academy at Ezhimala on the basis of their All-India Rank on the Joint Entrance Examination. Those entering the service through the National Defence Academy route must pass a separate entrance exam conducted by the Union Public Service Commission. These naval cadets, after graduating from the National Defence Academy, join a fourth-year class of cadets at the Indian Naval Academy to complete the training curriculum. All officers who graduate from the Indian Naval Academy are awarded bachelor of technology (B.Tech) degrees. This is a unique feature of the navy's officer training regime that distinguishes it from the other two services.

Executive officers then specialize in navigation and direction, gunnery and missile warfare, anti-submarine warfare and communications, and electronic warfare. Naval aviation candidates complete aviation training with the IAF. Submariners are trained separately. Engineering and electrical officers also undergo further specialized training at Indian Naval Station Shivaji and Indian Naval Station Valsura respectively. The first class of B.Tech officers graduated from the naval academy in 2013.

With this new system of recruitment and education, the Indian Navy is striving to keep pace with global technological progress in computing and Internet technology. The goal is to preserve the prestige of executive officers in this high-tech age by giving them legitimate authority, rather than appearing less educated than the officers as well technically qualified men from the electrical and engineering branches. In this, the navy has largely succeeded.

It has also sought to build greater camaraderie and cohesion among various branches by merging the cadet training of military and engineer officers. Much like the Royal Navy's Selborne-Fisher scheme, introduced in 1903, the Indian Navy's training and recruitment reforms too have failed to assuage the grievances of the technical branches who have remained where they started.[56] Naval engineers and electrical officers still lack executive powers. For example, only the commanding officers of technical training establishments have the authority to discipline men. Other engineering and electrical officers can only be members of a court martial through special administrative mechanisms.

The navy's reforms are still young, so it is too early to comment on their long-term effects. However, this author feels that, even in the age of AI and machine-learning, greater seamanship skills—such as ship-handling in restricted waters or navigating without modern gadgets—would add more prestige to the stature of an executive officer than acquiring a B.Tech degree. The Indian Navy does focus on seamanship training. Officers graduating from the naval academy undergo 24 weeks of sea training with the First Training Squadron at Kochi, where cadets also train on board two sail ships, INS *Sudarshini* and INS *Tarangini*.

The personnel branch, headed by the chief of personnel (one of the principal staff officers at NHQ), handles all promotions and postings. The total naval strength is roughly 60,000. The majority of sailors hail from the northern states, with only around 30 per cent coming from coastal towns. This is likely because coastal states are economically better off than the hinterland states and offer more job opportunities for young people. The Indian Navy's 6,000 officer cadre includes officers from every Indian state, as per official defence recruitment policy.

The children of noncommissioned officers make up almost 20 per cent of the navy's officer cadre. This is due to the Indian Navy–managed education available at all naval stations. The schools are quite egalitarian: officers' and sailors' children study together, providing equal opportunity for upward mobility.[57]

Promotion System

Up to the rank of commander, promotions in the Indian Navy are timebound. The ranks of captain and above are based on a pyramidical promotion structure involving selection boards. Officers face their first selection board at the rank of captain, after completing 18 or 19 years of service—usually when they are in their early 40s. Those who are not promoted get two more opportunities to be considered by the board. Every year, only 20 per cent of officers eligible for promotion make the rank of captain, 0.6 per cent make rear admiral, 0.3 per cent make vice admiral, and only 0.2 per cent become commanders-in-chief (C-in-C).[58]

Those who do not make the select list become so-called time-scale captains after completing 26 years of service. Captains on the select list are automatically promoted to the rank of commodore. All select-list and time-scale captains or commodores retire at age 56. Only select-list captains are considered for flag ranks, based on their performance at sea. Rear admirals are bifurcated into command and staff streams. Only command-stream officers can go on to become C-in-Cs or the chief of naval staff.

Although a few good officers do get left behind, the system is largely fair. Generally, an officer's career profile is evident from the type of ship he serves and commands. Officers who command aircraft carriers or other frontline ships and those who complete command courses abroad, especially in the United States and United Kingdom, are most likely to become flag officers.

As far as rank-and-file sailors are concerned, the Indian Navy fills the electrical and engineering branches with bright young diploma holders. These sailors make up maintenance teams that service engines, power generation, propulsion, air conditioning, auxiliaries, sensors (including radar), and onboard weapons systems. The Indian Navy strives to ensure that its tooth-to-tail ratio—the number of personnel required to supply and support each combat soldier—remains low so that it can spend more on combat platforms.

Indian Coast Guard

The Indian Navy and the Indian Coast Guard (ICG) have operated as a joint force since 1977. The ICG was created to ensure the security of the maritime zones around India, while the navy focused on war-fighting duties. Initially, the navy transferred two small naval frigates—INS *Khuthar* and INS *Kirpan*—and five small coastal patrol boats with crew to support the new coast guard. The navy mentored the fledgling ICG, training its officers and sailors at naval establishments.

Since the 2008 Mumbai terrorist attacks (26/11), considerable efforts have been made to streamline India's coastal security apparatus, including encouraging functional synergy among different actors. A new coastal security architecture has emerged in which the Indian Navy serves as the hub for overall maritime security, including coastal and offshore security, and the ICG is the nodal agency for coastal security in territorial waters and for coordination between central and state marine agencies. Under this new structure, states have taken on a newly significant role in maritime security, including as direct stakeholders. The Ministry of Home Affairs (MHA) has collaborated with state governments to form a Marine Police Force in coastal states.[59] The central government is also contemplating transferring the ICG from the Ministry of Defence to MHA.

Conclusion

The Indian Navy, which began 70 years ago as a part of a collective Commonwealth force, has evolved into a formidable navy with capability to project power in its region. The modern navy has imbibed sea power lessons from three major maritime powers—Britain, the Soviet Union, and the United States—learning from each the nuances of sea warfare and warship design and construction.

India's relationship with the Royal Navy was a continuation of its colonial legacy. Its experiences with the Soviet Navy were largely transactional and tactical. The India–US relationship, initiated in the early 1990s, is different; as its intellectual mentor, the US Navy has culturally and operationally influenced the Indian Navy more than any force since the decline of the Royal Navy.

As a cost-intensive service, the navy's demands have always been difficult for the Indian government to meet. However, the navy's direct impact with foreign policy has likely forced the government to understand that naval demands are not limited to security considerations alone. It is mainly this perspective that has led the navy and central government to work together over the past seven decades. Despite fiscal constraints and its preoccupation with border disputes, India has developed a powerful regional navy with experience not just in operating but also in building the twin essentials of a modern naval power: aircraft carriers and nuclear-powered submarines. The result of their sustained collaboration is clear. The 130-ship Indian Navy is well on its way to becoming a 175-ship force by 2027.[60]

Today, India exhibits a strong maritime posture in the Indian Ocean region. Its Information Fusion Centre provides a comprehensive picture of threats and challenges in the Indian Ocean to stakeholders across the region. This domain knowledge enhances maritime security in the region and helps the Indian Navy maintain a 'positive and favorable maritime environment' in the face of natural disasters.

During India's era of isolation, the navy's interactions with other services remained significant. With the institutionalization of the joint architecture, the Indian Navy's challenges are likely to increase. Its plans will now be scrutinized as part of a tri-service framework. The concept of joint theatre command, which is still in its infancy, will impact the existing command-and-control structure in the navy, likely leading to massive changes.

One area where the navy needs improvement is research and development. And its reliance on naval technologies of the late twentieth century remains a big lacuna in its force levels. It is still chasing the naval products of the second and third industrial revolutions. The Indian Navy has to start imagining operations with modern technologies, including artificial intelligence and autonomous air and underwater vehicles. Swarms of 3-D-printed drones are likely to operate at sea in the coming years. Disruptive technologies will also impact the training and personnel policies of the navy.

India must rethink its force structure for the decades to come. Otherwise, its dreams of being a sea power and a domestic producer of naval armaments will remain elusive and it may find itself seeking another mentor in half a century.

Notes

1. Walter C. Ladwig, "Drivers of Indian Naval Expansion," in *The Rise of the Indian Navy, Internal Vulnerabilities, External Challenges*, ed. Harsh, V. Pant

(London: Ashgate Publishing, 2012), 56. Also see, "Ensuring Secure Seas: Indian Maritime Strategy," *Indian Navy Strategic Publication* (NSP 1.2), October 2015, https://www.indiannavy.nic.in/sites/default/files/Indian_Maritime_Security_St rategy_Document_25Jan16.pdf.

2. Adm. Karambir Singh, "Chief of the Naval Staff: Navy Focused on Contributing to Blue Economy," *FICCI Press Release,* April 23, 2021, https://ficci.in/pressrele ase-page.asp?nid=4153.

3. Arun Prakash, "Mastering the Seas," *The Indian Express*, March 2, 2018, https:// indianexpress.com/article/opinion/columns/mastering-the-seas-china-india-naval-services-chabahar-port-5083316/.

4. James R. Holmes, Andrew C. Winner, and Toshi Yoshihara, *Indian Navy Strategy in the Twenty First Century* (London: Routledge, 2009): 67.

5. Ashley J. Tellis, "Securing the Barrack: The Logic, Structure and Objectives of India's Naval Expansion," *Naval War College Review* 43, no. 3 (Summer 1990): 77–97, p. 78.

6. Dinakar Peri, "Quad Navies Enjoy High Degree of Interoperability: Navy Chief," *The Hindu,* April 14, 2021, https://www.thehindu.com/news/national/quad-nav ies-enjoy-high-degree-of-interoperability-navy-chief/article34320013.ece.

7. Iskander Rehman, "India's Aspirational Naval Doctrine," Carnegie Endowment for International Peace, October 15, 2017, https://carnegieendowment.org/2012/ 10/15/india-s-aspirational-naval-doctrine-pub-49694.

8. Rehman, "India's Aspirational Naval Doctrine."

9. Rear Admiral Satyindra Singh, *Under Two Ensigns: Indian Navy from 1945–50* (New Delhi: Oxford & IBH, 1986).

10. Pushpindar Singh, *Fly Navy—An Illustrated Story of Indian Naval Aviation* (Delhi: Society for Aerospace Studies, 2006), 35.

11. "The Darkening Horizon," *Economic Weekly* (October 26, 1957), 1376–1377.

12. Srinath Raghavan, *India's War: World War II and the Making of Modern South Asia* (New York: Basic Books, 2016).

13. Greg Kennedy, "British Sea Power and Imperial Defence in the Far East: Sharing the Seas with America," in *Sea Power and the Asia Pacific: The Triumph of Neptune?,* ed. Geoffrey Till and Patrick C. Bratton (London: Routledge, 2012), 195–236.

14. As quoted by C. Raja Mohan, "Beyond Idealism: Geopolitics of the Nehru Raj," NMML Occasional Paper, no. 48 (2015), 2.

15. Harsh V. Pant, "Indian Navy's Moment of Reckoning: Intellectual Clarity Need of the Hour," *Maritime Affairs: Journal of the National Maritime Foundation of India* 5, no. 2 (2010), 32–46.

16. George Schuster, "India's World Role: II," *The Spectator* (November 19, 1943), 474–475.

17. George Schuster, "India's World Role: I," *The Spectator* (November 12, 1943), 450.

18. Srikant B Kesnur, "Adhar Kumar Chatterji—The Admiral Who Shed his Vice and Built the Navy," *Naval Despatch* (Winter 2020).

19. Raju G.C. Thomas, "The Sources of Indian Naval Expansion," in *The Modern Indian Navy and the Indian Ocean: Developments and Implications,* ed. Robert H. Bruce (Perth: Center for Indian Ocean Regional Studies, 1989), 97.

20. Thomas, "Indian Naval Expansion," 96.

21. Singh, *Fly Navy*, 35.

22. 'Chapter 9: "Of Funds and Finances—The Naval Budget," https://www.indiann avy.nic.in/sites/default/themes/indiannavy/images/pdf/chapter9.pdf.

23. 'Chapter 9: "Of Funds and Finances—The Naval Budget,"

24. Cmde. Gopal Suri, "Trincomalee: India's Call," *VIF* (April 27, 2017), https://www. vifindia.org/article/2017/april/27/trincomalee-india-s-call.

25. Yogesh Joshi, "Sailing through the Cold War: Indian Navy's Quest for a Submarine Arm, 1947-67," *India Review* 17, no. 5 (2018), 476–504, p. 490.

26. Interview with Adm. V. Bhagwat, October 20, 2020.

27. G.M. Hiranandani, *Transition to Guardianship: The Indian Navy 1991–2000* (New Delhi: Lancer, 2010), xxii.

28. Yogesh Joshi, "Sailing through the Cold War," 492.

29. Adm Karambir Singh, "Dynamics of Security in Indo-Pacific," *Naval Despatch*, 2020.

30. The bilateral experience was repeated in 1995 and 1996. After a brief break in 1998 due to conduct of peaceful nuclear test by India and US imposed sanctions, the Malabar exercise was back in 2002. Australia and Japan also were a part of the Malabar series in 2007, presenting the blueprint of Quadrilateral (Quad) grouping of four democracies that is now the lynchpin of US strategy in the Indo-Pacific.

31. USN-IN established a "Joint Strategic Vision for the Asia Pacific and Indian Ocean Region." in 2015, which states: "We affirm the importance of safeguarding maritime security and ensuring freedom of navigation and over flight throughout the region, especially in the South China Sea."

32. Enrico D'Ambrogio, "The Quad: An Emerging Multilateral Security Framework of Democracies in the Indo-Pacific Region," *European Parliamentary Research Service,* March 2021, 1–12, https://www.europarl.europa.eu/RegData/etudes/ BRIE/2021/690513/EPRS_BRI(2021)690513_EN.pdf.

33. Allan Westcott, "Introduction," in *Mahan and Naval Warfare: Selections from the Writings of Rear Admiral Alfred T. Mahan,* ed. Allan Westcott (New York: Dover Publications Inc, 1999), V. Apart from the widely read, "Influence of Seapower upon History 1660–1783," Mahan wrote a series of books such as *"The interest of America in Sea Power—Present and Future," "The Influence of Seapower upon French Revolution and Empire," "The Life of Nelson—The Embodiment of Sea Power of Great Britain," "Lessons of the War with Spain," and "The Problem of Asia and its Effect upon International Policies."*

34. Michael Pugh, "Is Mahan Still Alive?" *The Gregg Centre, The Journal of Conflict Studies* 16 (1996), 109-124, http://journals.hil.unb.ca/index.php/jcs/article/view/ 11817/12640. US politician Henry L. Stimson once remarked of the US Navy that

it frequently seemed to "retire from the realm of logic into a dim religious world in which Neptune was God, Mahan his prophet, and the United States Navy the only true church".

35. James Goldbrick and Sudarshan Y. Shrikhande, "Sea Denial Is Not Enough: An Australian and Indian Perspective," *The Interpreter* (March 10, 2021), https://www.lowyinstitute.org/the-interpreter/sea-denial-not-enough-australian-and-indian-perspective.

36. Thomas P. Barnett, "Blast from the Past-India's 12 Steps to World Class Navy," US Navy Proceedings, July 2001, http://thomaspmbarnett.squarespace.com/globlog ization/2010/8/6/blast-from-my-past-indias-12-steps-to-a-world-class-navy-200.html#ixzz6zOU776Jc.

37. A. Wess Mitchell, "The Curzonian Imprint on Indian Foreign Policy," *The Hindustan Times*, June 12, 2021.

38. Arun Prakash, "Tweet: This Badly Worded PIB Release Would Have You Believe That Our Navy Is Absent from an IN-USN Exercise??," *@arunp2810*, June 23, 2021, https://twitter.com/arunp2810/status/1407507862742437888?s=20.

39. Ministry of Defence, "IAF and USN in IOR," *Press Information Bureau*, June 22, 2021, https://pib.gov.in/PressReleaseDetailm.aspx?PRID=1729451.

40. "Bipin Rawat Puts Third Aircraft Carrier on Backburner Citing Costs: A Look at How Absence of the Behemoth Will Impact Indian Navy," *Firstpost*, February 18, 2020, https://www.firstpost.com/india/cds-gen-bipin-rawat-puts-third-aircraft-carrier-on-backburner-citing-cost-issues-a-look-at-how-the-absence-of-the-behemoth-will-impact-indian-navy-8053521.html.

41. M. Matheswaran, "A Third Aircraft Carrier for India: Budget Versus Necessity," *The Interpreter* (October 13, 2020), https://www.lowyinstitute.org/the-interpre ter/third-aircraft-carrier-india-budget-versus-necessity.

42. Sarbjeet S. Parmar, "India's Aircraft Carriers: Potency and Numbers," *RSIS*, 12 Sep, 2023, https://www.rsis.edu.sg/rsis-publication/rsis/indias-aircraft-carriers-potency-and-numbers/

43. Ashley J. Tellis, "Does India need aircraft carriers?" *ThePrint*, https://youtu.be/6BficVBrqls?si=YhuApi0iZqSn0eB3

44. Geoffrey Till, *Seapower: A Guide for the Twenty-First Century* (Great Britain: Frank Cass, 2004).

45. Official website of Lloyds of London: The World oldest marine insurance market-place, https://www.lloyds.com.

46. Hiranandani, *Transition to Guardianship*, xx.

47. Cmde. K.N. Vaidyanathan, "Design and Construction of Warships," *Indian Defence Review* 22, no. 1 (2012), http://www.indiandefencereview.com/news/des ign-and-construction-of-warships/.

48. Hiranandani, *Transition to Guardianship*, 120.

49. Hiranandani, *Transition to Guardianship*, 121.

50. Sujeet Samaddar, "Disruptive Technologies and the Navy," Theme address at FICCI conference, 2017, https://www.linkedin.com/pulse/disruptive-technolog ies-navy-sujeet-samaddar/.

51. Surendra Singh, " 'Rukmini' Keeps Eye on Dancing 'Dragon' at Sea," *The Economic Times*, July 14, 2018.

52. Satish Soni, "Technology Requirements for the Indian Navy," *USI Journal*, April–June 2017, https://usiofindia.org/publication/usi-journal/technology-requireme nts-for-the-indian-navy/.

53. The case was closed by CBI in 2013.

54. Deepshikha Gosh, "Two Officers Died in Fire on Board Submarine INS Sindhuratna, Confirms Navy," *NDTV*, February 28, 2014, https://www.ndtv.com/ cheat-sheet/two-officers-died-in-fire-on-board-submarine-ins-sindhuratna- confirms-navy-552152.

55. Hiranandani, *Transition to Guardianship*.

56. Edward Dodd, "Engineering Men: Masculinity, the Royal Navy and the Selborne Scheme." Master's Thesis, Memorial University of Newfoundland School of Graduate Studies, October 2015, https://research.library.mun.ca/9795/1/the sis.pdf.

57. Interview with Capt. D.K. Sharma, VSM (retd.), Former Spokesperson and Public Relations Officer of the IN.

58. Interview with Capt. D.K. Sharma, VSM (retd.).

59. Himadri Das, "Strengthening Maritime Security and Coastal Security in India by States and Union Territories," *Naval Despatch*, Winter 2020, 132-142.

60. The Navy's Maritime Capability Perspective Plan (MCPP) for 2012–27, envisaged a 200-ship navy. The plan has been revised due to a sudden fall in the naval budget from 18 per cent in 2012 to approximately 13 per cent in the financial year at the time of writing, 2019–20.

4

The Indian Air Force

Rahul Bhatia and Shibani Mehta

Introduction

The No. 1 Squadron of the Indian Air Force (IAF) was formed at Drigh Road, Karachi, on 1 April 1933. Equipped with four Westland Wapitis, it was what US defence analyst George Tanham described as a 'partial squadron' with a shortage of educated recruits and only enough technicians to form one flight.[1] Today, in contrast, the IAF has 31 combat squadrons, each with 16 aircraft plus two trainers, and a sanctioned strength of 42 fighter squadrons, all with an expanding inventory.[2] One of the oldest independent air forces, the IAF has engaged in a variety of conflicts, from high-end, regular conventional warfare during World War II to counterinsurgency and counterterrorism operations. It operates first-rate equipment and shows determination to build its global reach and status. The aim of this chapter is to analyse whether the IAF is an effective fighting force by examining its foundation and stated role, its performance in conflict, force structure, and acquisition programme. The chapter addresses the key question of whether the IAF's capacity is sufficiently balanced to tackle the security challenges posed by its main adversaries and contemplates possible reforms.

Founding of the IAF

The interwar years witnessed significant shifts in British strategic thinking about India. While scaling back its defence commitments after World War I—and not anticipating the second—Britain sought to make India more responsible for its own defence.[3] Chief of Staff General Sir

Rahul Bhatia and Shibani Mehta, *The Indian Air Force* In: *Institutional Roots of India's Security Policy*. Edited by: Milan Vaishnav, Oxford University Press. © Oxford University Press 2024.
DOI: 10.1093/oso/9780198894612.003.0004

Andrew Skeen chaired a committee in 1925 to study the Indianization of the Indian Army's officer corps—a step that was welcomed by the growing nationalist campaign in India. One of the committee's recommendations was that Indian cadets should be accepted for officer training at the Royal Air Force (RAF) College Cranwell and then be commissioned in an air arm of the Indian Army. However, Air Vice Marshal Geoffrey Salmond—then Air Officer Commanding in India—advocated for an independent air force instead, one that would be equal to the army.

A radical shift from the RAF's own approach to air power, the proposal was met with strong opposition and was widely debated until Lord Birkenhead, Secretary of State for India, approved the creation of an Indian air force on 5 April 1928.[4] In the following two years, the first six officer cadets began their training at RAF College Cranwell in September 1930. The Indian Air Force was established on 8 October 1932, and the six flight cadets were commissioned the same day.

Until 1936, the IAF was kept small, confined to supporting RAF operations with reconnaissance and ground attack operations against tribes in the North-West Frontier Province between India and Afghanistan. The IAF entered World War II in September 1939 with only one full squadron. As the war progressed, more Indians underwent pilot training in the UK with the intention of assessing their 'quality under active service conditions'. This proved useful during the Burma campaign in 1942, when Indian airmen became known for their professionalism.[5] In recognition, the IAF was granted the prefix 'Royal' on 12 March 1945. During this time, the IAF expanded from a single squadron force of 16 officers and 269 airmen in 1939 to a nine-squadron force that, in July 1945, included 1,638 officers.[6]

After partition in August 1947, the assets of the Royal Indian Air Force were divided between the new states of India and Pakistan, giving India six fighter squadrons and one transport squadron. Air Marshal Sir Thomas Elmhirst was appointed the first Chief of the Air Staff on the condition that he would be given a fully independent service.[7] The political leadership decided to build a balanced force: a fighter force for air defence and a strike force with offensive capabilities. The air force would additionally provide air combat and transport support to the army and the navy. The First Kashmir War, however, arrested the IAF's desired expansion as the budget was no longer available.

The early 1950s witnessed the distinct severance of formal imperial ties when the IAF dropped its 'royal' prefix, and Air Marshal Subroto Mukerjee became the first Indian officer Chief of the Air Staff. At this time, the IAF possessed six fighter squadrons of Spitfires, Vampires, and Tempests, one B-24 bomber squadron, one C-47 Dakota transport squadron, one Auster AOP flight, a communications squadron at Palam, and a growing training organization.

Stated Role

At first, the mission of the IAF was not distinct from the armed forces' broader objective to protect India from external threats. This, however, translated into serious ambiguity about the role of the IAF and often compelled improvisation in the field. A turning point in the rather slow doctrinal evolution of the IAF came after the 1965 war with Pakistan. Under the leadership of Air Chief Marshal Pratap Chandra Lal, the IAF made deterrence and the protection of Indian sovereignty the key drivers of its mission. As a result, air defence and close air support took precedence over offensive action. The victory against Pakistan in the Bangladesh Liberation War in 1971 was attributed to these priorities, which continued to guide the IAF for much of the following two decades.

Until the early 1990s, the IAF had a tactical orientation and operated in the army's shadow when it came to budget share and bureaucratic clout. But its mindset began to shift following the first Gulf War in 1991. The use of air power to simultaneously interfere and influence land and sea operations in the Gulf War placed air power, for the first time, on equal footing with land and sea power in modern combat. Air power eliminated Iraq's air weapons, cut off and immobilized the Iraqi Army, and helped the US-led coalition ground forces achieve their objectives in a very short time. Its critical role in the war sparked a global debate about the function of air power in national security, boosting the IAF's confidence and giving it cause to view itself as a professional instrument of military power with significant influence on strategy.[8] The army, however, may not have shared that view.

In the Kargil War of 1999, the IAF maintained combat air patrols along the length of the Line of Control (LoC), coordinated air strikes to precede ground strikes, and conducted precise electronic surveillance to provide useful signals intelligence to the army.[9] Despite this, there was considerable tension between the two services before, during, and even after the war. The army believed that the air force had dawdled over its requests; air force officers, meanwhile, argued that the army was not forthcoming about operational realities and made unrealistic demands, such as using attack helicopters in high-altitude areas. In addition to tensions between senior officers and underlying inter-services rivalry, the execution of joint operations was further complicated by institutional structures that did not facilitate joint planning, training, and information sharing.[10]

During the early 2000s, several senior IAF officers underscored the importance of air power during the Kargil War, arguing that its employment quashed the orthodox thinking of escalating conflict and turned the tide in India's favour. It is important to note that after the Kargil War, India's defence structure underwent comprehensive reforms. Scholars write that the IAF's success in the 1999 war prompted greater consideration of air power's strategic role, as it had helped to defuse potential nuclear escalation. As part of that desire to dominate escalation in future conflicts, India began to view air power as its principal strategic advantage.[11] This argument carried through to the 2012 IAF doctrine, which marked the metamorphosis of the IAF from a predominantly tactical air force into a semi-strategic force with adequate full-spectrum capability. It makes a clear link between air power and national security, explaining to a far greater extent the role that air power plays. Over the next decade, the IAF began to see itself in terms of 'aerospace', as a service that commands the skies and beyond. The 2022 doctrine delves into the significance of aerospace power for India's national security and the country's future. It recognizes that the IAF constitutes the core competence, while acknowledging the valuable contributions of the air divisions of other services, civil aviation, and space agencies towards this collective prowess. Although the doctrine emphasizes the necessity for cohesive warfighting strategies, it also underscores the importance of preserving the distinctive nature of air power, which can provide crucial backing to ground and maritime forces. Furthermore, the document asserts that air power can effectively execute offensive strikes deep within enemy territory to disrupt logistics and critical installations.[12]

The IAF's Capability and Performance
Over the Years

Over the course of the last eight decades, the IAF's capabilities have varied. So too has its relative performance as per its stated role. This section covers both of these aspects through the lens of the five conflicts the IAF has been involved in: the First Kashmir War in 1947–48, the Sino-Indian War of 1962, the Second Kashmir War in 1965, India's role in the Bangladesh Liberation War of 1971, the Kargil War in 1999, and the Balakot air strikes and subsequent skirmishes in 2019. It also examines the IAF's capability in assisting the Indian government in maintaining internal security and providing disaster relief.[13]

First Kashmir War (1947–8)

Despite its limited capabilities, the fledgling IAF was pressed into service in the First Kashmir War in 1947. At the time, there was only one reliable all-weather road to Srinagar, and it ran through Pakistan. The only way to provide military assistance to the city—and to prevent it from being captured by Pakistani irregulars—was to airlift troops in. The IAF famously airlifted an entire brigade of the Indian Army to Srinagar in just five days, preventing the town from being captured.[14] Meanwhile, Spitfire fighters and Tempest fighter-bombers were used to strafe the Pakistani irregulars on their way to Srinagar, greatly slowing their advance and giving Indian soldiers time to set up defensive positions.[15] As the conflict progressed, the IAF established an air-bridge to Poonch, supplying provisions to the soldiers stationed in the area and evacuating refugees. These flights continued throughout the war.[16]

Later in the conflict, as Pakistani forces advanced towards Leh, the IAF was instrumental in relieving the garrison there, airlifting troops to the area despite the harsh terrain. During the subsequent siege of Skardu, IAF Tempests were widely used for close air support and to airdrop supplies. While the air force was not permitted to bomb targets in Pakistan, it did carry out air strikes against a communications station and a runway in Gilgit, putting both out of action. Overall, the IAF played an important role in support of the Indian Army, undertaking missions ranging from reconnaissance and close air support to transportation and air-dropping supplies. The IAF made crucial contributions to the defence of Srinagar, Poonch, and Leh, and undoubtedly influenced the amount of territory the army was able to control.[17]

Sino-Indian War (1962)

During the Sino-Indian War of 1962, the IAF was not utilized for combat operations. Instead, it was used to transport supplies and soldiers, as well as for evacuations. The decision to not use offensive air power in the war has been the topic of enduring debate in India, with many analysts arguing that the IAF could have carried out strategic bombing and provided close air support, potentially altering the course of the war.[18] However, the political leadership at the time considered the use of air power to be too risky and escalatory in nature, with New Delhi fearing that Beijing might retaliate against Indian cities and supply lines. Thus, the combat arm of the IAF remained on high alert but unused throughout the war.[19]

The air force did play a key role in keeping the army supplied before and through the war. While it displayed ingenuity in transporting weapons, such as AMX-13 tanks, to the front line, its supply drops were not very accurate due to the terrain.[20] In addition to its transport and supply duties, the IAF also performed reconnaissance, and its helicopters were instrumental in the evacuation of retreating Indian troops.[21]

Second Kashmir War (1965)

The war in 1965 came at a time when India was still grappling with the political vacuum left by Prime Minister Jawaharlal Nehru's death the year before, and its armed forces were being re-equipped and re-organized following their defeat against China in 1962.[22] At the start of the war, the IAF possessed 26 fighter squadrons and four medium bomber squadrons, although many of these were understaffed, understrength, and made up of aging or obsolete aircraft. Further, the IAF lacked reliable radar cover and coordination. On the other hand, the Pakistani Air Force (PAF) fielded modern F-86 Sabre fighters and supersonic F-104 Starfighters, as well as an effective radar-controlled air defence network.[23] Through the course of the war, the IAF undertook air-support operations using Mystère ground attack and Hunter and Vampire fighter aircraft while Gnat fighters were deployed in an air defence role. Further, Canberra medium bombers were used to carry out night raids on Pakistani airfields. The IAF was mainly used in the Chhamb area during the war and devoted most of its missions to aiding ground operations, undertaking reconnaissance in addition to search and destroy missions.[24]

The IAF's actions in the 1965 war damaged or destroyed several Pakistani tanks, vehicles, guns, and supply trains, and took an overall toll on the Pakistani war effort.[25] But its overall performance left much to be desired. It was not able to establish air superiority over the better-equipped PAF and suffered a higher attrition rate.[26] Furthermore, due to poor logistical arrangements and technological issues, the IAF lost a significant amount of its fleet on the ground to Pakistani air raids in the initial days of the conflict. This resulted in the IAF focusing on protecting its bases for the remainder of the war. Despite the political leadership's aspirations to use air power to support Indian offensive actions, such as in the Lahore sector, the IAF could only undertake defensive operations like combat air patrols.[27]

The Bangladesh Liberation War (1971)

When India went to war in 1971, the capabilities of the IAF had been improved significantly. Unlike during the war in 1965, the IAF was now larger—fielding 35 combat squadrons—and it was better equipped with more modern aircraft, including Soviet-made MiG-21 fighters and Sukhoi-7 fighter-bombers. The IAF's obsolete aircraft had been mostly phased out. In addition, the air force had taken measures to improve its air-defence network and its coordination with the army.[28] The IAF was able to neutralize the lone PAF F-86 squadron based in East Pakistan within two days, thereby establishing complete air superiority in the eastern theatre.[29] This allowed the air force to carry out a range of logistical operations in support of the army, hastening India's advance towards Dhaka. Apart from this, the IAF also struck key military targets in East

Pakistan; it famously hit the governor's house in Dhaka while a high-level meeting was in progress, prompting the governor, Dr A.H. Malik, and his cabinet to resign on the spot.[30]

In the western theatre, the IAF began its operations soon after the initial PAF strikes on Indian airfields. India's response to the PAF strikes was measured and the IAF aimed to maintain pressure on the PAF. Special care was taken to keep the attrition rate of the IAF low. Limited strikes were carried out against Pakistani airfields through the day and night. The air force used its newly acquired Sukhoi-7s—an all-weather day/ night-capable fighter-bomber—for such missions, along with Hunters, Canberras, and MiG-21s. MiG-21s and Gnats also provided cover for ground-attack missions.[31] These strikes gradually weakened the PAF and forced it to go on the defensive.[32]

The IAF was highly effective against Pakistani Army targets as well. It made a vital contribution at the battle of Longewala, where IAF Hunters repeatedly strafed Pakistani tanks, destroying a majority of them. The air force also played a major role in blunting the Pakistani offensive at Fazilka, striking Pakistani armour, supply and ammunition dumps, and lines of communication. Overall, one could say that the IAF performed well and that it played a key role in India's quick victory in the east and its defence in the west.[33]

The Kargil War (1999)

During the Kargil conflict, the IAF launched Operation Safed Sagar, carrying out reconnaissance and strafing missions in support of the Indian Army. The IAF's air campaign in Kargil faced unique operational challenges. It had to hit targets in mountainous terrain at elevations of 14,000 to 18,000 feet. The targets in question were usually small encampments of troops and ammunition dumps, which had to be spotted and accurately targeted against a backdrop of rocks and snow. Further, given that helicopters could not be used in an offensive role due to their service ceiling, all air strikes had to be carried out by fighter aircraft. These had to remain 6,000 to 8,000 feet above the high ridgelines to avoid missiles and were forbidden from crossing the LoC. Because of these limitations, many of the IAF's munitions missed their mark. As the conflict progressed, however, the air force was able to effectively adapt and hit important targets, especially with the introduction of Mirage 2000s to the front. Overall, the IAF was able to strangulate the supply lines of the occupying Pakistani forces through reconnaissance and air strikes—thus playing a pivotal role in India's ultimate victory.[34] In addition, the IAF also helped ferry weapons, supplies, and reinforcements to the front lines, as well as evacuating casualties.[35]

Balakot and Subsequent Skirmishes (2019)

Although retaliatory air strikes against Pakistan had been considered following the Parliament attack in 2001 and the Mumbai attacks in 2008, the IAF was only given the all-clear to carry out air strikes in 2019 as a punitive response to the Pulwama terrorist attack. For this, a strike force of 12 Mirage 2000s made a shallow incursion across the LoC to drop their ordinances on a Jaish-e-Mohammed training camp near the town of Balakot in a remote area of Khyber Pakhtunkhwa. While the actual damage caused by the air strike remains unclear, five SPICE-2000 bombs were supposedly dropped on the target.[36]

The next day, Pakistan retaliated by dispatching JF-17s and Mirage-IIIs to hit Indian Army positions in Nowshera, with PAF F-16s providing cover. The PAF F-16s engaged India's Mirage 2000s and Sukhoi Su-30MKIs, although both sides' aircraft stayed strictly on their side of the LoC, manoeuvring to try and get a shot at the other side without exposing themselves. Given the superior range of the PAF's Advanced Medium-Range Air-to-Air Missile (AMRAAM) missiles, IAF fighters were unable to take any shots at Pakistan's F-16s without putting themselves in danger. The PAF F-16s reportedly launched four or five AMRAAMs that missed their mark, although later in the engagement an IAF MiG-21 was downed.[37]

While the Balakot episode demonstrated the IAF's ability to strike Pakistani territory, it also exposed the relative weakness of the IAF's fighter aircraft. The IAF was outgunned, with Pakistan's AMRAAM-equipped F-16s and the Saab 2000 airborne early warning and control aircraft being the difference. Further, the IAF suffered many technical deficiencies. The Su-30MKI's radar failed to pick up PAF fighters, the

Mirage 2000s failed to fire their MICA missiles due to a glitch, and a jammed MiG-21 radio resulted in the aircraft being shot down.[38]

Capability in Aiding the Government

Humanitarian Assistance and Disaster Relief

A key aspect of the IAF's aid to the government is its role in humanitarian assistance and disaster relief (HADR) operations. Over the last two decades, the air force has become a mainstay in disaster relief operations. Its primary function is transporting relief materials and medical equipment, along with disaster response and medical personnel to affected areas. It has also performed other functions that range from surveying affected areas and air-dropping food packets in remote locations to rescuing and evacuating disaster victims. The air force was most notably involved in relief operations following the devastating Indian Ocean tsunami in 2004, when it ferried relief material to and within the Andaman and Nicobar Islands.[39] More recently, the IAF was heavily involved in operations following the Uttarakhand floods in 2013.[40]

The air force has also taken part in disaster relief operations overseas. In the aftermath of the 2004 tsunami, the IAF assisted operations in both Sri Lanka and the Maldives.[41] In 2014, the air force further helped alleviate a drinking water crisis in the Maldives.[42] The IAF has also been deployed regularly to transport emergency supplies and relief material to countries in South and South East Asia following natural disasters. In addition to its role in disaster relief, the IAF has regularly evacuated Indian nationals stranded abroad during conflicts.[43]

The air force's HADR mandate greatly increased during the COVID-19 pandemic and it was called on to assist in various capacities. Its transport fleet was used to ferry medical personnel and medical supplies across the country.[44] The IAF also created quarantine facilities at its bases, and evacuated Indian citizens stuck in countries such as China[45] and Iran.[46] During India's deadly second COVID-19 wave, when the country faced a shortage of medical oxygen, the air force was instrumental in transporting ventilators, oxygen cylinders and concentrators, and cryogenic containers. These operations included sorties that brought medical equipment from abroad as well as transporting it within the country.[47]

Given that HADR operations usually involve a limited number of light- and medium-utility helicopters, they rarely seem to have any discernible impact on the IAF's capabilities. Even in the event of a large calamity, such as a devastating earthquake, the IAF may deploy some medium- and heavy lift transport aircraft to undertake a few flights, briefly keeping them from their regular duties. However, as part of India's response to its second COVID-19 wave, the IAF pressed 12 heavy lift and 30 medium lift aircraft into service for a month and a half.[48] This included a significant portion of the IAF's strategically important heavy lift IL-76 and C-17 aircraft, which undertook a number of international flights to transport necessary medical equipment.[49] The temporary absence of such aircraft would have dented the IAF's capabilities to undertake a strategic airlift, as C-17s and Il-76s are usually employed to quickly transport weapons, soldiers, and equipment to the front. This could have been critical if continuing tensions with China in Eastern Ladakh had necessitated such an airlift.

Internal Security

For decades, the IAF was frequently employed in the maintenance of internal security, particularly in the north-eastern states. For instance, Ouragan fighter-bombers were used against Naga insurgents in 1956. Similarly, Vampire fighter-bombers were employed against rebels in the erstwhile North-East Frontier Agency in 1960.[50] More notably, in 1966, the Indian government used offensive air power against the Mizo National Front (MNF), an insurgent group in Mizoram. The MNF had started an uprising in 1966 and overrun many important towns in Mizoram, including Aizawl.[51] This prompted India's political leadership to undertake drastic actions: Ouragan and Hunter combat aircraft were deployed to strafe MNF positions while soldiers were airlifted in. Although the IAF's actions may have caused civilian casualties,[52] the use of air power resulted in a breakthrough that allowed Indian security forces to promptly retake territory from the MNF.[53]

Since the 1960s, however, the IAF has rarely been used to handle matters of internal security. While the government tried using attack helicopters in anti-terrorist operations in the Kashmir Valley in 2000, the missions were not considered successful and the IAF was subsequently withdrawn.[54] The Indian government also considered using air power against Naxalite insurgents in 2010 but ultimately decided against it.[55] While some continue to advocate for the use of air power against the Naxalites,[56] there does not seem to be any concrete evidence to suggest that it would have a significant impact. Further, as former Air Marshal Narayan Menon has argued, the use of the IAF in internal security operations would detract from its primary responsibilities and dilute its core values. The use of air power also poses the risk of collateral damage and further escalation.[57]

The IAF itself seems to be opposed to the use of air power against the Naxalite insurgents. In 2010, P.V. Naik, then Air Chief Marshal, stated that he was not in favour of using air power in anti-Naxalite operations because the IAF was not trained for limited lethality. The IAF's weapons were meant for foreign adversaries rather than domestic insurgents.[58] The air force, however, does continue to support the Indian paramilitary forces fighting the insurgency, deploying Mi-17 helicopters for reconnaissance, transportation, and casualty evacuation.[59] Although these Mi-17 helicopters are equipped with light machine guns and fly with Garud commandos—the IAF's special forces unit—on board, the IAF has laid out strict rules of engagement: helicopters can only engage Naxalite insurgents in a proportional response if they are fired upon.[60]

Force Structure

Commands, Squadrons, and Current Inventory

In the early 1950s, tensions with Pakistan prompted the sanctioned number of IAF squadrons to be increased from six to 15. The next expansion came after the Sino-Indian War of 1962, which jolted the Indian government to drastically increase the size of the IAF. The approved number of squadrons was then increased to 45 (although the actual force often lagged behind), initiating an extensive build-up. The Second Kashmir

War in 1965 added further urgency to the expansion. India's operations in the Bangladesh Liberation War in 1971 revealed a much-improved and more capable air force. The force level of the IAF increased to about 40 squadrons in the early 1970s and it remained around there through the 1990s.[61] In the twenty-first century however, the force level of the IAF has declined. Currently, it has around 31 combat squadrons, although the IAF's sanctioned strength remains at 42.[62]

The IAF squadrons are deployed across the country based on an assessed threat pattern. This threat pattern is constantly being reviewed, and operational units are moved around the country accordingly. The IAF's usual peace-time deployment changes to a war-time deployment when its units are activated. Overall, the air force's operational units fall under the operational control of five geographical commands:[63]

- Central Air Command, Allahabad
- Eastern Air Command, Shillong
- Western Air Command, New Delhi
- Southern Air Command, Thiruvananthapuram
- South Western Air Command, Gandhinagar

Apart from these five geographical commands, the IAF also maintains two functional commands: one for maintenance in Nagpur and another for training in Bengaluru.[64]

The IAF inventory today consists of seven types of combat aircraft, with 12 squadrons of Sukhoi Su-30MKIs forming its backbone (see Table 4.1). In addition, the air force has three Mikoyan MiG-29UPG squadrons, three Dassault Mirage 2000 squadrons, six SEPECAT Jaguar squadrons, and three Mikoyan-Gurevich MiG-21 Bison squadrons, which are to be retired imminently.[65] The IAF has also recently raised two Hindustan Aeronautics Limited (HAL) Tejas squadrons[66] and two Dassault Rafale squadrons.[67]

Apart from its combat squadrons, the IAF has a range of transport aircraft. These include the older Ilyushin IL-76 as well as the recently acquired Boeing C-17 Globemaster III and Lockheed Martin C-130J Super Hercules, which have given the IAF strategic airlift capabilities.[68] The IAF also operates smaller transport aircraft such as the Antonov AN-32, the Hawker Siddeley HS 748, and the Dornier 228. In 2023, the air force

Table 4.1 Combat Aircraft in the IAF Over the Years

Combat Aircraft	Type	Country of Origin	Years of Service
Westland Wapiti IIA	General purpose	United Kingdom	1932–42
Hawker Audax	Army cooperation	United Kingdom	1941–3
Westland Lysander	Army cooperation	United Kingdom	1941–3
Hawker Hurricane IIB	Fighter	United Kingdom	1942–6
Bristol Blenheim I	Light bomber	United Kingdom	1942–5
Vultee Vengeance I	Dive-bomber	United States	1943–4
Supermarine Spitfire Mk. VII—XIX	Fighter	United Kingdom	1945–57
Hawker Tempest II	Fighter-bomber	United Kingdom	1946–55
Consolidated B-24 Liberator	Heavy bomber	United States	1948–67
de Havilland Vampire FBMk. 52	Fighter-bomber	United Kingdom	1948–65
Dassault Ouragan (Toofani)	Fighter-bomber	France	1953–67
Dassault Mystère IVA	Fighter-bomber	France	1957–73[a]
Hawker Hunter FMk. 56	Fighter	United Kingdom	1957–96[b]
English Electric Canberra	Medium bomber	United Kingdom	1957–2007[c]
Folland Gnat/ HAL Ajeet	Light fighter	United Kingdom/ India	1960–91[d]
Mikoyan-Gurevich MiG-21FL/Bis	Fighter	Soviet Union	1963–present[e]
HAL HF-24 Marut	Strike aircraft	India	1967–90[f]
Sukhoi Su-7 BM	Fighter-bomber	Soviet Union	1968–85
SEPECAT Jaguar IS/ IB/IM	Strike aircraft	United Kingdom/ France	1979–present
Mikoyan-Gurevich MiG-23BM/MF	Fighter-bomber	Soviet Union	1981–2009[g]
Mikoyan-Gurevich MiG-25R	Reconnaissance	Soviet Union	1981–2006[h]
Mikoyan MiG-27 M	Strike aircraft	Soviet Union	1985–2017[i]
Dassault Mirage 2000 H	Multirole fighter	France	1985–present
Mikoyan MiG-29UPG	Air superiority fighter	Soviet Union/ Russia	1987–present[j]
Sukhoi Su-30MKI	Multirole fighter	Russia	1997–present[k]

Table 4.1 Continued

Combat Aircraft	Type	Country of Origin	Years of Service
HAL Tejas Mk.1/1A	Multirole light fighter	India	2016–present[l]
Dassault Rafale	Multirole fighter	France	2020–present[m]

This table has been mainly sourced from the Indian Airforce's Website: "Our Journey" https://indianairforce.nic.in/history/ Any information that has been sourced from elsewhere has been cited separately.

[a] "Dassault Mystere IVA," *Bharat Rakshak*, February 27, 2019, https://www.bharat-rakshak.com/IAF/Galleries/Aircraft/Vintage/Fighters/Mystere/.

[b] Saikat Datta, "Rest Over, Upgraded Sukhois Set to Fly Again," *The Indian Express*, September 27, 2002, https://indianexpress.com/article/news-archive/rest-over-upgraded-sukhois-set-to-fly-again/.

[c] Snehesh Alex Philip, "Untold Story of an IAF Canberra & Its Crew, 60 Years before Wing Commander Abhinandan's MiG," *ThePrint*, October 6, 2020, https://theprint.in/defence/untold-story-of-an-iaf-canberra-its-crew-60-years-before-wing-commander-abhinandans-mig/227141/.

[d] Tanham and Agmon, *The Indian Air Force: Trends and Prospects*, p. 65.

[e] Huma Siddiqui, "MiG 21: The Fighter Jet That Arrived in India in 1963 and Still Plays a Major role," *The Financial Express*, February 27, 2019, https://www.financialexpress.com/defence/mig-21-the-fighter-jet-that-arrived-in-india-in-1963-and-still-plays-a-major-role/1500436/.

[f] Roblin, "India's Disappointing Marut Jet Fighter Proved Itself in Combat."

[g] "Final touchdown for IAF's MiG-23 fighter jets," *India Today*, March 6, 2009, https://www.indiatoday.in/latest-headlines/story/final-touchdown-for-iafs-mig-23-figh ter-jets-41197-2009-03-06.

[h] Shiv Aroor, "Farewell, the MiGnificent Flying Machine," *Indian Express*, April 16, 2006, http://archive.indianexpress.com/news/farewell-the-mignificent-flying-machine/2537/.

[i] "MiG-27 Goes into History: Legacy of Indian Air Force's Bahadur Valiant," *India Today*, December 72, 2019, https://www.indiatoday.in/india/story/mig-27-goes-into-history-legacy-of-indian-air-force-s-bahadur-valiant-1631924-2019-12-27.

[j] Singh Raminder, "Air Defence Aircraft MiG 29 to Give IAF Complete Mastery over South Asian Skies," *India Today*, August 15, 1986, https://www.globalsecurity.org/military/world/india/baaz.htm.

[k] "Su-30 Flanker," *FAS*, May 27, 1998, https://nuke.fas.org/guide/india/aircraft/su-30.htm.

[l] P.R. Sanjai, "Tejas Inducted in IAF after 33 Years."

[m] Philip, "IAF Inducts Rafale Today."

began inducting the Airbus C-295 medium tactical transport aircraft to replace its HS 748s.[69]

Additionally, the IAF has a full suite of helicopters including Cheetah and Chetak light utility helicopters, Mi-17 and Dhruv medium utility helicopters, and Mi-25/35 attack helicopters.[70] The air force has recently begun to induct more advanced helicopters such as the HAL Prachand, an indegeniously designed light attack helicopter.[71] It also received a boost in the form of 22 Boeing AH-64E Apache attack helicopters and 15 Boeing Chinook CH-47F heavy lift helicopters.[72] Apart from this, the IAF operates Ilyushin IL-78 aerial refuelling tankers and two kinds of airborne warning and control systems—the Israeli-made Phalcon system affixed on Beriev A-50 aircraft and the indigenous Netra early warning system fitted on Embraer-145 jets.[73]

The IAF currently employs a diverse range of combat aircraft. This is not a recent development, but indicative of a historical trend. The IAF fielded up to 11 types of aircraft in the 1980s.[74] The multiplicity of combat aircraft types in the IAF is not by design, however. It is the result of several factors, including political choices, resources available to the government, the IAF's preferences, and the geopolitical environment.[75] Regardless, the multiplicity of aircraft types has resulted in budgetary, management, maintenance, organizational, and training challenges for the IAF.[76]

An ideal mix of combat aircraft is understood to be three to four types, and the IAF does slowly seem to be moving in this direction. The future of Indian air power is set to revolve around four combat aircraft: the Sukhoi Su-30MKI, the HAL Tejas, the Dassault Rafale, and a fourth platform that is yet to be acquired. The remaining aircraft—including the MiG-29UPG, the Mirage 2000, and the Jaguar—are only likely to be add-ons for as long as they can be sustained.[77]

The Role of the Government and a Drive Towards Self-Reliance

The IAF's force structure is heavily influenced by decisions taken by the Indian government. The government determines the force levels of the air force and the military hardware with which it is equipped. When it comes to the procurement of military hardware, the IAF is responsible for submitting its operational requirements to the Ministry of Defence. Once these requirements are accepted, the government takes the process forward in accordance with the latest Defence Acquisition Procedure. While the air force submits its recommendations during the trial phase of the procurement process, the final decision ultimately rests with the government.[78] This defence acquisition process has often meant that India's armed forces do not acquire the most advanced hardware possible.

It has, however, allowed the Indian government to fulfil the important objective of increasing India's self-reliance when it comes to weapons and equipment.[79]

Since the early days of independence, the Indian government has sought to diversify the sources of IAF equipment and increase self-reliance in the defence space. The strategy was partially driven by fears that reliance on Britain and the United States for defence equipment could leave India in a vulnerable position during a conflict. For instance, during the First Kashmir War, New Delhi was apprehensive that Britain and the United States might limit military supplies to India. This fear was realized in 1951, as continuing tensions between India and Pakistan prompted Britain to hold up supplies of the Vampire's Goblin engine to India in order to limit the IAF's capabilities and reduce tensions.[80] Initially, India approached European countries to reduce its dependency on British and US equipment, purchasing the Ouragan and Mystère aircraft from France.

By the 1960s, however, India increasingly looked to the Soviet Union to service the needs of the IAF. This was propelled by three main factors: the Soviet Union was willing to sell India advanced combat aircraft, it allowed defence purchases to be made with staggered rupee payments, and, most importantly, Moscow agreed to license the manufacture of combat aircraft in India without any political preconditions.[81] Furthermore, the geopolitical environment during the second half of the twentieth century catalysed the Indo-Soviet defence partnership. The United States—which had provided military aid to India during the Sino-Indian War in 1962—imposed an arms embargo on the subcontinent at the outbreak of the Second Kashmir War in 1965. It remained apprehensive about selling India arms until the mid-1980s. The Soviet Union, on the other hand, never stopped supplying arms to India, even when New Delhi was at war.[82] Overall, the partnership with the Soviet Union deepened over time and Moscow emerged as the principal supplier of the air force.[83] Even today, the IAF's fleet is mainly of Soviet (and now Russian) origin.

India has also sought to increase its self-reliance by building up its own aerospace capabilities. This has translated into the license manufacture of aircraft such as the MiG-21, and later the Jaguar and the Su-30MKI.[84] India's mission of self-reliance has also encouraged the development and manufacture of indigenous fighter aircraft such as the HAL Marut and Tejas. The projects to develop both the Marut and the Tejas were extremely ambitious undertakings. While the Marut was an underwhelming aircraft that was already outdated at the time of its induction, the Tejas—which came out of the Light Combat Aircraft programme—has garnered a warmer response from the IAF.[85]

Recruitment, Training, and Maintenance

A technologically intensive service, the IAF maintains high standards for the induction of personnel. Personnel are selected through a four-step testing process spread over many days that gauges a candidate's intelligence and psychological and medical fitness. Based on the candidate's performance on written tests, physical activities, personal interviews, and their medical results, an All-India Merit List is compiled and selected candidates are invited to join one of the IAF training establishments.[86] As of February 2021, the IAF consists of nearly 150,000 personnel.[87]

Personnel functions are spread across three branches within the IAF. They are:

Flying branch:

- Fighters
- Transports
- Helicopters

Ground duty (technical) branch

- Mechanical
- Electronics

Ground duty (non-technical) branch

- Administration
- Accounts
- Logistics
- Education
- Meteorology

In 2022, the Indian Government launched the Agnipath scheme, a recruitment initiative for short-term service in the armed forces. This program permits selected candidates to join the IAF under the Air Force Act of 1950 for a fixed term of four years, during which they will hold a unique rank within the air force.[88] Notably, this rank will be distinct from the existing ones, with only 25 percent of participants being retained in the service after completing their tenure.

In 2023, the Ministry of Defence announced new regulations facilitating the inclusion of women in the IAF through the Agnipath scheme, encompassing both combat and non-combat positions. Upon the fulfillment of their designated roles, female recruits will be eligible for induction both in combat and non-combat roles.[89] While the new scheme potentially offers multiple benefits, its implementation remains a work in progress, at the time of writing. Allowing the model to adapt with necessary adjustments is vital to ensure it remains relevant.

The IAF takes pride in having a highly educated and technically trained officer corps that can absorb complex information and operate high-technology equipment. With respect to training, the 2012 doctrine outlined two objectives: to provide the individual the knowledge and skills to operate air power assets, and to promote professional military education that connects theory to war-fighting abilities. To this end, the courses and syllabi were reviewed and revised to address existing limitations. For instance, the growing importance of information dominance in warfare led to the foundation of the Information Warfare School, a cyber training institute at the air force station outside of Bengaluru. These objectives are emphasized again in the lastest doctrine.[90]

Fighter pilots of the flying branch have traditionally dominated the service's leadership.[91] IAF fighter pilots log an average of 200 flight hours per year in a variety of air-to-air and surface attack mission profiles. Training at the squadron level focuses mainly on air defence, aerial combat, and airfield attack, with less emphasis placed on counter-land missions. Jasjit Singh, a former IAF air commodore and prominent military scholar, points out that pilot training is frequently ad-hoc in nature, subject to constant experimentation, and altered to meet equipment shortages, often with serious consequences.[92] In the mid-1960s, the IAF established a three-stage training programme. The HAL HT-2 (and later the HAL HPT-32 Deepak) served as the basic trainer aircraft, while the HAL HJT-16 was used for both intermediate and advanced training, even though it proved inadequate for the latter. Pilots were then trained on Hunter or MiG-21 combat aircraft for six months, where they would be exposed to high-speed manoeuvres before joining operational squadrons.

The lack of an advanced jet trainer (AJT) was apparent. In fact, the committee chaired by Air Chief Marshal Denis La Fontaine that investigated IAF aircraft accidents between April 1977 and August 1982 concluded that human error, due to 'lack of knowledge or skill', was one major reason for the large number of accidents. The absence of an AJT was blamed for the high rates of error. An AJT was finally inducted into the IAF in 2008. Nonetheless, losses have continued even since the induction of the AJT. In 2012, India grounded its fleet of Mirage 2000s for nearly two months after an engine malfunction caused two crashes in less than 10 days. Additionally, aircraft simulators were reported to be critically deficient; one-third of them were non-operational.[93]

The strength of an air force is determined not only by the prowess of its pilots but also by the quality of its machines. While technology may determine direction, the ability to maintain technology dictates how long the air force can proceed in that course. Capital and knowledge intensive, air power maintenance depends on the combined serviceability of aircraft, availability of spare parts, and reliability of weapon systems. A mixed inventory that includes everything from legacy assets to state-of-the-art platforms creates significant challenges, especially when dealing with obsolescence due to system fatigue, corrosion, or even humidity. In the late 1990s, India experienced an acute spare parts crunch due to inventory reduction in the Central Asian and Eastern European countries that had earlier provided spares. Cognizant of the challenge, the IAF is establishing new maintenance standard operating procedures that synchronize procurement, training, and operational cycles to improve quality assurance of its assets. Additionally, it is engaging the private sector to fill the gaps.[94]

Certain cultural traits that the IAF inherited from the RAF decades ago continue to run deep.[95] In 2017, when the IAF was called out for its discriminatory study-leave policy that favoured officers, IAF authorities cited British-era rules in their defence, stating that only officers are entitled to the 'privilege' of study leave. Another troubling trend has been pilots leaving the air force to join private airlines that offer better salaries. More than 200 mid-career IAF pilots opted for premature separation from service during 2018–19 alone. Replying to a question in the Lok Sabha in March 2021, the Minister of State for Defence said the number of pilots in the IAF was 3,834, against a sanctioned strength of 4,239.[96] With the existing shortage of about 400 pilots and the challenge of retaining young, qualified ones, the concern becomes even greater in the context of competition with the civil aviation sector. A similar trend was revealed by data from an internal survey. In a poll of IAF sergeants with a service bracket of 13 to 20 years, 32 per cent of the respondents said airmen tend to leave the service after 20 years 'due to lack of a suitable environment', while 25 per cent believed that civilian life offers better prospects. Other reasons to leave the service included frequent movement (19 per cent), slow career progression (17 per cent), and poor pay (7 per cent).[97]

As an institution, the IAF should incorporate the career aspirations of its personnel with its broader organizational goals if it wishes to maintain a high-quality professional force. For instance, the IAF could consider policies that ensure the minimum strength of pilots is maintained to carry out operational roles. Media reports from 2020 suggested that senior officials were reviewing the IAF's promotion policy to remove stagnation at the group captain rank, a critical career juncture.[98]

Conclusion

All things considered, the IAF is a capable and effective combat arm. According to Ashley J. Tellis of the Carnegie Endowment for International Peace, the IAF 'remains exemplary among air forces in the developing world' and 'increasingly stands in favorable comparison with its peers in developed countries'.[99] Capable of a full spectrum of operations, the IAF has played an important role in nearly every conflict in which India has been involved. Today, however, it faces challenges because of its numerical strength, force structure, budget, and personnel issues.

The IAF has historically enjoyed air superiority over both its principal adversaries: Pakistan and China. But over the last two decades, India's quantitative and qualitative advantage in the air has been drastically eroded. The IAF currently faces some 350 combat aircraft to the west from Pakistan and about 200 combat aircraft to the north from China's Western Theatre Command.[100] Although two successive air force chiefs have asserted that the IAF was prepared for a 'two front war' with Pakistan and China, it is far outnumbered in such a worst-case scenario.[101] Further, the proposed formation of five Integrated Theatre Commands—to operationally combine India's tri-service personnel and assets—could result in the IAF's assets being divided between theatres, thereby diminishing its operational advantage in interchangeable strategic and tactical roles. Differences between the three services over the proposed integrated theatre commands came out in public in 2021 when then Chief of Defence Staff, General Bipin Rawat, called the air force a supporting arm of the army. The Chief of the Air Staff at the time responded saying that air power's role in integrated defence cannot be diminished, making it clear that the IAF has no desire to be tethered to an air support role under the army; it envisions a greater role.

Given that both China and Pakistan will continue to improve their air capabilities, and that the IAF itself performed inadequately in its brief encounter with the PAF after the Balakot incident, the IAF needs to modernize quickly. The acquisition of the Rafale is a step in the right direction. As a 4.5-generation multi-role combat aircraft, it is considered to be amongst the finest fighters in the world. Its avionics, radar, and weapons systems are more advanced than anything in either China's or Pakistan's inventory.[102] However, 36 Rafales will not be enough to plug the gaps in the IAF's capabilities. The Indian government needs to equip the IAF with several more squadrons of modern fighter aircraft. While a proposal to acquire 114 4.5-generation fighter aircraft is in the works,[103] progress on it has been slow.[104] If the Medium Multi-Role Combat Aircraft process[105]—India's last attempt at acquiring modern fighter aircraft—is anything to go by, it could take more than a decade for such a deal to be finalized.

For the time being, the Indian government has placed an emphasis on indigenous production to modernize the IAF. At the centre of this is the decision to acquire 220 indigenously produced Tejas Mark I and Mark IA aircraft.[106] Although the Tejas would be an upgrade to the MiG-21, the IAF has been opposed to the indigenous fighter from its first flight in 2001. The IAF has argued that the Tejas has several deficiencies and lacks the level of performance required for surviving contested airspace in the event of a war.[107] In 2017, the IAF even highlighted to the Indian government that the Tejas has a much lower endurance, a significantly smaller weapons payload, a greater maintenance requirement, and about half the lifespan compared to its competitors, such as the Saab JAS 39 Gripen and the Lockheed Martin F-16.[108] Despite this, New Delhi has chosen to go ahead with the Tejas, probably because it is cheaper than its more capable, albeit expensive, international competitors.[109]

In a bid to improve upon the Tejas, India is developing the Tejas Mark II. The new fighter features a more powerful GE 414 engine that will give it a longer range and greater payload capacity. It will also be equipped with a superior radar, better avionics and an advanced electronic warfare suite.[110] Apart from this, India is also undertaking an ambitious project to develop a fifth-generation Advanced Medium Combat Aircraft (AMCA). India hopes to equip its air force with at least six squadrons of the Tejas Mark II and seven squadrons of the AMCA starting in the 2030s.[111] Given India's drawn-out process of developing and manufacturing indigenous aircraft, delays can be expected in the induction of both fighters.[112]

Ultimately, the acquisition of any aircraft will depend on the resources the government is able to spare. But experts argue that the IAF's plans reflect a disregard for fiscal reality. In 2020, then Air Chief Marshal RKS Bhadauria had suggested that the IAF would be able to raise its strength to 36-38 combat squadrons by 2030. However, the additional 320-odd fighter types that would be required for this would cost upwards of $45 billion, or around 68 per cent, of the $65.9 billion defence budget for the fiscal year 2020–1 (see figure 4.1). An audit by the Comptroller and Auditor General of India in 2019, which examined 11 contracts of capital acquisition signed between 2012 and 2013 and 2017 and 2018, found that the current acquisition system was unlikely to support the operational preparedness of the IAF, and recommended that the Ministry of Defence structurally reform the entire acquisition process.[113] Military analyst and former Air Marshal V.K. Bhatia is of the opinion that the IAF needs to create additional financial, design, and manufacturing capacities with the

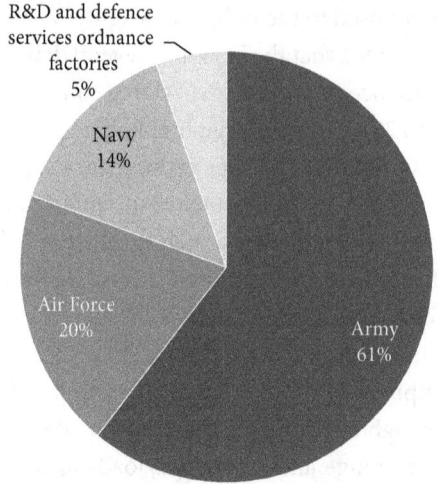

Figure 4.1 Budget of Defence Services (2021–22)

In 2021–22, the total allocation to the three forces (including pensions) was 4.78 trillion rupees. Expenditure for the Army includes expenses on Border Roads Organization and Jammu and Kashmir Light Infantry. Expenditure for Navy includes expenses on Coast Guard Organization.

Sources: Union Budgets 2011–22; PRS Legislative Research

Aeronautical Development Agency (ADA) and HAL to achieve its acquisition targets.[114]

The IAF is at the forefront of India's military modernization effort, as reflected in the level of technology, capital expenditure, and diversity of imports. In its overall budget allocation for 2021–22, modernization comprises 52 per cent of the total IAF budget, while maintenance makes up just 10 per cent (see figure 4.2). Yet the decline in personnel numbers (19 per cent of the service budget) due to critical shortcomings, such as poor pay and delayed promotions, pose a key challenge to the IAF's expansion.[115] Nevertheless, a simple comparison of the budgets of India's principal defence services indicates that the IAF is investing greater resources into modernization when compared to either the army or the navy (see figure 4.3).

As India's strategic interests grow and its neighbourhood becomes increasingly contested, the country must step up its defence preparedness. The IAF, as the country's premier instrument of power projection, can influence the outcome of conflict. But its emphasis on technology as the key to modernization and transformation, despite structurally weak

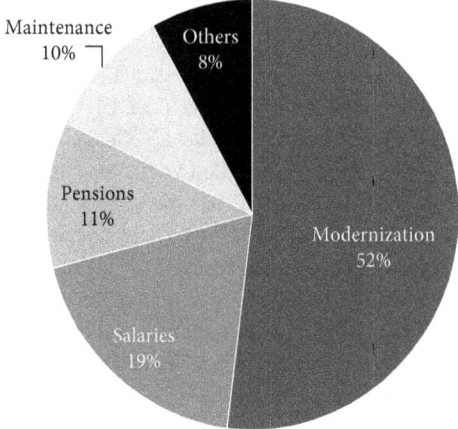

Figure 4.2 Composition of Air Force Budget (2021–22)

The IAF has been allocated 940.78 billion rupees for the year 2021–22 (including pensions). Salaries include civilian employees. The IAF's funds allotted for modernization are calculated from the following heads of the capital outlay: (i) Aircraft and Aeroengine, (ii) Heavy and Medium Vehicles, and (iii) Other Equipment.

Sources: Union Budgets 2011–22; PRS Legislative Research

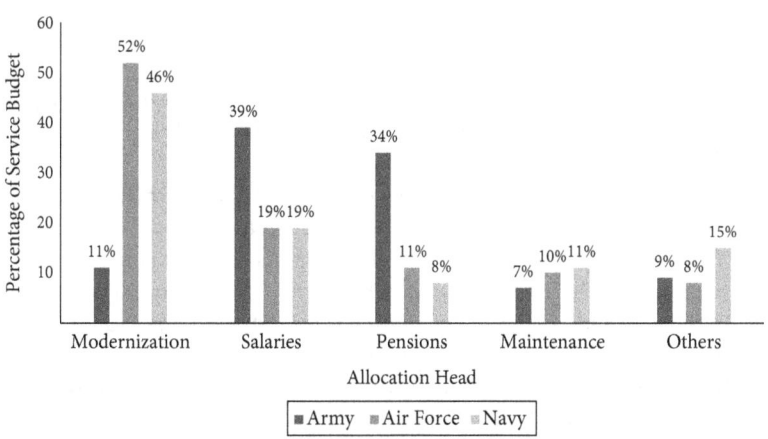

Figure 4.3 Budget Comparison of India's Defence Services (2021–22)

Sources: Union Budgets 2011–22; PRS Legislative Research

processes, reduces the incentive for organizational change. To be an effective and capable force with significant influence in its sphere, the IAF must marry modernization and organizational planning to enhance capacity sufficiently and alter the balance with its main adversaries.

Notes

1. George K. Tanham and Marcy Agmon, *The Indian Air Force: Trends and Prospects* (Santa Monica: Rand, 1995), 13–16. Also see Table 4.1.

2. The Rafale aircraft was inducted into the 17 "Golden Arrows" Squadron in September 2020 followed by its induction in 101 Squadron of the Eastern Air Command in July 2021. See also: K.T. Sebastian, "How Many Does IAF Need?" *Deccan Herald,* August 20, 2020, https://www.deccanherald.com/opinion/main-article/how-many-does-iaf-need-876291.html.

3. Vipul Dutta, "War and Indian Military Institutions: The Emergence of the Indian Military Academy," in *Culture, Conflict and the Military in Colonial South Asia,* ed. Kaushik Roy and Gavin Rand (London: Routledge, 2018), 239–57.

4. Peter Devitt, "The Royal Indian Air Force, 1932—1947," Royal Air Force Museum blog, August 15, 2020, https://www.rafmuseum.org.uk/blog/royal-indian-air-force/.

5. No. 1 Squadron IAF was sent to fly tactical reconnaissance operations from Toungoo in Burma (Myanmar) on February 1, 1942.

6. Bisheshwar Prasad, *Expansion of Armed Forces and Defence Organisation* (New Delhi, 1956), 153.

7. Before 1947, the commander in chief of the Indian Army administered control over both the army and air force.

8. Ramesh V. Phadke, "Response Options: Future of Indian Air Power Vision 2020," *Strategic Analysis* 24, no. 10 (2001): 1795–812.

9. Benjamin S. Lambeth, *Airpower at 18,000: The Indian Air Force in the Kargil War* (Washington DC: Carnegie Endowment for International Peace, 2012), 9–34. https://carnegieendowment.org/files/kargil.pdf.

10. Anit Mukherjee, "Fighting Separately: Jointness and Civil–Military Relations in India," *Journal of Strategic Studies* 40, no. 1–2 (2016): 6–34.

11. Christina Goulter and Harsh Pant, "Realignment and Indian Airpower Doctrine," *Journal of Indo-Pacific Affairs,* January 2, 2020, https://www.airuniversity.af.edu/Wild-Blue-Yonder/Article-Display/Article/2007488/realignment-and-indian-airpower-doctrine/#sdendnote27sym.

12. Doctrine of the Indian Air Force, *Indian Air Force,* 2022, https://indianairforce.nic.in/wp-content/uploads/2023/01/2MB.pdf.

13. "Handbook on RTI Act," *Indian Air Force,* 2005, https://indianairforce.nic.in/sites/default/files/HandbookOnRTIAct2005%20-%20latest%20%2827jun19%29.pdf.

14. Jasjit Singh, *Defence from the Skies: 80 Years of the Indian Air Force* (New Delhi: KW Publishers, 2013), 53–55.

15. "1947–1948 Kashmir Operations: An Air Force Perspective," *Indian Air Force.* https://indianairforce.nic.in/content/1948-ops.

16. Arjun Subramaniam, "Crucial Role IAF Played in Early Days of 1947–48 Pakistan War," *ThePrint,* October 26, 2018, https://theprint.in/opinion/crucial-role-iaf-played-in-early-days-of-1947-48-pakistan-war/140390/.

17. Singh, *Defence from the Skies*, 55–64.

18. Vijay K. Bhatia, "Airpower across the Himalayas: A Military Appreciation of Chinese and Indian Air Forces," *Policy Brief, S. Rajaratnam School of International Studies* (2013): 2, www.jstor.org/stable/resrep05787.

19. R. Sukumaran, "The 1962 India-China War and Kargil 1999: Restrictions on the Use of Air Power," *Strategic Analysis* 27, no. 3 (July–Sept. 2003): 332–43.

20. P.C. Lal, "1962 War: The Role of the IAF," *Indian Defence Review*, February 17, 2021, http://www.indiandefencereview.com/interviews/1962-war-the-role-of-the-iaf/.

21. Arjun Subramaniam, *India's Wars: A Military History 1947–1971* (Noida: HarperCollins India, 2020), 429–38.

22. Subramaniam, *India's Wars: A Military History 1947–1971*, 477–504.

23. Ramesh V. Phadke, "Air Power in the 1965 Indo-Pakistan War: An Assessment," *Journal of Defence Studies* 9, no. 3 (July–Sept. 2015): 121–22. http://idsa.in/jds/9_3_2015_AirPowerinthe1965IndoPakistanWar.html.

24. Phadke, "Air Power in the 1965 Indo-Pakistan War," 122–31.

25. Phadke, "Air Power in the 1965 Indo-Pakistan War," 122–31.

26. A.K. Tiwary, "IAF Defeated PAF in 1965 War," *Indian Defence Review* 22, no. 1 (Jan–Mar. 2007), http://www.indiandefencereview.com/spotlights/iaf-defeated-paf-in-1965-war/.

27. Rudra Chaudhuri, "Indian 'Strategic Restraint' Revisited: The Case of the 1965 India-Pakistan War," *India Review* 17, no. 1 (March 29, 2018): 55–75.

28. Singh, *Defence from the Skies*, 55–64.

29. Singh, *Defence from the Skies*, 55–64.

30. A.K. Tiwary, "1971 Air War: Battle for Air Supremacy," *Indian Defence Review*, November 15, 2017, http://www.indiandefencereview.com/spotlights/1971-air-war-battle-for-air-supremacy/2/.

31. Subramaniam, *India's Wars: A Military History 1947–1971*, 724–29.

32. Singh, *Defence from the Skies*, 161–67.

33. Singh, *Defence from the Skies*, 149–61.

34. Benjamin S. Lambeth, *Airpower at 18,000*, 9–34.

35. Jagjit Singh, "Kargil War: Role Played by the Indian Air Force," *Indian Defence Review*, February 2, 2019, http://www.indiandefencereview.com/interviews/role-played-by-the-indian-air-force/.

36. Arjun Subramaniam, *Full Spectrum* (Noida: HarperCollins India, 2020), 904–12.

37. Arjun Subramaniam, *Full Spectrum*, 912–17.

38. Snehesh Alex Philip, "Never Mind Balakot, IAF Is Worse off than Pakistan Air Force on Pilot Strength," *ThePrint*, May 07, 2019, https://theprint.in/defence/never-mind-balakot-iaf-is-worse-off-than-pakistan-air-force-on-pilot-strength/231826/.

39. "Aid to Civil Power," *Indian Air Force*, May 13, 2021, https://indianairforce.nic.in/content/aid-civil-power.

40. "Operation Rahat," *Indian Air Force*, May 13, 2021, https://indianairforce.nic.in/content/op-rahat-0.

41. "Aid to Civil Power," *Indian Air Force*.
42. "Maldives in Water Crisis after Fire at Treatment Plant," *BBC News*, December 5, 2014, https://www.bbc.com/news/world-asia-30344155.
43. Constantino Xavier, "Safe Homecoming," *Force*, May 2017, 46–48, https://carneg ieendowment.org/files/Force_May_2017-Constantino_Xavier.pdf.
44. "IAF'S Support Towards Fight Against Covid-19," Press Information Bureau, Ministry of Defence, April 20, 2020, https://pib.gov.in/PressReleasePage. aspx?PRID=1616467.
45. "IAF Relief Flight Evacuates Indians, Foreigners from Virus-hit Wuhan," *Hindustan Times*, February 27, 2020, https://www.hindustantimes.com/india-news/iaf-airforce-relief-flight-evacuates-indians-foreigners-from-virus-hit-wuhan/story-EQmAS8583Ze3uGzDvqxADO.html.
46. Elizabeth Roche, "IAF Plane with 58 Indians from COVID-19 Hit Iran Lands at Hindon Airbase," *Mint*, March 10, 2020, https://www.livemint.com/news/india/iaf-plane-with-58-indians-from-covid-19-hit-iran-lands-at-hindon-airbase-115 83815048304.html.
47. Manjeet Negi, "Covid-19: Indian Air Force Ferries 11,000 Oxygen Concentrators, 2,950 Ventilators," *India Today*, May 25, 2021, https://www.indiatoday.in/india/story/covid-19-indian-air-force-ferries-11-000-oxygen-concentrators-2-950-ventilators-1806858-2021-05-25.
48. Shreya Dhoundial, "55 Times Around the Globe: That's The Distance IAF Has Covered In Fight Against Covid-19," *News18*, May 27, 2021, https://www.new s18.com/news/india/55-times-around-the-globe-thats-the-distance-iaf-has-covered-in-fight-against-covid-19-3781889.html.
49. "Indian Air Force Flown 1,400 Hours in 21 Days to Boost Oxygen Supply," *Mint*, May 12, 2021, https://www.livemint.com/news/india/indian-air-force-flown-1-400-hours-in-21-days-to-boost-oxygen-supply-11620815947801.html.
50. Narayan Menon, "Air Power against the Maoists," *Indian Defence Review* 27, no. 3 (Oct–Dec 2012), http://www.indiandefencereview.com/news/air-power-agai nst-the-maoists/0/.
51. David Buhril, "50 Years Ago Today, Indira Gandhi Got the Indian Air Force to Bomb Its Own People," *Scroll*, June 28, 2016, https://scroll.in/article/804555/ 50-years-ago-today-indira-gandhi-got-the-indian-air-force-to-bomb-its-own-people.
52. Buhril, "50 Years Ago Today."
53. Arjun Subramaniam, *Full Spectrum*, 151–57.
54. Menon, "Air Power against the Maoists."
55. "Govt. May Revisit Mandate on Use of Air Force against Maoists," *The Hindu*, April 7, 2010, https://www.thehindu.com/news/national/lsquoGovt.-may-revi sit-mandate-on-use-of-Air-Force-against-Maoistsrsquo/article16364640.ece.
56. Anil A. Athale, "Enlist the Army to Fight the Naxalites!," *Rediff*, April 9, 2021, https://www.rediff.com/news/column/enlist-the-army-to-fight-the-naxalites/ 20210409.htm.

57. Menon, "Air Power against the Maoists."
58. "IAF Chief Not in Favour of Air Attack in Anti-Maoist Operations," *The Hindu*, April 7, 2010, https://www.thehindu.com/news/national/IAF-chief-not-in-fav our-of-air-attack-in-anti-Maoist-operations/article16364529.ece.
59. "Air Force to Lend Support for Anti-Naxal Operations," *The Hindu*, June 8, 2016, https://www.thehindu.com/news/national/air-force-to-lend-support-for-antina xal-operations/article4763722.ece.
60. Shishir Gupta, "MoD Clears IAF's Rules of Engagement with Naxals," *The Indian Express*, November 1, 2009, https://indianexpress.com/article/news-archive/ web/mod-clears-iafs-rules-of-engagement-with-naxals/.
61. Tanham and Agmon, *The Indian Air Force: Trends and Prospects*, 59–62.
62. Huma Siddiqui, "Indian Air Force Will Have 35 -36 Combat Squadrons by Mid 2030s Says IAF Chief," *Financial Express*, October 6, 2022, https://www.financial express.com/business/defence-indian-air-force-will-have-35-36-combat-squadr ons-by-mid-2030s-says-iaf-chief-2701254/.
63. Interview with Manmohan Bahadur.
64. See "Maintenance Command," Indian Air Force, https://indianairforce.nic.in/ maintenance-command/; and "Training Command," Indian Air Force, https:// indianairforce.nic.in/training-command/ .
65. Ajai Shukla, "IAF to Increase Squadron Strength; 3 More to Be Inducted in 2020," *Business Standard*, January 18, 2020, https://www.business-standard.com/arti cle/economy-policy/iaf-to-increase-squadron-strength-3-more-to-be-induc ted-in-2020-120011801028_1.html.
66. Wilson Thomas, "IAF Operationalises Second LCA Squadron, Inducts First LCA Tejas in FOC Standard," *The Hindu*, May 27, 2020, https://www.thehindu.com/ news/national/tamil-nadu/iaf-operationalises-second-lca-squadron-inducts- first-lca-tejas-in-foc-standard/article31685568.ece.
67. Ajit K. Dubey, "IAF's Second Rafale Squadron to Get Operational by July 26," *ANI News*, July 13, 2021, https://www.aninews.in/news/national/general-news/ iafs-second-rafale-squadron-to-get-operational-by-july-2620210713203554/.
68. Vijay Mohan, "Behind Massive Build-up at LAC Is the IAF's Never-seen-before Airlift Capability," *The Tribune*, June 29, 2020, https://www.tribuneindia.com/ news/nation/behind-massive-build-up-at-lac-is-the-iafs-never-seen-before-airl ift-capability-106054.
69. Dinakar Peri. "IAF Inducts C-295 Transport Aircraft, Starts Phasing Out Legacy Avro Aircraft," *The Hindu*, September 25, 2023, https://www.thehindu.com/ news/national/first-c-295-aircraft-inducted-into-indian-air-force/article67343 776.ece.
70. "Our Strength," Indian Air Force, https://indianairforce.nic.in/content/our- strength.
71. Saurav Anand, "IAF Inducts First Made-in-India Light Combat Helicopters," *Mint*, October 3, 2022, https://www.livemint.com/news/india/iaf-inducts-first- made-in-india-light-combat-helicopters-11664807466198.html

72. "Boeing Completes Delivery of Apache, Chinook Helicopters to IAF," *The Hindu*, July 10, 2020, https://www.thehindu.com/business/boeing-completes-delivery-of-apache-chinook-helicopters-to-iaf/article32046094.ece.

73. Rajat Pandit, "India Plans Major Indigenous Project for Six Powerful 'eyes in the Sky' AWACS," *The Times of India*, December 16, 2020, https://timesofindia.ind iatimes.com/india/india-plans-major-indigenous-project-for-six-powerful-eyes-in-the-sky-awacs/articleshow/79766365.cms.

    See also Dinakar Peri, "IAF to Adopt New Process to Lease Refuelling Aircraft," *The Hindu*, April 10, 2021, https://www.thehindu.com/news/national/iaf-to-adopt-new-process-to-lease-refuelling-aircraft/article34292349.ece.

74. Tanham and Agmon, *The Indian Air Force: Trends and Prospects*, 73.

75. Interview with Sushant Singh.

76. Tanham and Agmon, *The Indian Air Force: Trends and Prospects*, 73.

77. Interview with Arjun Subramaniam.

78. Interview with Manmohan Bahadur.

79. Tanham and Agmon, *The Indian Air Force: Trends and Prospects*, 61–62.

80. Singh, *Defence from the Skies*, 66.

81. Singh, *Defence from the Skies*, 66.

82. S. Nihal Singh, "Why India Goes to Moscow for Arms," *Asian Survey* 24, no. 7 (July 1984): 707–20. https://www.jstor.org/stable/2644184.

83. Tanham and Agmon, *The Indian Air Force: Trends and Prospects*, 76.

84. "Our History," *Hindustan Aeronautics Limited*, https://hal-india.co.in/Our%20 History/M__111

85. Sebastien Roblin, "India's Disappointing Marut Jet Fighter Proved Itself in Combat," *The National Interest*, August 13, 2017, https://nationalinterest.org/blog/indias-disappointing-marut-jet-fighter-proved-itself-combat-21875. See also: P. R. Sanjai, "Tejas Inducted in IAF after 33 Years," *Mint*, July 01, 2016, https://www.livemint.com/Politics/UuAGjJYaTiuZvqo7OLZlOO/Indian-Air-Force-inducts-first-squadron-of-LCA-Tejas.html.

86. Air Force Academy (AFA), Air Force Administrative College (AFAC), Air Force Technical College (AFTC), Flying Training Establishments (FTE), and the National Defence Academy (NDA). See also https://afcat.cdac.in/AFCAT/Train ing.html.

87. This information was tabled in a written reply in the Rajya Sabha https://pib.gov.in/Pressreleaseshare.aspx?PRID=1696144.

88. "Detailed Brief," Indian Air Force. https://indianairforce.nic.in/wp-content/uplo ads/2022/06/Detailed-BRIEF-13-JUN-22.pdf

89. Parikshit Luthra, "Indian Air Force, MoD Agniveer: Women Can Now Join Air Force – DMA," CNBCTV18, Accessed June 12, 2023, https://www.cnbctv18.com/india/indian-air-force-iaf-mod-agniveer-women-can-now-join-air-force-dma-16914871.htm#.

90. Indian Air Force, *Doctrine of the Indian Air Force*, January 2023, 69, https://ind ianairforce.nic.in/wp-content/uploads/2023/01/2MB.pdf.

91. Benjamin S. Lambeth, "India's Air Force Evolves," *Air Force Magazine*, March 2015, 62–66.
92. Singh, *Defence from the Skies*, 274.
93. "Trouble with Spares, Absent Pilot Trainers Puts the Mirage in Critical Condition," *India Today*, May 7, 2012. https://www.indiatoday.in/magaz ine/defence/story/20120507-mirage-fighter-fleet-in-critical-condition-758 190-2012-04-27.
94. "IAF Looks for Industry Help to Tackle Obsolete Assets Challenge," *The Asian Age*, November 16, 2019. https://www.asianage.com/metros/kolkata/161119/ iaf-looks-for-industry-help-to-tackle-obsolete-assets-challenge-1.html.
95. Benjamin S. Lambeth, "India's Air Force Evolves," 62–66.
96. Lok Sabha Unstarred Question No.4692, https://eparlib.nic.in/bitstream/ 123456789/985541/1/AU4692.pdf.
97. Bhartesh Singh Thakur, "Why Airmen Are Leaving Indian Air Force," *The Tribune,* May 9, 2020, https://www.tribuneindia.com/news/nation/why-air men-are-leaving-indian-air-force-82569.
98. Rahul Singh, "Air Force Could Give Quicker Promotions in Retention Plan," *Hindustan Times*, February 24, 2020, https://www.hindustantimes.com/india- news/air-force-could-give-quicker-promotions-in-retention-plan/story-RGD V8jBNEuOxq6OiwigaeN.html.
99. Ashley J. Tellis, *Troubles, They Come in Battalions: The Manifold Travails of the Indian Air Force* (Washington DC: Carnegie Endowment for International Peace, 2016), 5–6.
100. Harsh V. Pant and Angad Singh, "Rafale Jets Won't Save India's Air Force," *Foreign Policy*, August 10, 2020, https://foreignpolicy.com/2020/08/10/rafale- jets-wont-save-indias-air-force/.
101. Elizabeth Roche, "Air Force Fully Prepared for Two-Front War, Says IAF Chief Bhadauria," *Mint*, October 05, 2020, https://www.livemint.com/news/india/ fully-prepared-for-two-front-war-iaf-chief-11601892500129.html.
102. Snehesh Alex Philip, "IAF Inducts Rafale Today, Here's How the Deadly Fighter Jets Will Boost India's Air Power," *ThePrint*, July 29, 2020, https://theprint.in/ defence/iaf-inducts-rafale-today-heres-how-the-deadly-fighter-jets-will- boost-indias-air-power/470043/.
103. Manjeet Negi, "IAF to Soon Move Rs 1.4 Lakh Crore Deal for Govt Approval," *India Today*, January 31, 2021, https://www.indiatoday.in/india/story/iaf-to- soon-move-rs-1-4-lakh-crore-deal-for-govt-approval-1764509-2021-01-31.
104. Interview with Sushant Singh.
105. In 2007, India floated a global tender for the procurement of 126 medium mul- tirole combat aircraft (MMRCA) to replace the IAF's aging Mig-21s. Six fighter aircraft submitted bids for the contract and the Rafale was eventually chosen in 2012. However, the deal was nixed in 2015 as negotiations were still ongoing.
106. "IAF Receives First LCA Tejas Trainer Aircraft from HAL, Eyes Additional 97 Fighter Jets," *Mint*, October 4, 2023, https://www.thehindu.com/news/national/ air-force-likely-to-get-123-lca-tejas-by-2024-25/article17532355.ece.

107. Ajai Shukla, "Tejas versus JF-17 Thunder," *Business Standard*, May 6, 2021, https://www.business-standard.com/article/opinion/tejas-versus-jf-17-thun der-121050601415_1.html.

108. Sudhi Ranjan Sen, "Tejas Far Behind Competitors, Not Enough to Protect Indian Skies: IAF," *India Today*, November 10, 2017, https://www.indiatoday.in/ mail-today/story/tejas-indian-air-force-f-16-mig-21-fighter-planes-ajit-doval-1083350-2017-11-10.

109. Tellis, *Troubles, They Come in Battalions*, pp. 27–32.

110. Rahul Bhatia, "India Needs to Fix Its Indigenous Fighter Before Building Stealth Aircraft," Carnegie India, August 10, 2022, https://carnegieindia.org/2022/08/ 10/india-needs-to-fix-its-indigenous-fighter-before-building-stealth-aircr aft-pub-87643.

111. "IAF Plans to Have 125 Advanced Combat Jets," *The Tribune*, October 7, 2020, https://www.tribuneindia.com/news/nation/iaf-plans-to-have-125-advanced-combat-jets-152029.

112. Shishir Gupta, "Indian ADA to Roll Tejas Mark II Prototype with F-414 Engine by 2024 End," *Hindustan Times*, July 21, 2023, https://www.hindustantimes. com/india-news/indian-ada-to-roll-tejas-mark-ii-prototype-with-f-414-eng ine-by-2024-end-101687323394817.html.

113. "Report No. 3 of 2019: Performance Audit Report of the Comptroller and Auditor General of Indian on Capital Acquisition in Indian Air Force," Comptroller and Auditor General, February 13, 2019.

114. Rahul Bedi, "IAF's Fanciful Ambitions Now Risk Exceeding India's Declining Defence Budget," *The Wire*, October 7, 2020, https://thewire.in/security/iaf-figh ter-aircraft-budget-bhaduria.

115. Union Budget 2021–22. See also Figures 4.2 and 4.3.

PART II
INTELLIGENCE

Part II examines two of India's premier intelligence agencies—the externally-oriented Research and Analysis Wing (R&AW) and the domestically-oriented Intelligence Bureau (IB). Although both agencies loom large within India's security apparatus, there is a dearth of systematic analyses of their capacity, organization, evolution over time, and operational effectiveness. Drawing on a range of sources—including government documents, media accounts, memoirs, and interviews—this part aims to shed light on two key institutions which have largely existed in the shadows, evading both popular scrutiny and parliamentary oversight.

5

The Research and Analysis Wing

Shreyas Shende and Rudra Chaudhuri

Introduction

The Research and Analysis Wing (R&AW), India's external intelligence agency, has been in operation for over five decades. It was created through an executive order issued by Prime Minister Indira Gandhi in September 1968. The R&AW works alongside the Indian Ministry of External Affairs (MEA), much like the UK's MI6 works alongside the British Foreign, Commonwealth, and Development Office, and its budget is allocated through the MEA. While the primary focus of the organization is to collect intelligence within the Indian subcontinent, its officers and networks are spread across the world. The Indian prime minister is the agency's primary customer.

Yet, despite its centrality, the R&AW has no constitutional status in India. In short, it legally does not exist. There is no official history of R&AW. The little that is known about this organization can be gleaned from a handful of memoirs that have been authored by its former serving officers, and which largely focus on covert operations.[1] To date, there has not been a single debate in the Indian Parliament about the R&AW and there are no select parliamentary committees that look into the affairs of the R&AW.[2] As a former senior official has written, such agencies 'have also been exempt from disclosure under the Right to Information Act on the basis of national security considerations'.[3] Attempts to introduce a degree of parliamentary oversight have had no effect whatsoever. Unlike in the United Kingdom or other parts of the world, India has no structure that can also serve as a 'surrogate' for public opinion on intelligence matters.[4] There is no institutional bridge between the public and intelligence agencies like the R&AW.

Shreyas Shende and Rudra Chaudhuri, *The Research and Analysis Wing* In: *Institutional Roots of India's Security Policy*. Edited by: Milan Vaishnav, Oxford University Press. © Oxford University Press 2024. DOI: 10.1093/oso/9780198894612.003.0005

In keeping with the general theme of this volume, this chapter focuses primarily on the organizational aspects of the R&AW. While the chapter dips in and out of the many covert operations that have been detailed in existing accounts, its aim is to provide a clearer—and perhaps drier—institutional account of one of India's principal security institutions. The R&AW's involvement in operations, from the creation of Bangladesh in 1971 to its increasing global footprint, has been well documented in existing narratives[5]—many of which serve as a basis for parts of this chapter. Further, this chapter is based on a careful survey of media reports on and analyses of the organization—conducted since 1980—and a selection of government reports that have advocated for the reorganization of Indian intelligence. Lastly, it relies on interviews with former serving officers and experts.

The chapter is divided into three sections. The first outlines the history and the core objectives of the R&AW. The second shines light on its organizational structure and provides an account of recruitment policies as well as human and financial resources. In the concluding section, the authors analyse the agency's need for change and reform.

Raison d'Etat and History

The R&AW was carved out of the IB, the Indian Intelligence Bureau, on 21 September 1968.[6] Officially known as the Research and Analysis Wing of the Cabinet Secretariat, its officers were hitherto part of the external wing of the IB. With an initial strength of 200–250 officers, it was led by Rameshwar Nath Kao, the erstwhile head of the IB's external branch.

India's shocking defeat in the 1962 Sino-Indian War and Pakistan's surprise covert military infiltration into Jammu and Kashmir in 1965—which ultimately led to the outbreak of war—served as the principal reasons for the creation of an organization dedicated to the collection of external intelligence. P.N. Haksar, then Secretary to Indira Gandhi, played a crucial role in creating the R&AW.[7] He unhesitatingly advocated for the creation of such an organization. Kao was trusted by the Prime Minister—the only person to whom he was answerable—but also had the institutional background for the task at hand. An officer in the Indian Police Service (IPS) since 1940, he went on to head the Aviation Research Centre (ARC).

Created with the help of the US Central Intelligence Agency (CIA) in 1962, the ARC was responsible for signals and technical intelligence and even possessed a fleet of its own aircrafts. Kao retired in 1977 and died in 2002, leaving taped recordings of his accounts within the R&AW. To date, however, they remain undisclosed. He is nothing short of a legend in the services. Ironically, for someone who advocated the creation of a historical wing within the R&AW, he also championed the secretive nature of this unique institution—a tradition that continues today.

Unsurprisingly, what mattered most in the creation of the R&AW was trust. Personalities mattered more than institutional structures. The R&AW was never meant to follow bureaucratic protocols, norms, and rules. It was set up with the explicit intent to remain a dependable agency that reported directly to the prime minister. Indira Gandhi had, in fact, commissioned Kao to outline the structure of a new foreign intelligence agency. Kao studied the CIA closely and took inspiration from its design.[8]

From the very beginning, the R&AW was Kao's institutional baby.[9] Gandhi made sure to place the newly formed organization under the direct control of the Prime Minister's Office, ensuring that Kao 'not only had the prime minister's confidence but had unmediated access [to her] as well'.[10] Such access helped ameliorate the struggles that define much of the Indian administrative state.

Gandhi tasked Kao to create a truly 'multi-disciplined' organization that 'should not draw its higher personnel exclusively from the IPS'.[11] Both Kao and his successor, K. Sankaran Nair, stressed that the R&AW 'should not become just another police organization'.[12] Gandhi exempted the organization from the 'purview of the Union Public Service Commission (UPSC) in matters of recruitment and promotions'.[13] Yet to this day, with the exception of one R&AW chief who came from the Indian Postal Service, every other R&AW chief has been a police officer.

During the R&AW's early days, Kao and Nair set up 'separate analysis and operational desks', modelled on Western intelligence organizations.[14] By separating intelligence collection from analysis, the R&AW was able to provide unvarnished intelligence to its key customers. Over the next several decades, the R&AW's self-styled approach diverted significantly from Western intelligence agencies. The lack of parliamentary oversight and the agency's general unwillingness to engage with experts outside its ranks stand at odds with the inner workings of the CIA or MI6.[15]

To be sure, the R&AW, according to Jairam Ramesh '[fell] victim to a bureaucratic tussle' soon after it came into existence.[16] Kao immediately raised these issues with Haksar,[17] and was given 'full powers and independence from the usual bureaucratic scrutiny'.[18] In addition, and by design, the R&AW was kept out of the purview of any formal accountability mechanisms. It operated and continues to operate in a 'legal vacuum'.[19]

In 1969, Haksar advocated providing the R&AW with as much operational freedom as possible, free from administrative controls. He noted that the R&AW chief should be

> appointed as Additional Secretary, it is in the interests of security and efficiency of work that he [the R&AW chief] should function as such with all the powers, including financial powers normally exercised by Additional Secretaries and the Organization should be treated as an integral part of the Cabinet Secretariat.[20]

He further argued that 'with matters relating to the Organization's administration, establishment and finances, a separate Administrative Cell should be created in the Cabinet Secretariat'. This cell 'should work under the Additional Secretary and should examine establishment and financial proposals made by the Research and Analysis Wing in consultations with its concerned officers'.[21] Hence, from the very beginning, it was clear that the R&AW chief would enjoy considerable powers to exercise their authorities in service of national security. The funding for the R&AW was always to be channelled through the MEA, a practice that continues even today. Indeed, as former senior officers make clear, its 'budget has actually never been a limitation for the organization'.[22]

Kao's first priority was to strengthen the R&AW's capacity for collecting intelligence in Pakistan and China.[23] All foreign desks that were previously located within the IB 'were transferred to R&AW'.[24] Yet the 'intelligence collection and covert action capabilities relating to Pakistan and China', from within the IB, were found to be inadequate.[25] Kao's immediate task then was to build up and strengthen R&AW's covert action capabilities, including its capability 'for covert action in East Pakistan'.[26] From the very beginning, Kao knew that the crisis unfolding in East Pakistan would be 'the first serious test for his agency'.[27] Along with proving the efficacy of the organization, he also had to demonstrate the necessity for the R&AW to exist separately from the IB. After all, officers who joined the R&AW were considered traitors by those still in the IB.[28]

The R&AW played a crucial role in the creation of Bangladesh. Much of this had to do with Kao's own position and influence at the time. As a noted historian of the 1971 war underlines, Kao played a strategic role in shaping Gandhi's own 'position on the crisis'.[29] In April 1971, Kao was given charge of a coordination committee mandated to oversee all 'questions pertaining to the Bangladesh movement, including political, military, [and] administrative'.[30] Yet, as an organization, the R&AW had limited success in collecting strategic intelligence outside of India's immediate borders. It could not gauge the intentions of the United States, which ultimately played an all-important role in shaping West Pakistan's advances.[31]

Kao, along with Nair, set up the R&AW's technical branches—a Monitoring Division to collect technical intelligence (TECHINT) and a Cryptography Division.[32] In 1971, the R&AW also created a psychological warfare (PSYWAR) division, termed the 'information division', which included professionals from the Ministry of Information and Broadcasting.[33] The early efforts to set up these divisions played a crucial role in the 1971 war. By the early 1970s, the R&AW had several thousand personnel.[34] Similarly, its annual budget had grown from close to 20 million rupees at the time of its formation, to an estimated annual budget of 300 million rupees in the early 1970s.[35]

Compared to strategic intelligence, the R&AW had greater success with TECHINT. The Monitoring and Cryptography Divisions were generally thought to be effective.[36] These divisions helped produce usable intelligence for its primary consumers: the Indian Army and the Indian government. It trained Bengali freedom fighters in secret training camps on the border and designed an active propaganda campaign to ensure that international audiences were sensitized to the atrocities being committed in the East.[37] In short, its first major operation was a success.

Yet the R&AW's main objectives were still unclear. The focus remained on India's immediate neighbourhood. Deploying officers and cultivating agents in Pakistan, China, Nepal, and independent Bangladesh was of primary importance. Closer to home, the R&AW was tasked to ensure Sikkim's accession[38]—a monarchy granted special status at the time of Indian independence.[39] G.B.S. Sidhu, an IPS officer, headed a three-man

R&AW team sent to Gangtok in 1973. They connected with the Sikkim Congress, which in turn played a crucial role in supporting accession with India in 1975.[40]

During the Indian Emergency (1975 to 1977), the R&AW's role was brought into sharp relief. Kao regularly updated Gandhi on the apparent role of the 'foreign hand' in India's domestic affairs. The intelligence in question was clearly manipulated, though it remains unknown whether the producers or the consumers were responsible for such manipulation. The CIA, the main target of Gandhi's regime, had, in fact, very little to do with India at the time. This is well substantiated in archival records de-classified over the last decade.[41]. Further, the Emergency provided an op-portunity for the Soviet KGB to cement ties with India. The KGB invested in an extensive active measures campaign, planting articles in the Indian press about the CIA's alleged activities in India.[42] The campaign worked. Gandhi was convinced that the CIA wanted to oust her just like 'Chile's CIA-backed general Augusto Pinochet ousted Salvador Allende.'[43] None other than Yuri Andropov, the KGB chief at the time, approved 'Indian active measures operation' in April 1975 'to publicise fabricated evi-dence of CIA subversion.'[44] The R&AW's counter-intelligence capabilities were either limited or turned a blind eye to the KGB's widespread and well-funded campaign. Interestingly, in terms of planted articles in the press, the KGB's active measures campaign declined from 1,980 stories in 1976—when Gandhi was in power—to 411 in 1977, when she lost the general election in a dramatic reversal of fortune.[45]

Ironically, towards the end of the Emergency, Kao advised Gandhi that she would win the elections to follow. However, Gandhi and the Congress Party badly lost the elections, ushering in a ramshackle coali-tion of political parties opposed to the Emergency known as the Janata government.

Understandably, incoming Prime Minister Morarji Desai was wary of the R&AW given its proximity to Gandhi. Desai 'drastically reduce[d] [the R&AW's] strength and budget'.[46] This was in part due to the criti-cism levelled against the R&AW and its 'alleged interference in domestic politics'.[47] Reportedly, when the Desai-led government sought to find in-stances of the R&AW's abuses of power at Gandhi's instructions, it was hard pressed to find any records proving misdeeds.[48] In 1977, K. Sankaran Nair—also a member of the IPS—succeeded Rao as R&AW chief. He resigned three months into the job when his position was downgraded by a world-weary Desai.[49] Nair was replaced by N.F. Suntook, who was then Chairman of the Joint Intelligence Committee (JIC).[50] Political unease about the R&AW also translated into internal problems. Rising discontent among staff personnel led to strikes—the first for India's external intelligence agency[51]—before it finally created an R&AW Employees Association.[52] These were early days, and systems of management were still in the making.

The Janata government's stint in power was short lived. Gandhi won the 1980 elections soon after the coalition crumbled. Whilst Suntook remained in post, Kao returned to the Cabinet Secretariat as a senior adviser to the prime minister in 1981.[53] Since the very beginning, when it was created by executive order, the R&AW's fate has been closely entwined with the political leader of the day. This was, and continues to be, in keeping with the very nature of the organization.

Kao and Nair, who had retired but continued to provide input, used this time to resume direct recruitment and complete the 'constitution of the cadre'.[54] The 'detailed service rules' for a Research Analysis Service (RAS), first created in 1971 and suspended by Desai, were formalized,[55] and the RAS cadre constituted at Kao and Nair's suggestion.[56]

The new rules defined 'job requirements and the required personality traits' for the RAS cadre.[57] Fresh recruits were asked to 'develop language expertise' and undergo rigorous training, 'including physical toughening in the training institutes of various security forces'.[58] The aim was to introduce a degree of transparency into the hiring process. At the same time, the government passed the Intelligence Organizations Act in September 1985. The Act barred officials of any Indian intelligence organization from being 'a member of or ... associated in any way with' unions or any class of political associations.[59] After nearly two decades, the RAS cadre was 'formally constituted with lateral entrants drawn from the IAS, IPS and other services including the armed forces'.[60]

In short, the close relationship with the prime minister had paid off. Kao's second priority was creating the Policy and Research Staff in the Cabinet Secretariat. This served as a precursor to the National Security Council Secretariat, which was finally established in 1999.[61] These swift decisions were possible because of the flexible nature of the R&AW's foundational structure. To this end, remaining outside the traditional scrutiny of administrative processes served the organization well. It could make and take decisions and effect them with little delay.

By the 1980s, the R&AW's purview had shifted from India's immediate land borders to include Sri Lanka, Afghanistan, and even further afield to Africa. In Sri Lanka, the agency supported Tamil militant organizations,[62] such as the Liberation Tigers of Tamil Eelam (LTTE).[63] That this strategy ultimately backfired is another matter altogether.[64] In Afghanistan, it forged close working relations with the KhAD, the Afghan security and intelligence agency created and trained by the KGB.[65] They coordinated activities even as the Berlin Wall collapsed in 1989 and the KGB morphed into the Russian FSB in 1995. India's growing footprint in Africa, especially in the decolonized countries of Ghana and Namibia and in apartheid South Africa, can be attributed to Suntook's personal interest in that part of the world.[66] Whilst the R&AW closely coordinated with the MEA, its top leaders had a fair degree of latitude in determining its areas of operations. Prior to his retirement in 1983, Suntook set up a separate division—led by the maverick officer B. Raman—that focused on the growth of Sikh separatism, the Khalistan movement, and its ties to the Pakistani Inter-Services Intelligence (ISI).[67]

With the goal of checking the ISI's growing involvement in both Sikh separatism and the future of Jammu and Kashmir, Suntook's successor, G.C. Saxena—also an IPS officer—reactivated the R&AW's contacts with 'Sindhi, Pashtun, and Baloch nationalists in Pakistan'. This was done at the direct order of Indira Gandhi,[68] but the policy of 'undercutting Pakistan's influence' continued under her successor and son, Prime Minister Rajiv Gandhi.[69] During this period, the R&AW also opened two new desks: Counter Intelligence Team-X and Counter Intelligence Team-J, which were created to 'wreak havoc in Pakistan and make [Pakistan's] activities in Punjab "prohibitively expensive"'.[70]

Political leadership and top officers' personal interests determined the R&AW's areas of interests and operations. As previously mentioned, this cut both ways. In the early 1990s, Prime Minister Narasimha Rao sought to cultivate better relations with both China and Myanmar. In 1993, India and China signed the first in a series of milestone agreements that sought to bring 'peace and tranquility' to the contested 3,488-kilometre-long border.[71] With this in mind, Rao ordered the closure of the R&AW's eastern operations.[72] Further, in an effort to mend ties with Pakistan, Rao reportedly reduced 'the lethal angle to India's covert action in Afghanistan and Pakistan'.[73] Rao, according to one notable academic, took this decision to avoid a 'conflict with Pakistan over Kashmir, or in Afghanistan', given India's dire economic situation at the end of the Cold War.[74]

In the late 1990s, Prime Minister Inder Kumar Gujral followed suit. He shut down the counter-intelligence teams that were 'aimed at Pakistan'.[75] Between 1990 and 1999, the R&AW was led by seven chiefs—a period of instability for India's premier external intelligence agency. India's political turmoil, which witnessed six changes in the prime ministership, clearly resulted in equally quick successions in leadership at the R&AW. Finally, in 1999, A.S. Dulat was appointed chief. Although he retired from the R&AW a year later in 2000, he continued to serve as an advisor to the government of Prime Minister Atal Bihari Vajpayee until 2004.

These were crucial years not only for the R&AW but also for India's entire intelligence apparatus.[76] The surprise infiltration in Kargil in 1999 led to major restructuring in the R&AW, propelling it into the twenty-first century.

Organizational Structure and Human Resources

The R&AW is headed by a chief at the rank of Secretary in the Government of India. This is similar to other arms of government like the MEA, which is led by the foreign secretary, or the Home Ministry, which is led by the home secretary. In 2020, 14 additional secretaries were placed in charge of different sections of the R&AW. The government has also approved a rank known as special secretary for three positions in the organization. These are considered on a case-by-case basis. Of the R&AW's cadres, 40 to 50 per cent remain at the rank of undersecretary, deputy secretary, or director. Promotions are a problem for the organization, given the limited senior posts available. Most officers are still seconded from other services and ministries. This personnel structure, as senior officers argue, has done little to create a professional intelligence service. There is 'no breaking-in period' for those seconded. There is also little training available to them, unlike for those that are directly recruited into the organization. The latter are sent to commando training, attached to the Border Security Force units for short periods, given language training, and even sent for short courses to the Jawaharlal Nehru University and other premier educational institutions.[77] Most R&AW officers broadly undergo two forms of training: basic and field.[78] Basic training consists of geostrategic analyses and learning the basics of intelligence and espionage. During field training, officers are 'attached to military units to learn tactical intelligence' and they learn 'infiltration, interrogation and how to avoid capture'.[79] Some officers are also sent to other countries for language training.

From what can be gleaned from open sources, the R&AW has four region-specific desks, each headed by a joint secretary: a Pakistan desk, a China and South East Asia desk, a Middle East and Africa desk, and a desk for other countries.[80] In addition to this, an additional secretary for special operations[81] and the head of ARC report directly to the R&AW chief.[82] However, and interestingly, the ARC has a separate and much larger budget than the R&AW.[83] The Special Service Bureau, raised in 1963 in the aftermath of the 1962 India–China war, reported directly to the R&AW.[84] In addition to these responsibilities, the R&AW also ensures 'security for India's nuclear program and keeping details about nuclear detonations quiet'.[85]

In late 1998, a key change was made to India's security-making process: the creation of the National Security Council. Prime Minister Vajpayee's principal secretary, Brajesh Mishra, became India's first National Security Adviser (NSA).[86] This brought a layer of political oversight to the unfettered access the R&AW chief had long enjoyed to the Prime Minister's Office. The chief was now required to report to the NSA who, in turn, reported to the prime minister. In April 1998, the NSA was given a secretariat. The Joint Intelligence Committee (JIC) was morphed into the newly established National Security Council Secretariat (NSCS), under the leadership of the NSA.[87] For an organization that had enjoyed such close proximity to the prime minister of the day, this was a significant organizational change. The NSA, a political appointee, became the country's *de facto* intelligence and security tsar. In June 2019, the NSA's rank in the government was elevated to that of a cabinet minister. In previous years, it was pegged to that of a junior minister or a minister of state.

Yet the main organizational change to the R&AW took place in the aftermath of the Kargil conflict—a surprise attack by regular Pakistani military personnel disguised as Kashmiri militants in the summer of

1999. The Kargil crisis was broadly branded as an intelligence failure.[88] The Kargil Review Committee (KRC), set up in July 1999, noted that the 'R&AW facility in Kargil area did not receive adequate attention in terms of staff of technological capability'. As a result, 'intelligence collection, coordination and follow-up were weak'.[89] One of the key issues that the KRC noted was the R&AW's feeble human intelligence (HUMINT) capabilities.[90] The committee also highlighted the 'lack of coordination between the R&AW and the Army'.[91] This was, in no uncertain terms, the organization's moment of reckoning.

In April 2000, the government constituted a Group of Ministers (GoM) to re-examine issues pertaining to security and intelligence. Four task forces were set up, including one dedicated to intelligence.[92] An Intelligence Coordination Group (ICG) was created, chaired by the NSA in an attempt to provide systematic intelligence oversight.[93] This added yet another layer of internal oversight to the workings of the R&AW. The organization's freedom of manoeuvre had been seriously limited. This was a far cry from Haksar and Kao's initial designs to provide the R&AW with as much latitude as possible.

In 2003, the government set up a Technical Coordination Group (TCG), with the aim to 'oversee technical requirements and resources'.[94] Another outcome of the KRC report and the GoM's suggestions was the creation of the National Technical Research Organization (NTRO). Established in April 2004, this is India's equivalent of the US National Security Agency.[95] The National Security Adviser was the main customer for all of these new organizations, and the changes resulted in the NSA becoming a 'powerful coordinator of intelligence'.[96] The R&AW chief was no longer the principal security actor, advising the government or the prime minister of the day on matters of external intelligence. He—and all of the chiefs have, indeed, been male so far—had become *one* of the many guardians of India's national security.

For those who held senior positions in the R&AW during the first decade of the twenty-first century, it had become clear that, organizational changes aside, there was little concerted effort in terms of coordination. While the NSCS centralized information and operations, there was—and, indeed, continues to be—a clear lacuna in coordination efforts. The IB and the R&AW were often at odds in their appreciation of threats. Senior officers needed to develop personal relations with those in the MEA and other government ministries to get a clearer sense of common priorities. The institutional mechanisms for coordination were as good as non-existent. In addition, there was almost no coordination with the primary consumers of intelligence. The consequences of the lack of coordination were perhaps most apparent in India's dealings with Nepal, as Maoists sought to oust the Nepalese monarchy. For an entire year, senior R&AW officers coordinated with the Maoists, with the MEA and the NSA brought into this process much later. The lack of coordination also meant that differing perceptions of the Nepalese Maoists were being peddled in the Joint Intelligence Committee. The IB argued that those in Nepal supported the Maoists in India. The R&AW disagreed. This tussle fed into India's muddled approach to Nepal as the Maoists marched into Kathmandu.[97]

Further, it was also increasingly clear that little was being done by way of perspective planning. A senior management group, made of special and additional secretaries, had been created in the R&AW in the mid-2000s. However, the group spent most of its time on administrative matters—threats were rarely discussed. K.C. Verma, then chief of the R&AW, understood the challenges the organization faced. The balance between bureaucratic manoeuvrings and the actual time spent on developing a threat-based advance had tilted squarely to the former. Verma's successor, Sanjeev Tripathi, understood this well too, and initiated a process to address the gap. The results remain unknown.

In 2008, the lack of coordination and the need to focus on new and emerging threats was underlined when gunmen trained by the Pakistani establishment tore across the city of Mumbai. The central question was simple: How could this have happened? Was this an intelligence failure? A post-mortem of the attacks made clear that the lack of coordination was a root cause in the failure to anticipate or detect the gunmen, who came by sea from Karachi. Reportedly, the R&AW and the IB had received intelligence that an attack was conceivable, but the agencies failed to share the intelligence. The IB did not have access to foreign internal intelligence, and there was no streamlined process by which diplomats in the MEA could be in regular contact with those in the R&AW.

Following the 2008 Mumbai attacks, the JIC was 'directed to focus more on the immediate or short-term intelligence inputs'. The NSCS 'reverted to more in-depth, policy-oriented prognoses relating to intelligence and national security priorities'[98] The 2008 terrorist attack—as a stark example of a 'national intelligence and security lapse'—did not spur the kind of inquiry that should have taken place; the response was limited to a probe of how the Mumbai police responded to the attack.[99]

In 2011, the government appointed a task force on national security led by former cabinet secretary Naresh Chandra. However, the task force report was not made public. The commission was 'discarded' as soon as the Bharatiya Janata Party–led government came to power in 2014.[100] There have been reports about major changes in India's intelligence apparatus, such as closing the ARC and splitting its assets between the Indian Air Force and the NTRO. Reportedly, these changes are designed to 'enhance intelligence-gathering on China's military capacities in the Tibet plateau'. However, there is no evidence in the public domain about whether and when such restructuring has actually taken place.[101]

What is clear is that the R&AW suffers from a shortage of qualified personnel. According to one report published in 2013, the deficit in the number of officers was close to 40 per cent.[102] This shortage allegedly included a shortfall of around '130 management-level staff'. Crucial positions across India's borders with Afghanistan and Pakistan were staffed by those 'who have never served in those countries, pointing to a deepening lack of area and language skills'.[103] The situation seems to have improved in the last three to four years. Of the 9,000 officers needed in the service, 7,500–8,000 were in position.[104] Yet, as a senior officer insists, this has not helped the need for greater coordination with the consumers of intelligence or with the MEA, the key ministry it works alongside.

Former R&AW officers have recommended workforce planning to mitigate the human resource issues that plague the organization.[105] The R&AW, reportedly, does not 'pay enough attention towards developing HUMINT'.[106] For instance, the training period for fresh recruits, roughly six months, is too short to create an effective workforce. The initial R&AW officers, on the other hand, underwent extensive training—they would spend 'close to three years in training before they were permitted to take up desk assignments'.[107] In addition to concerns around shortened training periods, the gulf between those on deputation from various civil services—including, primarily the IPS—and those who were directly recruited has led to a 'constant and debilitating tussle' within the R&AW.[108] The primacy of the IPS within the R&AW does not just affect the organization at the lower and mid-levels; disaffection with the police services has also been documented at the senior additional secretary level.[109] Excessive focus on deputing officers from the various services also results in limited space for specialists. The R&AW's 'intake of scientists, cyber analysts and linguists is below required levels' and the lack of lateral entry options 'reduces the agency's ability to recruit off the market'.[110] Cadre management, as a former R&AW officer notes, is essential for both the quantitative and qualitative needs of the agency—ensuring that there are no excessive vacancies and creating well-trained officers with specialized skill sets.[111]

With workforce planning that focuses on direct recruitment, extensive training, and mid-career reviews, human resource issues in the R&AW should be addressed in the medium to long term.[112]

Conclusions

Intelligence failures are more easily recounted than successes. The latter remain unknown to the general public. But failures are widely established. The R&AW has played a crucial role in every major diplomatic manoeuvre since the early 1970s. From the creation of Bangladesh and Rajiv Gandhi's reset with China in 1988 to rebuilding human assets in Pakistan in the twenty-first century and shaping international negotiations, the R&AW's hand is clear. Its shortcomings—in Sri Lanka, for instance, or its inability to detect surprise attacks in 1999 and 2008—have been widely recounted. Given the opaque nature of the organization, there is very little point in assessing its performance in terms of its operations that remain in the shadows. Instead, this concluding section focuses on the authors' analysis of what more can be done to improve the administrative functioning of this crucial organization.

First, there is a desperate need to engage more with the public. This is particularly crucial in a democracy. In turn, being a part of the public's active imagination has every potential to better serve the R&AW's own cadres, and potentially make the organization more effective. Levels of engagement with parts of the public—whether academics or journalists—have traditionally relied on personal relationships between senior officers and those in their social orbits. Only a few maverick officers have sought out those in the academy or in public policy. In a world in which open-source intelligence (OSINT) is seen to be as important as traditional forms of intelligence, greater interaction with the public sphere has every potential to expand the agency's collective mind space.[113] As Jonathan Evans, the former head of MI5, recounts, greater openness increases public confidence. Just as importantly, it 'helps [the MI5] do our job of protecting national security'.[114] The challenges of today—whether it is terrorism, radicalization, or cyberwarfare—cannot and should not be left to the mandarins who live in the shadows. As John Sawers, the former head of MI6, argues, one of the main reasons for commissioning an official history of the organization was 'to increase public understanding of SIS [MI6]'.[115]

Today, MI5 and MI6 have a website for their respective organizations, as does the CIA. The CIA library is a treasure trove of declassified information on the agency's analyses, up to the late 1970s. This is all easily accessible on the Internet.

Greater transparency has often been derided by those in Indian intelligence. 'India is not a mature democracy,' they argue. Yet being more open does not necessarily have to compromise national security, no matter how chaotic a democracy might be. Rather, it should be seen as an investment in a surgical declassification process. Greater transparency requires creativity and foresight, with the view to giving the public an insight into an organization that has more to lose in the shadows than to gain in partial public sunlight. It is worth recounting, at this point, that Kao himself championed a historical division within the R&AW.

Second, and relatedly, greater openness has the potential to prevent intelligence failures. The 1999 crisis in Kargil and the 2008 attacks in Mumbai have been largely attributed to the lack of coordination among agencies or the inability to cipher actionable intelligence, as underlined in this chapter. But another key factor is the sheer failure of imagination. Ideationally, the spectre of the Pakistani Army breaking away from a customary agreement, by which the two sides stepped away from their physical locations in the winter months, or the inkling that 10 well-trained and die-hard gunmen could start a journey in Karachi and end up in a hotel in Mumbai were considered outside the realm of possibility. Preparing for such surprises is never easy. Intelligence will fail. That is the nature of the beast. Yet greater public engagement with experts in and out of India can provide better strategic intelligence and add a dose of realism to intelligence officers' perceptions of how nation states are meant to behave.

The R&AW would be well served to bring in academics and experts to independently provide forensic analysis of failures. As Robert Jervis makes clear, 'all too often, intelligence and critics rely on intuitive ways of thinking and rhetorical forms of exposition. More careful, disciplined, and explicit reasoning will not automatically yield the right answers but will produce better analysis.'[116] To be sure, Jervis, an academic, was commissioned by the CIA to write a post-mortem of American intelligence failures in assessing the fall of the Shah in Iran and the miscalculation surrounding Iraq's nuclear weapons programme prior to the 2003 US-led intervention. Both accounts were finally declassified and published as academic texts in 2010. In the case of Iran, his conclusion was startling. The CIA believed the Shah, as an autocrat, would use extreme force to quell the Islamic revolution. This was their primary frame of analysis. They did not for a moment guess that the Shah, for a variety of reasons, would shy away from using violence against his own population. The CIA had failed to anticipate the revolution; instead they internalized what had become an article of faith.[117] As Jervis concludes, 'Analysts, re-examine your assumptions and beliefs; managers, create an environment conducive to analyzing foreign affairs, not just reporting them.'[118] There are never any simple answers to the question of failure, as the CIA's critique of Jervis's report—also published—underlined. The key lies in the willingness to involve external actors who can introspect on behalf of institutions that are often systematically hypnotized into their social world and social understandings of the past, the present, and the future.

Third, this analysis of the R&AW clearly shows the need to include those outside the police services. Secondments to the organization from other services also do little to promote a culture of professionalism. The existing training apparatus is almost non-existent—only three months of training—for this category of officers. Direct recruitment into the organization ought to make up a primary percentage of the R&AW cadre. Training institutes should be professionalized instead of being treated as a 'dumping ground', as officers have made clear. Prospective, threat-based planning ought to be built into the R&AW's research and policy curriculum. Indeed, the R&AW could take a leaf out of the MEA's playbook. The MEA's Policy Planning and Research (PP&R) Division, usually led by a joint secretary with a team of two to three serving officers (at the level of director and deputy secretary), could be replicated by the R&AW. A permanent division should be created to constantly assesses strategic futures and to work closely with the MEA's PP&R Division through an established institutional channel.

Fourth, as previously mentioned, a systemic issue that afflicts India's intelligence apparatus at large—and thereby the R&AW as well— is its weak 'intelligence coordination capabilities and structures'.[119] Historically, there has been distrust between the R&AW and the IB, with the IB director even trying to scuttle the R&AW's plans to recruit priority personnel at the time of its formation.[120] Reportedly, this kind of competition between the two agencies continues even today. As a former R&AW chief notes, cooperation between the IB and the R&AW is productive at times, but this is not always the case.[121] Bureaucratic tussles between the R&AW and the MEA have also been highlighted.[122] Indeed, as has been written, the 'bane of intelligence agencies' includes 'turf-battles' and 'poor coordination'.[123]

In the best-case scenario, a sense of mistrust and lack of communication between various agencies can create unnecessary bureaucratic hurdles. In the worst-case scenario, however, a lack of coordination between various organizations can lead to serious crises—such as Kargil in 1999.[124] An Institute for Defence Studies and Analyses task force noted that intelligence agencies tend 'to work in watertight compartments' with 'no institutionalized system for coordinated action or for information sharing'.[125] This 'silo mentality' that exists between the various intelligence agencies was also highlighted by the GoM.[126] While there have been attempts to rectify the institutional inadequacies that exist in India's larger intelligence apparatus, most—as the reports make clear—are 'crisis-driven reviews, retrospective in nature, rather than need-based broad perspective plans to reform and revamp'.[127] Weekly meetings at the JIC provide some room for coordination, but much more needs to be done to break down organizational, cultural, and institutional barriers to greater and timely cooperation.

Lastly, the singular lack of a comprehensive review of India's intelligence apparatus—one that is not driven by crisis or is retrospective in nature—stems, in part, from the lack of accountability when it comes to intelligence agencies like the R&AW. Usually, in instances of security failures, no person or agency is held accountable.[128] A persistent recommendation has been to institute a mechanism for parliamentary oversight.[129] This is, unsurprisingly, not a popular view within the R&AW. Clearly, a balance needs to be struck between maintaining secrecy and providing a necessary degree of oversight.

The authors would like to thank Dikshita Venkatesh for her research assistance.

Notes

1. A notable exception is a 2020 book by Yatish Yadav. See: Yatish Yadav, *RAW: A History of India's Covert Operations* (Chennai: Westland Publications, 2020).
2. *Note*: this conclusion is based on an extensive rendering of Lok Sabha questions and debates between 1984 and 2021 and Rajya Sabha questions and debates between 1995 and 2021.
3. Arvind Gupta, *How India Manages Its National Security* (New Delhi: Penguin Random House, 2018), 210–11.
4. M. Hamid Ansari, *By Many A Happy Accident: Recollections of a Life* (New Delhi: Rupa, 2021), 279–80.
5. For an excellent introduction to R&AW's operational activities, see Yadav, *RAW*.
6. Jairam Ramesh, *Intertwined Lives: P. N. Haksar and Indira Gandhi* (New Delhi: Simon & Schuster, 2019), 121.
7. Ramachandra Guha, *India after Gandhi: The History of the World's Largest Democracy* (New Delhi: Pan Macmillan India, 2017), 432.
8. K. Sankaran Nair, *Inside IB and RAW: The Rolling Stone that Gathered Moss* (New Delhi: Manas Publications, 2008), 155.
9. Nair, *Inside IB and RAW*, 154.
10. Srinath Raghavan, *1971: A Global History of the Creation of Bangladesh* (Ranikhet: Permanent Black, 2013), 57.
11. Nair, *Inside IB and RAW*, 154.
12. IDSA Taskforce, *A Case for Intelligence Reforms in India* (New Delhi: Institute for Defence Studies and Analyses, 2012), 42.
13. B. Raman, *The Kaoboys of R&AW: Down Memory Lane* (New Delhi: Lancer, 2013), 73.
14. Nair, *Inside IB and RAW*, 155.
15. See: "History of the CIA," Central Intelligence Agency, last updated October 5, 2020, https://www.cia.gov/legacy/cia-history/.
16. Ramesh, *Intertwined Lives*, 122.
17. Ramesh, *Intertwined Lives*, 122.
18. Ramesh, *Intertwined Lives*, 122.

19. IDSA Taskforce, *Intelligence Reforms*, 33.
20. Ramesh, *Intertwined Lives*, 121.
21. Ramesh, *Intertwined Lives*, 122.
22. Interview with a former Senior Officer, October 13, 2020 [hereon referred to as 'A'].
23. Chris Ogden, *Indian National Security* (New Delhi: Oxford University Press, 2017), 46.
24. Nair, *Inside IB and RAW*, 155.
25. Raman, *The Kaoboys of R&AW*, 8.
26. Raman, *The Kaoboys of R&AW*, 9.
27. Raghavan, *1971*, 57.
28. Yadav, *RAW*, 1.
29. Raghavan, 1971, 66.
30. Zorawar Daulet Singh, *Power and Diplomacy: India's Foreign Policies during the Cold War* (New Delhi: Oxford University Press, 2017), 282.
31. Rudra Chaudhuri, "India," in *Routledge Companion to Intelligence Studies*, ed. Robert Dover, Michael S. Goodman, and Claudia Hillebrand (Oxon: Routledge, 2014), 186. Also see Raman, *The Kaoboys of R&AW*, 39.
32. Raman, *The Kaoboys of R&AW*, 10. Also see, Nair, *Inside IB and RAW*, 155.
33. Raman, *The Kaoboys of R&AW*, 12.
34. Chaudhuri, "India," 185.
35. Ryan Shaffer, "Unravelling India's Foreign Intelligence: The Origins and Evolution of the Research and Analysis Wing," *International Journal of Intelligence and Counter-Intelligence* 28, no. 2 (11 March 2015): 260.
36. Raman, *The Kaoboys of R&AW*, 10–11.
37. Raman, *The Kaoboys of R&AW*, 9–12.
38. Guha, *India after Gandhi*, 480.
39. Guha, *India after Gandhi*, 480.
40. Deb Mukharji, "A Comprehensive Account of the History of Sikkim since 1947, That Lays to Rest Any Suggestion of the Forcible Annexation of the State," *Indian Express*, June 23, 2019, https://indianexpress.com/article/lifestyle/books/writ ten-on-the-wall-sikkim-annexation-5795298/. Also see: Sudipta Bhattacharjee, "An Insider Account of Sikkim Turning from Monarchy to Indian State," *The Telegraph*, February 21, 2019, https://www.telegraphindia.com/culture/books/ an-insider-account-of-sikkim-turning-from-monarchy-to-indian-state/cid/ 1685143.
41. See: Rudra Chaudhuri, "Re-Reading the Indian Emergency: Britain, the United States and India's Constitutional Autocracy, 1975–1977," *Diplomacy & Statecraft* 29, no. 3 (20 August 2018), 481-82. .
42. Christopher Andrew and Vasili Mitrokhin, *The World Was Going Our Way: The KGB and the Battle for the Third World* (New York: Basic Books, 2005), 327.
43. Katherine Frank, *Indira: The Life of Indira Nehru Gandhi* (London: Harper Perennial, 2007), 375. *Note:* the fullest record of Gandhi's paranoia with regards

to the CIA and Allende can be found in: Pakenham to C.O. Hume, New Delhi, 7 January 1976, NA FO 37/1724.

44. Christopher Andrew and Vasili Mitrokhin, *The Mitrokhin Archive II: The KGB in the World* (London: Allen Lane, 2006), 326–27.

45. Andrew and Mitrokhin, *The Mitrokhin Archive II*, 333.

46. Raman, *The Kaoboys of R&AW*, 48.

47. Srinath Raghavan, "After 50 Years of RAW, There Are Still No Declassified Documents or an Official History," *ThePrint*, September 18, 2018, https://thepr int.in/opinion/why-was-raw-formed-and-what-has-india-learnt-after-50-years-of-its-existence/119811/. Also see, Avinash Paliwal, *My Enemy's Enemy: India in Afghanistan from the Soviet Invasion to the US Withdrawal* (Noida: HarperCollins Publishers, 2017), 54.

48. Raman, *The Kaoboys of R&AW*, 54–5. K. Sankaran Nair outlines how the Morarji Desai government tried to connect him and Indira Gandhi's son, Sanjay Gandhi, to alleged financial misappropriation. See: Nair, *Inside IB and RAW*, 171.

49. Nair, *Inside IB and RAW*, 170–4. Also see: Raman, *The Kaoboys of R&AW*, 55.

50. Raman, *The Kaoboys of R&AW*, 57–8.

51. Raman, *The Kaoboys of R&AW*, 115. Also see, Shaffer, "Unravelling India's Foreign Intelligence," 267.

52. Shaffer, "Unravelling India's Foreign Intelligence," 267. Also see, Ashoka Raina, "RAW Employees Announce Pen-Down Strike," *India Today*, December 31, 1980, updated on December 18, 2014, https://www.indiatoday.in/magazine/ind iascope/story/19801231-raw-employees-announce-pen-down-strike-773687-2013-11-30#:~:text=On%20November%2027%2C%20RAW%20employees,dis content%20to%20the%20public%20eye.

53. Raman, *The Kaoboys of R&AW*, 72.

54. Raman, *The Kaoboys of R&AW*, 133.

55. IDSA Taskforce, *Intelligence Reforms*, 43.

56. IDSA Taskforce, *Intelligence Reforms*, 43.

57. IDSA Taskforce, *Intelligence Reforms*, 43.

58. IDSA Taskforce, *Intelligence Reforms*, 43.

59. Government of India, "Act No. 58: The Intelligence Organizations (Restriction of Rights) Act, 1985," September 6, 1985, 1, http://legislative.gov.in/sites/default/files/A1985-58.pdf.

60. Anand Arni, "In Its Sixth Decade, R&AW Needs to Look at the World outside Terrorism," *The Telegraph*, October 3, 2018, https://www.telegraphindia.com/opinion/in-its-sixth-decade-r-aw-needs-to-look-at-the-world-outside-terror ism/cid/1670832.

61. Arni, "In Its Sixth Decade," 191–96. Also see, Nitin A. Gokhale, *R. N. Kao: Gentleman Spymaster* (New Delhi: Bloomsbury India, 2019), 218.

62. Shivshankar Menon, *Choices: Inside the Making of India's Foreign Policy* (Haryana: Penguin Random House India, 2016), 129.

63. Menon, *Choices*, 125–29.

64. Menon, *Choices*, 129.
65. Paliwal, *My Enemy's Enemy*, 38.
66. Raman, *The Kaoboys of R&AW*, 77.
67. Raman details the issue of 'Khalistani terrorism' in Chapter 10 in his book: Raman, *The Kaoboys of R&AW*.
68. Paliwal, *My Enemy's Enemy*, 54.
69. Paliwal, *My Enemy's Enemy*, 62.
70. Paliwal, *My Enemy's Enemy*, 62.
71. Menon, *Choices*, 26.
72. Jayshree Bajoria, "RAW: India's External Intelligence Agency," Council on Foreign Relations, November 7, 2008, https://www.cfr.org/backgrounder/raw-indias-external-intelligence-agency.
73. Paliwal, *My Enemy's Enemy*, 95.
74. Paliwal, *My Enemy's Enemy*, 95.
75. Bajoria, "RAW: India's External Intelligence Agency."
76. Chaudhuri, "India," 187–89.
77. Interview with [A].
78. R. Prasannan and Namrata Biji Ahuja, "Spies Rule the Roost: In Its 50th Year, R&AW Is at the Centre of Massive Overhaul of Intelligence Apparatus," *The Week*, November 11, 2018, https://www.theweek.in/theweek/cover/2018/11/03/spies-rule-the-roost.html.
79. Prasannan and Ahuja, "Spies Rule the Roost."
80. Bruce Vaughn, "The Use and Abuse of Intelligence Services in India," *Intelligence and National Security* 8, no. 1 (1993): 8. Also see: Prasannan and Ahuja, "Spies Rule the Roost."
81. Vaughn, "The Use and Abuse of Intelligence," 8.
82. Praveen Swami, "RAW to Shut Down Its Covert Air Wing, Assets Will Go to NTRO and IAF," *Indian Express*, September 18, 2015, https://indianexpress.com/article/india/india-others/raw-to-fold-its-covert-air-wing/. Also see: Josy Joseph, "Panel Suggests Merging Aviation Research Centre with RAW," *Times of India*, July 11, 2012, https://timesofindia.indiatimes.com/india/Panel-suggests-merging-Aviation-Research-Centre-with-RAW/articleshow/14813688.cms.
83. Interview with [A].
84. "Intelligence Bureau to Get 2,000 SSB Staffers as Govt Approves Border Snoop Plan," *Mint*, September 7, 2017, https://www.livemint.com/Politics/8vZWysLyJAZ6Pi1aoef0EP/Intelligence-Bureau-to-get-2000-SSB-staffers-as-govt-approv.html.
85. Shaffer, "Unravelling India's Foreign Intelligence," 260.
86. Manoj Joshi, "Lacking Innovation, National Security Council is Unlikely to Make a Mark," *India Today*, December 7, 1998, https://www.indiatoday.in/magazine/defence/story/19981207-national-security-council-unlikely-to-make-a-mark-due-to-lack-of-innovation-827477-1998-12-07.
87. Chaudhuri, "India," 188.

88. Srinath Raghavan, "Intelligence Failures and Reforms," *Seminar India*, July 2009, https://www.india-seminar.com/2009/599/599_srinath_raghavan.htm.

89. "Kargil Review Committee Report," Kargil Review Committee, 2000, http://nuclearweaponarchive.org/India/KargilRCB.html.

90. IDSA Taskforce, *Intelligence Reforms*, 26.

91. IDSA Taskforce, *Intelligence Reforms*, 27.

92. Janani Krishnaswamy, "Why Intelligence Fails?" *The Hindu Centre for Politics and Public Policy*, Policy Report no. 3, (2013), 3.

93. Chaudhuri, "India," 189.

94. Chaudhuri, "India," 189.

95. IDSA Taskforce, *Intelligence Reforms*, 90–91.

96. IDSA Taskforce, *Intelligence Reforms*, 93.

97. Interview with [A].

98. IDSA Taskforce, *Intelligence Reforms*, 95.

99. IDSA Taskforce, *Intelligence Reforms*, 27.

100. Saikat Datta, "Intelligence, Strategic Assessment and Decision Process Deficits," Henry L. Stimson Center (2018), 112, https://www.stimson.org/wp-content/files/InvestigatingCrisesIntelligence.pdf.

101. Swami, "RAW to Shut Down Its Covert Air Wing, Assets Will Go to NTRO and IAF."

102. Praveen Swami, "Five Years after 26/11, Intelligence Services Still Crippled by Staff Shortage," *The Hindu*, November 26, 2013, https://www.thehindu.com/news/national/five-years-after-2611-intelligence-services-still-crippled-by-staff-shortage/article5391698.ece. Another 2013 report notes that R&AW's personnel numbers around 12,000 (including drivers, secretaries, etc.). See: "Counter-Terrorism in India," *The Economist*, September 7, 2013, https://www.economist.com/asia/2013/09/07/do-lali.

103. Swami, "Five Years after 26/11."

104. Prasannan and Ahuja, "Spies Rule the Roost."

105. For instance: Anand Arni, Shibani Mehta, and Pranay Kotasthane, "India's External Intelligence Agency: Managing the Human Resources Challenge," Takshashila Institution, January 2019, https://takshashila.org.in/wp-content/uploads/2019/01/TDD-Managing-the-HR-Challenge-AA-SM-PK-2019-New.pdf.

106. Manoj Joshi and Pushan Das, "India's Intelligence Agencies: In Need of Reform and Oversight," Observer Research Foundation, ORF Issue Brief no. 98 (July 2015), 4, https://www.orfonline.org/wp-content/uploads/2015/07/IssueBrief_98.pdf.

107. Joshi and Das, "India's Intelligence Agencies," 10.

108. IDSA Taskforce, *Intelligence Reforms*, 44.

109. Sandeep Unnithan, "Getting a Raw Deal," *India Today*, November 19, 2009, https://www.indiatoday.in/magazine/radar/story/20091130-getting-a-raw-deal-741338-2009-11-19.

110. Joshi and Das, "India's Intelligence Agencies," 5.

111. Arni, Mehta and Kotasthane, "India's External Intelligence Agency," 13.

112. These recommendations have also been made by former intelligence officers. For instance: Arni, Mehta, and Kotasthane, "India's External Intelligence Agency."

113. On the advantages of OSINT, see: Christopher Hobbs, Matthew Moran, and Daniel Salisbury, *Open-Source Intelligence in the Twenty-First Century: New Approaches and Opportunities* (New York: Palgrave Macmillan, 2014).

114. Christopher Andrew, *The Defence of the Realm: The Authorized History of MI5* (London: Allen Lane, 2009), xvi–xvii.

115. Keith Jeffery, *MI6: The History of the Secret Intelligence Service 1909–1949* (London: Bloomsbury, 2010), pp. vii–viii.

116. Robert Jervis, *Why Intelligence Fails: Lessons from the Iranian Revolution and the Iraq War* (Ithaca: Cornell University Press, 2010), 1–6.

117. Jervis, *Why Intelligence Fails*, 72–75.

118. Jervis, *Why Intelligence Fails*, 108.

119. Chaudhuri, "India," 190.

120. Nair, *Inside IB and RAW*, 155.

121. A. S. Dulat, Asad Durrani, and Aditya Sinha, *The Spy Chronicles: RAW, ISI and the Illusion of Peace* (Noida: HarperCollins Publishers, 2018), 47.

122. For instance: Raman, *The Kaoboys of R&AW*, 245. Also see: Singh, *Power and Diplomacy*, 270, 321.

123. Krishnaswamy, "Why Intelligence Fails?" 8.

124. IDSA Taskforce, *Intelligence Reforms*, 27.

125. IDSA Taskforce, *Intelligence Reforms*, 85.

126. Manoj Joshi, "The Unending Quest to Reform India's National Security System," Policy Report, S. Rajaratnam School of International Studies (March 2014), 5, https://www.rsis.edu.sg/wp-content/uploads/2014/09/PR140301_The_Unending_Quest_to_Reform_India_National_Security_System.pdf.

127. IDSA Taskforce, *Intelligence Reforms*, 17.

128. Joshi and Das, "India's Intelligence Agencies," 3.

129. For instance: IDSA Taskforce, *Intelligence Reforms*, 31. Also see, Joshi and Das, "India's Intelligence Agencies," 8.

6

The Intelligence Bureau

Praveen Swami

Introduction

Late in 1887, the embers of the Indian Rebellion of 1857 still glowing, Frederick Temple Hamilton-Temple-Blackwood, the 1st Marquess of Dufferin and Ava and the Viceroy of India, laid out a new blueprint to surveil the restive land that was—as he put it—'exceptionally exposed to political intrigues or danger'.[1] He wrote, 'The arrangements for the collection of secret and political intelligence have been, except perhaps in the Punjab, very imperfect, but I have now prepared a scheme which will, I hope, result in obtaining much more systematic and complete information from all parts of India.'

The new organization drew on the experience of the General Superintendent of Operations for the Suppression of Thuggee and Dacoity, a paramilitary force that had waged a relentless and often savage war against bandits preying on travellers.[2] Lord Dufferin's new Special Branch, though, had a far broader mandate: 'collecting and recording the intelligence received, and of initiating or conducting at the instance of the Government of India, such inquiries as may be needed in special cases'.

Economy of resources, Lord Dufferin noted, would be key: 'the formation of a large detective staff would be open to very serious objections' and 'a more extended employment of special and secret agents would lead to unsatisfactory results'. Existing government institutions, like police and political officers, would form the backbone of the Special Branch, along with 'special agencies of the lowest possible strength'.

That small agency created in 1887 is now India's largest intelligence service, the Intelligence Bureau. Its functions span an extraordinary range of issues.

Praveen Swami, *The Intelligence Bureau* In: *Institutional Roots of India's Security Policy*. Edited by: Milan Vaishnav, Oxford University Press. © Oxford University Press 2024. DOI: 10.1093/oso/9780198894612.003.0006

In addition to its counterterrorism and counter-intelligence roles, the Intelligence Bureau liaises between police forces across the country on significant threats to state security and order; monitors critical sectors of economic activity; conducts background investigations on contenders for high office, such as judges; provides assessments on the likely consequences of public policy; and even surveils political life, elections, and the activities of non-governmental organizations. Its work is driven by the sweeping mandate of its principal consumer of intelligence, the Ministry of Home Affairs, as well as the special needs of the office of the National Security Advisor and, through them, the prime minister.

As former police and intelligence officer K.S. Subramanian has pointed out, 'Perhaps no other intelligence agency in the world, including those in the Anglophone former colonies, undertakes such wide-ranging internal political intelligence collection as the Indian IB does, at least not on a continental scale.'[3]

More than a century and a quarter after its creation, however, this chapter argues that fundamental asymmetries of ends and means have led the Intelligence Bureau to something of a cul-de-sac. Several of the Intelligence Bureau's core functions have met with competition from state and private-sector organizations, often with competencies exceeding those of the bureau itself. Perhaps more importantly, and as the following pages endeavor to show, the bureau remains understaffed and under-resourced. This anaemia has been compounded by a long-standing inability to engage in the kinds of thorough capacity development and reform that many in India's intelligence community have called for.

A necessary caveat is that the literature on the Intelligence Bureau is, at best, thin. Furthermore, the organization is not subject to government declassification practices, such as they are. Parts of this chapter rely on interviews with serving and retired Intelligence Bureau officials, who are legally bound not to speak on these issues. Since these interviews are, by their nature, unverifiable, they are not cited.

The Intelligence Bureau in Context

In 1953, B.N. Mullik—the second Director of the Intelligence Bureau in independent India—authored the new nation state's first-ever crime survey. His foreword offers a rare glimpse into the new intelligence leadership's understanding of India. There was, he observed, an uptick in the economy; agrarian production had improved; Hindu–Muslim communal violence had ended; and even India's communists had succeeded in nothing more significant than staging a tram workers' strike. The report called for a plethora of measures to enhance policing, from improving the quality of training to the introduction of forensic science. Yet, Mullik looked at the future with concern: 'The old fear, which the police used to inspire amongst the criminals, has largely been dissipated and surveillance over criminals has become extremely difficult.'[4]

Like many of his generation, Mullik viewed the new India emerging around him with suspicion: the world seemed suffused with existential threats to the fragile, new state. The fundamental role of the Intelligence Bureau was to examine those threats—and guide the state's coercive assets in the right direction.

From the moment of its genesis, the British Imperial state had conditioned the Intelligence Bureau to think of itself in this role. Former Intelligence Bureau officer Amiya Samanta has noted that the 1872 assassination of Richard Bourke, the Earl of Mayo and Viceroy of India, crystallized Imperial concerns over the rise of political Islam and Hindu nationalism. This helped fuel the Intelligence Bureau's creation, as 'a detective police for political purposes', designed to prevent another 1857-like uprising against Imperial authority.[5]

The historian Christopher Bayly has ably documented the earlier intelligence preoccupations of the British Empire, ranging from harvesting information on populations and politics to exploring and defending the frontiers of India.[6] Now, intelligence-gathering was to serve the task of policing a restive population.

By the early 1900s, the Intelligence Bureau had become increasingly focused on combating revolutionary terrorist movements. The bureau worked closely with the British, including MI5's Indian Political Intelligence Office and Imperial Police, to penetrate Indian nationalist cells in the United Kingdom, United States, and East Asia. The intelligence it assembled was critical in dismantling several terrorist cells, leading to successful prosecutions in the 1917 Hindu–German Conspiracy trial in San Francisco.[7]

It was not until 1933, however, that the Intelligence Bureau began to acquire an independent intelligence-collection capability—promptly spawning clashes with the new provincial assemblies elected in 1935. As Samanta writes:

> Many important secret and top secret files, relating to the Non-cooperation and Civil Disobedience movements, were sent to the office of CIO of the Intelligence Bureau, which was statutorily secured from ministerial interference, or to the Governor's secretariat, either for destruction or for transfer to more secured places. The Provincial Governments frequently complained of spying on them by the Central Intelligence.[8]

The Crisis after Independence

Left in 'a tragi-comic state of helplessness' by the large-scale removal of files and dislocation of personnel in 1947, newly independent India's intelligence services consisted of little more than 'the office furniture, empty racks and cupboards, and a few innocuous files dealing with office routine'.[9] The bureau, thus, played a marginal role in the great events that shaped India from 1947, remaining on the sidelines of the war in Jammu and Kashmir and the military intervention in Hyderabad.

From the records of the commission that investigated the assassination of Mohandas Gandhi, it is also clear that the Intelligence Bureau's capacity to gather intelligence on hostile political movements was, at best, limited. Though the Intelligence Bureau received information from the Uttar Pradesh Police on possible threats to Gandhi's life, it was able to do little more than pass it along to the Bombay Police. Similarly, the bureau appears to have had no ability to evaluate or act on intelligence gathered by the Poona Police.[10]

The bureau's lack of capacity—both to independently gather information and to assess it—was brutally exposed in the build-up to the Sino-Indian War of 1962. Although the Intelligence Bureau set up several small posts to monitor Chinese logistical infrastructure, it lacked the analytical capabilities to assess the looming threat posed by China. The official Indian history of the war of 1962 notes that Mullik, then chief of the

Intelligence Bureau, was among several key officials who failed to challenge ill-founded political assessments that

> ... [t]here might be isolated clashes here or there, but the Chinese would not escalate these into a war. War between India and China would escalate on a global level with the potential of a nuclear conflagration and therefore China would desist from it.[11]

Even though the disaster of 1962 resulted in the creation of a dedicated external intelligence service—the Research and Analysis Wing—the Intelligence Bureau did begin to register genuine successes at home as it slowly rebuilt its capacities after independence.

Years of Revival

Jammu and Kashmir was among the theatres where the expanding Intelligence Bureau registered its most significant successes. Inderjit Singh Hasanwalia, Prime Minister Jawaharlal Nehru's hand-picked choice to lead the Intelligence Bureau's stations in Jammu and Kashmir, developed a formidable reputation. Hasanwalia is, among other things, credited with bringing a peaceful conclusion to the crisis involving the disappearance of a holy relic from the shrine of Hazratbal in Srinagar, which sparked large-scale riots.[12] Indeed, Hasanwalia's influence increasingly made him an adversary of the state's political patriarch, Sheikh Mohammad Abdullah.

This surge in the Intelligence Bureau's capacity engendered several similar conflicts across the country, centred around the agency's role as an instrument of the Congress Party. In 1963, for example, the Intelligence Bureau ordered the Gujarat Police to surveil the Swatantra Party, a right-wing formation opposed to the ruling Congress. In response to queries from Gujarati Chief Minister Balwantrai Mehta, the home minister responded that government was compelled to keep watch over persons 'who habitually opposed the policies of the government in position'.[13]

From the 1970s, the Intelligence Bureau's role in political surveillance—often of dubious legality—expanded steadily, with successive Directors of the Intelligence Bureau becoming enmeshed in the government's efforts to undermine opponents.

These operations brought the bureau into considerable disrepute during the 1975–77 period of Emergency Rule under Prime Minister Indira Gandhi. The findings of the L.P. Singh Committee, which was set up to consider reforms after the Emergency came to an end, are still secret—but the committee is believed to have neither assigned personal responsibility for violations of the law by the intelligence services, nor advised measures to reform them.

For better or worse, though, the Intelligence Bureau continued to acquire an ever-increasing role in government—particularly under Prime Minister Rajiv Gandhi, who is reputed to have insisted on being briefed by the director of the agency almost every morning on everything from internal security threats to political dissent. According to the senior bureaucrat N.N. Vohra, the centrality of the Intelligence Bureau to the prime minister's functioning had finally arrived:

> ... when [Prime Minister] Indira Gandhi, impelled by power politics, weakened the Home Minister's role [and] the Director of the Intelligence Bureau was asked to report directly to the prime minister on certain matters. From then on, successive Directors of the Intelligence Bureau did not find it obligatory to look to the Home Minister for direction and control.[14]

The Intelligence Bureau's national security function also grew dramatically during this period. The organization played a central role in the management of insurgencies in India's north-east, the Liberation Tigers of Tamil Eelam, and the Punjab crisis that began in the mid-1980s. Even though there were several significant successes, particularly in influencing the leadership of north-eastern insurgencies, the bureau's record was far from perfect. Notably, it failed to predict the scale of impact of the jihadist rising in Kashmir in 1988.

Among the Intelligence Bureau's more significant successes was the 1986 peace deal with the Mizo insurgent leader, Laldenga, which brought an end to an insurgency that had lasted over two decades. Intelligence Bureau and Research and Analysis Wing assets were jointly used to bring Laldenga back to India from Pakistan, where he was living under the protection of the Inter-Services Intelligence, Pakistan's premier intelligence agency. The operation ended in elections that resulted in Laldenga's installation as chief minister.[15]

The Intelligence Bureau also succeeded in arriving at a peace deal with the Tripura insurgent B.K. Hrangkhawl—an operation that, among other things, involved operating deep inside Bangladesh, where Hrangkhawl enjoyed none-too-covert military support.[16]

From an early stage, the Intelligence Bureau also became involved in combating Pakistani espionage operations. In 1951, the agency arrested Shadi Lal Kapur, a junior ministry of external affairs officer recruited by Pakistan's Intelligence Bureau. The case, interestingly, generated some early bitterness between the intelligence services of two countries. Although New Delhi agreed to the quiet withdrawal of the Pakistani diplomatic officer handling Kapur, Islamabad expelled an official in retaliation.[17]

From a relatively early stage, the two countries engaged in a high degree of visible and obtrusive surveillance of each other's diplomats, seeking not just to limit the possibilities of espionage but to restrict social contact altogether. This kind of surveillance work has sometimes verged on the farcical: in 2018, Indian diplomats in Islamabad complained their doorbells were being rung late at night with the alleged intent to harass.[18]

Among the most important of the Intelligence Bureau's counterespionage operations was the arrest of then Brigadier Zaheer-ul-Islam Abbasi, Pakistan's defence attaché in New Delhi, in 1988, on charges of providing funding for terrorists in Jammu and Kashmir.[19] Abbasi, as a major general, was later charged in Pakistan for his role in an Islamist-led attempt to stage a coup d'état against Prime Minister Benazir Bhutto.

From the accounts of officers involved in these operations, it is clear they were achieved despite infrastructure that left more than a little to be desired. Writing of his experience running counter-insurgency intelligence operations through Subsidiary Intelligence Bureau stations (the Intelligence Bureau's state-level offices) in the north-east, O.N. Shrivastava wrote:

> the Intelligence Bureau was really poorly off in terms of resources. The administration had just two cars, communication was only through wireless sets which involved enciphering and deciphering at both

ends, the only means of pushing intelligence from the field to the IB Headquarters was through registered post, and the only way of getting through to any of the SIBs in the North-East was through lightning phone calls, which had their limitations.[20]

Precisely how significant the Intelligence Bureau's role as a producer of tactically useful intelligence, though, remains disputed. For example, the bureau is said to have played a key role in Operation Black Thunder, where Khalistan terrorists were successfully flushed out of the Golden Temple in Amritsar. K.P.S. Gill, the police officer credited with the defeat of the Khalistan insurgency, has suggested these counterterrorism contributions were at best fitful:

> ... despite continuous inputs from the IB, the State intelligence apparatus remained crucial for a complete picture of events. I must confess, moreover, that the extraordinary cooperation with the IB during the Black Thunder episode is not something that happens often. The relationship between State and Central agencies tends to be mixed. They often operate independently of each other, and at least occasionally, at cross purposes...[21]

Following the Mumbai attacks of 2008, similarly, evidence emerged that the Lashkar-e-Taiba unit responsible for the operation had been successfully infiltrated by the Jammu and Kashmir Police.[22] This breakthrough allowed the Intelligence Bureau to subsequently monitor the attack as it happened, gathering critical evidence.

In general, the criminal justice dividends from these intelligence operations remained low, with the state police forces responsible for turning Intelligence Bureau cases into prosecutions often failing to competently gather and assess the material. Few cases, until the founding of the National Investigation Agency (NIA) in 2009, ended in prosecutions. The cost in human suffering was enormous: in one case, 127 men accused in 2001 of possessing ties to the proscribed Islamist group Students' Islamic Movement of India were acquitted at the end of a trial that lasted 19 years.[23] The quality of intelligence that led to arrests in cases like these has never been audited, because of the absence of an oversight and assessment system.

The Intelligence Bureau, from the 1950s on, also came to play a controversial role in conducting background checks on appointees to high office, in particular judges of the High Court and Supreme Court. The decision to use the Intelligence Bureau for this role appears to have been motivated by the need for central authorities to be able to form an independent assessment of a candidate's suitability and financial probity. This has occasionally resulted in an intense furore, since such checks are conducted with no legal authority; in 2020, for example, reports emerged that one candidate, Saurabh Kirpal, was deemed unfit to hold judicial office since he was gay and lived with a foreign partner.[24]

Nonetheless, the Intelligence Bureau has emerged as the executor of New Delhi's political will. In a country with no real federal police—and a constitution that granted the states authority over law and order—the agency drew power from its position as the sole repository of information flows from across the country. The director of the Intelligence Bureau served as a kind of patriarch for the Indian Police Service, whose elements were scattered across the states. No other organization had either the means or the mandate to execute these functions.

Towards a Cul-de-Sac

Eight years ago, as the Intelligence Bureau turned 125, India's now National Security Advisor—and former Intelligence Bureau Director—Ajit Doval, noted that the last thorough review of the organization's objectives and methods had taken place in the 1980s, under his predecessor M.K. Narayanan. Pointing to new and changing circumstances with which the bureau had to contend, he made the case for a review of India's intelligence services which:

… should attempt to architect [sic.] new doctrines, suggest structural changes, aim at optimisation of resources and examine administrative and legislative changes required for empowerment of intelligence agencies. While intelligence agencies in developed countries frequently attempt this exercise, the Indian intelligence has rarely made a conscious effort in this direction.[25]

To many of his contemporaries, this advice might have seemed misplaced: the Intelligence Bureau had acquitted itself well in a succession of crises. In the build-up to the Kargil war, the agency had generated intelligence on the training of Pakistani soldiers for war—information the Indian Army chose to ignore.[26] The bureau had successfully helped multiple police forces unravel the Indian Mujahideen, the architects of the most successful urban jihadist bombing campaign the country had ever seen.[27]

Perhaps most importantly, the Intelligence Bureau had presided over the steady degradation of the Kashmir insurgency to a point where, by 2008, violence had diminished to negligible levels.[28] From the account of former Intelligence Bureau officer Amarjit Singh Dulat, it is clear the Intelligence Bureau succeeded both in significantly penetrating the jihadist movement and in inveigling the state's political elite to cooperate with India.

The Intelligence Bureau had, moreover, made significant progress in modernizing its technical capabilities, particularly during the tenure of Nehchal Sandhu, who served as Director from 2010 to 2012. New communications intelligence capabilities, built up from the early 2000s, were critical to Intelligence Bureau contributions to a range of operations, among them the investigation into the attack on the Indian Parliament in 2001.

Yet, as the decade progressed, it became evident that the Intelligence Bureau's place of prestige—as the government's core instrument of national security–related decision-making and execution—had begun to diminish. The Intelligence Bureau slowly became one of many influences on government decision-making, rather than the critical actor it was from the 1960s through the 1990s.

Indeed, the frequency of consultation between the director of the Intelligence Bureau and the prime minister is reputed to have diminished steadily through the 2000s. To understand why, four issues are key.

Anaemic Spies

First, the Intelligence Bureau is a modest operation: the government committed funding of 25.75 billion rupees for the organization for

2019–20—some $300 million—which is less than one-third, for example, of the 74.97 billion rupees allocated to the Delhi Police alone.[29] Perhaps more importantly, just a tiny fraction of that sum—835 million rupees—was available for capital investments like technology and infrastructure. The Intelligence Bureau's means are in stark contrast to those of major intelligence agencies in the West; the Federal Bureau of Investigation, for example, sought $9.8 billion in funding for the 2021 fiscal year.[30]

The relatively small budget of the Intelligence Bureau means it has largely failed to enhance, or upgrade, its human resources. In 2013, Parliament was informed that some 8,000 positions in the organization were unfilled, out of a sanctioned staff strength of 26,867.[31]

Although former Home Minister P. Chidambaram authorized a programme to address staffing issues, the Intelligence Bureau's new training facility in New Delhi's Dwaraka area is believed to barely produce enough recruits to cover organic attrition—which is, in turn, the consequence of a shortage of competent instructors.

For the Intelligence Bureau, staffing problems have been so acute that it has been unable to consistently and adequately staff small groups of personnel in its state-level offices dedicated to counterterrorism, first conceived of during Ajit Doval's term as Director of the Intelligence Bureau.

In addition, training is rudimentary. In the course of three months, new recruits to the Intelligence Bureau learn only the basics of their tradecraft, in addition to receiving general instruction on national security challenges. There is no infrastructure for systematic instruction in languages, regional cultures, analytic methods, or technology; few venues exist for mid-career skill acquisition.[32] In some areas, such as cyber, in-house technology is limited. Though efforts have been made to fill the gaps by recruiting companies and individuals on contracts, the gains have been minimal.

Efforts to make cutting-edge technological resources available to the Intelligence Bureau have been driven by the creation of the National Technical Research Organization (NTRO), which controls the hardware, as it were, that meets the needs of the Intelligence Bureau, the Research and Analysis Wing, and other agencies. Although the reasons for centralizing technology are understandable—funding, after all, is not limitless—there has been considerable discontent about the resulting priorities and focus.

The second key challenge is the emergence of new institutions that fulfil the Intelligence Bureau's traditional remits. The Intelligence Bureau's import to counterterrorism investigations, for example, has diminished as state forces have acquired access to technological resources that the bureau alone once commanded. The Telangana Police and the NIA have, for example, been central to several recent investigations of jihadist cells, needing little or no assistance from the Intelligence Bureau.[33] Indeed, the NIA has begun to develop an independent intelligence capacity of its own—which, should it be given a formal architecture, would significantly degrade the Intelligence Bureau's role.

The lack of a clear demarcation of the Intelligence Bureau's domestic security role has meant that it often competes with the NIA to produce results on high-profile counterterrorism cases, sometimes creating schisms in the police forces they partner with. NIA officers claim the Intelligence Bureau's lack of attention to the need to produce evidence that will withstand scrutiny in court has undermined the wider legitimacy of the counterterrorism effort.

Third, political parties have secured access to new streams of information, ranging from professionally conducted opinion polls to expertise provided by think tanks and non-governmental organizations. In addition, many Indian political parties have developed a cadre of organic intellectuals, whose assessments are more trusted by the leadership than those of government institutions. Increasingly, the Intelligence Bureau is just one of many providers of information and analysis. As noted earlier in this chapter, the funding available to the Intelligence Bureau for capital acquisitions is now extremely modest; in time, it is likely that the bureau's dependence on the NTRO will increase.

Barring its control of the Multi-Agency Centre—India's national counterterrorism database, which is fed by subsidiary centres operated at the state level in coordination with police forces—the Intelligence Bureau has no means to direct the shape and priorities of India's domestic intelligence efforts.

Fourth, with its focus on investigations and policing, the Intelligence Bureau lacks the domain expertise needed to conduct the assessment and analysis that the government needs to navigate an increasingly complex world. Though precise numbers are hard to estimate, of some 30-odd joint director–level officials—the critical level of senior executive

authority—only nine operate in national-security domains where policing must be a primary skill, like counterterrorism. Even the joint directors responsible for the Multi-Agency Centre have no real competence
in the technology domain. Yet the Intelligence Bureau has, despite decades of debate, failed to recruit professionals from outside its own cadre
and the Indian Police Service.

An Institutional Malaise

Part of the problem is that 'there is no mechanism to assess the product-
ivity of our two apex intelligence agencies,' the bureaucrat Vohra writes.[34]
'In the absence of a mechanism to evaluate the quality of intelligence
generated by the Intelligence Bureau,' he notes, 'its contribution and use-
fulness in national security management has largely depended on the
professional competence of those appointed by the Director.'

This, former Police and Intelligence Officer Subramanian has noted,
has not always had roseate consequences, in large part because:

> The IB does not possess any special qualifications or expertise to con-
> duct the kind of socio-political analysis that it does routinely for the
> ruling elite. The top officers are mainly from the Indian Police Service
> (IPS), who are generalists recruited by the UPSC and trained at the
> National Police Academy.... The glamour or mystique arises from the
> classification given to IB reports such as 'secret' or 'top secret', which
> helps prevent questions as to their sources.[35]

Accusations like these might overstate the case, but they underline the
capability deficits that will likely shape the organization's future. K.P.S.
Gill and others have argued that the Intelligence Bureau's limited human
resources may present an insurmountable obstacle to its utility as a
frontline provider of information. Gill wrote:

> An illusion of 'intelligence' may be created by monitoring urban and
> political gossip centres and such 'intelligence' may even be quite useful
> in drafting general risk assessments—but the real substance of oper-
> ational intelligence flows from the grassroots, from rural and mofussil

concentrations, or from the most degraded and neglected areas of the urban complex.[36]

Necessary Transformations

The Intelligence Bureau's transformation into a modern intelligence service necessarily depends on whether a future government decides to create a legislative foundation for its existence and functioning. There has been occasional interest in providing the Intelligence Bureau with a legal framework. Former Minister for Information and Broadcasting Manish Tewari twice sought to introduce a private member's bill in Parliament to establish legislative oversight of the operations of the intelligence services.[37] However, no political party in India, in or out of power, has supported such reform.

These questions have gathered urgency as India's Supreme Court grapples with pleas that the intelligence services may have illegally surveilled the mobile phones of dozens of journalists, opposition politicians, and activists using technology provided by the Israeli NSO Group.[38] The targets include some that could be considered legitimate foreign and domestic intelligence targets—including foreign diplomats, world leaders, and subjects of ongoing counterterrorism enquiries—but some are citizens subjected to surveillance in apparent violation of the law. The Indian government has, so far, declined to state who was surveilled, for what reasons, or, indeed, if such surveillance took place at all.

In key ways, the core problem is that the Intelligence Bureau remains an instrument of the Home Ministry; it is 'merely an adhoc administrative arrangement by the Executive', as one study described it.[39] Its legal basis is the 1925 Rules of Business of the Government, which attached the bureau's director to the Home Department 'for administrative convenience'. The director was expected to provide, 'either on his own initiative or on request, information relating to the security of India to other Departments'.[40]

Following the Kargil conflict, the Indian government appointed four task forces to review national security. Based on these recommendations, a Group of Ministers concluded that:

Internal security disorders cannot be effectively managed unless central intelligence agencies provide timely operational intelligence to enable security forces to launch operations. Upgradation of the central intelligence agencies, notably the Intelligence Bureau (IB), as well as the intelligence apparatus in the States is essential in this regard.[41]

The specific recommendations of the Group of Ministers on intelligence reforms remain classified. However, it is believed that no recommendations were made for institutional reform, except advocating that the organization cease to be treated as an appendage of the Ministry of Home Affairs.[42] The Intelligence Bureau has since been made the nodal agency for counterterrorism intelligence work and provided with an expansive—but remarkably vague—charter: the protection of the Constitution.[43] Even though Ajit Doval went on to become National Security Advisor in 2014—becoming, arguably, the most powerful incumbent that office has ever seen—his 2012 call for extensive reforms has not been acted upon.

It takes little imagination to see that the absence of a legislative foundation for the Intelligence Bureau has left it vulnerable to abuse by the executive branch. Allegations that the organization remains enmeshed in large-scale surveillance targeting the political opposition and even judges, accurate or otherwise, remain widespread.[44]

The status quo, it is clear, does something even more detrimental: it creates incentives to ensure the worst possible outcomes. The lack of a clear legislative mandate for the Intelligence Bureau means it has no genuine accountability, and thus no abiding incentives for reform or growth. The path of transformation might well lead to a smaller Intelligence Bureau, where its means are more suited to its ends—but one whose information-generating and analytic capabilities are truly exceptional. Failure to act will ensure that India continues to work with an intelligence apparatus designed for a feudal world that has long since vanished.

In some key senses, the Intelligence Bureau is an artefact of an anaemic state, which lacks the institutional resources to gather and assess information on its own situation. In a landscape where state capacities have expanded and developed, the bureau's very *raison d'être* needs careful reconsideration.

Notes

1. Dufferin to Viscount Cross, Secretary of State for India, Foreign Department No. 179 of 1887 (November 15, 1887).
2. Mike Dash, *Thug: The True Story of India's Murderous Cult* (London: Granta, 2005).
3. K.S. Subramanian, "Intelligence Bureau, Home Ministry, and Indian Politics," *Economic and Political Weekly* 40, no. 21 (May 2005): 2147–50, https://www.jstor.org/stable/4416668.
4. National Crimes Record Bureau, "Crime in India—1953: General Situation in the Country," 1953, https://ncrb.gov.in/sites/default/files/GENERAL%20SITUAT ION%20IN%20THE%20COUNTRY.pdf.
5. Amiya Samanta, "Growth of Intelligence Institutions in British India," *Indian Police Journal* 59, no. 4 (October–December 2012): 11.
6. C.A. Bayly, *Empire and Information: Intelligence Gathering and Social Communication in India, 1780–1870* (Cambridge: Cambridge University Press, 2009).
7. Samanta, "Growth of Intelligence Institutions," 12.
8. Samanta, "Growth of Intelligence Institutions," 12.
9. Lieutenant-General L.P. Sen, *Slender Was the Thread* (New Delhi: Orient Longman, 1994), 27–29.
10. Jeevan Lal Kapur, *Report of the Commission of Inquiry into the Conspiracy to Murder Mahatma Gandhi* (New Delhi: Government of India Press, 1969), 124–38.
11. P.B. Sinha and A.A. Athale, *History of the Conflict with China, 1962* (New Delhi: History Division, Ministry of Defence), 415.
12. Praveen Swami, *India, Pakistan and the Secret Jihad* (London: Routledge, 2009), 30.
13. <REF:JART>K.S. Subramanian, "Intelligence Bureau, Home Ministry and Indian Politics," 2148.
14. N.N. Vohra, *Safeguarding India* (Harper Collins: New Delhi, 2016), 59.
15. O.N. Shrivastava, "My Experience of Life and Work in IB," *Indian Police Journal* 59, no. 4 (October–December 2012): 69.
16. Shrivastava, "My Experience of Life and Work in IB," 70.
17. K.M. Singh, "A Lengthy History of Espionage Tactics," *News18*, June 1, 2020, https://www.news18.com/news/india/a-lengthy-history-of-espionage-tactics-when-pakistan-double-crossed-india-after-nehrus-generosity-2647615.html.
18. Iain Marlow, "Ring the Doorbell and Run: How Nuclear Rivals India and Pakistan Harass Each Other," *The Economic Times*, March 16, 2018, https://economictimes.indiatimes.com/news/defence/ring-the-doorbell-and-run-here-is-how-nuclear-rivals-india-pakistan-harass-each-other/articleshow/63327292.cms?from=mdr.
19. K.M. Singh, "A Lengthy History of Espionage Tactics."
20. Shrivastava, "My Experience of Life and Work in IB," 70.

21. K.P.S. Gill, "Observations on India's State and Central Intelligence Apparatus," *Indian Police Journal* 59, no. 4 (October–December 2012): 87.

22. Praveen Swami, "The Unknown Kashmiri Spy Who Penetrated Lashkar-e-Taiba before 26/11," *Firstpost*, November 26, 2018, https://www.firstpost.com/india/the-unknown-kashmiri-spy-who-penetrated-lashkar-e-taiba-before-2611-and-how-india-dishonoured-him-5620291.html.

23. Bilal Kuchay, "127 Indian Muslims Charged with 'Terror' Acquitted after 19 Years," *Al-Jazeera*, March 9, 2021, https://www.aljazeera.com/news/2021/3/9/127-indian-muslims-charged-with-terror-acquitted-after-19-years.

24. Maneesh Chhibber, "IB Checks Delhi HC Judge Candidate'S Facebook Profile for Proof of Sexual Orientation," *ThePrint*, October 22, 2019, https://theprint.in/judiciary/ib-checks-delhi-hc-judge-candidates-facebook-proof-sexual-orientation/309592/.

25. Ajit Doval, "India's Intelligence Services: Imperatives for Change," *Indian Police Journal* 59, No. 4 (October–December 2012): 33.

26. Praveen Swami, "Skeletons in the Generals' Cupboards," *The Hindu*, August 12, 2009, https://www.thehindu.com/opinion/lead/Skeletons-in-the-Generalsrs quo-cupboards/article16874698.ece.

27. Shishir Gupta, *Indian Mujahideen: The Enemy Within* (New Delhi: Hachette, 2011).

28. Praveen Swami, "New Kashmir Sees Lull in Violence but Jihadi Elements May Take Advantage of Political Vacuum," *Firstpost*, April 14, 2020, https://www.firstpost.com/india/new-kashmir-sees-lull-in-violence-but-jihadi-elements-may-take-advantage-of-political-vacuum-classified-govt-data-shows-peace-can-be-deceptive-7904361.html.

29. "Union Budget (2020–21)—Police," *OpenBudgets*, undated, https://openbudge tsindia.org/dataset/police-2020-21-budget/resource/47e97ec4-cb84-400c-a1d9-7b4dc1935cd1.

30. Christopher Wray, "FBI Budget Request for Fiscal Year 2020," *FBI.gov*, April 4, 2019, https://www.fbi.gov/news/testimony/fbi-budget-request-for-fis cal-year-2020.

31. "Over 8,000 Vacancies in IB for Want of Eligible Candidates," *Press Trust of India*, March 12, 2013, https://www.business-standard.com/article/pti-stories/over-8-000-vacancies-in-ib-for-want-of-eligible-candidates-113031200299_1.html.

32. Anand Arni, Shibani Mehta, and Pranay Kotasthane, "India's External Intelligence Agency: Managing the Human Resources Challenge," Takshahila Institution Discussion Document, January 2019, https://takshashila.org.in/resea rch/takshashila-discussion-document-indias-external-intelligence-agency1. They note that these problems also dog India's external intelligence operations.

33. Praveen Swami and Nikita Doval, "The Day after the Dreams," *Firstpost*, March 1, 2019, https://www.firstpost.com/india/the-day-after-the-dreams-6180151.html.

34. Vohra, *Safeguarding India*, 60.

35. Subramanian, "Intelligence Bureau, Home Ministry and Indian Politics," 2147.

36. Gill, "Observations on India's State and Central Intelligence Apparatus," 87.

37. "Manish Tewari's Bill Sought to Regulate IB, RAW, NTRO's Operations," *The Times of India*, July 18, 2013, http://timesofindia.indiatimes.com/articleshow/21134566.cms?utm_source=contentofinterest&utm_medium=text&utm_campaign=cppst.

38. Krishnadas Rajgopal, "Pegasus Case: SC to Pass Interim Orders," *The Hindu*, September 13, 2021, https://www.thehindu.com/news/national/pegasus-row-wont-file-detailed-affidavit-centre-tells-sc/article36425644.ece.

39. IDSA Task Force, *A Case for Intelligence Reforms in India* (New Delhi: Institute for Defence Studies and Analysis, 2012), 32.

40. K.C. Verma, "Intelligence Bureau," *Indian Police Journal* 59, no. 4 (October–December 2012): 25.

41. *Report of the Group of Ministers on National Security* (New Delhi: National Security Council Secretariat, 2000), 45.

42. Praveen Swami, "Stalled Reforms," *Frontline*, May 9, 2003, https://frontline.thehindu.com/the-nation/article30216803.ece.

43. Verma, "Intelligence Bureau," 25.

44. "Police Should Ask Intelligence Bureau about Phone Tapping of Judges: Arvind Kejriwal," *The Economic Times,* November 4, 2016, https://economictimes.indiatimes.com/news/politics-and-nation/police-should-ask-intelligence-bureau-about-phone-tapping-of-judges-arvind-kejriwal/articleshow/55245927.cms?utm_source=contentofinterest&utm_medium=text&utm_campaign=cppst.

PART III
INTERNAL AND BORDER SECURITY

Part III examines the roles played by various organizations responsible, under the Ministry of Home Affairs (MHA), for India's internal and border security—the armed paramilitary forces, the security forces safeguarding India's many borders with neighboring countries, and the counter-insurgency forces trained to deal with armed insurrections. Following a general review of the central government's paramilitary forces, this part turns its attention to several specialized units: the Indo-Tibetan Border Police and Sashastra Seema Bal; the Border Security Force; and the Assam Rifles and Rashtriya Rifles.

Each chapter delves into the history, structure, and organization of these forces as well as their varied interactions with one another.

7

India's Central Paramilitaries

Paul Staniland

Introduction

India has a vast security apparatus. Its conventional military, which is aimed at foreign rivals, and its regular police forces, who interact daily with citizens across India, have occupied researchers' attention for years. But the fastest-growing part of the security establishment is the Ministry of Home Affairs' (MHA) armed paramilitary forces, which are used to maintain internal security and guard international borders.[1] They are, in comparative perspective, an unusually large and prominent feature of India's security landscape. This chapter explores their origins and growth.

There are seven paramilitaries under the MHA: the Assam Rifles (AR), the Border Security Force (BSF), the Central Industrial Security Force (CISF), the Central Reserve Police Force (CRPF), the Indo-Tibetan Border Police (ITBP), the National Security Guard (NSG), and the Sashastra Seema Bal (SSB). Technically speaking, the Assam Rifles is a central paramilitary force and the NSG is a special task force under MHA administrative control but Ministry of Defence (MoD) operational control, drawing personnel on deputation from other forces. The remaining five forces are formally categorized as Central Armed Police Forces (CAPFs). For brevity's sake, this chapter will generally refer to all seven outfits as CAPFs.

This chapter provides an overview of these forces. It briefly explores their origins and historical evolution and then focuses on their functions in recent decades (especially since 1990). Wherever possible, it also draws on recent research on their personnel composition and fatalities.[2]

The most politically important forces are the BSF and the CRPF, which have been involved in intensive counter-insurgency operations

Paul Staniland, *India's Central Paramilitaries* In: *Institutional Roots of India's Security Policy.* Edited by: Milan Vaishnav, Oxford University Press. © Oxford University Press 2024. DOI: 10.1093/oso/9780198894612.003.0007 in Jammu and Kashmir, Punjab, the north-east, and—in the case of the CRPF—anti-Naxalite operations and communal riot suppression. The Assam Rifles has played a key role in the north-east, while the ITBP is an important force along the extended Line of Actual Control (LAC) with China. The CISF guards various public facilities; the NSG is a small and highly specialized force used for hostage situations, counterterrorism, and protection of senior politicians; and the SSB guards the Indo-Nepal and Indo-Bhutan borders. In their areas of operations, these organizations can be enormously important—in contexts of insurgency, for example, they are some of the most visible manifestations of state power. As the largest of the paramilitaries with the broadest range of tasks, the CRPF merits particular attention.

This chapter advances a broader argument that the central paramilitaries' political importance is one of several reasons to study India's MHA more intensively. Opaque to outsiders, and thus little researched, the MHA is one of India's so-called power ministries: in addition to controlling paramilitaries that are larger than most nations' entire militaries, it is deeply involved in border control, managing foreigners' visits, domestic intelligence-gathering, central language policy, and centre-state relations, among other hugely important topics.[3]

India's Security Landscape and the Central Paramilitaries

India has a three-tiered security structure. The MoD directs the Indian Army, Navy, and Air Force in standard conventional military operations, with a focus on Pakistan, China, and the Indian Ocean region. The army has been substantially deployed in counter-insurgency (COIN) operations in border regions (i.e. Jammu and Kashmir, Punjab, and various parts of the north-east), but also maintains a central and resource-intensive role in conventional operations. Law and order is a state responsibility under the constitution, so state police forces are expected to manage standard law-enforcement operations. These are staffed by a blend of Indian Police Service (IPS) and state-specific personnel.

These military and state-level police are used for a variety of roles. But multiplying demands have led to the expansion of a set of paramilitary forces that can fill the gaps between the military and state police, as well as reduce the burden on both. Some of these forces—specifically the Assam Rifles and the CRPF—organizationally predate decolonization, while the rest were created to manage new security threats and challenges. The 1960s were a decade of creation and expansion, with the BSF, the ITBP, and the SSB emerging to manage different border areas as it became clear that India faced enduring rivalries with China and Pakistan. From this period onwards, one can broadly distinguish between border forces—the Assam Rifles, the BSF, the ITBP, and the SSB—and those that operate away from India's borders, most importantly the CRPF (see Table 7.1).

Manpower Trends

As scholar Devesh Kapur has noted, India's armed paramilitary forces have grown enormously over time. Data remains somewhat rough: in government reports, there is not always reliable data on the actual strength compared to the sanctioned strength, and some years neither is reported for a particular force (this is especially common for the Assam Rifles). There can also be discrepancies across sources—for instance, the 2018 Chidambaram Report identifies the Assam Rifles' sanctioned strength as 66,412, while the 2018–19 MHA Annual Report puts it at 63,905. Nevertheless, the overlying trend is unambiguously one of massive expansion over time.

Figure 7.1 provides a sense of the paramilitaries' expansion from 1988 to 2018, using reported sanctioned size. It does not include the CISF and NSG, since they are not of great political importance, focusing instead on the five paramilitary forces that are central to the management of internal security and external borders. These data are drawn primarily from the annual reports of the MHA, supplemented by parliamentary reports and questions. Though in some years there are missing data or some ambiguity about the reported size being actual or sanctioned, the basic trend is extremely clear: the CAPFs have grown substantially since the late 1980s.

Table 7.2 shows the starting and end points of these data and the percentage increases between 1988 and 2018. India's population has grown roughly 63 per cent since 1988, but the CAPFs (including the NSG and the CISF) have grown by an average of about 134 per cent—more than

Table 7.1 Central Paramilitaries at a Glance

	Date of Founding	Total Sanctioned Strength	Battalions	Border areas[a]
Assam Rifles	1835 (Cachar Levy); 1917 (Assam Rifles)	65143[b]	46	1,631 kms (Myanmar)
Border Security Force	1965	263,905[c]	192	6,386.36 kms (Pakistan, Bangladesh, Line of Control)
Central Industrial Security Force	1969	152,049[d]	N/A[e]	N/A
Central Reserve Police Force	1939 (Crown Representative's Police); 1949 (CRPF)	324,824[f]	246	N/A
Indo-Tibetan Border Police	1962	89,437[g]	60	3,488 kms (China)
National Security Guard	1984	10,844[h]	N/A	N/A
Sashastra Seema Bal	1963 (Special Service Bureau)	97,244[i]	73	1,751 kms (Nepal), 699 kms (Bhutan)

[a] Parliamentary Standing Committee on Home Affairs, *Working Conditions in Border Guarding Forces (Assam Rifles, Sashastra Seema Bal, Indo-Tibetan Border Police and Border Security Force)*, Report No. 214, December 12, 2018, https://rajyasabha.nic.in/rsnew/Committee_site/Committee_File/ReportFile/15/107/214_2019_11_11.pdf.

[b] Ministry of Home Affairs (MHA), *Annual Report, 2018–19* (New Delhi: Government of India, n.d.), https://www.mha.gov.in/sites/default/files/AnnualReport_18_19.pdf.

[c] MHA, *Annual Report, 2018–19.*

[d] Parliamentary Standing Committee on Home Affairs, *Working Conditions in Non-Border Guarding Forces (Central Industrial Security Force, Central Reserve Police Force and National Security Guard)*, Report No. 215, December 12, 2018, https://rajyasabha.nic.in/rsnew/Committee_site/Committee_File/ReportFile/15/107/215_2019_11_14.pdf.

[e] Parliamentary Standing Committee on Home Affairs, *Working Conditions in Non-Border Guarding Forces* notes on p. 7 that there are 339 units deployed; CISF does not use a battalion structure.

[f] MHA, *Annual Report, 2018–19.*

[g] MHA, *Annual Report, 2018–19.*

[h] Parliamentary Standing Committee on Home Affairs, "*Working Conditions in Non-Border Guarding Forces.*"

[i] Sashastra Seema Bal, "Home Page," SSB official website (accessed June 25, 2020), https://ssb.nic.in/index1.aspx?lsid=37&lev=2&lid=9&langid=1&Cid=0

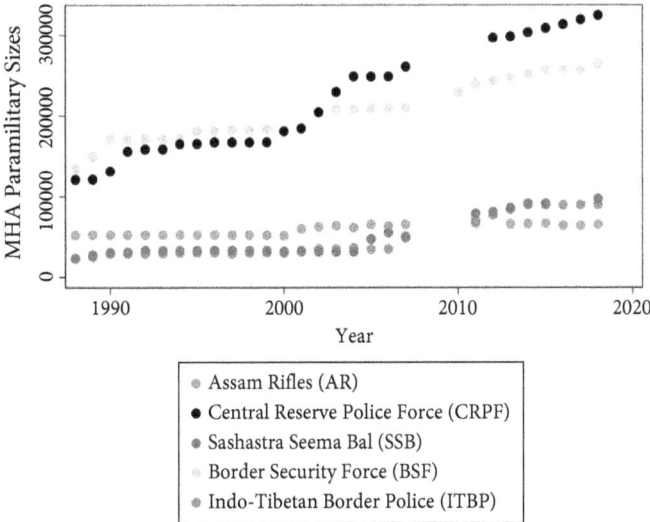

Figure 7.1 Growth Trends in Five CAPFs

Source: Author's analysis of annual reports of the MHA, supplemented by parliamentary reports and questions.

Table 7.2 Change in CAPF Sanctioned Sizes, 1988–2018

	1988	2018	% Change
AR	52,067	65,143	25.11
BSF	135,544	263,905	94.70
CISF	66,102	152,049	130.02
CRPF	120,979	324,824	168.50
ITBP	23,419	89,437	281.90
NSG	7,563	10,844	43.38
SSB	23,244	97,244	318.36
Total	428,918	1,003,446	133.95

Source: Author's analysis of annual reports of the MHA, supplemented by parliamentary reports and questions.

twice the rate of population growth. Sanctioned sizes are not the same as actual sizes; in the contemporary period there are indications that vacancies run about 10 per cent. But this does not change the obvious upward trajectory.[4]

Although there has been a general increase across the board in both force sizes and budgets, there is substantial variation. The Assam Rifles has expanded the least, while the specialized border-oriented SSB and ITBP have expanded dramatically, approximating tripling their sizes. The CRPF has also grown dramatically, more than doubling between 1988 and 2018. The BSF lies in between, at nearly double its previous size. The SSB and ITBP expansions likely have something to do with reforms and rationalization of India's border-management strategy. The CRPF has become a heavily used force, deployed in India's various areas of insurgency (it is also used to provide election security and manage other forms of violence) and dramatically growing in turn. Though the CISF's political insignificance means it warrants less attention in this analysis, that force also shows substantial expansion as it moves away from being primarily aimed at protecting public-sector undertakings to a broader mission that reflects the growth of India's economy, including the proliferation of airports and private-sector installations.

Spending Trends

The increase in manpower is also reflected in the CAPF's rising expenditures over time, which are more reliably reported than the sanctioned sizes. Figure 7.2 shows the increase in nominal spending on five CAPFs, in crore rupees. These are all drawn from MHA Annual Reports, which account for actual expenditures by force going back to 1988. These data, which are more consistent than the manpower numbers, tell a story of even more dramatic growth.

Table 7.3 examines shifts in nominal spending from 1988 to 2018. The rupee saw its value inflated by roughly 750 per cent from 1988 to 2018, so clearly spending on CAPFs dramatically outpaced inflation—total spending ballooned by almost 60-fold. The acceleration began towards the end of the first United Progressive Alliance (UPA) government, expanding from roughly 130 billion rupees in 2007–8 to 377.24 billion rupees by 2013–14. This trend continued under the government of Prime Minister Narendra Modi, growing from 424.28 billion rupees in 2014–15 to 711.14 billion rupees in 2018–19.

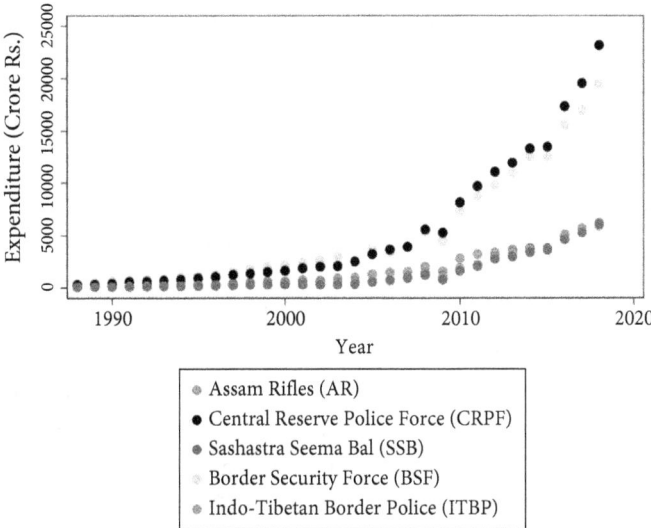

Figure 7.2 Nominal Spending on CAPFs

Source: Author's analysis of annual reports of the MHA.

Table 7.3 Trends in CAPF Spending

Force	1988	2018	% Change
AR	139.59	5,899.67	4126.43
BSF	435.95	19,469.77	4366.06
CISF	119.55	9,220.91	7613.02
CRPF	321.82	23,126.24	7086.08
ITBP	76.9	6,190.72	7950.35
NSG	26.15	1,115.72	4166.62
SSB	73.13	6,050.39	8173.47
Total	1,193.09	71,143.42	5862.96

Source: Author's analysis of annual reports of the MHA.

Note: All amounts are in nominal, crore rupees.

Over the last 15 years, an internal security leviathan has been born. The MHA's spending in general has grown dramatically. PRS Legislative Research, which tracks the functioning of the Indian Parliament, reports that MHA expenditures expanded annually by an average of

15 per cent between 2010–11 and 2020–21, with police expenditures (most of which go to the CAPFs) tracking that annual growth rate at 12 per cent.[5] By comparison, the MoD grew just 9 per cent over that same period.

Understanding Growth

What is driving this expansion? And why has it seemingly attracted so little political attention compared to debates over India's defence budget? Some key drivers are clearly functional: the intensification of insurgencies in the late 1980s and early 1990s placed further demands on India's internal security apparatus, given a further fillip with the re-surgence of the Naxalite insurgency in the 2000s. Porous borders and ongoing international tensions with Pakistan also put a stress on border-guarding agencies. At the same time, the MHA has surely had bureau-cratic incentives to expand its power and budget. Its large, expensive paramilitary forces provide opportunities to do both. Home ministers also tend to be very powerful, and they operate in a political role that is more politically central and sensitive—including recurrent allega-tions that they use the Intelligence Bureau for surveillance and political management—than most defence ministers. The clout of current Home Minister Amit Shah and past home ministers like P. Chidambaram has been substantial.

One reason for the relative lack of political controversy around this growth is that the MHA's budget, despite expansion, is still dramatic-ally smaller than the defence budget. The costs of the paramilitaries do not involve massive weapons systems or far-flung naval operations, so the tensions surrounding defence budgeting are far less relevant to the MHA. A second reason is that the MHA's operating domains are often murky, hidden by layers of secrecy, and involve fundamental questions of counter-insurgency, state repression, and border management that can be insulated from public oversight and justified in the name of national security and counter-subversion. This is a less technocratic domain than conventional weapons platforms; instead, it touches on some of the most delicate and (intentionally) opaque issues in Indian politics.

Recruitment

The MHA's recruitment policy differentiates across multiple dimensions. First, there is a geographical basis, as laid out in 2015:

1. 60% of vacancies are allotted amongst States/UTs on the basis of population ratio.
2. 20% of vacancies in the Border Guarding Forces (BGFs) (BSF, ITBP, SSB and Assam Rifles) are allotted to border districts, which fall within the responsibility of the Force.
3. 20% of vacancies in BGFs are allotted to areas affected by militancy, i.e. J & K, north-eastern States and naxal affected areas. The districts/areas affected by militancy are notified by the Government from time to time.
4. In Forces, other than BGFs, 40% vacancies are allotted to militancy affected areas i.e. J&K, north-eastern States and naxal affected areas. The district/areas affected by militancy are notified by the Government from time to time.[6]

Second, there is a preference for ex-servicemen:

10% of the vacancies in Group A, B & C in CAPFs and AR are reserved for Ex-servicemen apart from reservation as applicable under the relevant Rules to SC/ST/OBC [Scheduled Tribe/Scheduled Caste/Other Backward Class] candidates. Concessions in height and chest to the candidates from some specified states/areas/regions/category are also provided as per the provisions in the respective Recruitment Rules/ schemes.[7]

Third, there are categories set aside for SC/ST personnel in recruitment.[8] As of the mid-2010s, there had been difficulties filling these categories. Various special recruitment drives have been launched to attempt to meet these quotas.

Fourth, there have been efforts to create women-only units (like the CRPF's Mahila battalions and the SSB's Mahila companies) in order to improve relations between the forces and female populations. As of early 2019, the MHA reported that women represented 2.77 per cent of the

CRPF, 2.16 per cent of the BSF, 6.04 per cent of the CISF, 2.36 per cent of the ITBP, 2.56 per cent of the SSB, and 1.33 per cent of the Assam Rifles.[9] A parliamentary committee has expressed deep dissatisfaction with the CAPFs' inability to attain its targets for female recruitment.[10]

While there are little long-term data on the nature of several of these categories (though, in recent years, the MHA's annual reports have provided valuable information on some), scholar Drew Stommes and the author have used the BSF's and CRPF's commemorative publications on killed-in-action personnel to crudely map out their regional composition.[11] This is a messy and incomplete picture that should only be taken as a suggestive first step: further data collection will be necessary to make confident claims. In addition to concerns about data quality, these figures also assume that fatalities are roughly proportional across the force; in very small states, this will be a particular problem. Nevertheless, the data at least provides preliminary insights into the basic regional spread of the forces' recruits relative to India's population. Dead force members' next of kin addresses have been used as proxies for their likely state and district of origin.

Given the explicit strategy of over-representing border states, it is not surprising that the BSF appears to have historically been over-represented by personnel from Jammu and Kashmir, Uttarakhand, Himachal Pradesh, Haryana, Tripura, Punjab, Manipur, Meghalaya, Nagaland, Assam, Rajasthan, and Sikkim, with under-representation from Maharashtra, Tamil Nadu, Odisha, Karnataka, Madhya Pradesh, Andhra Pradesh, and Jharkhand; West Bengal and Kerala are proportional to population. More surprising is under-representation from border states, Gujarat, Bihar, Uttar Pradesh, and Mizoram. The dominance of the north-east, northern hill states, and states bordering Pakistan (especially Punjab and Jammu and Kashmir) is reassuring for data quality: these are precisely the types of states where the government has intentionally set up quotas for representation.

The CRPF paints a more surprising picture. There is a preference for recruits from conflict-affected states but not border states. There is (tentatively) over-representation from Manipur, Himachal Pradesh, Jammu and Kashmir, Uttarakahand, Haryana, Tripura, Punjab, and Assam, with relative under-representation from Maharashtra, Tamil Nadu, Chhattisgarh, West Bengal, Karnataka, and Madhya Pradesh. Uttar

Pradesh, Bihar, Jharkhand, and Rajasthan are proportional. The north-eastern states, Punjab, and Jammu and Kashmir make sense given their histories of conflict. But states like Himachal Pradesh and Uttarakhand are more surprising since they lack any current or past insurgency. It seems possible that these historically 'martial' areas have family histories or social networks that encourage joining security forces more so than in Gujarat, Andhra Pradesh, or Goa.

With all the caveats that are necessary in using these data, they do suggest a fairly clear core of internal security force recruitment, heavily drawn from India's smaller border states. The vast states that make up so much of India's population tend to be either proportionately repre-sented or under-represented; it is relatively small states like Himachal, Uttarakhand, Punjab, Manipur, and Jammu and Kashmir that are over-represented in the CAPFs. More research will need to be done to deter-mine what explains this variation—state strategy in targeting border and/ or conflict areas is obviously a key determinant but not sufficient on its own. States with larger or more diversified economies may see propor-tionately lower recruitment to the CAPFs, for instance, or historical re-cruiting networks may contribute to regional biases.

The rest of this chapter provides an overview of several key paramili-tary forces. As the largest force, the CRPF merits particular attention, as do the border-guarding forces, with a focus on the BSF and the Assam Rifles due to their active participation in major counter-insurgency campaigns. The chapters that follow offer deeper analysis of these latter forces. Given the CISF and NSG's extremely specialized roles, they are not discussed further.

Central Reserve Police Force

With roots in the twilight of British rule, the CRPF was originally con-ceived as a force for managing riots and situations in which a state needed assistance in restoring order. It continued this role into inde-pendence, while also adding border management to its mandate in the 1950s. The killing of 10 CRPF personnel at Hot Springs in a clash with Chinese forces in October 1959 was a crucial moment in the escalation of China–India tensions that led to the 1962 war. The CRPF's deployment expanded dramatically in the 1960s, when it became deeply involved in counter-insurgency operations: a commemorative publication of the CRPF notes a death in Nagaland (then part of Assam) in 1960 during a clash with Naga militants. Other deaths from counter-militancy operations occurred in Jammu and Kashmir, the North-East Frontier Agency, Manipur (then part of Assam), Tripura, Mizoram (then part of Assam), and Andhra Pradesh during the 1960s. The CRPF also took casualties during the 1965 war with Pakistan.

In the 1970s, the CRPF was deployed to West Bengal, Nagaland, Andhra Pradesh, Manipur, Mizoram, Assam, and Bihar, among others, and took part in the 1971 Indo-Pakistani War. Thus, though India's so-called counter-insurgency era did not begin in earnest until the mid-1980s (and largely ended, in this author's estimation, in the mid-2010s), the CRPF was on the front lines of the earlier waves of revolt that challenged Delhi. It also was involved in putting down the 1974 railway strike.

The 1980s saw the CRPF put into action in Punjab, Assam, and Jammu and Kashmir, as well as continuing various activities in the north-east and in support of state-level anti-Naxalite operations. In the last 15 years, it has become the front-line central force pushing back Naxalite mobilization in central India, especially Chhattisgarh and Jharkhand, where the MHA has led a major offensive against the insurgent Communist Party of India (CPI-Maoist). This emphasis on counter-Naxalite operations has included the creation of a set of specialized battalions aimed at overcoming the difficult terrain and specific operations of the CPI-Maoist. Between 2008 and 2011, 10 of these CoBRA (Commando Battalion for Resolute Action) battalions were raised specifically for jungle counter-insurgency.[12]

While the army, the BSF, and the Assam Rifles, plus state police forces, have all played a major role in COIN operations, the CRPF is the common denominator across essentially all of India's insurgencies. It has been deployed across the country, in roles ranging from a hasty stopgap (as in Jammu and Kashmir in 1989–90) to a long-term, deeply dug-in presence (as in contemporary Naxalite-affected areas). The distribution of CRPF forces is regularly shifting, but data from 2018 showed 38 per cent of battalions engaged in anti-Naxalite operations, 26 per cent in Jammu and Kashmir, 15 per cent in the north-east, 7 per cent acting as Rapid Action Forces (more on that later), and 14 per cent deployed elsewhere.[13] While these percentages regularly fluctuate, the basic posture is likely to be broadly similar at present. The CRPF has grown to a sanctioned strength of over 324,000 people, though the actual number of personnel in the force has been consistently below that. This represents a 168 per cent increase in sanctioned manpower since 1988—a dramatic growth that has been accompanied by even higher expenditures.

Per data from the CRPF's commemoration of its fatalities up to 2016, the deadliest states for CRPF personnel have been Jammu and Kashmir, Chhattisgarh, Manipur, Punjab, Assam, Tripura, and Jharkhand. This shows the extent of the CRPF's activities, spanning the hot spots of various insurgencies against the Indian government. These fatalities are concentrated from the late 1980s, when conflicts in Assam, Jammu and Kashmir, and Punjab added to existing insurgencies in the northeast, until roughly 2010, when a major offensive was launched against Naxalite forces in interior India. The deadliest districts for the CPRF include Srinagar, Dantewada, Bijapur, Amritsar, South Tripura, Tarn Taran, Narayanpur, Pulwama, and Imphal—a broad swath of India that demonstrates the reach of the CRPF.

While counter-insurgency is the main occupation of the CRPF, it has also been used in a wide variety of other ways. The waves of communal riots that hit India in the late 1980s and early 1990s led to the creation of Rapid Action Force (RAF) battalions in October 1992, which are located in areas where there are credible fears of clashes and disturbances.[14] The initial stock of 10 RAF battalions has been expanded to 15. The CRPF is a particularly useful force for preventing or responding to communal tensions and violence. State police forces are often seen as political, communal, or otherwise unreliable, so a central presence can seem more trustworthy (though this does not mean that central forces are necessarily neutral arbiters).

This does not exhaust the force's long list of uses. Over time, it has become engaged in providing security for elections, assisting with huge public pilgrimages, and defending Parliament, among other tasks.[15] Moreover, the CRPF was part of the Indian Peacekeeping Force in Sri Lanka and has contributed personnel to other overseas missions, such as duties in Haiti and Kosovo.[16]

Heavy usage of the force has led to important critiques. First, the living conditions of CRPF personnel are often abysmal, and the high tempo of operations limits time away from duty. The force has limited and often very slow promotion pathways and there are tensions between those who rise within the CRPF and members of the IPS who join on deputation.[17] The large number of vacancies in the CRPF also limits the force's capabilities.

Second, the CRPF has been accused of human rights violations and a heavy-handed approach to security. This should not come as a surprise considering its origins in colonial policing. It lacks both the training and resources of the conventional military and the focus on everyday interactions that ideally would characterize regular policing. Counter-insurgency operations are, in the best of circumstances, difficult to pursue without serious abuses—and those circumstances rarely apply to the CRPF's operations.

Border Security Force

In contrast with the all-purpose CRPF, the BSF was built with a special-ized task in mind: managing India's borders with Pakistan (then both east and west) in the wake of the 1965 Indo-Pakistani War. That conflict, as well as the events that led to it, made clear the limits of state-level police forces' ability to control India's potentially hostile borders with Pakistan. The BSF was given a greater level of central control, training, and arma-ment specifically for this task. Founded in 1965, it took several years to stand up substantial forces, but fairly quickly was able to manage its duties.

Today, the BSF is responsible for the India–Pakistan and India–Bangladesh borders, as well as operations with the Indian Army along the Line of Control (LoC) dividing the Indian- and Pakistani-administered portions of Jammu and Kashmir. The force has two major sets of po-tential responsibilities. During peacetime, it is responsible for security, control over transit, and anti-smuggling and law enforcement activities along the border. In these tasks, the BSF is often deployed in very chal-lenging terrain with limited amenities. Different borders present a var-iety of challenges, from cross-LoC infiltration and Pakistani shelling in Kashmir to intercepting smugglers on the border with Bangladesh. The BSF is responsible for more territory than any other border-guarding force, including the most challenging border zones. During wartime, the BSF is supposed to hold areas that are not sorely pressed, protect flanks and vital installations, and fight against paramilitaries on the other side.[18]

These are major operations. The BSF played a part in the 1971 and 1999 Indo-Pakistani Wars and has been heavily involved in regular exchanges of gunfire along the LoC. This role, however, has expanded beyond border-guarding into high-intensity counter-insurgency actions in Jammu and Kashmir and the north-east, as well as a limited role in anti-Naxalite operations in interior India. The size of the force has nearly doubled since 1988, as shown previously in Table 7.1—both border security and counter-insurgency have become increasingly challenging, and the BSF has consequently grown substantially. Like the other CAPFs (aside from the Assam Rifles), India's counter-insurgency era saw the BSF expand, especially since a number of these insurgencies included cross-border sanctuary and/or transit, requiring an emphasis on border management and control.

According to available data, there were three major peaks in BSF fatalities: 1971, the early 1990s, and the early 2000s. The first coincides with the 1971 Indo-Pakistani War, during which the BSF was heavily engaged on the border with East Pakistan.[19] The early 1990s and early 2000s were both periods of very intense violence in Jammu and Kashmir; the early 1990s also witnessed a substantial insurgency in Punjab. The BSF's focus on Jammu and Kashmir is apparent in the data: it is, by far, the deadliest state for the BSF, with (according to these data), more than four times as many deaths as the next state (Punjab). Within Jammu and Kashmir, Srinagar, Baramulla, Rajouri, Kupwara, and Pulwama districts have been the bloodiest. The BSF's role in the north-east includes operations in Tripura, Manipur, Assam, West Bengal, and Meghalaya.

The BSF has received critiques similar to the CRPF. Its counter-insurgency activities in Jammu and Kashmir were notorious among many Kashmiris for brutality (for instance, its Papa II interrogation facility is alleged to have been the site of extensive torture). A parliamentary report in 2018 identified numerous concerns, ranging from the quality of housing to the incidence of suicide within the force to the extremely high tempo of operations that limits rest.[20] The growth of the CAPFs has not been matched by equivalent levels of infrastructure or internal mobility, making the forces less capable and more internally aggrieved than a simple examination of changes in size and budget might suggest.

Sashastra Seema Bal and Indo-Tibetan Border Police

The two least-known MHA paramilitaries are the SSB and the ITBP, both of which manage borders that (at least until recently) were much calmer than the frontiers with Pakistan, Bangladesh, or Myanmar. Both have interesting origins in the 1960s but have become more institutionalized and far larger in recent decades.

The SSB—initially called the Special Service Bureau—was created in March 1963 after the war with China to play a 'stay-behind role' in future wars and to engage in national integration and security provision in remote border communities.[21] Given the difficulties of fully projecting state power into these areas, the SSB was intended to be a force multiplier that could build civic defence programmes, reduce Chinese intelligence penetration, and train villagers in firearms. Over time, the SSB's remit expanded well beyond the border with China to include Rajasthan, Mizoram, Nagaland, Meghalaya, Tripura, and Jammu.[22] According to the SSB, during this phase (prior to the reorganization of its role), the SSB covered over 9,917 kilometres of India's borders, divided among 10 divisions, within which were various layers of geographical reach.

After the 1999 Kargil conflict, the government reorganized its border guards so that a single force would be responsible for each border.[23] The SSB was renamed the Sashastra Seema Bal in 2001 and assigned first to the India–Nepal border and then in 2004 to the India–Bhutan border. Along with this shift in responsibility, the force has massively expanded. The distinctive aspect of the SSB's remit is that India's border with Nepal is quite open and its border with Bhutan border also looks very different than the hostile Pakistan border or challenging Bangladesh and Myanmar borders. While difficulties like smuggling and human trafficking remain an issue, there are not cross-border insurgencies or severe geopolitical tensions.

The ITBP similarly has its roots in the 1962 war with China, being raised on 24 October 1962.[24] The wars of the 1960s had a huge effect not just on India's conventional military forces but on its entire border security apparatus. The ITBP was originally intended to operate as a kind of guerrilla border force that could battle the Chinese even in places where conventional combat would disadvantage India. It also took part in the 1965 and 1971 wars with Pakistan. As the initial shock of the 1962 war faded, the ITBP was reorganized in 1978 to be a more standard border-guarding force, albeit one that continued to be trained in internal-security operations.[25]

The ITBP was assigned to exclusively guard the India–China border as part of the post-Kargil reforms in 2004. It is responsible for keeping watch over a huge swath of territory, much of it challenging terrain that is difficult to access. As with the SSB, the ITBP has grown dramatically over time, almost tripling in size since 1988. The ITBP is tasked with managing the movement of people, preventing criminal activity, generating intelligence on Chinese activities along the LAC, and pursuing various civic action programmes in border areas. As of 2018, the ITBP had established 176 border outposts. As recent events along the LAC suggest, however, the India–China boundary is in places poorly defined, subject to different understandings, and not thoroughly manned or continually patrolled, given the terrain and weather.

The ITBP has also been given other duties. Several battalions of the ITPB have been involved in anti-Naxalite operations in Chhattisgarh (somewhat curiously justified by the MHA on the grounds that duties outside of the ITBP's areas of altitude operation are good for the health of the forces; it is unclear that these health benefits apply to fighting Naxalites in Chhattisgarh).[26] The ITBP has helped safeguard VIPs and important state installations (though these roles are supposed to be eventually eliminated in favour of specialized CISF and NSG forces). The ITBP has also been deployed in Afghanistan to provide security for Indian diplomatic installations, and to various UN peacekeeping operations around the world. The force has also provided support to mountain pilgrimages.

Both the SSB and ITBP have fewer issues with stagnant promotions than the CRPF and the BSF, since they are in rapid expansion mode. Nevertheless, housing, equipment, medical care, and the provision of basic amenities in both border forces have been the subject of criticism. They have been something of an afterthought in discussions about India's security establishment, but the growing importance of the India–China boundary, recurrent tensions with Nepal, and the influx of funding suggest that both forces may take on more prominent roles in the coming years.[27]

Assam Rifles

The Assam Rifles is quite different from the other forces. The MHA refers to it officially as a Central Paramilitary Force rather than a CAPF, and it has a different structure of ranks. This is largely due to its operational control by, and integration with, the Indian Army, even as it administratively and budgetarily falls under the MHA. Roughly 80 per cent of its officers are on deputation from the army and its rank structure is more aligned with the army than the other MHA CAPFs.[28]

The Assam Rifles—originally named the Cachar Levy—has a long history beginning in 1835. After independence, the Assam Rifles was initially assigned to the Ministry of External Affairs, which controlled the North-East Frontier Agency. In 1965, the force was reassigned to the MHA. However, it is operationally under the control of the Indian Army's Eastern Command, with the Assam Rifles Headquarters located in Shillong. An army lieutenant general commands the force. As of 2018, specific sectors are in Nagaland (IGAR North), Manipur (IGAR South), Assam/Mizoram/Tripura (IGAR East), and Arunachal Pradesh (25 Sector AR).[29]

In recent years, a dispute over whether the Assam Rifles should be entirely moved to the MHA has highlighted the curious nature of the force.[30] The MHA has pushed back against suggestions about shifting the balance of officers more towards Assam Rifles cadres as opposed to army officers on deputation, arguing that interoperability between the Assam Rifles and the army requires a major role for army officers and the force's continued integration within the army's chain of command. The Assam Rifles' core duties are counter-insurgency, the management of the Myanmar border, and a role in the planning for hostilities with China.[31]

The Myanmar border has been a fairly porous site of smuggling, movement of people, and cross-border operations for a variety of insurgent groups, especially but not exclusively the various Naga rebel factions. This is incredibly challenging terrain, with jungle and mountains, and a long history of resistance and rebellion. As with the other central forces, the Assam Rifles has been repeatedly accused of human rights abuses and impunity in its counter-insurgency operations.

The Assam Rifles is the oldest MHA-linked central paramilitary. It is both highly specialized and limited geographically. Perhaps as a consequence, it has experienced the least growth in sanctioned manpower since 1988—about a 25 per cent increase, far below the other paramilitaries. However, this may reflect the Assam Rifles' longer period of service, as well as the less expansive strain on the force; it has grown from 17 battalions in 1960 to 46 at present.[32]

The Assam Rifles is an unusual force in the Indian context. Its future seems to hinge on turf battles between the MHA and MoD. The insurgencies in the north-east that have occupied its attention since the 1950s are in severe decline, and the future force posture towards China may be in flux in the aftermath of India's recent tensions with China.

Internal Security and Politics

Internal conflict and policing are fundamental to India's politics. The MHA is the core ministry responsible for central policy towards both of these responsibilities, with vast security forces, a large intelligence network, and numerous legal and bureaucratic powers at its disposal. Under the current Modi government, Home Minister Amit Shah is an extraordinarily powerful figure. The central paramilitaries reflect the MHA's growth as a power ministry: both the size of the forces and the budget allocated to them have grown enormously, especially over the last 15 years. The second UPA government and post-2014 Modi government have both driven this trend, reflecting a focus on hardening India's internal security and border apparatuses.

This process has been accompanied by an expansion of surveillance powers, continued allegations of human rights violations, and substantially reduced (though not eliminated) insurgent violence in the core areas of revolt. While scholars have produced numerous studies of India's foreign policy, service provision, civil society, and electoral and party politics, the country's vast internal security structure has received surprisingly little study. This chapter makes clear how crucial the central paramilitaries are to understanding Indian politics, especially its insurgencies and border zones. To understand their political role, future research must grapple with both the role of the paramilitaries and the MHA more broadly.

Notes

1. Devesh Kapur, "The Worrying Rise of Militarization in India's Central Armed Police Forces," *ThePrint*, November 29, 2017, https://theprint.in/opinion/worrying-rise-militarisation-indias-central-armed-police-forces/19132/.
2. Paul Staniland and Drew Stommes, "New Data on Indian Security Force Fatalities and Demographics," *India Review* 18, no. 3 (2019), https://www.tandfonline.com/doi/abs/10.1080/14736489.2019.1616261.
3. For specialized work, see M.D. Sharma, *Paramilitary Forces of India* (New Delhi: Gyan Publishing House, 2008); Omar Khalidi, *Khaki and Ethnic Violence in India: Army, Police and Paramilitary Forces During Communal Riots*, 2nd Revised edition (Gurgaon: Three Essays Collectives, 2010); Bibhu Prasad Routray, "Internal Security Challenges and Role of the Central Armed Police Forces," in *India's Military Modernization,* eds. Rajesh Basrur, Ajaya Kumar Das, and Manjeet Singh Pardesi (New Delhi: Oxford University Press, 2013), 169–95.
4. For this average 10% vacancy level, see Lok Sabha, Unstarred Question no. 592, June 14, 2019, http://164.100.24.220/loksabhaquestions/annex/171/AU592.pdf.
5. Parliamentary Research Services, "Demand for Grants 2020–21 Analysis: Home Affairs," https://prsindia.org/budgets/parliament/demand-for-grants-2020-21-analysis-home-affairs.
6. Lok Sabha, Unstarred Question No. 6337, May 5, 2015, http://loksabhaph.nic.in/Questions/QResult15.aspx?qref=16590&lsno=16; see also Lok Sabha, Unstarred Question No. 2655, August 1, 2017, http://164.100.24.220/loksabhaquestions/annex/12/AU2655.pdf.
7. Lok Sabha, Unstarred Question No. 2550, December 15, 2015, http://loksabhaph.nic.in/Questions/QResult15.aspx?qref=26929&lsno=16.
8. Lok Sabha, Unstarred Question No. 1191, March 3, 2015, http://loksabhaph.nic.in/Questions/QResult15.aspx?qref=13111&lsno=16
9. Ministry of Home Affairs, *Annual Report, 2018–19* (New Delhi: Government of India, n.d.).
10. Parliamentary Standing Committee on Home Affairs, *Action Taken by Government on the Recommendations/Observations Contained in the Two Hundred Fifteenth Report on Working Conditions in Non-Border Guarding Central Armed Police Forces*, Report No. 220, December 11, 2019, 31, https://rajyasabha.nic.in/rsnew/Committee_site/Committee_File/ReportFile/15/122/220_2019_12_17.pdf.

11. Ministry of Home Affairs, *Warriors Remembered* (New Delhi: Government of India, 2015));)*BSF Martyrs: A Legacy of Pride and Valour* (New Delhi: Border Security Force, 2015).

12. MHA, *Annual Report, 2018–19*, 131.

13. Parliamentary Standing Committee on Home Affairs, *Working Conditions in Non-Border Guarding Forces*.

14. The list of 15 RAF battalions and their locations as of early 2019 can be found on pages 130–1 of the MHA, *Annual Report, 2018–19*.

15. http://crpf.gov.in/writereaddata/images/01/286042018..pdf

16. CRPF, *CRPF Samachar*, 2014, 15–16, https://crpf.gov.in/writereaddata/images/pdf/709115.pdf

17. Sanya Dhingra, "Modi Govt Plan to Merge CAPF, IPS Recruitment Exams Could End Animosity between Them," *ThePrint*, February 10, 2020, https://theprint.in/india/modi-govt-plan-to-merge-capf-ips-recruitment-exams-could-end-animosity-between-them/362646/.; Vijaita Singh, "End IPS Hegemony in Central Armed Police Forces, Says Parliamentary Panel," *The Hindu*, December 12, 2018, https://www.thehindu.com/news/national/end-ips-hegemony-in-central-armed-police-forces-says-parliamentary-panel/article25727367.ece.

18. Parliamentary Standing Committee on Home Affairs, *Working Conditions in Border Guarding Forces*, 68.

19. Staniland and Stommes, "New Data on Indian Security Force Fatalities and Demographics," 288–323.

20. Parliamentary Standing Committee on Home Affairs, *Working Conditions in Border Guarding Forces*; Parliamentary Standing Committee on Home Affairs, *Action Taken by Government on the Recommendations/Observations Contained in the Two Hundred Fifteenth Report on Working Conditions in Border Guarding Central Armed Police Forces*, Report No. 221, December 11, 2019.

21. Parliamentary Standing Committee on Home Affairs, *Working Conditions in Border Guarding Forces*, 24.

22. Sashastra Seema Bal, "SSB History," https://ssb.gov.in.

23. Abhimanyu Chakravorty, "Explained: Why Was the Sashastra Seema Bal Force Created?" *Indian Express*, February 17, 2016, https://indianexpress.com/article/explained/sashastra-seema-bal-ssb-news/.

24. Indo-Tibetan Border Police, "Origin of ITBP, the 'HIMVEERS,' and National Security," https://www.itbpolice.nic.in/Home/history_role.

25. Parliamentary Standing Committee on Home Affairs, *Working Conditions in Border Guarding Forces*, 47–8.

26. As of 2018–19, 8 battalions were deployed in anti-Naxal operations, per Parliamentary Standing Committee on Home Affairs, *Action Taken by Government on the Recommendations/Observations Contained in the Two Hundred Fifteenth Report on Working Conditions in Border Guarding Central Armed Police Forces*, 44.

27. There had been suggestions that the ITBP and SSB would be merged, but that does not appear to be occurring. See Press Trust of India, "Idea to Merge ITBP and SSB Not Under Consideration: Government," *The Hindu*, March 3, 2020, https://www.thehindu.com/news/national/idea-to-merge-itbp-and-ssb-not-under-consideration-government/article30974017.ece.

28. Parliamentary Standing Committee on Home Affairs, *Working Conditions in Border Guarding Forces*, 4.

29. Parliamentary Standing Committee on Home Affairs, *Working Conditions in Border Guarding Forces*, 5.

30. Nidhima Taneja, "Whom Does the Assam Rifles 'Belong' to?" *The Wire*, October 12, 2019, https://thewire.in/security/who-does-the-assam-rifles-belong-to; "Giving Total Control of Assam Rifles to MHA Will Adversely Impact Vigil: Army to Govt," *Economic Times*, September 30, 2019, https://economictimes.indiatimes.com/news/defence/giving-total-control-of-assam-rifles-to-mha-will-adversely-impact-vigil-army-to-govt/articleshow/71363588.cms?from=mdr.

31. Parliamentary Standing Committee on Home Affairs, *Action Taken by Government on the Recommendations/Observations Contained in the Two Hundred Fifteenth Report on Working Conditions in Border Guarding Central Armed Police Forces*, 68–9.

32. Assam Rifles, https://www.assamrifles.gov.in/english/newwindow.html?2030.

8

The Indo-Tibetan Border Police and the Sashastra Seema Bal

Jabin T. Jacob

Introduction

The Indo-Tibetan Border Police (ITBP) and the Sashastra Seema Bal (SSB), two of India's paramilitary forces, both came into being as a direct result of the 1962 Sino-Indian War.[1] The ITBP was raised on 24 October 1962, within days of the conflict with China breaking out. The SSB took shape in March of the following year. This genesis has shaped the role of both paramilitary organizations in significant ways. But while the ITBP has remained largely committed to the border with China, the SSB's focus has shifted specifically to India's borders with Nepal and Bhutan following the recommendations of the Kargil Review Committee. At the same time, mission creep has expanded the role of both the ITBP and the SSB in support of civilian administration, taking on additional responsibilities such as countering left-wing extremism.

This chapter examines issues around the control and restructuring of these two paramilitaries—including their origins, current roles, personnel recruitment, and working conditions—while also examining how and where they fit into India's overall security policy-making calculus. Unless separately referenced, this chapter relies on three primary *Sources:* the official websites of the ITBP[2] and the SSB,[3] annual reports from the central Ministry of Home Affairs (MHA), and a 2018 report by the Indian Parliament's Standing Committee on Home Affairs titled *Working Conditions in Border Guarding Forces.*[4] The latter document is particularly important, as it is the most recent available report presented to Parliament on the state of affairs in the ITBP and SSB.

Jabin T. Jacob, *The Indo-Tibetan Border Police and the Sashastra Seema Bal* In: *Institutional Roots of India's Security Policy.* Edited by: Milan Vaishnav, Oxford University Press. © Oxford University Press 2024. DOI: 10.1093/oso/9780198894612.003.0008

Over time, both the ITBP and the SSB have steadily accrued tasks far beyond their supposed specialized roles as border forces. Although it is difficult to pin down an authoritative or documented rationale for this shift, it can be argued that this is simply the result of the growth of the Indian state, its compounding responsibilities, and the myriad challenges it faces. The ITBP, SSB, and other Central Armed Police Forces (CAPFs) fall under the purview of MHA)—the same ministry responsible for internal security. Thus, it appears that when problems—such as left-wing extremism or providing security for elections—arise, those in charge often choose to redirect CAPF battalions from their original duties. Over time, this has become an accepted, institutionalized norm. Despite their evolving mandates, however, the organizational identities of the ITBP and the SSB remain strong.

Objectives, Roles, and Organization

The ITBP was formed with the express purpose of 'reorganizing the frontier intelligence and security set up along the Indo-Tibetan border'. Serving as a 'guerrilla-cum-fighting Force', it was supposed to be 'self-contained in supplies, communication and intelligence collection'. While it was involved in the 1965 and 1971 wars against Pakistan, by 1978 it had become 'a conventional border guarding force'.[5]

The SSB was similarly created with the objective of achieving 'total security preparedness' in the remote areas bordering China. Originally called the Special Service Bureau, it was founded by then Intelligence Bureau Director B.N. Mullik, who concurrently served as its director over two separate tenures. The SSB was also supposed to perform a so-called stay-behind role in the event of a war. Over time, however, the SSB's primary function has evolved from countering China to its present duties policing India's borders with Nepal and Bhutan.

The ITBP currently has 56 service battalions, four specialist battalions,[6] 17 training centres, and seven logistics establishments. As of the beginning of 2020, its sanctioned strength was 89,567 while its actual strength was 82,631.[7] The SSB currently has a sanctioned strength of 97,244 and actual strength of 78,809 personnel,[8] with 73 battalions[9] including two specialist battalions. In 2018–19, revised estimates of the ITBP's total expenditures totalled just over 62.46 billion rupees against a total budget of 62.47 billion rupees. Tentative expenditures for 2019–20 were over 62 billion rupees against a budget of more than 72 billion rupees. For the SSB, revised estimates put total expenditure in 2018–19 at about 60.92 billion rupees against a total budget of 61.26 billion rupees. The SSB's tentative expenditure for 2019–20 was 66.06 billion rupees against a budget of about 69.22 billion rupees.[10]

Despite the fact that it polices a longer border, the ITBP's strength is noticeably lower than the SSB's. This could be because the ITBP shares many of its responsibilities with the Indian Army. Despite its comparatively slimmer ranks, however, the ITBP enjoys greater financial resources than the SSB. Although there is no detailed breakdown of either force's budget expenditure, the difference likely stems from the fact that the ITBP polices especially demanding terrain and, thus, requires more specialized equipment.

The ITBP's current operational roles and responsibilities are defined under the Indo-Tibetan Police Force Act of 1992, and its rules were framed in 1994. The Sashastra Seema Bal Act and the SSB's rules, on the other hand, date only to 2007 and 2009, respectively. Roles and responsibilities are nearly identical for both paramilitaries:

> to safeguard the security of assigned borders of India and promote sense of security among the people living in border areas; prevent trans-border crimes, smuggling and any other illegal activity; prevent unauthorized entry into or exit from the territory of India; carry out civic action programme in the area of responsibility; and to perform any other duty assigned by the Central Government.

Interestingly, it was only in 2004 that the entire India–China boundary, comprising 3,488 kilometres (km), came fully under the ITBP's purview, when it replaced the Assam Rifles in Sikkim and Arunachal Pradesh. In this primary role, ITBP deployment also covers the states or union territories of Ladakh, Jammu and Kashmir, Himachal Pradesh, and Uttarakhand. In its early years, the SSB operated in North Assam, North Bengal, the hill districts of Uttar Pradesh, Uttarakhand, Himachal Pradesh, parts of Punjab, and Ladakh. Soon, however, its area of operations expanded to include Manipur, Tripura, and Jammu (1965), Meghalaya (1975), Sikkim

(1976), Rajasthan (1985), and finally southern West Bengal, Nagaland, and Mizoram (1989). At one point in time, its area of coverage included 15 states and nearly 10,000 km of India's international borders.[11] More recently, though, the SSB's mandate has been reduced to overseeing India's borders with Nepal (as of June 2001) and Bhutan (as of March 2004), covering a total length of 2,450 km. Today, SSB units in their primary operational role are stationed only in Uttarakhand, Uttar Pradesh, Bihar, West Bengal, Sikkim, Assam, and Arunachal Pradesh.

The SSB is the lead intelligence agency (LIA) on the borders it supervises. In 2020, there were two prominent instances when the SSB's intelligence functions were on display. The first had to do with preventing smuggling[12] and infiltration of people allegedly infected with COVID-19[13] during the country's stringent lockdown. The second involved preventing a terror attack[14] at the Ram temple *bhoomi poojan* (consecration of land) at Ayodhya in August.

The ITBP, however, is only the LIA 'along the Indo-China border in Jammu and Kashmir (Ladakh), Himachal Pradesh, and Uttarakhand'.[15] It has not, to date, assumed this role in Sikkim or Arunachal Pradesh, despite having replaced the Assam Rifles in 2004. This has been ascribed to both the Indian Army's reluctance to give up the role and a general lack of interest within the ITBP's leadership.[16]

Meanwhile, the ITBP's and SSB's twin injunctions to 'carry out civic action programme in the area of responsibility; and to perform any other duty assigned by the Central Government' have also been considerably expanded. Both organizations are, for instance, now involved in counter-insurgency and internal security roles—responsibilities it is not clear they are adequately trained for.

The ITBP is also specially tasked with security duties at various important national institutions, such as Rashtrapati Bhavan (the president's house), UpaRashtrapati Bhavan (the vice president's house), and the Lal Bahadur Shastri National Academy of Administration, as well as additional high-level protection duties.[17] Other prominent tasks include security and communication duties for Hindu religious pilgrimages to the Kailash Mansarovar and Amarnath, as well as deployment at the Rumtek Monastery in Sikkim. The ITBP had also been prominently involved in setting up quarantine camps in Delhi for people returning to India during the COVID-19 pandemic.[18] Other civic tasks for both organizations include elections-related responsibilities and border area development programmes.

The ITBP also has a role to play beyond India's borders. Since 2008, it has provided security for Indian diplomatic stations in Afghanistan, including the embassy in Kabul and four consulates in Kandahar, Jalalabad, Herat, and Mazar-i-Sharif. Small units of ITBP and SSB personnel are also occasionally deployed abroad as part of United Nations operations.[19]

Given the varied nature of the ITBP's tasks, it should not be surprising that slightly more than half of its battalions are deployed at the border. Out of its total of 56 battalions, only 32 ITBP battalions are engaged in border duties. Eleven others are deployed for internal security, plus eight battalions working on anti-Naxal operations. Five more are reserved for rest and recuperation. Out of the SSB's 73 battalions, 55 are operationally deployed, including two National Disaster Response Force battalions. The remaining 18 are reserve battalions.

Issues of Control

For both the ITBP and the SSB, the expansion of duties has led to two parallel developments. On the one hand, duties that overlap with other organizations have led to struggles over control and resources. On the other hand, some argue that the resources and capabilities of CAPFs should be increased in line with their greater standing.

For instance, consider the role of the ITBP and its relationship with the Indian Army. The army has, at least since 1986, been asking for operational command of the ITBP—especially since 1999, when a Chinese intrusion at Chip Chap in the Daulat Beg Oldi sector was reported after Indian troops had been diverted to the Kargil conflict with Pakistan. The army contends that its XIV Corps, based at Leh, Ladakh, should be in charge of all forces in the area.[20] The issue has given rise to an intra-governmental conflict that the political class has so far avoided addressing.[21] The MHA, to which all CAPFs report, has blocked the army's request on the grounds that peacetime border management should be carried out by central government police forces according to international norms. The army, the MHA claims, should deployed only in situations of actual war.[22]

One common refrain, often voiced by retired army officers, is that deploying the ITBP on the Line of Actual Control (LAC) sends the wrong message to the Chinese, who interpret it as an unstated declaration by India that it does not see the LAC as a high-enough priority for the army. This, they imply, only encourages Chinese adventurism. By contrast, the Indian government's reluctance has been attributed to fears that China would consider the army's presence to be excessively belligerent.[23] The MHA's reluctance has also been ascribed to the 'underlying resistance of the IPS [Indian Police Service] lobby to serve under any commander from the Army'. This resistance, it is argued, emerged despite the presence of many young ITBP cadre officers, who supposedly understood the value of operating under the army.[24] However, it is extremely unlikely that ITBP cadre officers—who are already resentful that they are unable to progress to the highest echelons of their own service because of the IPS presence—would be happy to add another layer of command. In fact, the principal rationale for keeping the two forces separate, according to the MHA, is to ensure that there is a system of checks and balances. Separate corroboration of facts by the two services would be undercut by putting the ITBP under the army's control.

Meanwhile, the parliamentary record shows that questions have been frequently raised about merging the ITBP or SSB with another CAPF—or even with each other. In March 2020, in response to a question jointly raised by five members of parliament in the Lok Sabha on the possibility of combining the ITBP and the SSB, the government replied that, while such an idea was mooted and 'informal consultations were held', no such proposal was under consideration 'at present'.[25] Despite these discussions, the plan's logic has never been apparent to the forces' themselves, given the declared government policy of 'one border, one force'.[26]

Personnel and Working Conditions

The ITBP and the SSB are divided into a number of different cadres. The General Duty cadre (GD) is the largest and most important component in both forces, supported by, among others, the Communication, Engineering, Ministerial, Motor Transport and Mechanics, Medical Officers, and Para-Medical cadres.

The recruitment processes for the ITBP and the SSB are broadly similar. The posts of constable (GD) and sub-inspector (GD) are handled by the Staff Selection Commission (SSC). The post of assistant commandant (GD) has been filled by the Union Public Service Commission (UPSC) since 2003.[27] To fill vacancies in paramilitary forces, one appointed CAPF serves as the hub, collating vacancies across all the CAPFs and reporting them to the appropriate recruitment agency, such as the SSC or the UPSC. Recruitment of tradesmen and all posts other than GD—such as communication, ministerial, education, stenographer, paramedical, and compassionate appointments in the two paramilitaries—is done at the respective departmental levels. Vacancies against promotions are supposed to be filled up by the Departmental Promotion Committee annually, per India's recruitment rules. The top echelons of both CAPFs are dominated by the IPS—about 80 per cent of the deputy inspector general positions belong to cadre officers, while the rest go to IPS officers. One rung above, at the inspector general rank, the breakdown is 50 per cent from each. Finally, the top jobs—director general and additional director general—are filled only by IPS officers. This causes much consternation among cadre officers in both organizations and is a consistent source of low morale and motivation. To add insult to injury, IPS officers joining a paramilitary are not required to undergo any sort of specialized training. For example, officers entering the ITBP do not necessarily have any training or skills in keeping with the organization's specialized role in the mountains and along the LAC.

The rank structure of both the ITBP and the SSB, in decreasing order of ranks, is given in Table 8.1.

The 2018 report of the Parliamentary Standing Committee, in fact, highlighted several serious problems in the way resources and incentives were made available and structured. Lack of promotional avenues and stagnation were a significant problem at multiple ranks in both the ITBP and the SSB.

Despite vacancies being notified, the committee pointed out that the MHA had not managed to fill them in the case of both CAPFs, with vacancies ranging from 7 per cent in the ITBP to 18 per cent in the SSB as of January 2019. Table 8.2 illustrates the difference between mandated time and actual time for promotions in the SSB GD cadre.

Table 8.1 Rank Structure of the ITBP and the SSB

Gazetted Officers
Director General
Additional Director General
Inspector General
Deputy Inspector General
Commandant
Second in Command (2I/C)
Deputy Commandant
Assistant Commandant

Subordinate Officers
Subedar Major
Inspector
Sub Inspector
Assistant Sub Inspector

Under Officers
Head Constable[a]

Enrolled Persons Other than Under Officers
Constable[b]

---

[a]There are also personnel in the ranks of Naik and Lance Naik below that of the Head Constable but these are holdovers of an earlier system and include those out of the reckoning for promotion due to injuries or medical conditions and waiting to complete their term of service.

[b]There used to be a category called "enrolled followers" that comprised such positions as the water carriers, for example. This category of the Group D services has now been abolished and recruitment starts directly at the Constable level.

The committee pointed out that despite the ITBP and the SSB both being in expansion mode, there was still some stagnation—namely, at the ranks of ITBP constable and assistant sub inspector, and SSB constable and head constable. In the ITBP, a constable in the GD cadre took 12 to 13 years to get promoted to the post of head constable instead of the mandatory five years, while it could take up to 10 years (instead of the required 6) for an assistant sub inspector (GD) to be promoted to sub inspector (GD). In the SSB, a constable had to wait 11 to 12 years to get promoted to the post of head constable—despite being told it would only take eight

Table 8.2 Promotions in the SSB

Promotional avenue available	Residency period	Actual time taken
Constable (GD) to Head Constable (GD)	8 years	11–12 years
Head Constable (GD) to Assistant Sub Inspector (GD)	5 years	8–10 years
Assistant Sub Inspector (GD) to Sub Inspector (GD)	6 years	6 years
Sub Inspector (GD) to Inspector (GD)	5 years	5–6 years
Inspector (GD) to Assistant Commandant (GD)	5 years	5–6 years
Assistant Commandant (GD) to DC	6 years	6 years
Deputy Commandant to Second in Command (2I/C)	5 years	5 years
Second in Command to Commandant	5 years	5 years
Commandant to Deputy Inspector General	3 years	3–4 years
Deputy Inspector General to Inspector General	4 years	6–7 years

years. Similarly, it took another eight to 10 years for a head constable to then become an assistant sub inspector, despite the required residency period being only five years. Explanations proffered by the MHA for delays in the SSB left the committee entirely unsatisfied.

In general, the problems with promotions and other anomalies in the command structure can be attributed to the lack of oversight. Despite the Department of Personnel and Training's existing guidelines that say cadre review should be carried out every five years, there has been no comprehensive cadre review of the SSB since its inception in 1963. By the ministry's own admission, there have only been partial reviews in 2011 and 2015. The ITBP's last cadre review was completed in 2019—nearly two decades after the previous review was held in 2001. Besides the problem that cadre reviews have been timed irregularly, they have also failed to account for changing requirements or circumstances—even when changes are announced, they have not been implemented.[28]

It is not surprising, then, that attrition is a serious issue in both organizations. Personnel leaving the SSB, either through voluntary retirement or resignation, cite reasons such as residing too long away from family, the inability to keep family at border outposts (BOPs), the lack of family accommodation at some battalion headquarters, and absence of proper education facilities for children. Better job prospects, family or personal illnesses, and other social and familial obligations were also commonly cited as reasons for exiting the force. To the former, the MHA has pointed out that several resignations were the result of young officers passing examinations for other services, including the Civil Services. The MHA attributed the massive increase in voluntary retirements among subordinate officers in 2016 and 2017 (see Table 8.3) to personnel waiting for the Seventh Central Pay Commission in order to leave with better benefits.

However, the number of resignations across the ranks has kept steady pace for many years, indicating that service conditions—including the lack of pay parity with other government services—were likely as much a factor in 2016 and 2017 as waiting for Pay Commission benefits. One notable exception is women, who have largely forgone voluntary retirement or resignation. While attrition in the ITBP is comparatively much lower, there was a parallel spike in voluntary retirement at the subordinate officer level in 2017, which has similarly been attributed to personnel waiting for the terms of the next Pay Commission.

An important aspect of working conditions in the two organizations is their grievance redressal mechanism.[29] Within the SSB, complaints largely pertained to accounts management, domestic problems, medical issues, transfer/service issues, promotions, and even uniforms. The ITBP, however, presents additional challenges.

The MHA's presentation to the Parliamentary Standing Committee offered details of various redressal mechanisms available to members of the ITBP, stating that only 27 out of 518 grievances received through their online portal were still pending resolution. Upon questioning by the committee, however, a specific problem became evident: dissatisfaction with India's new pension scheme.

From the ITBP's point of view, the problem is that the Indian Army—with which it operates in close quarters along the LAC—continues to enjoy the benefits of the old pension scheme. Within the ranks of the CAPFs, however, the new pension scheme has proven to be a major grievance—as has the lack of adequate feedback mechanisms or accountability from the leadership. Although the MHA claims that it has received only one online request for the old pension scheme to be restored, numerous complaints about the new pension scheme have been raised at the *sainik sabhas* (similar to town halls for CAPF personnel).[30]

Table 8.3 Voluntary Retirement and Resignation in the SSB

Year	Voluntary Retirement						
	Gazetted Officers		Subordinate Officers		Other Ranks		Total
	Male	Female	Male	Female	Male	Female	
2010	7	0	49	0	391	0	447
2011	1	0	35	1	276	0	313
2012	4	0	62	0	381	0	447
2013	13	0	56	1	269	2	341
2014	2	0	42	0	202	0	246
2015	1	0	13	0	47	0	61
2016	5	0	121	0	150	1	277
2017	8	0	232	0	248	2	490

Year	Resignation						
	Gazetted Officers		Subordinate Officers		Other Ranks		Total
	Male	Female	Male	Female	Male	Female	
2010	5	1	18	0	159	1	184
2011	6	0	7	0	93	6	112
2012	6	1	13	0	98	3	121
2013	12	0	32	0	85	0	129
2014	19	0	16	0	82	1	118
2015	17	2	18	0	84	1	122
2016	9	0	7	0	62	1	79
2017	10	0	5	1	41	1	58

Source: Standing Committee on Home Affairs, *Working Conditions in Border-Guarding Forces (Assam Rifles, Sashastra Seema Bal, Indo-Tibetan Border Police and Border Security Force)*, 214th Report, Rajya Sabha Secretariat, https://rajyasabha.nic.in/rsnew/Committee_site/Committee_File/ReportFile/15/107/214_2018_12_15.pdf.

Apparently, the availability of online grievance mechanisms does not necessarily guarantee accessibility.[31]

The committee's call for the ITBP's grievance mechanism to be 'robust' and for the mechanism to 'reflect a system of speedy and fair adjudication of grievances without delay' suggests that it perceived problems beyond what the MHA and the ITBP leadership presented. The committee specifically pointed out that a 'fair redressal of grievance of ITBP personnel would go a long way in motivating the force to face the challenging task and discharge entrusted duties without any worry and concern'.

Finally, postings remain a source of tension. Upon completing the required tenure at posts deemed 'hard areas' and 'extreme hard areas', CAPF personnel can utilize a built-in mechanism to request a transfer to a place of choice, depending on availability. However, at the deputy inspector general rank and above, non-field postings are usually monopolized by the IPS. Another issue is that units that are supposed to be on rest and recuperation are often diverted to internal security duties. Personnel returning from postings to challenging environments rarely get their mandated break or time for training.[32] The SSB, at least, has come up with an effective workaround: battalions are reconstituted for deployment in such a way that a third of the personnel have the opportunity to recuperate from a hard posting on rotation.[33]

Lacking the Basics

In their report, the Parliamentary Standing Committee detailed the ITBP's weapons and combat aid equipment, including bullet-resistant jackets and helmets, high-powered sport utility vehicles, mini excavators, clothing, and equipment for extreme cold and mountaineering equipment. (The report did not cover the status of the SSB's equipment.) The ITBP leadership sought to convey that their force was well equipped, with surveillance equipment, unmanned aerial vehicles, mine detectors, and explosive detection kits in use in Naxal-affected areas. Nevertheless, the committee declared itself 'extremely anguished to note that the ITBP... have not been equipped with basic training gadgets and facilities'.

Indeed, questions about the ITBP's lack of basic equipment are not new. Elsewhere, deficiencies in the supply of equipment have been acknowledged but ascribed to orders passed by the Ministry of Finance, such as a (subsequently lifted) 'ban on purchase of vehicles against condemned vehicles'.[34] Overall, however, many of these problems appear to have been resolved—for now.[35]

Other problems that impact retention rates—namely tough working conditions and poor or no facilities for housing and family stay—deserve closer attention. Issues range from the availability of regular medical facilities in distant BOPs,[36] the poor quality of food,[37] inadequate supply of electricity, and the lack of housing or accommodation for ITBP and SSB personnel. One acute problem is the lack of 'separated family accommodation', which means the families of personnel serving at BOPs or in the field are unable to make use of educational opportunities for their children.[38] Given the location of most SSB outposts, some argue that family accommodation should actually be built on site instead of requiring families to stay at the battalion headquarters.[39]

The lack of roads and telecommunication facilities was specifically highlighted as a problem for the ITBP. (The SSB, which operates along borders that are somewhat more amenable to physical infrastructure and habitation, has not reported similar issues.)

As of the end of 2018, nearly half of ITBP outposts—79 out of 177—were not connected by road.[40] Of the 73 road projects along the India–China boundary that the Indian government has identified as strategically necessary,[41] 25 are ITBP Priority Phase I roads but only 13 have been completed.[42] Of the remaining 35 general staff roads, 14 had been completed by the end of 2018. And of the 13 roads recommended by the China Study Group, only five had been finished by the end of 2018.[43] Even as construction of the remaining roads continues, the ITBP has proposed nearly 100 new roads—46 roads under its Priority Phase II plan, plus another 50 border roads under Priority Phase III—which are designed to facilitate road connectivity to all existing BOPs, as well as 47 new outposts.

Regular and reliable telephone and Internet connectivity has long been unavailable at ITBP outposts. In areas along the LAC with no mobile telephone connectivity, digital satellite phone terminals and satellite phones are available to the ITBP. Each member of a unit is allotted a fixed amount of free phone time, after which additional calls cost money.[44] Meanwhile, as late as the end of 2018, a proposal to provide fibre-optic connectivity to all ITBP outposts had not made it past consideration and remains dependent on a national plan to connect all villages through fibre-optic networks.

Performance

Tensions along the LAC over the past decade have kept the ITBP on its toes. Despite the lack of physical access and infrastructure along the LAC—as well as the aforementioned problems with personnel—it appears that the ITBP carries out its duties effectively and efficiently.

Although the Indian Army's standing request for permanent control over the ITBP remains a point of tension, the record also indicates that the two organizations have been able to coordinate their operations smoothly. The two forces jointly patrol sensitive areas along the LAC, with the army serving as the primary decision-maker. Following serious clashes between Indian and Chinese troops along the LAC in eastern Ladakh in 2020, the army recommended several ITBP personnel for commendations and gallantry medals.[45]

Along the India–Nepal border, there has so far been a high degree of cooperation between the SSB and Nepal's Armed Police Force (APF). But bilateral relations with Nepal have been affected, especially since the fuel blockade imposed by the Indian government in 2015[46] and Kathmandu's decision to release a new national map that showed parts of Uttarakhand State as Nepalese territory in 2020.[47] Tensions can be expected to increase here too.

Indeed, a question was raised in the Rajya Sabha over a reported clash in March 2017 between SSB personnel and Nepalese people at Lakhimpur Kheri on the Indo-Nepalese border. The apparent *casus belli* was Nepal's construction of a culvert in no man's land near a border pillar bridge. Individuals on the Nepalese side pelted SSB personnel with stones, but tensions were diffused after discussions by officials on both sides.[48] In 2020, multiple reported incidents involved SSB personnel at the India–Nepal boundary. Two Indians were shot and killed by the APF in separate incidents in July 2020, while Nepalese locals were accused of conniving with their local administration to erect fences on Indian territory.[49]

These incidents—which, until quite recently, were resolved by local authorities and, in many cases, continue to be solved the same way—are also now receiving greater media attention in both countries. The deterioration of bilateral ties mean such incidents could become intractable. Under the circumstances, the SSB's role along the border with Nepal will likely become both more challenging and more sensitive.

Meanwhile, it is entirely unclear whether the ITBP and the SSB are also effective in their non-core roles, such as in internal security duties. In fact, it is not even clear whether these roles are even assessed within the respective organizations or, if they are, what the criteria for success might be.

Training

Both the ITBP and the SSB have several training institutions across the country.[50] All ranks undergo about a year of basic training before they are operationally deployed. To be promoted, personnel must complete all the requisite courses for the next rank. But mission creep has meant that ITBP and SSB personnel have nearly as wide a training regime as the regular armed forces—from counter-insurgency and jungle warfare to high-altitude training and snow-craft to the handing of explosives. To train, the SSB must liaise closely with other government agencies including state police departments and the Indian Army. The ITBP, on the other hand, appears somewhat more self-sufficient and, in fact, trains personnel from other government agencies.

Psychological operations and perception management are largely absent from the SSB's list of specialized training programmes made available to senior and subordinate officers. These were part of the organization's original duties and surely remain important. In general, though, training in both forces appears slanted heavily in favour of physical fitness, while intellectual tasks receive less attention. Although modules from the Indian Institute of Management Indore and the Ministry of Defence-led Institute for Defence Studies and Analyses form part of the ITBP's Higher Strategic and Senior Management Courses, the lack of adequate language training should be worrying for the force. Familiarity with Tibetan and multiple dialects of Chinese will be essential if the organization is to carry out its lead intelligence agency role in full, or even simply to soothe tensions during crises on the ground.[51]

The Parliamentary Standing Committee report was, however, more concerned about the need 'to strengthen and rationalize the training regimes for CAPFs to handle new internal security challenges', suggesting that neither the duration of specialized training nor the capacity of SSB training institutions seemed adequate. It did not question what a force tasked with the security of a particular international border was doing tackling internal security challenges. In fact, both services have complained that continuous deployment on internal security duties have meant that even the one company within a battalion that is supposed to be on training is not spared any time.[52]

Conclusion

Considering the ITBP's and the SSB's place in India's national security architecture, there are at least three distinct issues that need greater attention as one looks to the future.

The first is state capacity itself. Overall, it can be argued that the ITBP and the SSB have adequately performed the tasks allotted to them, despite many constraints. The question remains whether they could do better if mission creep were eliminated and they were allowed to devote greater time, resources, and training to their primary tasks. In many ways, the use of the ITBP and the SSB for internal security duties reflects both the existence of state capacity (in terms of numbers to throw at a problem) as well as its absence (evidenced by the regular central or state government agencies' inability to handle certain situations, which necessitate additional deployment from CAPFs).

State capacity—or lack thereof—is also evident in the ITBP's and the SSB's issues with vacancies and stagnation in the ranks. Though there is ample capacity to assess requirements while drawing up budgets and sanctioned strengths, there is simultaneously an inability to actually conduct recruitment and implement rational and satisfactory promotion policies.

The second issue pertains to governance and human resources management within the CAPFs. The high degree of dissatisfaction with working conditions among the rank-and-file should be a major concern for policymakers in the MHA. Despite the ITBP and the SSB each being the equivalent in size to other countries' standing armies, there does not appear to be adequate thought given to planning, training, and staffing for the long term. The situation is aggravated by IPS officers who parachute in at the highest ranks; there is strong demand within both CAPFs for cadre officers to fill the upper echelons of leadership. In general, and as the 2018 Parliamentary Standing Committee report hints at, the IPS seems to suffer from a lack of empathy and commitment to addressing conditions within the CAPFs except in the most pro forma manner.

Cadre officers of the ITBP and the SSB have turned to the courts to achieve parity with Organized Group 'A' Services, especially their provision of Non-Functional Financial Upgradation (NFFU)—a perk that allows officers to receive salary raises even when they cannot be promoted due to the lack of vacancies.[53] However, although the Supreme Court upheld a 2019 decision by the Delhi High Court to bring the CAPFs under the Organized Group 'A' Services with access to NFFU,[54] implementation of this ruling has not yet begun. Unsurprisingly, this has been attributed to IPS officers who would rather preserve their privileges and postings on deputation in the various paramilitaries.[55] Even the committee's 2018 report did not directly address the NFFU question.

The third issue is of the role of the ITBP and the SSB in India's external security policies.

As India's bilateral relationships with neighbours China and Nepal deteriorate, the operational capabilities of the ITBP and the SSB will be increasingly put to the test. Given the qualitative change in the nature of confrontation between the Indian and Chinese armies in the summer of 2020 along the LAC in eastern Ladakh, it is time for the government to decide the nature and status of the LAC—is it still a peaceful border to be manned by the ITBP? Or is it now an active border with high potential for repeated violent clashes? If the latter is true, operational control over the ITBP could be shifted to the army. Any increase in the Indian Army's capabilities along the LAC in response to Chinese actions, must, in the interests of both balance and efficacy, be accompanied by a boost to the ITBP as well. This would require inter-agency and inter-ministerial coordination on a number of fronts. However, such a debate is yet to be fully joined in the public domain.[56]

While national security is always highlighted as a top priority of the central government, there appears to be little consideration of the specialized roles assigned to CAPFs or the skills they have developed. It is easier to throw available battalions at the next security problem that comes across policymakers' desks—whether it be left-wing insurgency or security for diplomatic establishments—than it is to question why forces originally raised for specialized border management have expanded well beyond past their original remit. Overall, rather than considering the rational design, structure, and expansion of these organizations, the government seems to prefer an ad hoc approach to the ITBP and the SSB. Naturally, national security policymaking will suffer the consequences.

Notes

1. This is the only security agency in India that goes by a name in Hindi, literally, "Armed Border Force".

2. Ministry of Home Affairs, "Indo-Tibetan Border Police—Home Page," ITBP official website, Last updated February 27, 2023, https://www.itbpolice.nic.in.

3. Sashastra Seema Bal, "Home Page," SSB official website, https://ssb.gov.in/.

4. Parliamentary Standing Committee on Home Affairs, *Working Conditions in Border Guarding Forces (Assam Rifles, Sashastra Seema Bal, Indo-Tibetan Border Police and Border Security Force)*, Report No. 214, December 12, 2018, https://raj yasabha.nic.in/rsnew/Committee_site/Committee_File/ReportFile/15/107/214 _2018_12_15.pdf.

5. Ministry of Home Affairs, *Annual Report, 2018–19*, (New Delhi: Government of India, 2019), https://www.mha.gov.in/sites/default/files/AnnualReport_English_ 01102019.pdf / https://www.itbpolice.nic.in/somepdfs/Citizen%20Charter.pdf.

6. The specialist battalions are deputed to the National Disaster Response Force.

7. Bureau of Police Research and Development, Ministry of Home Affairs, *Data on Police Organisations in India* (New Delhi: Government of India, 2020), 34, https:// bprd.nic.in/WriteReadData/userfiles/file/202101011201011648364DOPO01012 020.pdf.

8. Bureau of Police Research and Development, Ministry of Home Affairs, *Data on Police Organisations in India* (New Delhi: Government of India, 2020), 34, https:// bprd.nic.in/WriteReadData/userfiles/file/202101011201011648364DOPO01012 020.pdf.

9. It was reported in March 2021 that the government had sanctioned the raising of another 12 battalions, https://theprint.in/defence/govt-sanctions-12-new-ssb-battalions-to-fortify-nepal-bhutan-borders-tri-junction-area/615268/.

10. Bureau of Police Research and Development, Ministry of Home Affairs, "Table 4.1.5: Budget and Expenditure of CAPFS for the Financial Year 2018-2019 (revised) & Financial Year 2019–2020 (tentative) (Figures in Crores and Rupees)," in *Data on Police Organisations in India* (New Delhi: Government of India, 2020), 158, https://bprd.nic.in/WriteReadData/userfiles/file/2021010112 01011648364DOPO01012020.pdf.

11. Parliamentary Standing Committee on Home Affairs, *Working Conditions in Border Guarding Forces*.

12. What is termed as smuggling, it must be pointed out, is part of the general economic activity of the region that has carried on for generations across open borders. The SSB has, over time, refined its standard operating procedures to ensure greater sensitivity to local conditions and to prevent things from getting out of hand. Interview 3, 2020.

13. Ramashankar, "Officials Meet to Defuse Tension on Nepal Border," *The Times of India*, July 21, 2020, https://timesofindia.indiatimes.com/city/patna/officials-meet-to-defuse-tension-on-nepal-border/articleshow/77073711.cms.

14. "Security Beefed up on UP-Nepal Border for Ayodhya Event," *The Tribune India*, August 5, 2020, https://www.tribuneindia.com/news/nation/security-beefed-up-on-up-nepal-border-for-ayodhya-event-122445.

15. Lok Sabha, Unstarred Question No. 3333, July 28, 2009, https://eparlib.nic.in/bitstream/123456789/593860/1/73434.pdf.

16. Interview 1, 2020.

17. In its presentation before the Parliamentary Committee, stated that phasing the ITBP out of VIP protection duties was on the anvil.

18. Lok Sabha, Unstarred Question No. 3333, July 28, 2009, https://eparlib.nic.in/bitstream/123456789/593860/1/73434.pdf.

19. Lok Sabha, Unstarred Question No. 3286, December 6, 2016, https://eparlib.nic.in/bitstream/123456789/692093/1/44015.pdf. No contingent from the ITBP has been deployed in UN operations since 2019 when the ITBP contingent completed its deployment in the Democratic Republic of Congo in 2019. Interview 4, 2021.

20. Sujan Dutta, "Forget China Border. First Settle Domestic Row," *The Telegraph*, April 30, 2013, http://www.telegraphindia.com/1130430/jsp/nation/story_16843 423.jsp.

21. An exception is the Congress Party's 2019 election manifesto on national security written by former Northern Army Commander Lt. Gen. D. S. Hooda (retd) which reiterated the idea of 'one border, one force', with the army having operational control over the ITBP. The situation was 'not a recipe for success' according to the former senior military officer. "National Security Strategy for the Congress Manifesto by Gen Hooda," Indian National Congress, March 2019, https://www.scribd.com/document/407003561/National-Security-Strategy-for-the-Congress-Manifesto-by-Gen-Hooda#download.

22. The MoD too has been on record stating, "Border guarding forces are operationally placed under the Army only when security threat warrants it." https://eparlib.nic.in/bitstream/123456789/605667/1/108069.pdf

23. Sujan Dutta, "Forget China Border," April 30, 2013.

24. Quoted in Anil Bhat, "Management of Sino–Indian Ties on Table and Terrain," *Imphal Free Press*, May 28, 2013, http://kanglaonline.com/2013/05/management-of-sino-indian-ties-on-table-and-terrain/.

25. Lok Sabha, Unstarred Question No. 1944, March 3, 2020, http://164.100.24.220/loksabhaquestions/annex/173/AU1944.pdf.

26. Interviews, 2020. This policy is the result of the recommendations of the Kargil Review Commission.

27. The SSC and UPSC conduct combined examinations for all the CAPFs.

28. Interviews, 2020.

29. For an example of the apparent failure of this mechanism with specific reference to the BSF, see, https://www.youtube.com/watch?v=kStvsdivy0Y. See also with respect to the IA and other CAPFs, https://www.youtube.com/watch?v=qi7k dA4-xMM.

30. Interviews, 2020.

31. This is quite apart from security concerns about such networks. Unlike the SSB, the ITBP reports in detail about its initiatives in the domain of IT infrastructure and software applications, including the digitization of important processes such as Employee Personnel Information System, a grievance redressal application, a Vehicle Information System module, a Digital Budget Management System, Visitor's Management Software, E-Health Cards and so on with yet more applications under development.

32. In one particularly egregious instance, ITBP units were transferred from non-field areas to provide security for the Amarnath pilgrimage in 2017 as a temporary measure. The deployment was then extended owing to political tensions in the region and then for conduct of panchayat elections. It was two years before the ITBP units in question were pulled out of the state and then only onwards to their next field posting. Interview 2, 2020. In fact, this is simply part of a larger trend, where the deployment of CAPF battalions for internal security duties starts as temporary measure till the Central Reserve Police Force—under whose mandate internal security duties fall—can be deployed, but soon turns long term. Interviews, 2020.

33. Interview 3, 2020.

34. Rajya Sabha, Unstarred Question 379, November 26, 2014, https://rsdebate.nic.in/handle/123456789/642398?viewItem=search.

35. Interviews, 2020.

36. Consider the fact that there are well over 3,000 cases every year of SSB personnel falling ill because of water-borne diseases—enteric fever, diarrhoea, or dysentery, and viral hepatitis. Indeed, the lack of clean drinking water available at various BoPs is a serious issue—even Reverse Osmosis (RO) water filters are not available at all the BoPs, meaning that at many outposts' personnel were drinking groundwater contaminated by iron and arsenic.

37. For an infamous case involving the Border Security Force, see, *BBC News Hindi*. 2017. https://www.youtube.com/watch?v=kStvsdivy0Y

38. Interviews, 2020. The ITBP, for instance, has separated family accommodation only in three locations—Delhi, Dehra Dun, and Chandigarh.

39. Interview 3, 2020.

40. 180 as of October 2019. https://www.itbpolice.nic.in/PRO_new/Pro/Pro_doc/Raising%20Day%20Parade%202019.pdf

41. Standing Committee on Defence, Provision of All-Weather Road Connectivity under Border Roads Organisation (BRO) and Other Agencies up to International borders As Well As the Strategic Areas Including Approach Roads—An Appraisal, Report No. 50, Lok Sabha Secretariat, February 12, 2019, http://164.100.47.193/lsscommittee/Defence/16_Defence_50.pdf.

42. A later ITBP report of October 2019, however, puts the number at 11. https://www.itbpolice.nic.in/PRO_new/Pro/Pro_doc/Raising%20Day%20Parade%202019.pdf

43. Latest figures indicate that up to 60 roads of the 73 have been completed. https://www.itbpolice.nic.in/PRO_new/Pro/Pro_doc/Raising%20Day%20Parade%202019.pdf

44. The situation has considerably improved over the years—previously, an entire battalion would have to share a single satellite phone among its companies for several days at a time each. But even now, it appears to be the case that batteries can become faulty or run out leaving gaps in ability to communicate.

45. Interview 1, 2020.

46. "Nepal PM Wants India to Lift Undeclared Blockade," *NDTV*, November 15, 2015, https://www.ndtv.com/india-news/nepal-pm-wants-india-to-lift-undeclared-blockade-1243695.

47. Yubaraj Ghimire and Shubhajit Roy, "Nepal House Clears New Map Bill, Oli Calls for Talks, India Frosty in Response," *The Indian Express*, June 14, 2020, https://indianexpress.com/article/india/nepal-new-map-bill-india-response-6457736/.

48. Rajya Sabha, Unstarred Question 4452, April 12, 2017, https://rsdebate.nic.in/handle/123456789/673259

49. Kalyan Das, "Pillars Erected by Nepalese Citizens in No-Man's Land at India-Nepal Border Not Yet Removed," *Hindustan Times*, July 27, 2020, https://www.hindustantimes.com/dehradun/pillars-erected-by-nepalese-citizens-in-no-man-s-land-at-india-nepal-border-not-yet-removed/story-3FiAr14141HB3Ina3olK1K.html.

50. For a list of ITBP and SSB training institutions as well as others their personnel are sent to, see Bureau of Police Research and Development, Ministry of Home Affairs, *Data on Police Organisations in India* (New Delhi: Government of India, 2020), 226–27, https://bprd.nic.in/WriteReadData/userfiles/file/202101011201011648364DOPO01012020.pdf.

51. The situation is hardly better in the Indian Army itself though efforts have commenced in recent years to improve it.

52. Interviews, 2020.

53. The NFFU is an option by which if an officer of a particular year of entry into the Group A services gets promoted to the next rank, all Group A officers in the same year of entry will be upgraded to the same level in financial terms after two years from the date of the promotion, on a non-functional basis, that is, irrespective of whether they have been promoted or not. In the absence of NFFU as well as opportunities for promotion as shown here in the ITBP and SSB, but which is also the case in other CAPFs, officers in these services are doubly deprived.

54. Deeptiman Tiwary, "Give Paramilitary Officers Higher Grade Salary If You Can't Promote Them When Eligible: SC to Govt," *The Indian Express*, February 6, 2019, https://indianexpress.com/article/india/sc-upholds-hc-order-on-nffu-for-capf-officers-5571027/. See also Major Navdeep Singh, "Non-Functional Financial Upgradation and Today's Decision of the Supreme Court on it: An Explainer in Layperson Terms," *Bar & Bench*, February 5, 2019, https://www.barandbench.com/columns/non-functional-upgradation-capf-supreme-court-judgment.
55. Interviews, 2020.
56. See "At the Forefront, In the Background: The Indo-Tibetan Border Police in India's China Policymaking," ICS Wednesday Seminar, Institute of Chinese Studies, Delhi, June 16, 2021, https://www.youtube.com/watch?v=1aNyM3KMTMg.

9

The Border Security Force

Anirudh Deshpande

Introduction and History

In early May 1965, at a high level conference in Delhi, I was the lone voice from the police side to oppose the formation of the BSF. A few days later I was called to Delhi and asked to take over the responsibility of raising that force. I raised it and nurtured it for nine long years. To this day, I love the Force and my attachment for it is deep.

K.F. Rustamji
Founding Director General, BSF[1]

Nation states are defined and re-defined by their geographical, social, political, cultural, military, and, often, publicly imagined borders. In most cases, geography on the ground is quite different from what appears on official maps. And guarding these borders can be particularly difficult in some countries. In South Asia, the perception of borders is flexible— exemplified by the ill-defined Line of Actual Control (LAC) between India and China and the contested Line of Control (LoC) that separates India and Pakistan. To the battalions of the Border Security Force (BSF), stationed at inhospitable border outposts with their weapons and cold rations for company, the border is a live entity.

The nation state in South Asia is a colonial legacy. The partition of the Indian subcontinent was hastily executed by a boundary commission headed by an Englishman with no local experience. The China–India border is influenced by the contentious McMahon Line and colonial treaties between Tibet and Britain. Two centuries of colonial rule in South Asia altered the geographical, material, and intellectual conditions in the

Anirudh Deshpande, *The Border Security Force* In: *Institutional Roots of India's Security Policy.* Edited by: Milan Vaishnav, Oxford University Press. © Oxford University Press 2024. DOI: 10.1093/oso/9780198894612.003.0009 region. As a consequence, India in 1947 was left with two important *sets* of borders to settle.

This chapter provides an assessment of the BSF, from its origins in the mid-1960s to the present day. It begins by providing an overview of the context in which the BSF was created, tracing its evolution from the 1962 China–India war to the 1971 Bangladesh crisis to its expansion to non-traditional missions in more recent years. It then pivots to providing an organizational profile of the force, which is followed by detailed examinations of its recruitment procedures, training regimen, and human-resource management. The next two sections look at how the BSF has been used to win "hearts and minds" in border areas and its successes and failures in modernizing its force. The chapter concludes by providing a macro-assessment of its performance over six decades and priorities for reform.

The Formation of the BSF

Before the BSF was formed in 1965, the police forces of India's border states were entrusted with guarding their own borders. In an emergency, these forces were backstopped in an ad hoc fashion by units of the Indian Army and Central Reserve Police Force (CRPF) personnel. These state police forces usually dealt with trans-border crimes like cattle theft, abductions, murders, smuggling, land disputes, and incursions by foreign troops. Their system of border policing, later inherited and refined by the BSF, was based on establishing border outposts at regular distances or sensitive points and around-the-clock patrolling by typically ill-equipped armed border guards. Given their limited training and resources, state police forces performed as well as they could have under suboptimal conditions.

But the difficult circumstances created by the division of the Indian subcontinent in 1947 opened India's borders to a serious threat of infiltration. The ease with which criminals and gangs carried out the communal massacres of 1947 across states obviously serves as an important qualification. The country-wide events of 1946–8 exposed many flaws in the border policing arrangements of India's erstwhile princely states. Ultimately, as experiences especially in Kashmir and Gujarat proved, these forces were incapable of satisfactorily protecting India's borders against politically and militarily determined adversaries. State border forces were understaffed and financially under-resourced, carried obsolete weapons, and were improperly trained and disciplined for the task assigned them.[2]

The inadequacies of these border policing arrangements, highlighted by the Sino-Indian War in 1962, came to the fore in the border crises of 1965—the year in which the first full-scale *declared* war between India and Pakistan occurred. Available literature on the subject suggests that after the death of Prime Minister Jawaharlal Nehru in 1964, India's political future appeared uncertain. This provided a new opening to Pakistan, whose attempt in 1947–8 to seize the Kashmir Valley had been foiled by the Indian Army and the Kashmiri people. Consequently, Pakistani forces tried to re-draw the India–Pakistan border in the Rann of Kutch (in the state of Gujarat). When the Pakistani incursions began in January 1965, the State Reserve Police (SRP) proved too weak to fend off its better-armed adversary. Companies of the CRPF were rushed in to deal with the situation. These too proved inadequate. Finally, the Indian Army was deployed to repulse the invasion and restore the Indian national border in Gujarat. Had the army not been deployed in time, India would have ceded considerable territory to Pakistan. These incidents, as well as the lessons of 1962, highlighted the need for better border security; within a year, the BSF was raised.

In January 1965, under Prime Minister Lal Bahadur Shastri's overall supervision, the Emergency Committee of Secretaries set up a study group to examine 'the possibility of streamlining and reducing the multiplicity of para-military forces in border areas'.[3] Led by Lieutenant General Paramasiva Prabkhar Kumaramangalam, Vice Chief of the Indian Army, the study group submitted its report to the government in April 1965. This report was examined by General J.N. Chaudhari and Home Secretary Shri L.P. Singh, who together prepared the blueprint for the BSF.

After Pakistan's aggression in the Rann of Kutch, it had been decided that a 'small group consisting of an officer of high standing nominated by the Chief of the Army Staff, a Joint Secretary of the Home Ministry and the Inspector General of Police on Special Duty in the Home Ministry should go into the question of co-ordination and control of border security arrangements immediately'.[4] This was the second group of experts set up to advise the government on border issues. In early May 1965, a meeting of the home ministers and police chiefs of all the Indian States was held at the behest of the prime minister in Delhi. This meeting concluded with the prime minister's decision to raise a new central force dedicated to India's border defence.

In the end, the reports of both study groups were merged and submitted to an ad hoc group of secretaries, which met in New Delhi in November 1965. This committee examined the merged documents and came to 'certain conclusions' which formed the basis for the establishment of the BSF.

The tumultuous events of 1965 ultimately led to the official establishment of the BSF on 1 December 1965, under the leadership of its founding director general, the distinguished police officer K.F. Rustamji. The memorandum presented to the Committee of Secretaries earlier had included various details regarding the strength and deployment of the BSF. Particular attention was paid to the 'case of Punjab, Rajasthan and Gujarat', which comprised the border with West Pakistan. The BSF, it was planned, would not only protect the border with Pakistan but also instill greater confidence in the border population.[5]

The founders of the BSF were clear that establishing a special service to serve India's border needs 'would also enable the Army to keep away from the Border even in periods of some degree of tension'.[6] This would give security 'in depth' to the country. Just as the border conflicts with Pakistan had guided the process of raising the BSF, the state police's poor showing against the Pakistani Army informed the minimum number of battalions and critical equipment the BSF would need. Additional strength and reserve battalions were also mentioned in the memorandum.

Due to India's disturbed political conditions at the time, no men from the central forces could be released to raise the new battalions of the fledgling BSF. Hence, it was assumed, that the BSF would initially rely on available border state police battalions and reserves. Their poor training, inadequate equipment, and unsuitable manpower made Rustamji's task unenviable.[7]

Raising the BSF meant working with heterogeneous men and material and converting the whole mass into a competent, cohesive service. This was easier said than done.[8] The task of raising the foundational battalions of the BSF accompanied the work of finding suitable officers to lead them.

Emergency commissioned officers, who had served in the Indian Army during the 1962 crisis and the war of 1965, proved most suitable—the 'experience that these boys had acquired in the army was invaluable' to the young BSF.[9] From their ranks, 300 officers were selected to lead the first BSF battalions. Senior officers from the Indian Police Service (IPS) joined the service later.

From the outset, General Chaudhari opposed the idea of the BSF developing its officer corps from the Indian Army. The far-sighted general did not want the army to develop hegemony over the BSF, thereby eroding its peculiar character. Further, a group of army officers commanding a force independent of the army could, in the future, emerge as a challenge to democracy. Chaudhari thought the separation of duties between the army—primarily a combat organization—and the BSF—whose main role was border protection, not fighting an enemy army—was crucial.

Earlier, Rustamji had formed a team of senior officers who made up a sort of original general staff of the BSF, including reknown officers like Ranjit Singh, P.R. Rajgopal, K. Ramamurti, P.A. Rosha, Rajdeo Singh, Ran Singh, and R.S. Rathore. The BSF high command comprised Ashwini Kumar in Jalandhar, Ram Gopal in Srinagar, and P.K. Basu and Golak Majumdar in Kolkata. This team was 'full of ideas' and 'innovation'.[10] The officers, handpicked by the experienced Rustamji, on the basis of demonstrating 'courage that is not affected by rumors or setbacks, strength of mind to judge and not be stricken by panic at any important moment, health, mental ability and educational background and finally, the ability to be a leader of men'.[11] The inspiration here was the Indian Army, which, since the colonial period, has been considered an apolitical, secular, thoroughly professional and, therefore, reliable organization.

Grooming the service in its formative years was not easy. It depended on the cooperation of the Ministry of Finance, the Ministry of Home Affairs (MHA), and the men and officers of the BSF. Though funds in rupees were easily forthcoming, the economic conditions of the 1960s made it clear that foreign exchange for weapons or communications technology would not be available. This 'proved to be a blessing in disguise' because the technicians of the BSF were able to improvise the technology at their disposal and 'revolutionized the concepts in radio'—a remarkable feat for the young, cash-strapped service.

Special workshops and factories were set up to overcome the shortage of arms. In Tekanpur, the BSF started its own rocket programme. Under the guidance of eminent scientists like Vikram Sarabhai and future President of India A.P.J. Abdul Kalam, the BSF developed rockets with a range of 20 kilometres. Later research enabled the BSF to fire 'a rocket ninety kilometers from the base' in Pokharan.[12]

The war with Pakistan and the creation of Bangladesh in December 1971 were pivotal for the BSF. During the war, the BSF fought and 'fell shoulder to shoulder with the Army'. Although the BSF functioned under a separate enactment, its officers received commissions from the president. Prime Minister Indira Gandhi described 'their contribution to the war of liberation' as 'crucial', mentioning the BSF alongside the army, navy, and air force in her historic remarks on 16 December 1971 after Pakistan's surrender at Dacca.[13] The war, however, also underlined the need for a reorientation of the service. The events of 1971 had proved that the main aim of the BSF 'should not be frontal attacks on the enemy'. Instead, it should focus on making 'forward movements in such a manner that the great advantage that they have in the knowledge of the ground and local contacts would be' helpful. This required the 'ability to move fast and correctly over broken ground and the ability to use explosives and possess leadership at a lower level of such imaginative and aggressive nature that it can do the task allotted to it'.[14]

The BSF Beyond 1971

Though the BSF was created and trained to guard India's borders, it has been used by the MHA for various operations inside and outside of India. Soon after its foundation, it was put into action breaking a Delhi police strike in 1967. During the 1969 Gujarat riots and the 1989 Bhagalpur riots, the BSF deployed on short notice to bring the situation under control. They even organized community kitchens for displaced survivors.[15] During the 1974 railway strike, which threatened to disrupt commercial and non-commercial rail traffic throughout the country, the BSF successfully kept India's trains moving.

Since 1989, BSF battalions have been deployed against Islamist insurgents in Jammu and Kashmir and Maoist guerillas in the jungle tracts of central and eastern India. The BSF was also active against Khalistani terrorism in the Punjab (1989–1993) and in counter-insurgency operations in north-east India. In Kashmir, Punjab, and the north-east, the service has contended simultaneously with terrorism, smuggling, and border security. During the Kargil War (Operation Vijay), it informed the army about the intrusions at the Zojila Pass in March 1999 and helped recapture the peaks in July 1999.[16] The BSF also proved its credentials and operational efficiency during Operation Parakram, the stand-off between India and Pakistan in 2001–02.[17]

The BSF, between 1965 and thepresent, has expanded its duties far beyond border defence—from internal security to disaster management and United Nations peacekeeping missions abroad. Consequently, in response to its changing needs, the BSF has evolved into a multifaceted, quasi-military force. The contemporary BSF has developed its own artillery, air wing, surveillance equipment, water wing, and a veterinary section (which takes care of guard dogs, sniffer dogs, and camels in the Rajasthani and Gujarati deserts).[18] Having learned valuable lessons in counter-insurgency operations and urban warfare, the BSF has also raised its own commando units. Since its modest beginnings, the BSF has evolved into the largest border-guarding force in the world.

Organizational Profile

The BSF was accorded parliamentary legitimacy through the Border Security Force Act of 1968. Functioning under the MHA,[19] its duties and responsibilities can broadly be categorized into peacetime, wartime, and additional functions.

As a part of its peacetime role, the BSF seeks to promote a sense of security among people living in border areas and to prevent trans-border crime, including unauthorized entry or exit, smuggling, and other illegal activities. Its wartime functions include holding ground in less-threatened sectors, protecting vital installations (particularly airfields), extending the flanks of the army's main line of defence, and limited aggressive action against paramilitary or irregular forces.[20] The BSF may also be called upon to perform additional functions. These include internal security duties, election duties, counter-insurgency operations,

Table 9.1 Expansion and Evolution of the BSF's Strength and Structure

1965 (September 1)	25.5 battalions from border states form the initial ranks of the BSF
1965 (December 1)	BSF is formally raised
1966	19 additional battalions sanctioned
1967	8 more battalions sanctioned; the BSF stands at 52.5 battalions
1967	The BSF's 52.5 battalions are reorganized into 60 battalions, each with 6 service companies, 1 support company, and 1 headquarters company
1971	The first post group artillery regiment is formed
1972–1983	11 additional battalions are sanctioned, with significant additions made after the BSF's involvement in counter-insurgency duties in Punjab
1986	54 new battalions are sanctioned—25 for the western border and 29 for the eastern border
1990–1996	Amid rising insurgency in Jammu and Kashmir, 18 more battalions are raised for a total of 157 battalions.
2009–2016	29 new battalions are sanctioned, bringing the BSF's total sanctioned strength to 186 battalions—150 border-guarding battalions, 30 reserve battalions, 3 disaster management battalions, and 1 marine battalion

Source: Formulated on the basis of information found in Deshpande, *Border Security Force.*

anti-Naxalite operations, and disaster management and relief (see Table 9.1 for an overview of the BSF's expansion and evolution over the years).[21]

Raised in 1965 with an initial strength of 25 battalions and three companies, the BSF has grown dramatically over the past six decades (Figure 9.1 describes its organizational structure). According to the MHA's 2019–20 annual report, the force currently stands at 193 battalions, including four National Disaster Response Force battalions. Headquartered in New Delhi, its field formations include two special directorates general (Eastern Command and Western Command), a command headquarters for special operations at Raipur, 13 frontier headquarters, and 46 sector headquarters, in addition to its water wing, air wing, and other ancillary units.[22]

The Special Director General of the Western Command supervises the frontiers of Srinagar, Jammu, Punjab, Rajasthan, and Gujarat. The Special Director General of the Eastern Command is responsible for the frontiers of South Bengal, North Bengal, Shillong, Silchar, Tripura,

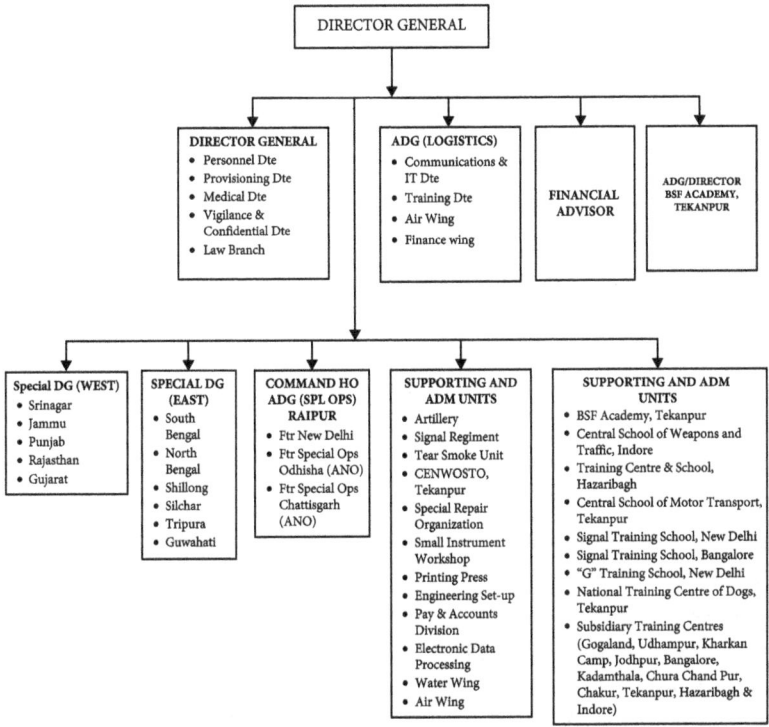

DIRECTOR GENERAL

DIRECTOR GENERAL	ADG (LOGISTICS)	FINANCIAL ADVISOR	ADG/DIRECTOR BSF ACADEMY, TEKANPUR
• Personnel Dte • Provisioning Dte • Medical Dte • Vigilance & Confidential Dte • Law Branch	• Communications & IT Dte • Training Dte • Air Wing • Finance wing		

Special DG (WEST)	SPECIAL DG (EAST)	COMMAND HO ADG (SPL OPS) RAIPUR	SUPPORTING AND ADM UNITS	SUPPORTING AND ADM UNITS
• Srinagar • Jammu • Punjab • Rajasthan • Gujarat	• South Bengal • North Bengal • Shillong • Silchar • Tripura • Guwahati	• Ftr New Delhi • Ftr Special Ops Odhisha (ANO) • Ftr Special Ops Chattisgarh (ANO)	• Artillery • Signal Regiment • Tear Smoke Unit • CENWOSTO, Tekanpur • Special Repair Organization • Small Instrument Workshop • Printing Press • Engineering Set-up • Pay & Accounts Division • Electronic Data Processing • Water Wing • Air Wing	• BSF Academy, Tekanpur • Central School of Weapons and Traffic, Indore • Training Centre & School, Hazaribagh • Central School of Motor Transport, Tekanpur • Signal Training School, New Delhi • Signal Training School, Bangalore • "G" Training School, New Delhi • National Training Centre of Dogs, Tekanpur • Subsidiary Training Centres (Gogaland, Udhampur, Kharkan Camp, Jodhpur, Bangalore, Kadamthala, Chura Chand Pur, Chakur, Tekanpur, Hazaribagh & Indore)

Note: ADG = Additional Director General; ADM = Administrative; ANO = Anti-Naxal Operations; CENWOSTO = Central Workshop and Store; DG = Director General; Dte = Directorate; Ftr = Frontier; SPL OPS = Special Operations

Figure 9.1   Organizational Structure of the Border Security Force (BSF)
Source: Parliamentary Standing Committee on Home Affairs, *Working Conditions in Border Guarding Forces,* p. 73

and Guwahati. Further, there are five Additional Directors General who supervise human resources, operations, logistics, special operations and anti-Naxalite operations, and the training academy. Chhattisgarh and Odisha are the only frontiers under the supervision of the Additional Director General at Raipur, who oversees special operations and anti-Naxalite operations.

The headquarters in New Delhi is divided into ten directorates, which deal with various aspects of the organization: personnel, operations, confidential and vigilance administrative, general, training, communication and information technology, provisioning, the air wing, and medical. There is also a law branch and the former Inspector General headquarters, which has been converted into a frontier headquarters at New Delhi.[23]

Recruitment Processes and Structure

In an attempt to make the BSF representative of India as a whole, its recruitment process was designed to showcase adequate representation from all states and regions. The Staff Selection Commission, with the help of India's Central Armed Police Forces (CAPFs), conducts recruitment for the non-officer ranks.[24] The Union Public Services Commission recruits for the post of Assistant Commandant (General Duty)—the enrty-level rank in the officer cadre. The BSF itself handles recruitment for the engineering, air wing, paramedical, veterinary, motor transport, water wing, and ministerial cadres.[25] As of 31 December 2019, the total strength of the BSF stands at 265,173 (see Table 9.2).

The BSF includes 5,215 women in its ranks. Women constables in combat roles were introduced in 2008. They are entrusted with and perform the same tasks as men, including all operational, security, and intelligence functions. Women sub-inspectors, a junior leadership role, were first inducted in 2010.[26]

The force also places a premium on providing job opportunities to youth from border and militancy-affected areas. Twenty per cent of the vacancies in India's border-guarding forces, including the BSF, are allotted to border districts, and an additional 20 per cent are allotted to districts and areas affected by militancy, including Jammu and Kashmir, the north-eastern states, and Naxalite-affected areas.[27] In 2018, the Parliamentary Committee on Home Affairs suggested the BSF recruit more heavily from the states and regions where the force is deployed to help mitigate personnel challenges, including frequent demands for long leaves, voluntary transfers, and resignations (Table 9.3 provides a summary of the rank structure within the BSF).

Table 9.2 Sanctioned and Actual Strength of the BSF

Sanctioned Strength			Actual Strength		
Gazetted	Non-Gazetted	Total	Gazetted	Non-Gazetted	Total
5,525	259,648	265,173	5,038	232,712	237,750

Source: MHA, *Annual Report, 2019–2020.*

Note: All figures are current as of December 31, 2019.

Table 9.3 Rank Structure and Hierarchy in the BSF

Officer Cadre	Director General
	Special Director General
	Additional Director General
	Inspector General
	Deputy Inspector General
	Commandant
	Second in Command
	Deputy Commandant
	Assistant Commandant
Other Ranks	Subedar Major
	Inspector
	Sub-Inspector
	Assistant Sub-Inspector
	Head Constable
	Constable

Source: "Payscale," Border Security Force Official Website, https://bsf.gov.in/Payscale?LangId=dHJ1ZQ==.

The 2018 Parliamentary Committee on Home Affairs offered suggestions to improve the BSF's recruitment policy, taking into account the challenges posed by frequent demands for long leaves, voluntary transfers, and resignations. In particular, the committee suggested that the MHA should align its policy with the geographical deployment of the BSF by recruiting more candidates from the states and regions where the force is deployed. This, the committee argued, would help in reducing not only the tendency to seek transfers to preferred locations, but also in addressing attrition to a certain extent.[28]

Training and Infrastructure

To train this formidable force, BSF founder Rustamji developed a programme unique to the role he envisioned for his force. While it drew upon elements from both the army and civilian police, it also helped to cultivate a distinct character for the BSF. The BSF's training regimen encompasses a comprehensive repertoire of courses that have been specifically designed for the force. It includes technical and practical combat skills in the initial stages, management and administration skills in the second phase, and conceptual and strategic skills at the top level of the force's hierarchy. The BSF also tries to synchronize existing training practices with new concepts in the domains of border guarding and border management.[29]

Over time, the training modules of the BSF have evolved into a sophisticated system that aims to address the diverse roles the force is asked to perform. The structure of these training courses, including 'basic', 'company collective', 'on the job', and 'specialized skill-based training', is described in Table 9.4.

Table 9.4 Training Patterns and Types in the BSF

Types of Training	
(a) Basic Training	12–53 weeks, depending on post.
(b) Mandatory In-Service Pre-Promotional Training	Periodic courses conducted for various ranks (executive cadre) to make them eligible for higher promotions.
(c) Company Collective Training	Periodic soldier training for the troops on ground for a duration of six weeks.
(d) On the Job Training	Training to enhance the professional knowledge of the soldier during their day-to-day work.
(e) Induction Training	Training organized for battalions due to be deployed along the India–Pakistan border, India-Bangladesh border, Line of Control, and for anti-infiltration, counter-insurgency and anti-Naxalite operations.
(f) New Weapon and Equipment Training	Training organized as and when new weapons and equipment are inducted in the force to meet the operational requirement.
(g) Specialized Trainings	Specialized modules for: (i) Assistant inspectorate of armament (assistant and deputy commandants) (ii) Ammunition technical officer (inspectors) (iii) Fleet management (assistant and deputy commandants) (iv) Driving and maintenance (constables) (v) Armourer (constables) (vi) Signal Training (communication cadre) (vii) Intelligence Training (constables to deputy inspect general level officers).

Source: Created on the basis of information found in Parliamentary Standing Committee on Home Affairs, *Working Conditions in Border Guarding Forces*, 88–9.

These programmes are conducted at different BSF training institutions across India.[30] The foremost institute, the BSF Academy at Tekanpur,[31] has been recognized as a Centre of Excellence by the MHA and envisions itself as a think tank and academic centre for border management, counter-insurgency, internal security, strategic planning, and human resource management. To serve the evolving needs of the organization, various wings have been established at Tekanpur, including training, administrative, and tactical. The latter is tasked with the critical function of evolving new concepts in border management and bridging the gap between training and realities on the ground. The Faculty of Studies at Tekanpur has been involved in formulating operational doctrines for the eastern and western theatres in consultation with field commanders. The Central School of Weapons and Tactics at Indore, among the oldest of the BSF's institutions, enrols the widest spectrum of trainees.[32] It trains not only BSF personnel but also officers and constabulary from different state and central police organizations in weapons skills and minor tactical training suited for armed and anti-insurgency operations. It too has been declared a Centre of Excellence by the Indian government.

With the expansion of the BSF and its evolving operational deployments, the government has established subsidiary training centres that serve the specific demands of the force, especially pertaining to counterterrorism, counter-insurgency, and anti-infiltration operations. The Training Centre and School,[33] located in Hazaribagh, offers training in counter-insurgency operations, counterterrorism operations, and explosives detection. The school's tactical wing trains subordinate officers from the BSF, including courses for platoon commanders and company commanders, and hosts various programmes specializing in commando operations. The BSF Institute of Disaster Response trains the BSF's National Disaster Response Force battalions, as well as other civil agencies. It also serves as a think tank focused on disaster response and coordinates all disaster response activities. The BSF's intelligence branch—the 'G' Directorate—is trained at the BSF 'G' Training School, which also offers intelligence training to other personnel on a regular basis. As the only central police force to have its own artillery, the BSF Academy at Tekanpur also houses its Artillery Training School.[34]

Human Resource Management in the BSF

Given its ever-expanding responsibilities and the dynamic operational environment, effectively personnel management has been a constant challenge for the BSF. Between 2015 and 2018, 12,096 BSF personnel either resigned or opted for voluntary retirement.[35] This high rate of attrition (owing to multiple factors, as detailed in Table 9.5) is a major concern that was also identified in the 2018 report by the Parliamentary Standing Committee on Home Affairs. The committee noted that, given the high rate of attrition, the BSF may have difficulty filling its vacancies within the required time frame, negatively impacting its operational efficiencies.[36]

Table 9.5 Reasons of Attrition in the BSF (2012–17)[a]

Reason of Attrition	Year					
	2012	2013	2014	2015	2016	2017
Superannuation	986	806	813	856	1,015	1,206
Voluntary retirement	3,471	3,495	2,067	511	3,132	6,001
Resigned from service	495	525	516	398	319	414
Invalidation (medical)	28	34	23	37	20	19
Dismissed on disciplinary grounds	146	101	99	87	59	60
Death in action	13	15	10	14	18	7
Suicide	40	38	46	27	24	38
Shoot-out	2	6	3	2	1	1
Accidental fire	1	02	3	0	1	2
Train accident	9	12	6	18	18	7
Vehicle accident	58	58	43	22	20	47
Drowning	1	7	8	2	5	5
Malaria	3	2	4	3	3	1
Illness	215	266	239	270	280	257
Death due to other reasons	76	85	39	83	87	51
Total	5,544	5,452	3,919	2,330	5,003	8,116

Source: Parliamentary Standing Committee on Home Affairs, *Working Conditions in Border Guarding Forces,* 74.

[a]Parliamentary Standing Committee on Home Affairs, *Working Conditions in Border Guarding Forces,* 74.

According to data published by the Bureau of Police Research and Development, the BSF has the third-highest number of vacancies (10 per cent) relative to its sanctioned strength; only the Sashastra Seema Bal and the Central Industrial Security Force reported higher vacancy rates.[37]

Another major challenge facing the force is the prevalence of suicide; more than 120 BSF personnel committed suicide between 2015 and 2018.[38] These unfortunate incidents have a deeply unsettling impact on the morale of the force. In this light, the standing committee has requested concerned ministries and agencies to help commanding officers monitor and address the stress levels of BSF personnel. However, there is an urgent need at the highest levels to identify specific factors that are leading to rising stress levels and declining motivation and to develop strategies that help personnel address these issues. The standing committee has recommended that the MHA consider creating dedicated posts in the medical cadre of the BSF to address mental health concerns in the force.[39]

One of the most important factors for motivation across the organizational spectrum is career growth and the prospect of rising through the hierarchy. Within the BSF, there is a huge divergence between the prescribed residency period and the actual time it takes to be promoted—especially from the rank of constable to head constable (see Table 9.6). This has limited promotional opportunities and stifled career growth. To ameliorate this situation, the Parliamentary Standing Committee on Home Affairs has recommended that, where possible, promotions are fast-tracked in alignment with the requisite residency period, and that personnel facing excessive stagnation in their career growth be provided with certain incentives to boost morale.[40]

Another grievance from the rank-and-file is that most of the higher posts—deputy inspector general and above—in the CAPFs, including the BSF, are filled by officers on deputation, especially from the Indian Police Service (IPS) (see Table 9.7). As one former additional director general of the BSF said, this leads to a

lack of connect of the policy level leadership with conditions on ground. Trained in policing, law and order duties, officers on deputation at higher ranks find themselves out of depth with the complexities and dynamics of border management, the ethos, and operational philosophy of a large organization like the BSF.[41]

Table 9.6 Divergence between Prescribed Residency Period and Actual Time Taken for Promotion in the BSF

Promotion From—To	Group 'A' service/ Residency Service	Actual Time Taken from Entry Grade
Inspector General to Additional Director General	30 years with 3 years as Inspector General	More than 35 years
Deputy Inspector General to Inspector General	24 years with 2 years as Deputy Inspector General	More than 33 years
Commandant to Deputy Inspector General	20 years with 2 years as Commandant	More than 28 years
Second in Command to Commandant	15 years with 5 years as Second in Command	More than 22 years
Deputy Commandant to Second in Command	10 years with 5 years as Deputy Commandant	More than 16 years
Assistant Commandant to Deputy Commandant	5 years as Assistant Commandant	More than 7 years
Inspector to Assistant Commandant	3 years as Inspector	10 years from Inspector
Sub-Inspector to Inspector	5 years as Sub-Inspector	5 years
Assistant Sub-Inspector to Sub-Inspector	6 years as Assistant Sub-Inspector or combined 10 years as Head Constable/ Assistant Sub-Inspector with 3 years as Assistant Sub-Inspector	The Assistant Sub-Inspector post was sanctioned in 2012, so it is too early to assess the stagnation.[a]
Head Constable to Assistant Sub-Inspector	5 years as Head Constable	10 years
Constable to Head Constable	8 years as Constable	20 years

Source: Parliamentary Standing Committee on Home Affairs, *Working Conditions in Border Guarding Forces*, 77

Note: Head Constables with 9 years of service and Assistant Sub-Inspectors with 18 years' service have recently been promoted as Assistant Sub-Inspector and Sub-Inspector, respectively.

In response, the 2018 Parliamentary Standing Committee on Home Affairs recommended that not more than 25 per cent of posts should be reserved for officers on deputation and that officers from the CAPF cadres should be given equal opportunity to reach the topmost ranks. The hope is that this move will boost the morale of the CAPFs while also providing a larger pool of qualified officers.[42]

Table 9.7   Method of Recruitment for Posts
over Deputy Inspector General in the BSF

Posts	Method of Recruitment
	BSF
Director General	0 per cent cadre 100 per cent IPS
Additional Director General	25 per cent cadre 75 per cent IPS
Inspector General	50 per cent cadre 50 per cent IPS
Deputy Inspector General	80 per cent cadre 15 per cent IPS 5 per cent army

Source: Created on the basis of information found in Parliamentary
Standing Committee on Home Affairs, *Working Conditions in
Border Guarding Forces,* 110

Winning Hearts and Minds

In order to successfully carry out its duties, the BSF must garner the support and cooperation of local populations along the border, engaging
their services and availing themselves of their knowledge to address local
problems. This strategy of 'winning hearts and minds' through public relations and community engagement is a key aspect of the BSF's shift from
border guarding to border management.

Under its community development programmes, the BSF consults
with village heads and panchayat members to develop measures that limit
cross-border criminal activities. In addition, the BSF has also played a significant role in implementing the Border Area Development Programme
(BADP), which aims to meet the unique developmental needs of people
living in remote, inaccessible areas along India's international border by
building essential infrastructure.[43] Under this programme, priority is
given to 'strategic villages' identified by the BSF that are located less than
10 kilometres from an international border.

The BSF has undertaken several civic action programmes across its
area of deployment. These are especially targeted at inaccessible and remote regions affected by terrorism or insurgency. The BSF collaborated

with the National Skill Development Corporation to provide skills-based training to people living in border areas. The force has also organized Bharat Darshan Tours, including for children from Jammu and Kashmir, in an effort to earn the confidence of the local people. As a part of its 'additional responsibilities', the BSF has also contributed its troops and resources towards disaster relief operations such as during the Gujarat Earthquake of 2001, the disastrous floods in Jammu and Kashmir in 2014, and the Uttarakhand Floods in 2013.[44]

Quest for Modernization

The BSF's first major initiative to upgrade its technology was between 1996 and 2002 when it introduced a number of advanced systems and devices such as night vision and handheld thermal imagery equipment in aid of its operational duties. Its first modernization plan was implemented between 2002 and 2010, marking the force's realization that 'manpower intensive border-guarding practices are no longer adequate, and the employment of suitable technologies is critical to assist the border guards'.[45] Its most recent modernization plan, which began in 2018, seeks to integrate cutting-edge technology, such as drones with night-vision capabilities, light bulletproof vehicles, and geostationary satellite phone terminals.

The BSF has also pursued a comprehensive integrated border management system, which includes utilizing technological solutions in regions where the construction of physical fences is unfeasible.[46] Further, the BSF has introduced a counter-insurgency operations planning system in Naxalite-affected areas, and is in the process of implementing border operations planning system software to identify likely infiltration routes and vulnerable areas. The force has also invested in GIS technologies in order to 'organize complex spatial environments with tabular relationships', thereby enabling faster and better-informed decision-making.[47]

The BSF air wing's new platforms have made it one of the prized assets of the MHA.[48] The water wing has also reinforced its capacities, with new boats that use a jet propulsion system and sensor-based control equipment that is currently deployed along the Sir Creek border in Gujarat.[49]

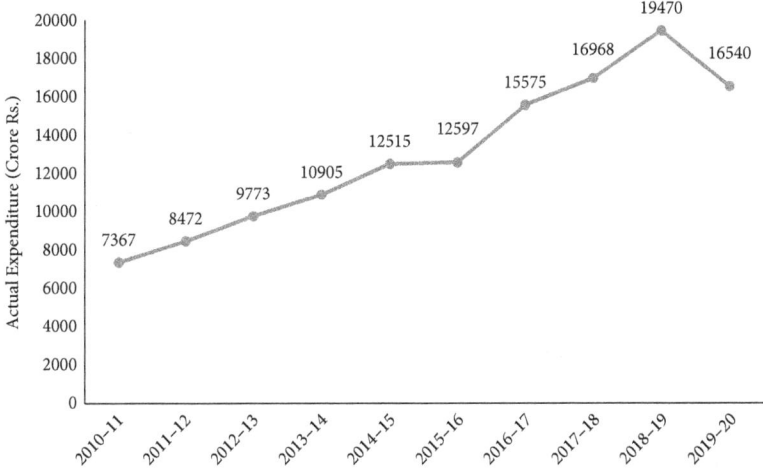

Figure 9.2 Actual Expenditure on the BSF
Source: MHA, *Annual Report, 2019-2020.*
Note: Amounts are in Rs. Crore

The budget of the BSF has grown in line with its expanding role and responsibilities. The BSF's actual expenditures increased from almost 74 billion rupees in 2010–11 to about 165 billion rupees in 2019–20 (see Figure 9.2).

Performance and Reform: An Assessment

India's borders pass through some of the most unforgiving terrain in the world—riverine areas, salt flats, creeks, deserts, forests, hills, marshes, and the snow-capped Himalayas. The challenges associated with securing India's borders are exacerbated by diverse ecological milieus, physical and socio-economic landscapes,[50] and the differing realities on the ground in each of these settings.[51]

The 2019–20 MHA annual report states that the objective of border management is to '[secure] the country's borders against interests hostile to the country', and institute 'systems that are able to interdict such elements while facilitating legitimate trade and commerce'.[52] The 2001 Report of the Group of Ministers on National Security emphasizes the necessity of interpreting the term 'border management' capaciously to include 'coordination and concerted action by political leadership, and administrative, diplomatic, security, intelligence, legal, regulatory, and economic agencies of the country to secure our frontiers', in addition to strengthening vigilance through robust surveillance infrastructure, and enhanced capacities of the border-guarding forces.[53]

Aligning with the principle of 'one border, one guarding force', the BSF is currently guarding 2,290 kilometres of India's border with Pakistan and 4,097 kilometres of India's border with Bangladesh. In addition, the BSF guards 237kilometres of the LoC under the operational control of the army.[54] In the decades since its inception, the BSF's functions and operations, however, have evolved—marking a transition from border guarding towards integrated border management, as noted above. The latter is a much broader concept, encompassing security, economic and social development, and trade relations. Further, though a specialized force armed and trained to man the international border, it has also been tasked with maintaining law and order in aid of state administrations. Its counter-insurgency and anti-infiltration operations have also been notable.[55]

The force has undoubtedly played a vital role in ensuring the integrity and security of the nation. However, scholars believe that, today, the force stands at a crossroads. It is faced with a multiplicity of challenges as it seeks to align its predominantly militaristic operational philosophy, organization, and training with a security environment that has significantly changed since its inception.

To begin with, its arming and training policy—especially in light of emerging challenges posed by asymmetric and non-conventional warfare, evidenced by terrorist attacks at Dinanagar [2015], Pathankot [2016], Nagrota [2016], and Uri [2016]—is in dire need of reform. While the western borders require aggressive domination, the eastern borders require the force to exercise restraint. Suitably designed pre-induction training before deployment in these regions therefore become critical. Given the growing interactions with the local populations, and to counter the perceptions of alienation between security forces and the inhabitants of border regions, some reformers recommend incorporating essential soft-skills trainings into the curriculum.[56]

Some experts have suggested that the initial benefits that accrued from a rapid, if irregular, expansion of the force have now saturated. Personnel are stagnating for long periods, resulting in dissatisfaction and demoralization. Untimely promotions, unplanned recruitment at the entry levels, and scarce higher-level posts have all resulted in limited upward mobility or career progression. Cadre-review exercises must be streamlined to better assess and incorporate the demands of the personnel.[57]

Other personnel management issues pertain to the adverse effects of strenuous service conditions and strain due to sustained deployment on operational duties. This problem, compounded by the shortage of adequate basic amenities and infrastructure at the border outpost level, imposes severe constraints on the efficiency of a force that has to constantly contend with 'zero error syndrome'.[58] Recent reports of disgruntlement among the personnel underline the urgency of addressing this concern.

The BSF is an important player in India's security matrix. But as the force has evolved and its mission has expanded, some aspects of its operationalization are undoubtedly in need of reform.[59] As it is often the sole face of the government in remote areas, perception management must also be one of its foremost concerns. However, criticisms notwithstanding, despite deep-seated organizational and resource constraints, the world's largest border-guarding force has lived up to the vision of its founders and has excelled in roles that have gone far beyond its conventional mandate in service of national security functions.

Notes

1. P.V. Rajagopal, ed., *The British, the Bandits and the Bordermen: From the Diaries and Articles of K. F. Rustamji* (New Delhi: Wisdom Tree, 2009), 243.

2. This section is based on the following: Government of India, "Memorandum for Consideration of the Emergency Committee of Secretaries," *BSF Documents Collection* (hereafter Memorandum); "Border Management," *Faculty of Studies, BSF* (Tekanpur, Gwalior, MP: BSF Academy, January 2010); Dr. Surindur Singh, *Growth and Functional Dynamics of Border Security Force* (Jammu: Trikuta Radiant Publications, 1999); D. Banerjea, ed., *Central Police Organizations Part II* (Kolkata/New Delhi: Allied Publishers in collaboration with The West Bengal National University of Juridical Sciences, 2005).

3. Memorandum, 2.

4. Memorandum, 2.
5. Anirudh Deshpande, ed., *The First Line of Defence: Glorious 50 Years of the Border Security Force* (New Delhi: Shipra Publications, 2015).
6. Memorandum, 4.
7. Memorandum, 9.
8. Rajagopal, 247–48.
9. Rajagopal, 250.
10. Rajagopal, 247–48.
11. Rajagopal, 249.
12. Rajagopal, 250–51.
13. Rajagopal, reflections on 'A National Memorial', 198, 16/1/1972.
14. Rajagopal, section on the Western Front, 14/3/1972, 178–79.
15. For details of these unfortunate events, see Deshpande, *The First Line of Defence*.
16. "J-K: BSF Pays Tributes to Kargil War Heroes," *Business Standard*, July 23, 2019, https://www.business-standard.com/article/news-ani/j-k-bsf-pays-tributes-to-kargil-war-heroes-119072300453_1.html.
17. "Army, BSF Hold Synergy Conference at Western Command," *Hindustan Times*, August 26, 2021, https://www.hindustantimes.com/cities/others/army-bsf-hold-synergy-conference-at-western-command-101629920594739.html.
18. Deshpande, *The First Line of Defence*.
19. Ministry of Home Affairs, "Central Armed Police Forces," Ministry of Home Affairs official website, https://www.mha.gov.in/central-armed-police-forces.
20. Anirudh Deshpande, ed., *Border Security Force: India's First Line of Defence— A Saga of Grit and Glory*, 2nd edn. (Delhi: Shipra Publications, 2018), 163–4, https://bsf.gov.in/EventsDocs/history-2021.pdf.
21. Parliamentary Standing Committee on Home Affairs, *Working Conditions in Border Guarding Forces (Assam Rifles, Sashastra Seema Bal, Indo-Tibetan Border Police and Border Security Force)*, Report No. 214, December 12, 2018, 72, https://rajyasabha.nic.in/rsnew/Committee_site/Committee_File/ReportFile/15/107/214_2018_12_15.pdf.
22. Ministry of Home Affairs, *Annual Report, 2019–2020* (New Delhi: Government of India, 2021), https://www.mha.gov.in/sites/default/files/AnnualReport_19_20.pdf.
23. Deshpande, *Border Security Force*, 167–68.
24. Deshpande, *Border Security Force*, pp. 169–70.
25. Parliamentary Standing Committee on Home Affairs, *Working Conditions in Border Guarding Forces*, 73–74.
26. Deshpande, *Border Security Force*, 168.
27. MHA, *Annual Report, 2019–2020*.
28. Parliamentary Standing Committee on Home Affairs, *Working Conditions in Border Guarding Forces*, 91.
29. Deshpande, *Border Security Force*, 217–20.

30. For details on the BSF's training institutions, please refer to Deshpande, *Border Security Force*, 180–94.
31. "BSF Academy Tekanpur," Border Security Force Official Website, https://ftruser. bsf.gov.in/FrontierAboutUs?FrontierId=MTc=.
32. "CSWT Indore," *Border Security Forces Official Website*, https://ftruser.bsf.gov.in/ FrontierAboutUs?FrontierId=MTg=.
33. "Training Centre and School," *Border Security Forces Official Website*, https://ftru ser.bsf.gov.in/FrontierAboutUs?FrontierId=MTY=.
34. "Artillery HQ," *Border Security Forces Official Website*, https://ftruser.bsf.gov. in/FrontierAboutUs?FrontierId=Mzg=; "BSF Frontiers," *Border Security Forces Official Website*, https://bsf.gov.in/FrontiersList?LangId=dHJ1ZQ==.
35. Sanjiv Krishnan Sood, "Reform and Revive," *Force: National Security and Aerospace Magazine*, https://forceindia.net/guest-column/reform-revive/.
36. Parliamentary Standing Committee on Home Affairs, *Working Conditions in Border Guarding Forces*.
37. "Demand for Grants 2021–22 Analysis: Home Affairs," *PRS Legislative Research*, 2021, https://prsindia.org/budgets/parliament/demand-for-grants-2021-22-analysis-home-affairs.
38. Sood, "Reform and Revive," *Force*.
39. Parliamentary Standing Committee on Home Affairs, *Working Conditions in Border Guarding Forces*, 74–76.
40. Parliamentary Standing Committee on Home Affairs, *Working Conditions in Border Guarding Forces*, 77–81.
41. Sood, "Reform and Revive," *Force*.
42. Parliamentary Standing Committee on Home Affairs, *Working Conditions in Border Guarding Forces*, 109–11.
43. Department of Border Management, "New Guidelines of Border Area Development Programme (BADP), 2020," *Ministry of Home Affairs official website*, https://www.mha.gov.in/sites/default/files/GuidelinesofBADP_17032 020.PDF.
44. For more details, please refer to: Deshpande, *Border Security Force*, 291–304.
45. Sood, "Reform and Revive," *Force*.
46. For more details, please refer to "Comprehensive Integrated Border Management System: Implementation Challenges," Observer Research Foundation (ORF) Paper, 2016, https://www.orfonline.org/research/comprehensive-integrated-bor der-management-system/.
47. Deshpande, *Border Security Force*, 251–71.
48. Presently it consists of Embraer-135 BJ, 02 AVRO (HS-748) aircrafts in fixed wing, and 06 ALH (Dhruv), 01 Cheetah, 06 Mi-17-IV and 08 Mi-17 V5 helicopters in rotatory wing.
49. Deshpande, *Border Security Force*, 234–50.
50. Arvind Gupta, *How India Manages Its National Security* (New Delhi: Penguin Random House, 2018).

51. Rajya Sabha TV (RSTV), *Security Scan: Guarding the Borders*, Video, March 29, 2018, https://www.youtube.com/watch?v=qFeq2YO4I30.

52. MHA, *Annual Report, 2019–2020.*

53. *Report of the Group of Ministers on National Security* (New Delhi: Institute for Defence Studies and Analysis, 2000), https://www.vifindia.org/sites/default/files/GoM%20Report%20on%20National%20Security.pdf

54. Parliamentary Standing Committee on Home Affairs, *Working Conditions in Border Guarding Forces,* 73.

55. Ananya Bhardwaj, "54 Years Since Formation, BSF'S Role Has Gone Far Beyond Protecting India's Borders," *ThePrint*, December 2, 2019, https://theprint.in/theprint-essential/54-years-since-formation-bsfs-role-has-gone-far-beyond-protecting-indias-borders/329295/.

56. Sood, "Reform and Revive," *Force.*

57. Sanjiv Krishan Sood, "To Keep India Safe, BSF Must Get Leaders from Its Own Ranks—Not The IPS." *Scroll.in*, December 1, 2018, https://scroll.in/article/904098/the-bsf-a-key-player-in-indias-security-matrix-needs-urgent-reforms-or-could-lose-its-edge.

58. "Job Stress Leading BSF Men to Sleep-Deprived Nomadic Life," *The Economic Times*, February 8, 2015, https://economictimes.indiatimes.com/news/politics-and-nation/job-stress-leading-bsf-men-to-sleep-deprived-nomadic-life/articleshow/46161877.cms?from=mdr.

59. Sood, "Reform and Revive," *Force.*

10

The Assam Rifles and the Rashtriya Rifles

Raghuveer Nidumolu and Srinath Raghavan

Introduction

The modern Indian state, from its origins as a colonial autocracy through its development as a post-colonial democracy, has had a long and continuous history of armed insurrections. The 'prose of counter-insurgency' was not only constitutive of the rationality of the colonial state,[1] but also the development of its sinews. Even in the best of times, at least a third of the colonial Indian army was deployed for internal security duties.[2] Indeed, modern counter-insurgency doctrines, strategies, and tactics owe an unacknowledged debt to the British Indian Army's experience in the subcontinent—institutional memory and learning that were transposed to other theatres of counter-insurgency in the age of decolonization, starting with British Malaya.[3]

The counter-insurgency practices of the post-colonial Indian state—and military—have not received sustained historical treatment. To be sure, there are discrete accounts of various campaigns, from the Naga insurgency of the 1950s to the Maoist violence of the present.[4] But the processes of institutional learning, adaptation, and change in countering insurrections have yet to be mapped and analysed in detail. This chapter focuses on a particular aspect of the development of the Indian state's capacity in dealing with insurgencies: the institutional innovation of creating two large and specialized counter-insurgency forces. The Assam Rifles (AR) and the Rashtriya Rifles (RR) have no counterparts in any other significant military today. This chapter offers a comparative analysis of the Assam Rifles and the Rashtriya Rifles along four dimensions: historical

Raghuveer Nidumolu and Srinath Raghavan, *The Assam Rifles and the Rashtriya Rifles* In: *Institutional Roots of India's Security Policy*. Edited by: Milan Vaishnav, Oxford University Press. © Oxford University Press 2024.
DOI: 10.1093/oso/9780198894612.003.0010

development, organizational structure, human resources, and performance and reforms. The analysis suggests that the Assam Rifles and the
Rashtriya Rifles present contrasting yet instructive models of specialized
counter-insurgency forces. Their capabilities and challenges also cast
into relief larger questions of state capacity and reform in the domain of
security.

Raison d'Etre of Counter-Insurgency Forces

Assam Rifles

The organization known today as the Assam Rifles has its origins in a
colonial-era outfit called the Cachar Levy. Named after region of Cachar
in Assam, the force was raised in 1835 to protect the regional tea gardens
and estates that were under the control and management of the British.[5]
The hill tribes of Assam periodically raided the tea gardens, which were
an important export and source of revenue for the British. 'In order to
meet the threat', writes the official historian of Assam Rifles,

> the British decided to raise a 'Levy' (or a militia body) as a separate force
> under the civil government and distinct from both the regular army and
> the armed police ... [It] was to be put on a better military footing than
> the police in order to enable them to replace regular troops in certain
> parts of the tribal border. It was to be officered by police officials and
> would thus serve as a cheap semi-military body. The men were to be
> drawn from the Bengal Civil Police, at first comprising all classes, from
> Bengal.[6]

From the outset then, the Cachar Levy's envisioned role entailed a
modicum of flexibility in operation—a quality that endures to date. It
was—and remains—fundamentally a police force operating under civilian authority, yet capable of performing the functions of a military
force. The Cachar Levy's main task was to guard the 'eastern frontier of
Assam from the Brahmaputra River at Nowgong southwards to Silchar'.
The responsibility of guarding the border with Burma was left to the
army.[7] Over time, with changing requirements, the Cachar Levy was reorganized and expanded. In addition to its regular duties, the force was

also deployed during WWI in place of reservists and Nepalese Gurkha battalions. The Cachar Levy was decorated for its service in the war and renamed the Assam Rifles.[8]

After India's independence, the role of the Assam Rifles continued to evolve. When north-east India became the locus of a series of ethno-nationalist insurgencies, starting with the Nagas in the mid-1950s, the Assam Rifles was deployed in a string of counter-insurgency campaigns. Owing to this experience, the Assam Rifles was also deployed to Sri Lanka in Operation Pawan in 1987—India's only overseas counter-insurgency campaign to date. In addition, it was used in a conventional role during the Sino-Indian War of 1962.

Currently, the Assam Rifles is deployed along India's 1,643-kilometre border with Myanmar.[9] It has also grown over time, consisting currently of 46 battalions. According to the Assam Rifles Rules (of 2010), the force is to safeguard 'the security of borders of India and promote a sense of security among the people living in border areas' as well as 'prevent[ing] trans-border crimes, smuggling, unauthorised entry into or exit from the territory of India and any other illegal activity'. The Assam Rifles is further responsible for 'sensitive installations, banks, persons of security risk' and to 'restore and preserve order in any area in the event of disturbance therein'.[10] The official website of the Assam Rifles lists its main tasks as:

> Conduct counter insurgency operations in the north-east and other areas where deemed necessary, under control of the army. During peace and 'proxy war', ensure security of the Indo-China and Indo-Myanmar borders. During war, rear area security in the TBA (tactical battle area). Act as penultimate interventionist force of the central government in internal security situation, under the control of army, when the situation goes beyond the control of central paramilitary operations.[11]

Thus, the flexibility of operations that distinguished the Cachar Levy continues to characterize the Assam Rifles' purpose to date.

Rashtriya Rifles

The Rashtriya Rifles, much like the Assam Rifles, was an innovation aimed at addressing a specific need: waging counter-insurgency campaigns in densely populated areas such as the Kashmir Valley. In the words of former Defence Minister George Fernandes, the role of the Rashtriya Rifles included 'discharging the functions of rear area security, counter insurgency operations, maintenance of law and order & aid to civil authorities and augmentation of the field force during war-like situations'.[12] Until that point, Indian counter-insurgency had used heavy weapons, including artillery and attack helicopters, in theatres like Sri Lanka where 'civilians and villages were few and far between'.[13] The Kashmir Valley, by contrast, was more densely populated. Reliance on heavy firepower was bound to increase civilian casualties—hence, the need for lighter, infantry-based forces.[14]

A second, broader imperative was to reduce the mounting burden of counter-insurgency on the Indian Army—one that was seen as detracting from its conventional war-fighting capabilities. The army also felt that the existing central paramilitary forces were unable to cope with the demands of fighting an insurgency. As Rajesh Rajagopalan points out, the need was to create a paramilitary force with the 'ethos' of the Indian Army. In other words, this force would be 'officered by army personnel, and work under the command of the army rather than the MHA [Ministry of Home Affairs]'.[15] The creation of the Rashtriya Rifles was given the go-ahead by the Rajiv Gandhi government in 1990. Initially, two sectors (HQs) with three battalions each (equivalent to an infantry brigade) were sanctioned.[16] In 2001, the Indian government approved the creation of 30 new battalions to relieve the Indian Army from its mounting counter-insurgency duties in the face of worsening internal security.[17] By 2005, the sanctioned strength of the Rashtriya Rifles was increased to 63 battalions.[18]

Organizational Structure

Assam Rifles

The Assam Rifles is commanded by a director general who holds the rank of lieutenant general (three-star) in the Indian Army. Its apex headquarters is known as Headquarters Directorate General of Assam Rifles (HQ DGAR). Since the force's operations are largely specific to north-east

India, HQ DGAR is located in Shillong, Meghalaya.[19] Next in the Assam Rifles' chain of command is the inspector general, an army officer at the of rank of major general (two-star). The inspector general, in turn, oversees the various sector HQs of the Assam Rifles, which are headed by army brigadiers (one-star).[20] There are a total of 18 sectors in the Assam Rifles.[21]

Currently, the AR operates under the dual control of the Ministry of Defence (MoD) and the Ministry of Home Affairs (MHA). While the executive and operational aspects of the Assam Rifles are overseen by the MoD, the administrative and financial aspects are under the purview of the MHA. A brief history of India's security challenges may help clarify why the current organizational structure, characterized by the dual ministerial control, has come into place.

In October 1950, communist China invaded Tibet. This immediately raised concerns about India's security in the north-east. The Himmatsinhji Committee, constituted in December 1950, was tasked with reviewing the security situation in the region. It made some pertinent recommendations regarding the organizational structure of the Assam Rifles. In effect, the committee recommended the expansion and concentration of troop forces in order to better manage the region. In addition,

> the Committee felt that in order to achieve greater mobility and greater efficiency Assam Rifles battalions should be reorganized into a Headquarter Wing and Rifle Wings of three platoons each—the number of wings varying according to the number of platoons authorized in the particular battalion.[22]

The command and control of the Assam Rifles involved four different agencies at this point. To ensure 'greater coordination', it was decided that the Governor, representing the Indian government, should 'review the problem of frontier security as a whole and that all proposals about the Assam Rifles which required the orders of the Government of India should be channeled through his secretariat'.[23] These recommendations were accepted by the government.

By that point, the Assam Rifles had become an important component of the army, with an 'increased operation commitment'. As time went by, 'the Assam Rifles became more and more involved with the Army, with no signs of its ever returning to the civilian fold'.[24] As Major General D.K. Palit notes in *Sentinels of the North-East*, a history of the Assam Rifles, the threat emanating from China has played a crucial role in keeping the Assam Rifles under the operational control of the armed forces. In addition, the insurgency in Nagaland led to more Assam Rifles battalions being placed under the control of the army. According to the Ministry of External Affairs (under whose control the force operated at the time), the force's increased military responsibilities meant that it was becoming too big to remain under civilian control. Yet, while the imperative for retaining the Assam Rifles under the military control was recognized, the MoD was averse to the idea of assuming full responsibility—apparently owing to concerns about heightened budgetary requirements.[25]

In 1969, an official study group was established to consider whether the Assam Rifles should be split into two different forces to perform the distinct tasks of securing the international border and ensuring internal law and order. However, the study group eventually decided against bifurcating the Assam Rifles in order to 'maintain and foster its military character'. The Governor of Assam would exercise superintendence and control over the force, with the army taking over the administrative responsibilities of the force whenever it operated under the army's 'operational control'.[26]

Debate over the reorganization of the Assam Rifles persists—and will be discussed subsequently in this chapter. Some argue forcefully that the Assam Rifles should come fully under the purview of either the MHA or the MoD. Others continue to advocate the present model of dual control.

Rashtriya Rifles

Categorizing the Rashtriya Rifles is equally complicated. Organizationally, it is seen as a paramilitary force. Yet it is better trained and equipped than a regular paramilitary. Nevertheless, it is not entirely identified as a military force either. As Rajagopalan notes, the Rashtriya Rifles is a modified infantry formation of the Indian Army with a very different administrative and organizational structure.[27] General K.V. Krishna Rao—a former chief of the army staff and governor of the erstwhile state of Jammu and

Kashmir—described the Rashtriya Rifles as a 'semi-military organ-ization'.[28] Its units are characterized by their all-arms nature. Support services, like the Army Service Corps and electrical and mechanical engineers, are available at the battalion level in the Rashtriya Rifles, even though they are only available at the brigade level for regular infantry battalions.[29]

The complicated organizational character of the Rashtriya Rifles may have arisen from the unique purpose for which it was constituted: tackling the problem of counter-insurgency in a densely populated grid. According to one report, the Rashtriya Rifles was initially not to have 'more than 25 per cent of its strength from the regular army. The remaining was to be made up of ex-servicemen and lateral inductees from other paramilitary forces and central police organisations'.[30] Although budget seemed to be an issue when it came to whether the Rashtriya Rifles would be moved fully under the MoD, raising and expanding the force was seen as unavoidable given the security situation.[31] As Lieutenant General Syed Ata Hasnain notes, the budget for the Rashtriya Rifles is 'additional to the Army budget under separate head'.[32]

The structure and organization of a Rashtriya Rifles battalion differs from that of a regular infantry battalion. A regular battalion consists of four combat companies and retains its heavy weapons (such as mortars), whereas a Rashtriya Rifles battalion consist of six companies without any heavy weapons. It may be noted, however, that troops operating as part of a Rashtriya Rifles battalion are trained to use heavy weapons too. Additionally, unlike regular units of the army, which were rotated in and out of the Kashmir Valley regularly, the Rashtriya Rifles only changes its personnel—the units remain continuously deployed in the same location. This gives it an edge in terms of its ability to understand the terrain and gather local intelligence. Currently, Rashtriya Rifles units operate under five force headquarters (similar to an infantry division): Victor (Kashmir Valley), Kilo (Kupwara and Baramulla), Delta (Doda), Romeo (Poonch and Rajouri), and Uniform (Udhampur). Each force is headed by an army major general (two-star).[33] At this writing, the Rashtriya Rifles has 65 battalions, with an approximate total strength of 65,000.[34]

Since a central purpose in creating the Rashtriya Rifles was to reduce the army's counter-insurgency and counterterrorism burden, the army could initially draw personnel from various regiments operating in mixed

Rashtriya Rifles battalions. However, various administrative difficulties, combined with the problem of creating a regimental ethos, has forced a reorganization of the force's battalions.[35] Today, rather than having mixed battalions, the infantry troops and commanding officer of each Rashtriya Rifles battalion are drawn from the same infantry regiment of the Indian Army. Troops from the supporting arms and services posted in these battalions are, of course, drawn from different corps and regiments.[36]

Given its unique nature and structure, the Rashtriya Rifles has also periodically experienced friction with other security agencies and local police forces. For instance, the MHA questioned the rationale for creating a new counter-insurgency and counterterrorism force in Kashmir, arguing that it suggests that 'internal rebellions were a permanent feature in India'.[37] In another instance, during the 1999 Kargil War, India's Border Security Force (BSF, another paramilitary force deployed along the border with Pakistan), refused to serve under the Rashtriya Rifles, which they considered nothing more than another paramilitary.[38]

Human Resources

Recruitment: Assam Rifles

The recruitment policy of the Assam Rifles has largely relied on locals familiar with the climate and terrain of north-eastern India. A majority of those recruited have been from Nepal, especially the Gurkhas. As of 1982, they had constituted 42.4 per cent of Assam Rifles' recruits, followed by those from Garhwal and Kumaon. Palit notes that, in the early 1900s, the Assam Rifles made an effort to recruit personnel from other ethnic and religious groups, but they did not prove to be as effective as the Gurkhas, Kumaonis, and Garhwalis.[39] In the 1880s, the recruitment of Nepalis was restricted in order to fill the Gurkha regiments of the Indian Army. But by 1891, the Indian government had granted the Assam Rifles permission to recruit soldiers from Nepal, after the recruitment of Cacharis, Jaruas, Nagas, Kukis, and Lushais had not translated into 'much success'.[40] The preference for the Gurkhas was also based on the dominant so-called martial races ideology, which stipulated that only certain communities in the subcontinent were suitable for military manpower. The British military elite were tremendously impressed by the Gurkha's resistance against the British in the Anglo-Nepalese War of 1814–16. Subsequently, British officials articulated a cocktail of climatic, geographical, and diet-based theories to explain the martial superiority of the Gurkhas—which, although officially discarded, persist to this day.[41]

In the 1950s, the Assam Rifles was expanded considerably through the recruitment of Garhwalis and Kumaonis, who 'had proved their success' and ensured their continuity in recruitment. While the Gurkhas, Kumaonis, and Garhwalis had proven their worth as a fighting force, the Assam Rifles had to look elsewhere for specialists such as radio operators, engineers, laboratory assistants, and other positions that required a higher degree of 'educational qualifications'. The Gurkhas were considered unfit. Therefore, personnel from Bengal and Kerala were recruited to fill those technical roles.[42]

From 1982, the Assam Rifles conducted its own recruitment drives. By 1985, it began recruiting from across India, although most recruits still came from the north-eastern states. In 2003 and 2004, for instance, the force sought to recruit constables from states such as Chhattisgarh, Madhya Pradesh, and Rajasthan.[43] Since 2011–12, however, recruitment has been centralized via the annual Staff Selection Commission examination, rather than being carried out by the Assam Rifles. The government has also sought to increase recruitment from border states and areas affected by militancy, with 20 per cent of vacancies being filled by personnel from border districts that 'fall within the responsibility' of the Assam Rifles and a further 20 per cent from 'militancy affected areas' as defined by the government.[44]

Under this new recruitment system, applicants are asked to provide their preference for their services. Applicants have begun opting for apparently 'softer' forces, such as the Central Industrial Security Force (CISF), rather than the Assam Rifles, which is perceived as a particularly tough assignment due to its counter-insurgency duties. Since the Assam Rifles is the only paramilitary force under the MHA—the others are police forces—its military character faces a serious risk of dilution owing to the change in recruitment patterns.[45]

Vacancies arising from attrition remains an important problem for the Assam Rifles. A standing committee report tabled in the Rajya Sabha in 2018 noted that unsatisfactory working conditions may be causing attrition.[46] As of 2019, out of a sanctioned strength of 66,408, there were 4,432 vacant posts. The standard government line is that the vacancies are due to factors such as retirement, resignation, death, or the creation of new posts, and that the government aims to fill these posts through existing recruitment mechanisms.[47]

The Assam Rifles also began recruiting women into its cadres at the recommendation of the Committee on Empowerment of Women. In a 2010–11 report entitled *Women in Paramilitary Forces*, the committee wrote that 'adequate representation' of women should be 5 per cent of the force's personnel—around 2,400 women soldiers.[48] However, by 2018, there were only 360 women in the Assam Rifles; 125 were posted to battalions and 235 were undergoing training. As of 2020, the total number of women has risen to 900—still far short of the prescribed target.[49]

If filling the rank-and-file of the Assam Rifles largely depended on recruiting personnel from local tribes in north-east India and Nepal, staffing its brass was rather more complicated. Until India's independence, British officers had occupied the commanding positions in the Assam Rifles. Later on, however, several officers from the Indian Army served as commandants on a deputation basis: these officers led the Assam Rifles for a limited period of time before returning to their regiments in the army. This deputation-based policy was in place until 1968, creating several problems. Ensuring continuity was a major concern for the Assam Rifles during this period. Officers were also unable to get to know their soldiers well. Furthermore, the army officers took a long time to get familiar with the traditions, customs, and overall ambit of civil regulations and procedures.[50]

Owing to recurrent recruitment problems, a new affiliation plan was drawn up in 1977. It stipulated which regiments of the Indian Army would officer which battalions of the Assam Rifles. In addition, army leadership noted that 'officers for Assam Rifles battalions including commandants would be selected from the panels of their affiliated regiments'.[51] Even to this day, 80 per cent of Assam Rifles officers are drawn from the Indian Army; only 20 per cent come from the Assam Rifles cadre. The Standing Committee on Home Affairs found this to be 'highly skewed'. The committee recommended that this proportion be reconfigured to 'strike a balance between the officers of the Indian Army and the Assam Rifles Cadre'.[52]

Recruitment: Rashtriya Rifles

Although the Rashtriya Rifles is a paramilitary force engaged in low-intensity counter-insurgency operations, it is made up of soldiers drawn from various regiments of the Indian Army on a deputation basis. At the time of its formation, personnel came from all branches of the army. Infantry soldiers constituted half of the paramilitary's personnel, with service corps, artillery, and armour making up another 10 per cent, and the remainder coming from other parts of the army.[53] These mixed regiments resulted in what Rajagopalan calls the 'bad apple' problem. Army battalions would rid themselves of the most troublesome soldiers in their regiments by sending them to the Rashtriya Rifles.[54] In addition, the constant rotation of troops caused issues of 'camaraderie and cohesion' in the field.[55]

These problems motivated a change in the recruitment pattern in the Rashtriya Rifles,. While still relying on deputation since 1990, each Rashtriya Rifles battalion is now composed of soldiers from a single infantry regiment.[56] The majority of the officers are also from the same regiment. In some cases, such as the engineering services, officers may be posted from different regiments, given the all-arms nature of the force. However, all commanding officers are from the same regiment.

Performance and Reform

Both the Assam Rifles and the Rashtriya Rifles have been mainstays of India's counter-insurgency campaigns in, respectively, the north-east India and Jammu and Kashmir. While established as paramilitary forces to relieve the Indian Army, both the Assam Rifles and the Rashtriya Rifles fall under the purview of the MoD—albeit to varying degrees, with the Indian Army providing only officers to the Assam Rifles and both officers and soldiers to the Rashtriya Rifles. Given the army's direct involvement in the operations of both paramilitaries, it is difficult to evaluate whether these forces have lessened the army's role in counter-insurgency operations. For example, the fact that both Assam Rifles cadres as well as Indian Army regiments are deployed in India's north-east makes it hard to isolate the Assam Rifles' performance.

In their annual reports, both the MoD and the MHA detail the 'achievements' of the Assam Rifles and the Rashtriya Rifles. But it is difficult to draw informative analytical insights or inferences from those data alone, or to judge the performance of these forces through either comparative or individual analysis. For instance, the reports typically offer absolute yearly numbers on weapons seized, insurgents captured or killed, and other such statistics. Since nearly all these metrics are dependent on insurgent capacity and activity, the lack of proper benchmarks makes evaluating the counter-insurgency performance difficult—even over a fixed timeline for one particular force. Moreover, given how different the theatres are in north-east India and Jammu and Kashmir, drawing a comparative analysis is also difficult.

Based on available MHA data, the number of insurgents killed or surrendered by the Assam Rifles fell between 2010 and 2011 and 2019 and 2020, and the number of insurgents apprehended appears to have declined somewhat as well (Figure 10.1).

According to data on military and militant fatalities in Jammu and Kashmir provided by the South Asia Terrorism Portal, the number of insurgents and terrorists killed sharply declined between 2000 and 2020 (Figure 10.2). However, the number of casualties was at a minimum in

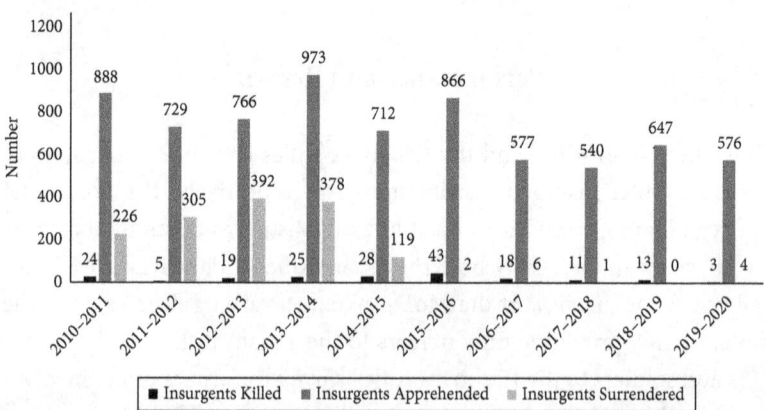

Figure 10.1 Insurgents Killed, Apprehended, and Surrendered (Assam Rifles)

Source: MHA annual reports, various years. The number of insurgents surrendered in 2018–19 is not available in MHA annual report for that year and has been marked as 0 for the sake of visualization.

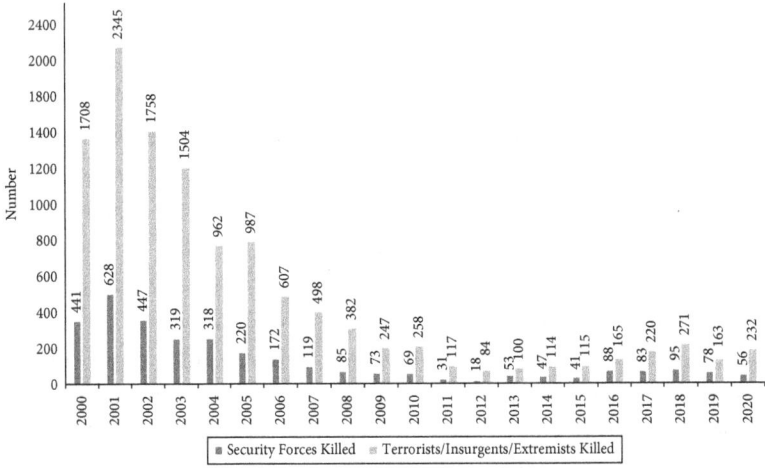

Figure 10.2 Security Forces vs. Non-State Actors Killed (Jammu & Kashmir)

Source: This data is taken from SATP and is for the entire state of Jammu and Kashmir, https://www.satp.org/datasheet-terrorist-attack/fatalities/india-jammukashmir. The data presented in MoD annual reports is patchy and discontinuous. Since RR is the main counter-insurgency and counter-terrorism force in J&K, these figures can be taken as an approximation of RR's performance.

2012 and seems to have returned to and stabilized at the level seen in 2009, with 232 terrorists, insurgents, or extremists killed in 2020.

However, inferring the paramilitaries' performance merely from the number of casualties could be misleading—the picture is rather more complicated.

Several variables that impact insurgency and counter-insurgency—including external support provided to insurgents in the form of safe havens, arms, and training—could be dependent on the state of India's bilateral relationships. External support for insurgencies in north-east India came in the past from China, Bangladesh, Myanmar, and Bhutan, provided either by the governments or other ally insurgent forces. However, recently improved relations with Bangladesh and Bhutan has mitigated this problem.[57] Since the 1980s, China too has stopped actively supporting insurgencies in north-eastern India.[58] In Kashmir, on the other hand, external support from Pakistan continues to flow in (although during the 2004–2007 composite peace process, there was a notable drop in the number of insurgents infiltrating India).[59]

Another factor is the ambiguous relationship between neutralization and area domination along the border versus in the hinterland, which complicates any analysis of a force's performance based solely on the body counts of insurgents. While a higher number of insurgent deaths might indicate the success of India's counter-insurgency operations, the body count may not necessarily serve as an accurate proxy for area domination. Counter-intuitively, a lower number of kills could also represent effective area domination by the security forces, because it could indicate lower levels of insurgent action due to effective control over the counter-insurgency grid. So, while border districts might register more infiltration and consequently a higher number of fatalities compared to the hinterland, this does not necessarily mean that the paramilitary deployed along the border is performing any better. Border areas may in fact be far more difficult to dominate than hinterland areas, given that border forces are the first line of defence against infiltrating militants. These complexities make it difficult to accurately evaluate the performance of the Assam Rifles and the Rashtriya Rifles, and continue to be the subject of much debate within the military and paramilitary forces themselves.

Reform: Assam Rifles

Two issues currently dominate discussions about reforming the Assam Rifles. The first has to do with bringing the force under the complete (administrative as well as operational) control of the MHA. As it stands today, the Assam Rifles is administratively controlled by the MHA while operational control rests with the MoD. Recently, the MHA proposed merging the Assam Rifles with the Indo-Tibetan Border Police (ITBP) to bring it fully under one ministry's control. Defence analyst Manvendra Singh has argued against the MHA taking full control, writing that the 'culture of Assam Rifles is operational' and that 'regimental rigidity has not set in'. He argued that bringing the Assam Rifles under the fold of the MHA could seriously affect the counter-insurgency performance of the force, which is largely dependent on 'deputationist Army officers'.[60] One report raised questions about the realities of merging the Assam Rifles with the ITBP, noting the different ethos of each force and the potential difficulty of integrating them effectively.[61]

If merging the Assam Rifles with the ITBP would make it a wholly border-guarding force, then the Standing Committee on Home Affairs' 2018 report on the Central Armed Police Forces essentially made the opposite suggestion: that the Assam Rifles be made a purely counter-insurgency force. It also recommended raising a separate force to guard the India-Myanmar border, which is currently one of the responsibilities of the Assam Rifles. The MHA, however, rejected this suggestion. It argued that a 'Border Out Post (BOP) type' deployment, in which a force would be placed at regular intervals to secure the border, would be impossible given the mountainous terrain. Rather, it chose to retain its current model, arguing that counter-insurgency operations in 'the hinterland are inextricably linked to the counter infiltration operations being undertaken at the border'.[62]

Reform: Rashtriya Rifles

While existing literature typically claims that the Rashtriya Rifles is an effective counter-insurgency force, the question of granting a permanent mandate to the Rashtriya Rifles has been a serious cause of concern to the MoD and a point of contention between the MoD and the Ministry of Finance. The Rashtriya Rifles, created to tackle the rise of militancy and insurgency in a specific time and place, was initially granted only a temporary mandate. Some have expressed concerns that not granting the Rashtriya Rifles a permanent mandate affected its modernization plans, with implications for its performance.[63] Others have argued that giving it a permanent mandate would constitute an implicit admission that internal strife was deeply entrenched. This issue remains unresolved, and it has resulted in 'grudging cooperation to [the Rashtriya Rifles] from the paramilitary forces, especially the Border Security Force'.[64]

As a part of the army's recent headquarters reorganization, the headquarters of the Rashtriya Rifles will be shifted from Delhi to the Northern Command in Udhampur, Jammu and Kashmir. This is essentially to reduce the so-called administrative burden of the Rashtriya Rifles and to enable it to focus more on operations. Given this reduction in scope, the Rashtriya Rifles will be led by an Additional Director General (a major general–rank army officer) rather than a Director General (a lieutenant general–rank army officer). To take care of procurement matters, a new sub-vertical will be created in the Infantry Directorate in New Delhi. This new structure is said to be similar to the way the Assam Rifles operates from their headquarters in Shillong.[65] Lieutenant General Syed Ata Hasnain has argued that it would be a mistake to treat the Directorate General of the Rashtriya Rifles (DGRR) like the Directorate General of the Assam Rifles (DGAR) for at least three reasons. First, Hasnain argues, the DGRR is 'lighter' and cannot function as Rashtriya Rifles' operational headquarters, as opposed to the DGAR, which is more like a 'Corps HQ of the Army'. Second, when the DGRR was moved to Srinagar, it was beset by inter-headquarter rivalries—specifically with the Army XV Corps. Finally, he argues that the XV Corps knows Kashmir best, so their primacy should not be meddled with.[66]

Conclusion

The Assam Rifles and the Rashtriya Rifles offer contrasting models of organizational history, structure, recruitment, and deployment of specialized counter-insurgency forces. Assessing their operational capabilities is no easy feat, yet one can observe with some confidence their relative advantages over the average infantry battalions that rotate in and out of counter-insurgency theatres. The brief analysis presented here underscores the need for more sustained examination of the operational capabilities of the Assam Rifles and the Rashtriya Rifles, including aspects that have not been broached in this chapter, such as doctrine, training, tactics, and technology.

Even as the Assam Rifles and the Rashtriya Rifles continue to be impacted by bureaucratic and organizational tussles, they represent important institutional experiments undertaken by the Indian security state. In these instances, rather than emulate models developed elsewhere, the Indian state has demonstrated its capacity for innovation. Yet this achievement obscures a harder truth: that the mere existence of these counter-insurgency forces represents the Indian state's continuing failure to elicit the consent of its governed people.

Notes

1. Ranajit Guha, "The Prose of Counter-Insurgency," in *Subaltern Studies: Writings on South Asian History and Society,* Vol. 2, ed. Ranajit Guha, (Delhi: Oxford University Press, 1983), 1–42.
2. Srinath Raghavan, "Protecting the Raj: The Army in India and Internal Security, c. 1919–39," *Small Wars & Insurgencies* 16, no. 3 (September 1, 2005): 253–79.
3. See Timothy R. Moreman, *The Army in India and the Development of Frontier Warfare, 1849–1947*, Studies in Military and Strategic History (London: Palgrave Macmillan UK, 1998), https://doi.org/10.1057/9780230374621; For a standard history of counterinsurgency that remains oblivious to this fact, see John A. Nagl and Peter J. Schoomaker, *Learning to Eat Soup with a Knife: Counterinsurgency Lessons from Malaya and Vietnam*, 1st edition (Chicago: The University of Chicago Press, 2005).
4. Vivek Chadha, *Low Intensity Conflicts in India: An Analysis* (Delhi: SAGE Publications India, 2005).
5. See "Section 2: History of Assam Rifles: 185 Years of Glory and Sacrifice," *Assam Rifles official website*, accessed August 5, 2021, https://www.assamrifles.gov.in/english/#.
6. D. K. Palit, *Sentinels of the North-East: The Assam Rifles* (New Delhi: Palit & Palit, 1984), 21.
7. Palit, *Sentinels of the North-East*, 22.
8. See "Section 1: History of Assam Rifles: 185 Years of Glory and Sacrifice," *Assam Rifles official website,* accessed August 5, 2021, https://www.assamrifles.gov.in/english/#.
9. Ministry of Home Affairs, *Annual Report, 2019–20* (New Delhi: Government of India, n.d.), 123, https://www.mha.gov.in/sites/default/files/AnnualReport_19_20.pdf.
10. "Assam Rifles Rules, 2010" (Ministry of Home Affairs, Government of India), 3, accessed August 13, 2021, https://upload.indiacode.nic.in/showfile?actid=AC_CEN_5_23_00025_200647_1517807326902&type=rule&filename=Assam%20Rifles%20Rules%202010.pdf.
11. See "Role and Tasks," *Assam Rifles official website*, accessed August 5, 2021, https://www.assamrifles.gov.in/english/newwindow.html?2030.
12. Vilas Baburao Muttemwar and George Fernandes, "Status of Rashtriya Rifles" (Lok Sabha Questions, November 22, 2001), http://loksabhaph.nic.in/Questions/QResult15.aspx?qref=34126&lsno=13.
13. "Rashtriya Rifles," *Bharat Rakshak*, accessed August 5, 2021, http://www.bharat-rakshak.com/ARMY/units/222-Rashtriya-Rifles.html.
14. "Rashtriya Rifles," *Bharat Rakshak.*
15. Rajesh Rajagopalan, "Innovations in Counterinsurgency: The Indian Army's Rashtriya Rifles," *Contemporary South Asia* 13, no. 1 (March 1, 2004): 28, https://doi.org/10.1080/0958493042000209852.

16. "Rashtriya Rifles," *Bharat Rakshak.*

17. A. Vijayaraghavan and Jaswant Singh, "New Battalions of Rashtriya Rifles" (Rajya Sabha Debates, July 27, 2001), https://rsdebate.nic.in/bitstream/123456789/20652/1/PQ_193_27072001_U508_p237_p237.pdf.

18. Rajamohan Reddy Mekapati and A.K. Antony, "Strength of Rashtriya Rifles" (Lok Sabha Questions, n.d.), http://loksabhaph.nic.in/Questions/QResult15.aspx?qref=37540&lsno=14.

19. See "Organization Structure" in "Welcome to Assam Rifles."

20. See "Section 3: History of Assam Rifles: 185 Years of Glory and Sacrifice," *Assam Rifles official website*, accessed August 5, 2021, https://www.assamrifles.gov.in/english/#.

21. See Appendix C of "Tender Notice of GP, B, C, F Rations and Carriage Contracts of Assam Rifles 2015–16," n.d., http://www.assamrifles.gov.in/DOCS/TENDER/Q%20Branch/Tender%20Notice%20of%20Assam%20Rifles%20Gp%20B,C%20and%20Carraige.pdf.

22. Palit, *Sentinels of the North-East*, 191.

23. Palit, *Sentinels of the North-East*, 192–93.

24. Palit, *Sentinels of the North-East*, 275.

25. Palit, *Sentinels of the North-East*, 275.

26. Palit, *Sentinels of the North-East*, 276–77.

27. Rajagopalan, "Innovations in Counterinsurgency," 25.

28. K. V. Krishna Rao, *In the Service of the Nation: Reminiscences* (New Delhi: Viking, 2001), 449.

29. Syed Ata Hasnain, "Rashtriya Rifles: The Story of Independent India's Finest Military Experiment," *Swarajya*, July 23, 2017, https://swarajyamag.com/defence/rashtriya-rifles-the-story-of-independent-indias-finest-military-experiment.

30. "Power Packed: Rashtriya Rifles Have Come a Long Way since Its Inception," *FORCE* (blog), March 11, 2019, https://forceindia.net/power-packed/.

31. Jaswant Singh to A. Vijayaraghavan in Rajya Sabha, "New Battalions of Rashtriya Rifles." See: https://rsdebate.nic.in/bitstream/123456789/20652/1/PQ_193_27072001_U508_p237_p237.pdf.

32. https://swarajyamag.com/defence/rashtriya-rifles-the-story-of-independent-indias-finest-military-experiment

33. Hasnain, "Rashtriya Rifles."

34. "Chapter Six: Asia," *The Military Balance* 121, no. 1 (January 1, 2021): 264, https://doi.org/10.1080/04597222.2021.1868795.

35. Rajagopalan, "Innovations in Counterinsurgency," 29–31.

36. Hasnain, "Rashtriya Rifles."

37. Rajagopalan, "Innovations in Counterinsurgency," 33.

38. Rajagopalan, "Innovations in Counterinsurgency," 34.

39. Palit, *Sentinels of the North-East*, 331, 333.

40. Palit, *Sentinels of the North-East*, 331.

41. Tejimala Gurung, "The Making of Gurkhas as a 'Martial Race,' in Colonial India: Theory and Practice," *Proceedings of the Indian History Congress* 75 (2014): 521–22. For a more detailed discussion on the construction of the martial race by the British, see the whole article.
42. Palit, *Sentinels of the North-East*, 332.
43. Arun Kumar, T. Govindan, and I.D. Swami, "Recruitment in PMF" (Lok Sabha Questions, August 5, 2003), http://loksabhaph.nic.in/Questions/QResult15. aspx?qref=63758&lsno=13; Also see "Annexure—I: Statement Referred to in Part (a) & (b) of Lok Sabha Unstarred Question No. 1775 For Answer on 20/7/2004" (Lok Sabha Questions, July 20, 2004), http://164.100.47.193/Annexture_New/lsq14/2/au1775.htm.
44. Ministry of Home Affairs, *Annual Report, 2011–12* (New Delhi: Government of India, n.d.), 186, https://www.mha.gov.in/sites/default/files/AnnualReport_11_12.pdf.
45. Interview with a former Director General of Assam Rifles (DGAR).
46. Parliamentary Standing Committee on Home Affairs, *Working Conditions in Border Guarding Forces (Assam Rifles, Sashastra Seema Bal, Indo-Tibetan Border Police and Border Security Force)*, Report No. 214, December 12, 2018, 16.
47. Pinaki Misra and Nityanad Rai, "Vacancies in Para Military Forces," Vacancies in Para Military Forces," (Lok Sabha Questions, July 2, 2019), http://loksabhaph.nic. in/Questions/QResult15.aspx?qref=1937&lsno=17.
48. Ministry of Home Affairs, *Annual Report, 2018–19*, 150, https://www.mha.gov. in/sites/default/files/AnnualReport_18_19.pdf.
49. MHA, *Annual Report, 2019–20*, 151.
50. Palit, *Sentinels of the North-East*, 281–82.
51. Palit, *Sentinels of the North-East*, 284.
52. Parliamentary Standing Committee on Home Affairs, *Working Conditions in Border Guarding Forces*, 9.
53. "Rashtriya Rifles," *Bharat Rakshak*.
54. Rajagopalan, "Innovations in Counterinsurgency," 31.
55. "Rashtriya Rifles," *Bharat Rakshak*.
56. Rajagopalan, "Innovations in Counterinsurgency," 31.
57. Udayon Misra, "ULFA: Beginning of the End," *Economic and Political Weekly* 44, no. 52 (2009): 13.; Praveen Kumar, "External Linkages and Internal Security: Assessing Bhutan's Operation All Clear," *Strategic Analysis* 28, no. 3 (July 1, 2004): 390–410, https://doi.org/10.1080/09700160408450144.
58. Subir Bhaumik, *Troubled Periphery: The Crisis of India's North East* (Delhi: SAGE Publications India, 2009), 163.
59. Happymon Jacob, *Line on Fire: Ceasefire Violations and India-Pakistan Escalation Dynamics* (New Delhi: Oxford University Press, 2019), 176.
60. Manvendra Singh, "Assam Rifles Operational Control Shouldn't Be under Home Ministry. Don't Mess with the Best," *ThePrint*, November 12, 2019, https://thepr

int.in/opinion/assam-rifles-control-shouldnt-be-under-home-ministry-dont-mess-with-best/319435/.

61. P.K. Chakravorty, "Assam Rifles: A Reality Check" (Delhi: Center for Land Warfare Studies, n.d.), https://indianarmy.nic.in/writereaddata/documents/claws06011119.pdf.

62. Parliamentary Standing Committee on Home Affairs, *Working Conditions in Border Guarding Forces*, 25.

63. M.V. Mysura Reddy, "Demand to Give Permanent Mandate to the Rashtriya Rifles," February 24, 2009, https://rsdebate.nic.in/bitstream/123456789/224 136/1/ID_215_20022009_p207_p207_26.pdf; Also see Manu Pubby, "Rashtriya Rifles in a Spot, Finance Ministry Objects to Permanent Mandate," *The Indian Express*, October 12, 2009, https://indianexpress.com/article/news-archive/web/rashtriya-rifles-in-a-spot-finance-ministry-objects-to-permanent-mandate/.

64. "Power Packed," 2019.

65. Shaurya Karanbir Gurung, "Army Rejig: Now ADG to Head Rashtriya Rifles," *The Economic Times*, April 1, 2019, https://economictimes.indiatimes.com/news/defence/army-rejig-now-adg-to-head-rashtriya-rifles/articleshow/68663165.cms?from=mdr.

66. Syed Ata Hasnain, "Army Reforms: Why Moving Rashtriya Rifles HQ to J&K Is Dangerous," *TheQuint*, September 12, 2018, https://www.thequint.com/voices/opinion/army-reforms-moving-rashtriya-rifles-hq-to-jammu-kashmir-unne cessary.

PART IV
POLICE AND INVESTIGATIVE AGENCIES

Part IV of this volume reviews the Indian police and the country's primary investigative agencies. Public order and most day-to-day aspects of internal security are the responsibilities of the Indian police force, which are under the supervision of India's various states. The chaper on the Indian police describes the history of the force, summarizes its organization and objectives, and outlines the multiple barriers that exist today to effective policing. The final chapter of the book analyses India's two premier investigation agencies: the Central Bureau of Investigation and the National Investigation Agency. This concluding chapter summarizes their role, describes their histories in the context of ongoing jurisdictional conflicts between the center and the states, and highlights issues relating to human resources, credibility, and institutional independence .

11

The Police in India

Akshay Mangla and Vineet Kapoor

Introduction

India's police are entrusted with maintaining public order and enforcing the law. From recording citizen complaints to investigating crimes, the police are essential to internal security and the criminal justice system. A classic example of street-level bureaucracy, police work involves a multitude of complex tasks that call for fine-grained judgement. Police agencies interact frequently with citizens, and officers are required to exercise discretion when handling cases.[1] Other street-level bureaucrats—such as schoolteachers, medical workers, or welfare officers—also must exercise discretion, but the police are distinct because they hold coercive authority and the mandate to enforce rules on society. They patrol and intervene across geographies and aspects of social life where citizens may not seek their presence. And, in the course of their everyday work, police must interpret laws that are often ambiguous and whose implementation may foster social conflict. As political scientist James Q. Wilson observed, 'These activities create special problems of administration, for they require the organization to deal with conflict over the meaning and importance of the law, the definition of "public order," and the trade-off between protecting individual rights and protecting the community.'[2] How police agencies negotiate these tensions can have material consequences for security provision, social welfare, and citizen trust in the state.[3]

This chapter presents an analytical appraisal of India's state police agencies and their relevance for India's internal security. In a large, multi-ethnic democracy such as India, with high rates of poverty and social inequality, the police occupy an essential role in the provision of security and crime control, as well as social welfare more broadly. How well are

Akshay Mangla and Vineet Kapoor, *The Police in India* In: *Institutional Roots of India's Security Policy.* Edited by: Milan Vaishnav, Oxford University Press. © Oxford University Press 2024. DOI: 10.1093/oso/9780198894612.003.0011 the police equipped to carry out their multiple mandates? What are the organizational capabilities, constraints, and cultures that shape how the police perform their core functions? These are the major questions animating this chapter. In it, we combine a macro-institutional view of the police force in India—its organizational structure and operations—with a micro-level understanding of police work from the perspective of frontline officers. We offer insights from the extensive literature on policing, along with administrative data and reports from government and non-governmental agencies. We also draw on extensive field research carried out in the state of Madhya Pradesh, where one of the authors currently serves in the state police,[4] to supplement the analysis with empirical materials. These include an original survey of 1,961 police officers, conducted in two rounds (2018 and 2020), which sheds light on officer perceptions and behaviours, as well as qualitative field research in three districts of Madhya Pradesh, including participant observation in eight police stations and two police training academies, and interviews of 46 police officers.

The chapter proceeds as follows. First, this chapter explores the organizational mandate and objectives of state police forces in India by tracing the agency's evolution from the colonial era to the post-independence period. Then, it examines the formal administrative design and procedures of the police, emphasizing the importance of organizational hierarchy. The next section discusses police administrative capacity, including human resources and physical infrastructure. Following that, it explores the informal culture and norms inside police agencies, which shape officer behaviour. Finally, the chapter analyses police performance in light of police organizational culture and resource constraints, including the policy implications of police reform proposals, before offering some concluding remarks.

Institutional Origins and Purpose of the Indian Police

The Constitution of India and various legal statutes set out the institutional objectives of the Indian police. These include law enforcement, crime control, and the maintenance of public order. However, much of what police agencies actually do goes beyond their traditional remit. From hearing citizen complaints, to adjudicating civil disputes, to extending humanitarian support, the Indian police have a diverse mandate and set of responsibilities.

The 1857 Mutiny and subsequent rebellions set the stage for the creation of a uniform administrative system of policing throughout India. The Government of India Act of 1858 transferred authority from the East India Company to the British colonial government. The chief objectives of the British Raj were to collect revenues and preserve public order in the service of the crown's economic exploits.[5] To meet these purposes, the colonial government introduced a system of policing, which gradually evolved as political conditions changed in the lead-up to independence.[6] The Madras Police Act of 1859 formalized the structure of a partly civil and partly military police organization, which formed the basis for police agencies across India.[7]

Shortly after the British Raj assumed control of India, reforms that had long been under discussion were inscribed in legislation, including the Code of Civil Procedure (1859), the Indian Penal Code (1860), the Code of Criminal Procedure (1861), and the Indian Evidence Act (1872). A police commission appointed in 1860 recommended sweeping institutional changes, including the elimination of military police. The resulting Police Act of 1861 established a civil police force overseen by provincial governments. At the local level, the district superintendent of police was made subservient to the district magistrate, the highest-ranking civil servant in the local bureaucracy.[8] These laws and structures formed the foundation of India's criminal justice system, and they continue to guide the police today. Colonial-era policing laws have garnered much criticism from civil society actors and political leadership. In response, legislators at the national and state levels have recently pressed for amendments that aim to better meet the contemporary demands of policing in a democracy.[9] At the time of writing, the fate of these proposed changes is uncertain.

Although the 1861 Police Act created a civil police force, the military police were never eliminated. Instead, the Raj drew a clear line between civil police units posted in police station houses (*thanas*) and the armed reserve police based in barracks. The latter retained its military character and were mainly summoned to quash communal disturbances or other threats to public order. Authority over rural policing was wrested away from landlords (*zamindars*) who traditionally policed the countryside through local headmen (*mukhias*) and watchmen (*chowkidars*) who resided in villages. Beginning with the 1870 Chowkidari Act, the duties of village police were reduced, as was the authority of village governments (*panchayats*) over policing functions. This centralization of authority in the hands of provincial governments enabled colonial authorities to maintain their top-down administrative control of the police. At the top of the hierarchy sat the Indian Imperial Police, the colonial predecessor to the Indian Police Service (IPS). To maintain British control over the force, posts within the Indian Imperial Police were closed to Indians until 1920.

India's colonial policing structure followed the Irish model, which emphasized accountability to rulers rather than local communities, the separation of the police from the civilian population, and the use of paramilitary arrangements to suppress peasant rebellions.[10] The civil police maintained separate police stations and living quarters from the public to help ensure that they would be responsive to state directives. According to criminal justice professor Arvind Verma and former IPS officer K.S. Subramanian, 'The structure stipulated clearly that there was no necessity for involvement of the community in anyway in the policing function.'[11] When criticisms of police malpractice reached the colonial leadership, Lord Curzon, then Viceroy of India, formed a police commission in 1902 to address the problem. The commission identified multiple defects such as substandard training, the use of oppressive tactics, and low public confidence in the police. Nonetheless, the commission endorsed the organizational principles set forth by the 1861 Police Act, which stressed centralized control and a militaristic hierarchy.[12]

The struggle for representative government, led by the Indian National Congress, drew mass support as disaffection with colonial rule grew during World War I. The police were summoned to curtail assemblies and crowds, employ force against rioters, and, together with municipal authorities, enforce licences for public meetings and processions. In addition to the civil police force, the armed reserve forces were frequently called upon to disperse crowds and maintain public order. In practical terms, this meant heavy-handed enforcement of rules to control public space, an orientation that persisted after independence. Less priority was afforded to investigating crimes and addressing the security needs of ordinary citizens.

Following independence, the overall organizational structure of the police remained unchanged, with its militaristic hierarchy and centralized command structure. But with the introduction of democracy in India, the mandate and operational modalities of policing underwent important changes. The police became implicated in the process of democratization and development.[13] For instance, their role in maintaining India's electoral democracy is evident. Indian police agencies help administer large-scale political events, including the world's largest elections, which are widely seen as being fair and credible in their execution. The management of collective violence is no small feat given India's diverse, multi-ethnic, and multi-religious social fabric.[14] Equally important, though, is the routine task of managing everyday, small-scale social conflict, a critical function of the police.

Indian democracy and the constitution also set important limits on the police's use of coercion in maintaining internal security. Police authority does not go unchallenged by society.[15] Agencies face pressure to demonstrate legitimacy in the eyes of the public, adding to their multiple mandates. The police are expected to perform social service functions and discharge other essential duties, such as disaster relief, that put them in regular contact with the general public. These facts, inextricably linked to internal security provision within a diverse social and political ecosystem, makes policing complex and greatly complicates the study of police organization and performance in India.

Formal Administrative Design of the Police

India's police are subject to the country's federal structure and the separation of powers between the central and state governments. According to the Seventh Schedule of the Constitution of India, policing and public order fall within the mandate of state governments. State police forces report to their Home Departments, which oversee crime control, prosecution, prison administration, and other internal security functions. The duty to manage internal security is shared with the central government's Ministry of Home Affairs (MHA). The MHA maintains a separate set of police forces and specialized branches, including investigative agencies like the Central Bureau of Investigation and intelligence entities such as the Intelligence Bureau.[16] The central government also has authority over police training and technical assistance for crime investigation, and it leads coordination among states during intelligence operations. Various central bodies, created under the MHA, work alongside state governments, such as the Bureau of Police Research and Development (BPRD), an apex body on policy and planning that supports police training and modernization. The MHA also oversees the recruitment, training, and employment conditions of officers in the IPS.

India's state police forces have a common administrative structure, with well-defined hierarchies, rules, and procedures that emphasize organizational coherence and chain of command.[17] Figure 11.1 illustrates the different organizational ranks in state police forces as well as the percentage distribution of police personnel within each category. At the top is an elite corps of gazetted IPS officers, who are nationally recruited on the basis of a highly competititve examination to serve in senior executive and managerial posts. The director general of police, the highest-ranking officer, oversees police activities throughout a state. The director general is supported by special directors general of police and additional directors general of police, followed by inspectors general, deputy

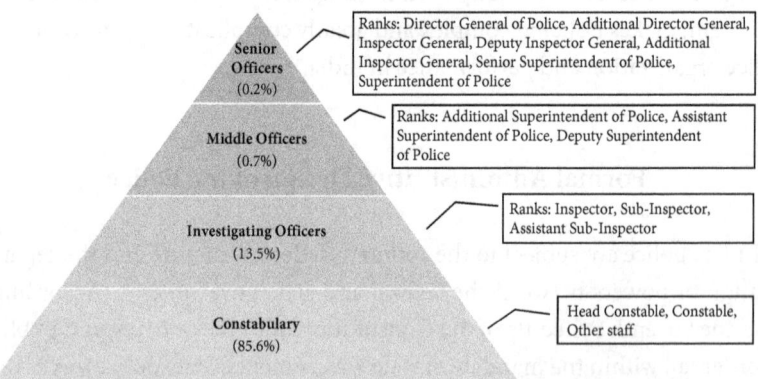

Figure 11.1 Police Officer Ranks and Percentage Distribution of Personnel in India

Source: Bureau of Police Research and Development (BPRD), Government of India (2018). Data indicate the percentage of actual police personnel strength within each rank.

inspectors general, and, lastly, superintendents of police, who oversee police districts. Functional responsibilities are allocated to different police branches, such as administration, training, crime, narcotics, traffic, cybercrime, intelligence, and crimes against women. Police branches are led by special directors general and additional directors general, while inspectors general and deputy inspectors general head sub-departments and oversee day-to-day branch operations.

Police authorities are organized into geographic jurisdictions within each state, including zones, ranges, and districts. Police zones are large jurisdictions overseen by an inspector general. Zones comprise multiple police ranges, which are overseen by deputy inspectors general. In turn, ranges are made up of multiple districts. Policing at the district level is managed by superintendents of police. For example, the state of Madhya Pradesh is divided into 11 zones, 15 ranges, and 52 districts. Each district has a team of gazetted officers from the State Police Services, including additional superintendents of police and deputy superintendents of police. Officers occupying these middle ranks assist the superintendent's office, overseeing assigned subdivisions of their districts and supporting the operations of functional branches at the local level. Likewise, each police station is assigned a geographic catchment area, over which it holds jurisdiction. The police station may be supported by multiple substations or outposts (*chowkis*), from which police staff conduct beats, monitor crime, and perform other field duties.

The subordinate ranks of the police consist of non-gazetted officers, recruited at either the state or district level. These ranks include inspector, sub-inspector, assistant sub-inspector, head constable, and constable. Officers at this level normally hold field postings at police stations, though they can also be assigned to support the district superintendent of police. There are important differences in the mandate, functions, and authorities vested in different subordinate officer ranks. The police station chief, known as the station house officer, is an inspector or sub-inspector who is responsible for managing the station's catchment area. Likewise, the authority to investigate crimes and file charge-sheets (*challan*) against accused parties is held by inspectors and sub-inspectors, which make up 14 per cent of the force. Constables and head constables are authorized to collect information from the public, conduct surveillance, guard vital installations, and perform other law-and-order duties, but they do

not have the power to investigate crimes (except for certain minor of-
fenses).[18] The constabulary constitutes the vast majority (87 per cent) of
police personnel.

In addition to the officer ranks, technical and other support staff are
assigned to police stations, districts, and branch offices. Each district also
has its own police line, a reserve that includes a store of resources (such
as uniforms, vehicles, communication equipment, and ammunitions)
as well as personnel. Police lines are headed by a reserve inspector, who
oversees the supply of equipment and extra personnel and assists the district superintendent with resources as needed.

Officers in the State Police Service occupy the middle-management
tier of the police hierarchy. These officers spend most of their careers in
the field supervising subdivisions, or clusters of stations known as circles. They are a chief conduit of information and managerial oversight
between senior ranks and police stations. At the top of the hierarchy, IPS
officers occupy the senior ranks. Altogether, the middle and senior ranks
account for less than 1 per cent of the force's personnel. India has around
4,000 IPS officers in all, more than 10 per cent of whom are normally on
deputation with the central government at a given time.

Administrative hierarchy and authority divisions are designed to facilitate a uniformity of purpose and adherence to chain of command
within the police. The top-down command structure—from police headquarters on down to the district and station level—enables large-scale coordination. The capacity to coordinate is critical for maintaining law and
order in Indian states, many of which are as populous as a large country.
Further, it enables the police to manage mass events, such as religious fes-
tivals, pilgrimages, public demonstrations, and protests, which happen
regularly in India. But the top-down command structure presents disad-
vantages as well. It places outsized authority in the hands of a small set of
IPS officers. Subordinates have little opportunity to participate in organizational decisions. Bottom-up communication and information-sharing
across hierarchical ranks and divisions can also be negatively impacted.

State police forces in India are also subject to a dual command structure, in which the state government and civilian bureaucracy both hold
authority over the police. The office of the director general of police reports to the MHA, which is overseen by the home secretary, a civil servant belonging to the Indian Administrative Service (IAS). Similarly, at
the district level, the superintendent of police operates under the district

magistrate (also an IAS officer). This system of dual control, stipulated in Sections 3 and 4 of the 1861 Police Act, provides for a clear separation of powers. While the superintendent directs the police, the district magistrate oversees judicial processes, which include issuing licences and arrest warrants. An exception to dual control is the commissionerate system used by some states, such as Maharashtra, Tamil Nadu, and Uttar Pradesh, a governance structure established for policing larger cities (those with populations above 1 million) and densely populated districts. The commissionerate system creates a uniform command structure under a commissioner of police, who holds complete executive authority.

There is a long-standing debate over the efficacy of dual control. Some view it as a hangover from colonial governance that enables bureaucratic interference while weakening the autonomous command structure of the police.[19] On the other hand, dual control may facilitate shared responsibility between the police and civilian bureaucracy, as well as inter-agency coordination. In the case of law-and-order management, for example, dual control encourages the superintendent and district magistrate to better coordinate their efforts.

Broadly speaking, police recruitment in India has four entry points: IPS officer, deputy superintendent of police, sub-inspector, and constable.[20] As one goes down the hierarchy, the rigour and professional oversight of selection declines. IPS recruitment takes place nationally under the aegis of the Union Public Service Commission. As with other all-India services, IPS candidates are required to have graduated from university and must pass an exceptionally rigorous, merit-based selection process involving national civil service examinations and interviews. Entry at the IPS level is extremely selective, with 150-200 candidates succeeding annually in recent years out of a pool of approximately one million applicants. The remaining three entry points into the police are overseen by state governments and the requirements vary somewhat depending on the state. Deputy superintendents are recruited into State Police Services, which have stringent requirements and meritocratic processes. Candidates must have graduated from university and are required to complete written examinations before being interviewed by the State Public Service Commission. Sub-inspector recruitment also occurs at the state level and is overseen by the state examination board. Eligibility requirements vary, but most states require candidates to hold a university degree and pass through a meritocratic assessment based on physical and written tests and interviews. Recruitment processes for constables are more uneven across states. Constables are typically selected at the district level through a selection board headed by the district superintendent. Most states require candidates to be at least 18 years old and to have completed grade 12, though some states only require completion of grade 10. Candidates must meet minimum physical requirements (such as height) and undergo physical and written examinations. The recruitment of constables is often alleged to be subject to manipulation and bribery.[21] Most states have adopted regulations to improve the integrity and transparency of recruitment processes, though implementation is uneven. Despite these issues, the recruitment of constables and other ranks is highly selective, with hundreds of thousands of applicants vying for a few hundred vacancies every year. Alongside the pecuniary benefits of government employment, the high demand for these posts also reflects the social status and recognition conferred on police officers.

Promotions within the police are nominally based on a combination of seniority and service performance. In reality, however, opportunities for promotion are scarce in the lower levels of the hierarchy, and upward mobility is limited. Constables normally expect to receive one promotion (to head constable) in their career, which takes 10 to 15 years. Few become investigating officers. IPS officers have considerably more opportunities for promotion, given the multiple ranks and charges available to them. Most IPS officers serve as district superintendents for five years before moving to higher-level post, often away from direct contact with the field.

Administrative Capacity: Police Infrastructure and Human Resources

Police work is personnel intensive, requiring officers to maintain a public presence and interact frequently with citizens. Yet India's state police forces suffer from significant shortfalls in staff. According to official sources, India has a police-to-population ratio (PPR) of 1.58 police officers per thousand people—on the low end even for a developing country.[22] That official PPR figure includes the State Armed Reserve Forces, a reserve contingent that is not posted in police stations, and as such, does not perform regular policing duties. Removing them from the tally, India's effective PPR is even lower—1.2 officers per thousand people. But this number too is somewhat misleading, because it includes the District Armed Reserve, a contingent that is typically summoned by the district superintendent to help maintain law and order, guard high-profile people, or take on other assignments that require a large force presence.

Against a low national average, there is some regional variation in the PPR across India. The more populous, northern states—including Bihar, Madhya Pradesh, Rajasthan, and Uttar Pradesh—have significantly lower PPRs in comparison to the rest of India. States with hilly terrain tend to have higher PPRs, particularly Jammu and Kashmir and the north-eastern states. Many of these territories are beset by insurgencies, separatist movements, and porous international borders, and—as a result—armed reserve units account for more than half of their police forces.

Figures 11.2 and 11.3 show, respectively, how the PPR in India has changed over time and its variation across states.

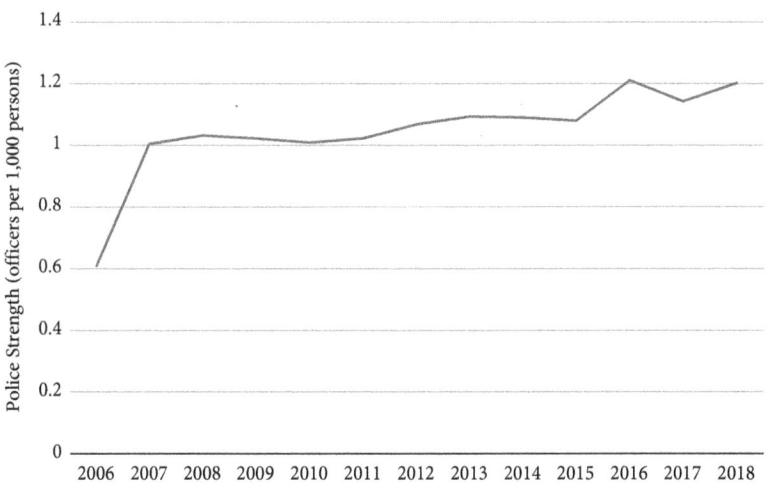

Figure 11.2 Police-to-Population Ratio in India (2007–18)

Source: BPRD, Government of India (multiple years); Population projections based on Census of India (2001; 2011).

Note: Calculated using the combined actual strength of the Civil Police force and District Armed Reserve.

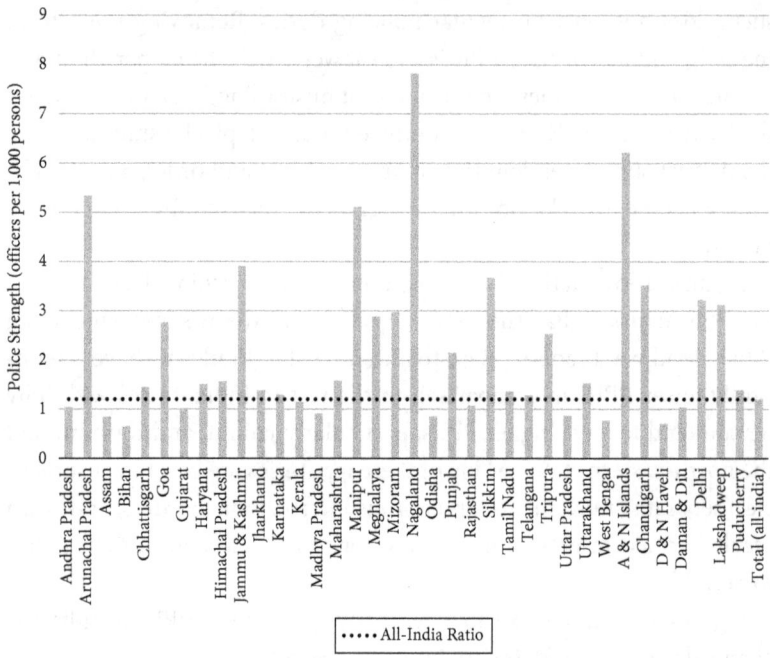

Figure 11.3 Police-to-Population Ratio across Indian States and Union Territories

Source: BPRD, Government of India (2018); Population projections based on Census of India (2011).

Note: Calculated using the combined actual strength of the Civil Police force and District Armed Reserve.

The personnel shortage is also evident in the police's vacancy rate. One-quarter of officially sanctioned posts are unfilled. Among constables, 20 per cent of sanctioned posts are vacant. For middle and senior officers, it is even higher—nearly 30 per cent.[23] Personnel shortfalls among investigating officers have a cascading impact on vital law enforcement duties, such as registering and investigating crimes, as well as important managerial functions like heading police stations and supervising subordinate officers.

The persistence of police vacancies presents a paradox given chronic personnel shortages and the large numbers of aspirants applying for such posts. One possible reason for the shortfall is that state governments may not have the fiscal resources to commit to so many permanent jobs. The cost of civilian police recruitment ultimately falls on the state exchequer, which must give final consent for expanding public employment. Additionally, some states exhibit a dearth of large-scale training capabilities, which can create bottleneckes for recruitment. The problem of vacancies may also be exacerbated by human resource policies. Among the police constabulary, a large proportion of constables get recruited into State Armed Reserve forces. These units typically act as a reserve force that operates on standby until called in for public order management and special operations (e.g, terrorist attacks and riots). They do not serve in police stations for routine law enforcement or assist with normal public-facing duties. Yet, the reserve forces consume a significant proportion of police posts, limiting the availability of officers to serve the public.

Along with aggregate shortfalls in staff, the recruitment of socially disadvantaged groups remains a challenge for India's police forces. State governments have approved the reservation of police posts for Scheduled Castes, Scheduled Tribes, and Other Backward Classes—three historically underrepresented groups. The allotted quotas differ widely across the states, partly as a consequence of their varying social demographics. With the notable exception of Karnataka, however, most states are far from meeting their official reservation quotas.[24]

The recruitment of women likewise merits attention. India's police forces are overwhelmingly comprised of men (Figure 11.4). The MHA has, on multiple occasions, issued advisories to state governments to increase women's recruitment. In 2013, the MHA stipulated that a quota of 33 per cent of posts be reserved for women, issuing guidelines that encouraged State Police Services to post female officers to police stations. Although many states have adopted these policy guidelines, only some have fully committed to to recruiting more women in line with quotas. Nevertheless, between 2004 and 2018, the overall number of women in the police more than quadrupled, from just under 40,000 to nearly 186,000. However, the proportion of women, while growing, remains low at just 9 per cent (Figure 11.5). There is a significant gap in instituting policies for the integration of women into the workplace and different job roles, limiting their career opportunities.[25] Even with greater female officer recruitment, the organizational culture of policing continues to be male-dominated, mirroring the patriarchal context in society more generally.

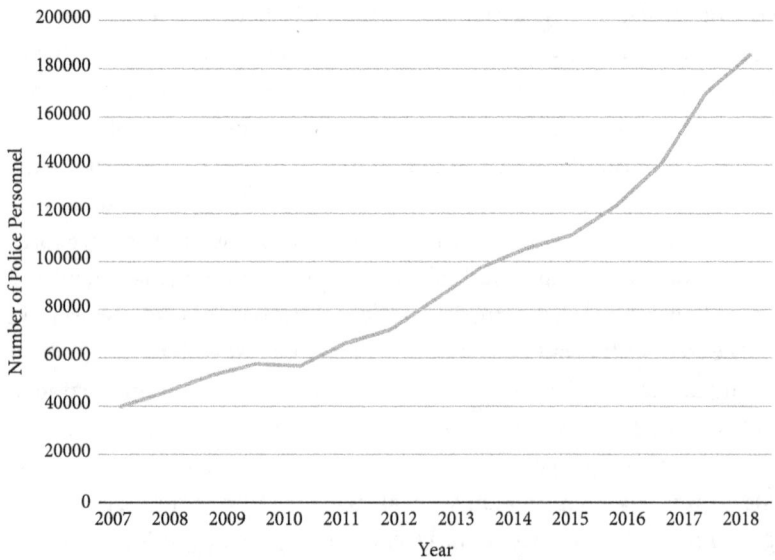

Figure 11.4 Number of Women in the Indian Police Force (2004–18)

Source: Data on Police Organizations in India, BPRD, Government of India (multiple years)

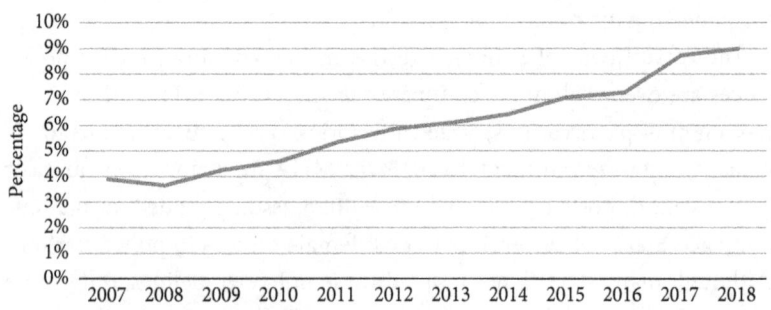

Figure 11.5 Proportion of Women in the Indian Police Force (2004–18)

Source: Data on Police Organizations in India, BPRD, Government of India (multiple years)

The inadequate provisioning of personnel impacts the police's ability to perform key functions and deliver quality services to the public. Compensating for shortfalls in staff, police officers have long workdays and erratic working hours. They have no regular days off during the week and precious few holidays to spend with their families. Station house officers are particularly overworked. Table 11.1 illustrates how station staff

Table 11.1 Time Use of Frontline Officers in Madhya Pradesh

Category of Activity	Number of hours spent on each activity in a typical workday	
	Station staff	Station house officer
Office / station-based work	4.9	5.0
Law and Order / Outside Duty	4.6	6.4
Travel	1.4	1.2
Crime investigation / Case work	1.2	1.1
Other miscellaneous work activities	0.7	1.3
Personal non-work activities (includes sleep)	11.2	9.0
Total work hours	12.8	15

Source: Police Officer Survey, Madhya Pradesh (2018); N = 1,941 officers.

and the station house officer spend their time, divided into six major categories, according to our survey of frontline officers.

Qualitative observations of police stations in Madhya Pradesh shed further light on the long hours that officers work, as well as the additional strains of inadequate staffing. On a typical day, most officers were observed reporting to the station for duty by 10:30 a.m., soon after which the morning roll call (*gadna*) took place. The head constable moharir, who works in consultation with the station house officer, assigned officers to their daily duties. Officer task assignments varied considerably depending on rank and responsibilities. For example, while many constables were placed on law-and-order duty, others were assigned to clerical work such as documentation or data entry. There was no fixed time for lunch; officers were observed eating at widely different times and locations. Evening roll call happened at approximately 6:00 p.m. Officers typically completed their duties and left for home by 11 p.m., having their dinner by midnight, just one indication of the immense strain the job poses on rank-and-file personnel.

The station house officer's hours were longer and even less predictable. After the morning roll call, the station house officer performed a series of administrative tasks, such as documenting case diaries for court, maintaining various station diaries and account books, liaising with senior officers, and giving guidance to sub-inspectors. After the evening roll call, the station house officer attended to cases reported to the station. He then typically left the station to patrol the catchment area, stopping at various outposts and beat checkpoints. Vehicle and alcohol checks, along with other law-and-order duties, made up the rest of the evening until midnight. Twice a week, the station house officer performed night duties, lasting from midnight until 5:00 a.m. These duties usually involved patrolling the catchment area or the police circle, an administrative area beyond the station. On more demanding days, there was little to no time for the station house officer to take proper rest.

Along with lengthy hours, the lack of personnel creates an uncertain and stressful work environment for officers.[26] Officers would get pulled into various tasks based on the immediate needs of the hour. If law-and-order duty called, they had to drop what they were doing at a moment's notice. When asked to escort politicians and other dignitaries, officers were required to spend long hours standing, often without food or water.

Field research verifies the deleterious effects of these excessively long workdays. In an open-ended survey question, frontline officers were asked to identify the worst aspects of police work. The most frequent responses mentioned having no days off, long hours on duty, and difficulty balancing work with family demands (Table 11.2). An understaffed and overworked police force is unlikely meet the everyday needs of citizens, with adverse effects on security provision. When officers are not available to hear citizen complaints or investigate crimes, it can diminish citizen expectations and deter them from reporting cases in the first place.

Poor human resource management is matched by inadequate physical infrastructure and equipment. State governments on average allocate 3 per cent of their annual budgets towards policing, of which the overwhelming majority (90 per cent) is spent on officer salaries and other

Table 11.2 Officer Perceptions on the Worst Aspects of Police Work

Officer Responses	Frequency of Response
'No day off'	54%
'Long working hours'	52 %
"Difficult to balance work with family demands"	33 %

Source: Police Officer Survey, Madhya Pradesh (2018); N = 1,941 officers.

fixed costs. Funding for infrastructure, technology, equipment, and other capital investments is extremely limited. Official data and reports suggest that most of India's 16,833 police stations are well equipped with vehicles, telephones, and wireless devices.[27] However, available studies of police stations, including our research in Madhya Pradesh, paint a very different picture. The Centre for the Study of Developing Societies, a New Delhi-based research institute, surveyed police in 21 states about the availability of physical infrastructure in their police stations. Contrary to official claims, 12 per cent of the officers surveyed said that their police stations had no drinking water, 18 per cent reported having no clean toilets, and 14 per cent reported having no public seating area.[28]

To supplement state police budgets, the central government introduced the Modernization of State Police Forces (MPF) scheme in 1969. Administered by the MHA, the MPF scheme aims to improve policing infrastructure to meet emerging challenges. Earmarked funds are used to upgrade police stations and outposts, as well as to provide computers and communication equipment, modern weaponry, traffic-control equipment, and forensic laboratories.[29]

The MPF scheme also supports the adoption of India's Crime and Criminal Tracking Networks and System (CCTNS). Initiated a year after the 2008 Mumbai terrorist attacks, the CCTNS is an ambitious programme to enable real-time information sharing and coordination through a sophisticated digital interface that tracks crime, warrants, arrests, missing persons, and other security information. CCTNS has become widely used by police forces across India—by April 2021, 15 out of 28 states (plus the Union Territory of Delhi) had adopted nearly all aspects of the CCTNS database, infrastructure, and technical personnel. In Madhya Pradesh, 90 per cent of the 180 police stations we surveyed reported having functioning Internet, and constables were frequently busy with CCTNS data entry.

Despite these improvements in technology, however, the MPF scheme remains highly underutilized. Comptroller and Auditor General reports over a five-year period revealed that more than 50 per cent of MPF funds went unused in 13 of the 22 states studied.[30]

In qualitative interviews, officers reported the perennial difficulties they experienced at work as a result of scarce resources (Figure 11.6). Many reported using their own private vehicles for beat patrols and other

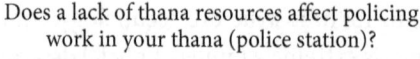

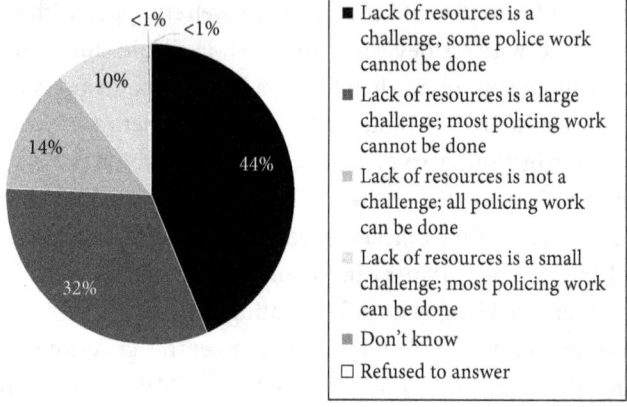

Figure 11.6 Officer Perceptions on the Impact of Resource Constraints on Police Work

Source: Police Officer Survey (2020), Madhya Pradesh

police work, while paying out of pocket for fuel expenses. Although officers can get reimbursed, many said that the reimbursement process was too lengthy and cumbersome to bother with. The inadequate availability of vehicles impeded critical tasks, such as investigating crimes or supporting victims in need of urgent medical attention. These observations were corroborated in the survey of frontline officers in Madhya Pradesh. When asked how the availability of resources impacted their work, more than three-quarters of officers reported that the lack of resources is a major challenge that restricts their ability to carry out some or all police work. Only 14 per cent of officers surveyed stated that resource provision was not a problem.

The Organizational Culture of Policing

The formal administrative structures and capacities of the Indian police exist alongside informal mechanisms of organizational culture—this includes the collective beliefs, norms, and values within an agency. Organizational culture conditions the behaviour of an agency's members in different ways.[31] Numerous studies show that norms in police agencies, what criminology professor Robert Reiner refers to as 'cop cultures', shape how officers understand their social environment, as well as their roles and responsibilities.[32] The organizational culture of police agencies is also closely connected to the occupational mandate of law enforcement. The potential use of force on the job makes police work unpredictable and dangerous.[33] According to Reiner, organizational culture provides officers with coping mechanisms, 'adaptive rules, recipes, rhetoric, and rites' for managing these daily tensions.[34] Police organizational culture may also help foster solidarity and the embrace of a common mission, while at the same time distancing the police organization from societal 'outsiders'.[35]

The culture of police agencies is hardly monolithic and may differ depending on the sociopolitical context. Police leadership and individual officers may respond in different ways to work-related tensions and uphold divergent priorities and styles of policing.[36] Frontline officers may experience diverse pressures at the local level and develop different subcultures in response to societal demands. The organizational norms of policing may vary across agencies, especially given the distinct political histories across Indian states.[37] Nevertheless, India's police agencies also share some common features, owing to the persistence of colonial institutional legacies of policing. Under the British Raj, the police were established to preserve order and stability rather than serve the public. As such, the police upheld a quasi-militaristic arrangement with highly centralized authority mechanisms and a culture that paid obeisance to hierarchy and status distinction between ranks.[38] A paternalistic orientation towards society encouraged officers to maintain their distance from ordinary citizens.[39] Likewise, social distance was preserved between officer cadres and the constables; the latter were deemed too close to society and therefore untrustworthy.

From the early stages of their careers, police officers are socialized into a highly stratified organizational hierarchy, which amplifies differences in social status and decision-making authority across ranks. Subordinates customarily salute senior officers and stand at attention until signalled to be at ease. Senior officers in the elite IPS corps receive heightened recognition, their superior status made palpable in organizational rituals and social practices. For example, senior officers have separate dining facilities and more generous housing allotments for their district field postings. During police training and other collective activities, senior officers normally take their meals separately and maintain minimal social interaction with subordinate officers.

At the other end of the organizational ranks, constables enjoy a lesser status within the police force. As criminology professor Beatrice Jauregui observes, squeezing labour out of constables while paying minimal attention to their welfare is an institutionally entrenched practice—one that reinforces the stark differences based on caste and socio-economic background.[40] Poor working conditions, inadequate housing, and the paucity of social welfare measures are material indicators of their lower status. Along with material differences, social distinctions between ranks are demarcated in duty assignments as well as mundane interactions and communication practices. Constables may be asked to serve as drivers and peons for senior officers; some get assigned to perform menial tasks unrelated to policing that go uncompensated, such as personal house cleaning and childcare.[41]

During our research in Madhya Pradesh, it was not uncommon to hear officers use the term 'constable' (*arakshak*) in a pejorative sense. Reflecting on her experience as a police trainee in Madhya Pradesh, a newly minted deputy superintendent of police remarked, 'The instructors here talk so roughly. It feels like we are some constables and not DSPs. They never give us any respect.'[42] Statements like these demonstrate that disrespecting constables is a normal, accepted practice within the police organization. Such behaviours expand the social distance between the elite senior officer corps and the subaltern rank-and-file officers, who typically have less formal education and lower socio-economic status. These status distinctions are salient among lower-ranked officers as well. The station house officer normally has a separate office with its own bathroom. Constables act as the station house officer's attendants, standing ready to fulfil their requests.

Related to the performance of hierarchy, the culture of police agencies in India puts a premium on discipline and compliance with orders and rules.[43] Officers are expected to arrive to duty sites punctually, irrespective of the time of day; failure to do so is taken as a sign of indiscipline. In our survey of police in Madhya Pradesh, frontline officers were asked to identify the three most important indicators of good police performance. Most officers (61 per cent) stated that 'arriving to work on time' came first, topping the list by a significant margin.

The importance ascribed to discipline and order is also evident from routine communication between officers and across organizational subdivisions of the police. Communication is a one-way street flowing from senior officers, who are empowered to give commands, to subordinates posted on the front lines, who are expected to obey commands. Subordinates rarely have the opportunity to express their thoughts. Pre-service training firmly establishes the norm of keeping silent, and any breach is perceived as a sign of poor discipline. Police academies have a formal curriculum on human rights, which in theory upholds freedom of thought and expression. However, this gets superseded by the informal, 'hidden curriculum', which restricts self-expression and discourages trainees from speaking, especially in the presence of senior officers.[44] These practices gain salience in officer field postings as well. In our field research, we observed the daily attendance and briefing sessions (*ganana*) held in police stations across multiple districts. Subordinate officers would line up and listen to the station house officer, who instructed them on the daily tasks requiring their immediate attention. At the end of the briefing, officers would be asked if they had any doubts—'Koi shaq?'—to which they were dutifully expected to reply, 'No, sir'.[45] In a similar vein, the sizable social distance between the IPS and front-line officers lends itself to gaps in communication and information exchange.[46]

Another feature of police organizational culture is the normalization of violence as a mode of policing. An institutional hangover from colonial policing, violence is commonly used to control society and extract confessions, particularly against poor citizens.[47] Police training, for example, affords more time to weapons and combat skills than conflict resolution or interpersonal skills.[48] The content of police training also departs from models of community policing, which encourage working partnerships between officers and the local populations they serve.[49] Police training is often haphazard and out of step with practical realities in the field. This is particularly the case for constables and other subordinate officers. After they receive mandatory pre-service training for 10 months, subordinate officers rarely receive any further structured training. By contrast, IPS officers are given high-quality professional training through the National

Police Academy in Hyderabad. This includes various kinds of pre-service training as well as in-service courses delivered by professional experts.

Institutional Performance, Accountability, and Reform Proposals

To evaluate the police's performance requires one to first define the object-ives and standards of policing, which itself raises fundamental normative and political questions. As professors Mark H. Moore and Anthony Braga suggest, 'One has to have an idea of the "good" or the "right" as it ap-plies to police operations.'[50] One must also identify the stakeholders who get to define the objectives of the police, as well as processes for reaching collective judgements. Under a democracy, the purpose of policing (and public administration more generally) is ultimately for citizens and their elected representatives to decide.

Policing is conventionally associated with the maintenance of public order, law enforcement, and the prevention and control of crime. The last of these—crime management—receives heightened attention in per-formance evaluations, which often rely on indicators such as the crime rate, arrests made by the police, and the rate of prosecution. Yet crim-inologists and practitioners have questioned whether these perform-ance indicators are useful or accurate.[51] Many crimes go unreported by citizens. The police may (or may not) register cases for strategic reasons, due to administrative incentives and political pressures to show a favour-able crime rate. There are also various confounding factors, both socio-economic and political, that impact criminal activity, making it difficult to draw causal inferences based on crime statistics.[52] These difficulties are likely compounded in India due to the inadequacy of data gath-ered through state police forces.[53] Further, it should be noted that po-lice agencies engage in a multitude of other activities, such as patrolling neighbourhoods, resolving local disputes, facilitating traffic movement, and assisting citizens in distress.[54] These activities are complex, diffi-cult to measure, and may not be readily tied to specific outcomes, even though the mode by which they are implemented matters to the public. As retired police officer David M. Gorby suggests, traditional perform-ance measures tend to rely on a reactionary model of policing and fail to represent the bulk of officer behaviours, including broader public service functions.[55]

With these caveats in mind, it is worthwhile, nevertheless, to explore crime statistics and related indicators, since these data are regularly collected by the Indian government and shape the public discourse around policing and citizen safety. Tables 11.3 and 11.4 present official data on crime and the associated performance indicators for 2011 to 2020, based on the *Crime in India* reports published annually by the National Crime Records Bureau (NCRB). The data are divided under two sets of criminal statutes, the Indian Penal Code (IPC) and Special and Local Laws (SLL). After declining between 2011 and 2014, the overall crime rate increased to previous levels by 2020. IPC crimes took on a much larger share of overall crimes, driven largely by property-related offences. The large jump in IPC crimes between 2019 and 2020 reflects violations of the government's COVID-19 lockdown policies.

The police are required by law to hear citizen complaints and record cognizable offences in a first information report (FIR). In practice, however, the police exercise considerable discretion when choosing whether to record FIRs. They may dissuade citizens from filing the FIR or even

Table 11.3 Crime Incidence and Rate (2011–20)

Year	Crime Incidence			Crime Rate (per 100,000 pop.)			IPC crimes as a share of overall crimes (%)
	IPC	SLL	Total	IPC	SLL	Total	
2011	2,325,575	3,927,154	6,252,729	192.2	324.5	516.7	37.2
2012	2,387,188	3,654,371	6,041,559	196.7	301.2	497.9	39.5
2013	2,647,722	3,992,656	6,640,378	215.5	324.9	540.4	39.9
2014	2,851,563	1,720,100	4,571,663	229.2	138.3	367.5	62.4
2015	2,949,400	1,761,276	4,710,676	234.2	139.9	374.1	62.6
2016	2,975,711	1,855,804	4,831,515	233.6	145.7	379.3	61.6
2017	3,062,579	1,944,465	5,007,044	237.7	150.9	388.6	61.2
2018	3,132,954	1,941,680	5,074,634	236.7	146.7	383.5	61.7
2019	3,225,701	1,930,471	5,156,172	241.2	144.3	385.5	62.6
2020	4,254,356	2,346,929	6,601,285	314.3	173.4	487.8	64.4

Source: Crime in India Report (2015, 2017, 2018, 2019), NCRB, Government of India; Census of India (2011) and *Estimated Mid-Year Population*, Registrar General of India.

Table 11.4 Charge-Sheeting and Cases Pending (2011–20)

Year	Share of criminal cases charge-sheeted (%)		Share of Criminal Cases Pending Police Action (%)	
	IPC	SLL	IPC	SLL
2011	78.8	93.4	27.2	6
2012	78.8	93.4	26.1	6.6
2013	79.5	94.3	27.2	6.7
2014	79.6	98.4	28	6
2015	77.7	98.1	28.4	6.5
2016	72.9	94.5	30.2	16.4
2017	70.7	92.8	29.1	18.7
2018	68.1	92.2	28.3	17.1
2019	67.2	93.3	29.3	18
2020	75.8	93.8	38.2	25.1

Source: *Crime in India Report* (2015, 2017, 2018, 2019), NCRB, Government of India

extract bribes.[56] These practices, which go against both official procedure and the law, likely result in the under-reporting of crimes.[57] After filing a FIR, the police are obligated to conduct an investigation, on the basis of which they produce a charge-sheet. As shown in Table 11.4, the share of cases that result in charge-sheeting has hovered between 68 and 78 per cent, meaning that more than one-fifth of cases each year result in no charges. In addition, a growing percentage of criminal cases lie pending each year, illustrating the uphill battle that aggrieved citizens (and accused parties) experience in seeking justice.

At the same time, it is important to situate police (in)action on criminal cases within the broader context of India's criminal justice system, which includes the prosecutor's office, judiciary, and penal system. As of 2021, India has a staggering 38.2 million cases pending in district courts and 5.8 million pending in high courts, adding almost 1 million cases annually over the past 15 years.[58] The backlog of court cases and long delays in judicial processes point to systemic weaknesses in the Indian justice system, of which the police are but one part.[59] Given these judicial pain points, in conjunction with the severe police personnel shortages, the

Table 11.5 Crimes against Women in India (2011–20)

Year	Incidence of Crimes Against Women			Rate of Crimes Against Women (per 100,000 female pop.)		
	IPC	SLL	Total	IPC	SLL	Total
2011			228,650			39.0
2012			244,270			41.7
2013			309,546			52.2
2014			337,922			56.3
2015			327,394			53.9
2016	325,652	13,302	338,954	53.0	2.2	55.2
2017	315,215	44,634	359,849	50.7	7.2	57.9
2018	323,345	54,932	378,277	50.3	8.5	58.8
2019	343,177	62,684	405,861	52.8	9.6	62.4
2020	311,354	60,149	371,503	47.3	9.1	56.5

Source: Crime in India Report (2015, 2017, 2018, 2019), NCRB, Government of India; and Census of India (2011) and Estimated Mid-Year Population, Registrar General of India.

police are likely to ration their time and may give less attention to more complex cases that trigger a protracted legal process.

Handling crimes perpetrated against women is an important part of police work. Table 11.5 shows the growing incidence and rate of crimes against women in India. These figures, however, likely grossly underestimate the true extent of the problem. A comparison of women's responses to national household surveys in India with the NCRB register suggests that 99 per cent of sexual violence cases go unregistered.[60] To be clear, under-reporting gender-based violence is a global problem.[61] In India, patriarchal norms, social barriers, and low trust in the police all likely prevent women from reporting crimes.[62] Growing public scrutiny regarding crimes against women has compelled India's central and state governments to adopt reforms meant to improve police responsiveness to women. Parliament enacted the Protection of Women from Domestic Violence Act in 2005, for the first time recognizing domestic violence—including physical, sexual, verbal, emotional, and economic abuse—in law. The act also provided civil remedies for those affected by domestic violence and identified the police's role in helping aggrieved persons gain access to social services.

State police forces have also adopted so-called Crimes Against Women cells, which oversee various gender-targeted initiatives. These include patrolling hot spots in police vehicles, establishing helplines for women, and forming all-women police stations (*mahila thanas*). The efficacy of these interventions demands careful study, and limited evidence available thus far points in multiple directions. A study based in Uttar Pradesh found that the introduction of all-women stations led to no improvement in crime registration, and may have even had the perverse effect of making it more difficult for women to file cases at regular stations.[63] Other research, conducted in Tamil Nadu, showed that all-women stations provided safe spaces where women felt more comfortable reporting cases and seeking resolution in family disputes, even if the stations were still less effective in registering crimes.[64] In Madhya Pradesh, the state govenment introduced the URJA program, an intervention that provided dedicated help desks for women's cases in police stations. A field-based study found that the UJRA women's help desk had a demonstrable impact on police registration of crimes against women, particularly when female officers were placed in charge of the desks.[65] In addition, police departments in several states have adopted quotas for the recruitment of women. Whether or not it improves the police's efficacy in handling crimes against women, improving gender representation within the police is a worthy objective itself. As noted earlier in the chapter, women account for less than 10 per cent of police personnel in India. Concerted efforts to recruit women will allow police agencies to draw from a wider talent pool and fill critical gaps in skills.

The ongoing struggle for women's security calls attention to how police agencies respond to structural inequalities in Indian society, which along with gender include caste, class, and religious differences. Although many state governments have introduced reforms to improve citizen access to justice, inequalities in police service delivery continue to surface, undermining public trust. These persistent inequalities have wider implications for citizen–state relations as well. Regular and systematic data on citizen perceptions of crime and police efficacy are unavailable at the national level. Nevertheless, surveys report low levels of public trust in the police, as well as an expectation that bribes are often necessary for police attention.[66] Low-income citizens in particular report experiencing heavy-handed police tactics.[67] Calls to enhance police responsiveness in

India highlight the need to reform internal processes and reshape how officers interact with women, landless labourers, lower castes, and other vulnerable groups.[68] In this regard, greater investment in police training is urgently needed. The 1971 report of the Gore Committee on Police Training highlighted the need to emphasize the social context of discrimination in India and to focus police training on communication, conflict resolution, and other so-called 'soft skills'.[69] Subsequently, two high-level committees recommended substantial structural and training related reforms to improve the democratic orientation, service delivery focus, and professionalism in police practice. These recommendations were picked up by BPRD, which has provided guidelines and strategies to strengthen police practices through improved training methodologies. Yet, efforts to adopt these guidelines are uneven. Some states have been more active than others in addressing the gap in 'soft skills' training, adopting victim-centric approaches and developing specialized services for marginalized sections of society, most notably to tackle crimes against women and children.

In the past two decades, certain states and the national institutes have intiated training reforms to address gaps in soft skills, community orientation, human rights, and ethics training. However, the pace has been slow and piecemeal in most endeavours. More recently, the National Police Academy and some states (e.g., Madhya Pradesh and Maharashtra, among a few others) have conducted a training needs analysis to address these issues and incorporate citizen-centric approaches and soft skills training.[70] These efforts are supported by BPRD, which has a committee dedicated to supporting the systematic adoption of training needs analysis across states and curricular changes in police training.

Beyond officer training, the National Police Commission produced eight reports on police reform in the 1970s, as well as a draft Model Police Act. However, none of the major recommendations were implemented by India's central or state governments. Echoing the work of previous commissions, the Malimath Committee's 2000 report recommended strengthening crime investigation capacity and separating it from the police's law-and-order functions. In 2006, the Supreme Court of India ruled in *Prakash Singh v. Union of India* that the state needed to replace the 1861 Police Act with new legislation to improve police accountability.

The court also issued seven legally binding directives, requiring the central and state governments to implement:

1. a State Security Commission to outline police performance criteria and shield officers from political interference;
2. a process of transparent, merit-based selection of the director general of police;
3. tenure (a minimum of two years) for superintendents of police, station house officers, and other operational posts;
4. the separation of crime investigation functions from law-and-order duties;
5. a Police Establishment Board to oversee transfers and promotions for field officers (below the rank of deputy superintendent);
6. a Police Complaints Authority to hear complaints against senior officers and address misconduct; and
7. a National Security Commission to oversee the selection of central police organization chiefs and to regularly review police effectiveness, capacity building, and personnel service conditions.

Likewise, the MHA drafted a Model Police Act in 2006, which aimed to improve police accountability and autonomy. A version of the act was subsequently adopted by several state legislatures, but core elements of the Supreme Court directives were diluted. In sum, numerous policy documents by the central and state governments have flagged the need for the police to incorporate good governance principles of transparency, accountability, and citizen responsiveness. However, their impact on day-to-day police practices is highly mixed and leaves vast scope for improvement.

Conclusion

An effective police force is a critical ingredient for citizen security in any functioning democracy.[71] This chapter has offered an appraisal of the Indian police's mandate and administrative capacity, along with its formal and informal organizational structures. It detailed the institutional barriers the police face to effective performance, particularly the lack of adequate personnel and resources, along with gaps in training and intra-organizational communications. It also outlined several proposals for police reform, many of which are promising.

India's incomplete efforts to fully implement police reforms points to underlying political and bureaucratic impediments. The political class in India has vested interests in maintaining control over public institutions, with potentially deleterious effects on overall governance and policy implementation. As the major coercive arm of the state, the police may be more vulnerable to such political meddling.[72] Politicians are often alleged to interfere in routine police work and encourage the selective implementation of the law, which provides them with a ready source of rents and political support. The growing criminalization of politicians in India likely makes matters worse, since the political and economic stakes for controlling the police are even higher.[73] Further, electoral strategies may foment social divisions and violence between groups, with the police being directed to turn a blind eye or even act as a co-conspirator.[74] A police force that operates independently and is responsive to citizen needs may pose a threat to politicians, their electoral strategies and networks. 'If there is one principle that unites Indian politicians,' Devesh Kapur and Milan Vaishnav contend, 'it is that a competent, autonomous police force is a threat to their common interests.'[75] Notwithstanding these constraints, the Indian police also has a demonstrated capacity for securing the public interest, notably in the maintence of order, prevention of collective violence, and not least of all, the administration of large-scale elections. Indeed, the stability and overall functioning of democracy in India, while far from perfect, is remarkable in comparison to other postcolonial settings, and the police have played an important role in this regard.[76]

However, the police also exhibit acute deficiencies and there an in urgent need for improvement in areas such as crime investigation and the treatment of marginalized social groups. The culpability for these deficiencies does not entirely lie with political actors. The police have a role to play as well and there is an urgent need to bring the voices of officers into the reform process, including constables, subinspectors, and others who serve on the front lines. The senior brass of the police administration in India possesses immense authority and status, and it is well positioned to press for institutional changes. Therefore, top officials must also share some responsibility for deficiencies in reform. While senior officers have closely guarded their superior status and employment benefits, the welfare shortcomings and inhumane work conditions faced by constables and other front-line staff are on open display. Indian citizens and civil society have good reason to demand more responsive and accountable policing. Public pressure to address crimes against women is an instructive example of the possibilities for reforms to gain tangible shape. In addition, the COVID-19 pandemic brought officers in closer contact with the public. Police officers expanded their roles in the realm of service provision, often taking personal risks to assist citizens in need. There are some early indications that police efforts during the pandemic were received favourably by some in the public.[77] By capitalizing on these developments, Indian policymakers may have an unparalleled opportunity to finally make police reform a reality.

Notes

1. Michael Lipsky, *Streel-Level Bureaucracy: Dilemmas of the Individual in Public Services* (New York: Russell Sage Foundation, 1980).
2. James Q. Wilson, *Varieties of Police Behavior: The Management of Law and Order in Eight Communities* (Cambridge, MA: Harvard University Press, 1978).
3. Tom R. Tyler, *Why People Obey the Law* (New Haven: Yale University Press, 1990).
4. One of the paper's authors, Vineet Kapoor, is a police officer in the Madhya Pradesh state cadre of the Indian Police Services.
5. Atul Kohli, *State-Directed Development: Political Power and Industrialization in the Global Periphery* (Cambridge: Cambridge University Press, 2004).
   Atul Kohli, *Imperialism and the Developing World: How Britain and the United States Shaped the Global Periphery* (New Delhi: Oxford University Press, 2019).
6. David H. Bayley, *Police and Political Development in India* (Princeton, NJ: Princeton University Press, 1969).; David Arnold, "The Police and Colonial Control in South India," *Social Scientist* 4, no. 12 (1976): 3–16.
7. Arnold, "The Police and Colonial Control in South India," 3–16.
8. Variations on this model existed throughout India. For example, the urban presidency towns of Madras, Bombay, and Calcutta adopted the Police Commissionerate system.
9. The proposed amendments include the Bharatiya Nyaya Sanhita Bill 2023 (to replace the Indian Penal Code of 1860), the Bharatiya Nagarik Suraksha Sanhita Bill 2023 (to replace the Code of Criminal Procedure of 1898), and the Bharatiya Sakshya Bill 2023 (to replace the Indian Evidence Act of 1872).
10. Dilip K. Das and Arvind Verma, "The Armed Police in the British Colonial Tradition," *Policing: An International Journal of Police Strategies & Management*

21, no. 2 (1998): 354–67.; The design of colonial policing in India was at odds with the prevailing approach of the Metropolitan Police in London, which aimed to work with local communities and build trust by responding to their needs.

11. Arvind Verma, and K.S. Subramanian, *Understanding the Police in India, Second Edition* (Gurgaon: LexisNexis, 2014).

12. Bayley, *Police and Political Development in India.*

13. Bayley, *Police and Political Development in India.*

14. Akshay Mangla, "The Indian Police: Managing Dilemmas of Internal Security," in *Internal Security in India: Violence, Order, and the State,* ed. Amit Ahuja and Devesh Kapur (New York: Oxford University Press): 240-259.

15. Beatrice Jauregui, *Provisional Authority: Police, Order, and Security in India* (Chicago: University of Chicago Press, 2016).

16. The Central Armed Police Forces under the MHA have several branches, including the Central Reserve Police Force (CRPF), Central Industrial Security Force (CISF), Border Security Force (BSF), Indo-Tibetan Border Police (ITBP) and the National Security Guard (NSG). See Chapter 7 in this volume for a detailed review.

17. BPRD, *Model Police Manual: Volumes 1, 2 and 3* (New Delhi: Bureau of Police Research and Development, 2016).

18. Some states give head constables the authority to investigate minor crimes.

19. Haridwar Rai, "Dual Control of Law and Order Administration in India: A Study in Magistracy and Police Relationship," *Indian Journal of Public Administration* 13, no. 1 (1967): 43–64.

20. For further discussion of police recruitment, including differences between states, see CHRI (2015).

21. Beatrice Jauregui, "Provisional Agency in India: Jugaad and Legitimation of Corruption," *American Ethnologist* 41, no. 1 (2014): 76–91.

22. Bureau of Police Research and Development, Ministry of Home Affairs, *Data on Police Organisations in India* (New Delhi: Government of India, 2019).

23. Bureau of Police Research and Development, Ministry of Home Affairs, *Data on Police Organisations in India* (New Delhi: Government of India, 2020)

24. Tata Trusts, *India Justice Report* (New Delhi: Tata Trusts, 2019).

25. Akshay Mangla, "Becoming the Police: Female Officers, Relational Work, and the Pursuit of Inclusion in India," Working Paper, Said Business School: University of Oxford, 2023.

26. D. Selokar, S. Nimbarte, S. Ahana, A. Gaidhane, and V. Wagh, "Occupational Stress among Police Personnel of Wardha City, India," *The Australasian Medical Journal* 4, no. 3 (2011): 114; Shweta Singh and Sujita Kumar Kar, "Sources of Occupational Stress in the Police Personnel of North India: An Exploratory Study," *Indian Journal of Occupational and Environmental Medicine* 19, no. 1 (2015): 56.

27. Bureau of Police Research and Development, Ministry of Home Affairs, *Data on Police Organisations in India* (New Delhi: Government of India, 2019).

28. CSDS, "Police Adequacy and Working Conditions," in *Status of Policing in India Report, 2019* (New Delhi: Common Cause and CSDS-Lokniti Program, 2019).

29. "Modernisation of State Police Forces (MPF) Scheme," Ministry of Home Affairs, Government of India, https://www.mha.gov.in/en/divisionofmha/police-modernisation-division/modernisation-of-state-police-forces-mpf-scheme.

30. CSDS, "A Study of Performance and Perceptions," in *Status of Policing in India Report, 2018* (New Delhi: Common Cause and CSDS-Lokniti Program, 2018).

31. Edgar H. Schein, "Culture: The Missing Concept in Organization Studies," *Administrative Science Quarterly* 41, no. 2 (1996): 229–40, doi: 10.2307/2393715.; John P. Kotter, *Corporate Culture and Performance* (New York, NY: Free Press, 1992); Geert Hofstede, "Attitudes, Values and Organizational Culture: Disentangling the Concepts," *Organization Studies* 19, no. 3 (1998): 477–93.

32. Robert Reiner, *The Politics of the Police* (Oxford: Oxford University Press, 2010).

33. Jerome H. Skolnick, *Justice Without trial: Law Enforcement in Democratic Society* (New York: John Wiley & Sons, 1966).

34. Reiner, *The Politics of the Police*.

35. Eugene A. Paoline, "Taking Stock: Toward a Richer Understanding of Police Culture," *Journal of Criminal Justice* 31, no. 3 (2003): 199–214.

36. Michael K. Brown, *Working the Street: Police Discretion and the Dilemmas of Reform* (New York: Russell Sage Foundation, 1988); Wilson, *Varieties of Police Behavior*.

37. In a related vein, Mangla finds that subnational differences in bureaucratic norms shape the how state education agencies operate services across India. Akshay Mangla, *Making Bureaucracy Work: Norms, Education and Public Service Delivery in Rural India* (New York: Cambridge University Press, 2022)

38. Verma and Subramanian, *Understanding the Police in India*.

39. Percival J. Griffiths, *To Guard my People: The History of the Indian Police* (London: Ernest Benn, 1971).

40. Beatrice Jauregui, "Lawfare and Security Labor: Subjectification and Subjugation of Police Workers in India," *Law & Social Inquiry* 9, no. 2 (2021): 1–29.

41. The misappropriation of constables' labour by senior officers, which has contributed to associational activity by constables, is examined in Jauregui, *Provisional Authority*.

42. Interview of DSP, 8 October 2019, Madhya Pradesh.

43. Qualitative interviews with field officers in Madhya Pradesh consistently revealed the importance of discipline (*anushasan*) as a norm within the police.

44. Vineet Kapoor, "Human Rights Education and Role Orientation of the Police in Democracy." PhD Thesis, School of Law, Rights and Constitutional Governance, Tata Institute of Social Sciences, 2018.

45. Qualitative observations in police stations in three districts of MP (Bhopal, Vidisha, and Indore), 2018–19.

46. Verma and Subramanian, *Understanding the Police in India*.

47. Rachel Wahl, "Justice, Context, and Violence: Law Enforcement Officers on Why They Torture," *Law & Society Review* 48, no. 4 (2014): 807–36, doi: 10.1111/lasr.12108.

48. Vineet Kapoor, "Human Rights Education and Role Orientation of the Police in Democracy."

49. D.P. Rosenbaum, "The Changing Role of the Police: Assessing the Current Transition to Community," in *How to Recognize Good Policing: Problems and Issues*, ed. Jean-Paul Brodeur (Thousand Oaks: Sage, 1998): 3-29; and Mark H. Moore, "Problem-Solving and Community Policing," *Crime and Justice* 15 (1992): 99–158, doi: 10.1086/449194.

50. Mark H. Moore and Anthony A. Braga, "Police Performance Measurement: A Normative Framework," *Criminal Justice Ethics* 23, no. 1 (2004): 3–19.

51. David Lilley and Sameer Hinduja, "Police Officer Performance Appraisal and Overall Satisfaction," *Journal of Criminal Justice* 35, no. 2 (2007): 137–50.; T.N. Oettmeier and M.A. Wycoff, "Police Performance in the Nineties: Practitioner Perspectives," *American Journal of Police* 13, no. 2 (1994): 21–49.

52. Abhijit V. Banerjee, Raghabendra Chattopadhyay, Esther Duflo, Daniel Keniston, and Nina Singh, "Improving Police Performance in Rajasthan, India: Experimental Evidence on Incentives, Managerial Autonomy and Training," *National Bureau of Economic Research*, Working Paper No. 17912, 2012.

53. Arvind Verma, "The Problem of Measurement of Crime," *Indian Journal of Criminology* 21, no. 2 (1993): 51–8.

54. According to studies of policing in the United States, crime-related activities account for only 10-20 per cent of time spent by officers. See Michael D. White, "Identifying Good Cops Early: Predicting Recruit Performance in the Academy," *Police Quarterly* 11, no. 1 (2008): 29.

55. David M. Gorby, "The Failure of Traditional Measures of Police Performance and the Rise of Broader Measures of Performance," *Policing: A Journal of Policy and Practice* 7, no. 4 (2013): 392–400.

56. Verma and Subramanian, *Understanding the Police in India*.

57. U. N. Rao and Arvind Tiwari, "A Study on Non-Registration of Crimes: Problems and Solutions," Bureau of Police Research and Development, Ministry of Home Affairs, (New Delhi: Government of India, 2016).

58. National Judicial Data Grid [URL: https://njdg.ecourts.gov.in/njdgnew/index.php].

59. Devesh Kapur and Milan Vaishnav, "Strengthening the Rule of Law," in *Getting India Back on Track: An Action Agenda for Reform*, ed. Bibek Debroy, Ashley J. Tellis, and Reece Trevor (New Delhi: Penguin Random House India, 2014).

60. NFHS-4, *National Family Health Survey-4* (Mumbai: International Institute for Population Sciences, 2015–16).; National Crime Records Bureau, *Crime in India* (New Delhi: Ministry of Home Affairs, Government of India, 2014–2016).

61. Charlotte Watts and Cathy Zimmerman, "Violence against Women: Global Scope and Magnitude," *The Lancet* 359, no. 9313 (2002): 1232–37.

62. Tata Trusts, *India Justice Report.*
63. Nirvikar Jassal, "Gender, Law Enforcement, and Access to Justice: Evidence from All-Women Police Stations in India," *American Political Science Review* 114, no 4 (2020): 1035-1054.
64. Mangai Natarajan, "Women Police Stations as a Dispute Processing System," *Women & Criminal Justice* 16, no 1–2 (2005): 87–106, doi: 10.1300/J012v16n01_04.
65. Sandip Sukhtankar, Gabrielle Kruks-Wisner, and Akshay Mangla, "Policing in Patriarchy: An Experimental Evaluation of Reforms to Improve Police Responsiveness to Women in India." *Science* 377, no. 6602 (2022): 191-198., doi: 10.1126/science.abm7387.
66. Juan Fernando Tellez, Erik Wibbels, and Anirudh Krishna, "Local Order, Policing, and Bribes: Evidence from India," *World Politics* 72, no. 3 (2020): 377–410.; CSDS, "A Study of Performance and Perceptions," in *Status of Policing in India Report, 2018* (New Delhi: Common Cause and CSDS-Lokniti Program, 2018).
67. Tariq Thachil, "Does Police Repression Spur Everyday Cooperation? Evidence from Urban India," *Journal of Politics* 82, no. 4 (2020): 1474-1489.
68. Tata Trusts, *India Justice Report.*
69. *The Gore Committee Report on Police Training*, Ministry of Home Affairs, Government of India, 1974.
70. Vineet Kapoor, "Human Rights Education and Role Orientation of the Police in Democracy."
71. Ian Loader, "Democracy, Justice and the Limits of Policing: Rethinking Police Accountability." *Social & Legal Studies* 3, no. 4 (1994): 521–44.
72. Steven I. Wilkinson, *Votes and Violence: Electoral Competition and Ethnic Riots in India* (New York: Cambridge University Press, 2006).
73. Milan Vaishnav, *When Crime Pays: Money and Muscle in Indian Politics* (New Haven, CT: Yale University Press, 2017).
74. Steven I. Wilkinson, *Votes and Violence*; K.S. Subramanian, *Political Violence and the Police in India* (New Delhi: SAGE, 2007).
75. Kapur and Vaishnav, "Strengthening the Rule of Law."
76. Devesh Kapur, "Why Does the Indian State Both Fail and Succeed?" *Journal of Economic Perspectives* 34, no. 1 (2020): 31-54.
77. CSDS, "Policing in the COVID-19 Pandemic," in *Status of Policing in India Report, Volume 2 2020-2021* (New Delhi: Common Cause and CSDS-Lokniti Program, 2021).

12

The Central Bureau of Investigation and the National Investigation Agency

Navneet Rajan Wasan

Introduction

India's Central Bureau of Investigation—also known as the Delhi Special Police Establishment (DSPE), its primary investigative wing—and the National Investigation Agency (NIA) are two of the Indian government's premier investigation agencies. The CBI investigates corruption-related, economic, and conventional offences, while the NIA exclusively handles terrorism-related and internal security crimes. This chapter examines the history of both agencies in the context of ongoing jurisdictional conflicts between Indian states and the central government, or centre. It also analyses core issues related to human resources, institutional credibility, and political interference. As both organizations share many commonalities, face identical challenges, and function in similar ways, this chapter focuses primarily on the CBI; the NIA is discussed where policies and issues substantially differ.

Objectives and Institutional Environment

Central Bureau of Investigation (Delhi Special Police Establishment)

In 1941, the Indian government set up the Special Police Establishment (SPE) through executive order to investigate corruption. At the time—the height of World War II—its jurisdiction extended to railways and

Navneet Rajan Wasan, *The Central Bureau of Investigation and the National Investigation Agency* In: *Institutional Roots of India's Security Policy*. Edited by: Milan Vaishnav, Oxford University Press.

involved the movement and supply of vital war materials. Headquartered in Lahore, it was led by a deputy inspector general. In 1943, by promulgation of Ordinance No. XXII and in exercise of the Emergency powers conferred on the Viceroy and Governor General of India,[1] it was constituted into an independent entity called the Special Police Establishment (War Department). The validity of this Ordinance was extended beyond the normal six-month period until it was finally repealed on 1 April 1946, and replaced on 25 September 1946, by the Special Police Establishment (War Department) Ordinance.[2] By 1 October 1946, this had mutated into the Delhi Special Police Establishment and, in November, was given statutory status through the Delhi Special Police Establishment Act, which continues to operate—albeit in amended form—to this day.

Section 2 of the Delhi Special Police Establishment Act vests it with jurisdiction to investigate notified offences in the Union Territories only. Section 5(1) of the Act provides for extension of its jurisdiction to other areas, including railway areas and states, for investigation of offences notified by the central government under Section 3. However, extension of the DSPE's jurisdiction is subject to a state government granting its consent under Section 6 of the Act. Even once the state has accorded consent to the DSPE, its anti-corruption authorities or State Vigilance Bureau continues to have concurrent jurisdiction to register cases under the Prevention of Corruption Act (PC Act) against public servants, including those employed by the central government. Thanks to an administrative arrangement, corruption cases related to public servants of the central government are normally investigated by the DSPE.

That the DSPE can investigate state-level cases has been a major area of controversy between the central government and the states, which maintain that it is an encroachment on their powers. On several occasions, state governments, often ruled by a political party other than that in power at the centre, have withdrawn their consent, citing Section 6 of the DSPE Act, thereby limiting DSPE officers' ability to investigate cases. For example, in Karnataka in the late 1970s, the government of Chief Minister Devaraj Urs recalled the general permission for DSPE investigations. Subsequently, the J. H. Patel government also withdrew consent on 15 December 1998, which continued for several years. Recent instances include the state governments of Mizoram (July 2015), West Bengal (November 2018), Andhra Pradesh (November 2018),[3] Chhattisgarh

(January 2019), Rajasthan (July 2020), Maharashtra (October 2020)[4], Kerala (November 2020), Jharkhand (November 2020), Punjab (November 2020) and Tamil Nadu (June 2023). However, withdrawal of consent does not prevent a constitutional court from using its inherent and extraordinary powers to order a DSPE investigation into individual cases for purpose of 'delivery of complete justice'.

Based on the recommendations of the Santhanam Committee on Prevention of Corruption and in view of the DSPE's increasing workload, the central government stood up the Central Bureau of Investigation (CBI) of the Ministry of Home Affairs (MHA) through an executive order, Resolution No. 4/31/61-T, on 1 April 1963, making the DSPE one of its divisions.[5] The creation of the CBI has been a controversial issue. The Constitution of India provides that only a state legislature is competent, in terms of Entry 2 of List II (State List) of the Seventh Schedule, to legislate on the subject of 'police'. The predominant view has been that the central government did not have the power to create or establish through executive action an investigative agency with police powers.

The matter has come under legal scrutiny on several occasions, with an aim to explore the possibility of affording statutory status to the CBI. In one such exercise, undertaken at the highest levels in 1970, the central government examined whether it could enact a law to create a police agency with investigative powers in respect of subject matters within the domain of the Union and Concurrent Lists in the Constitution. Solicitor General C.K. Daphtary expressed his opinion that 'investigation' in Entry 8 of the Union List did not have the same meaning as 'investigation' in the Code of Criminal Procedure.[6] Rather, the term referred only to a general inquiry for collecting information. Under the existing arrangement, the central government can only conduct an inquiry, whereas the abilities to investigate and prosecute an offence lie exclusively with State Police—as per Entry 2 of List II. Therefore, any law enacted by Parliament covering investigations would be unconstitutional under the doctrine of implied prohibition.

Niren De, then Attorney General of India, did not fully agree with these arguments, but he concurred that Parliament could not confer the powers to investigate offences to any agency other than the State Police without first amending the Constitution. In view of these opinions, no further action was taken in the matter.

In 1992, the Estimates Committee recommended that Parliament enact

a new law laying down the organizational structure of the CBI, functions to be discharged by it, types of offences which it can investigate
and providing for conferment of powers of Police laid down in Criminal
Procedure Code, 1973, on the members of the CBI.

The Committee also recommended a constitutional amendment that
would allow the CBI's jurisdiction to be extended to any state without
the consent of its government. A draft Constitution Amendment Bill
and a draft Bill on the CBI were sent to the Home Ministry on 12 June
1990, with no further action.[7] The Parliamentary Standing Committee
on Personnel, Public Grievances, Law and Justice made similar recommendations in March 2008.[8] These suggestions, too, proved to be
non-starters.

The question of whether the CBI could have been created through an
executive resolution also came up for detailed scrutiny before the Gauhati
High Court in 2007, when it quashed the MHA's 1963 resolution setting
up the CBI and rendered it unconstitutional. In its decision regarding
Navendra Kumar v. Union of India,[9] the Court examined several critical
questions about the legality of the CBI. For instance, it explored whether
the CBI was a constitutionally valid police force constituted under the
Union's legislative powers and empowered to investigate crimes. Further,
the Court asked whether a police force charged with investigating crimes
could be constituted by a resolution of the Ministry of Home Affairs as
opposed to dedicated legislation passed by Parliament. The Court also
considered whether the Delhi Special Police Establishment Act, a 1946
pre-independence law, allowed the Home Ministry to create a police
force in the name of the CBI.

The appellant in the case argued that the constitutional validity of the
CBI was in question since it was not a statutory body and its operations
interfered with the notion that law and order is a state subject under
the Constitution. With regard to the appellant's case, the High Court's
ruling notes:

[R]eliance was placed on the Constituent Assembly debates, dated
August 29, 1949, wherein Dr. B. R. Ambedkar had clarified that the

word '*investigation*', appearing in Entry 8 of List I (Union List) of the Seventh Schedule, which read, '*Central Bureau of Intelligence and Investigation*', would not permit making of an '*investigation*' into a crime by the Central Government inasmuch as '*investigation*' would be constitutionally possible only by a police officer under the Criminal Procedure Code (Cr.P.C.), *police* being exclusively a State subject and the word '*investigation*', appearing in Entry 8 of List I (Union List), would, in effect, mean making of merely an '*enquiry*' and not '*investigation*' into a crime as is done by a police officer under the Code. The word '*investigation*' is, therefore, according to the Constituent Assembly Debates, intended to cover general enquiry for the purpose of finding out what is going on and is not an *investigation* preparatory to the filing of a *charge sheet* against an offender, because it is only a police officer, under the Criminal Procedure code, who can conduct '*investigation*'.[10]

In essence, the appellant contended that:

the CBI may be treated to have been constituted by the Central Government under Entry 8 of the List-I (Union List); but there is no co-relation between the Entry 8 of List I and Entry 2 of List II inasmuch as Entry 8 of List I does not, in light of the Constituent Assembly debates, permit '*investigation*' of a crime in the manner as is, ordinarily, done by the police; whereas Entry 2 of List II permits enactment of laws relating to police.[11]

This distinction, the appellant argued, is important because the two entities described above are distinct and involve powers entrusted with different tiers of government.

[B]oth these entries are separate and distinct from each other and that the framers of the Constitution were well aware of the fact that they were enabling the Centre and State to create two separate authorities, one, which would be covered by Entry 8 of List I, and the other, which would be covered by Entry 2 of List II, and while 'investigation,' under Entry 2 of List II, would mean an '*investigation*' preparatory to the filing of a *police report*, commonly called *charge-sheet* or *final report*, under Section 173 (2) (i) of the Cr.PC, the other '*investigation*' would be in the form of merely an *inquiry* and not an *investigation*, which is conducted by a police officer under the Cr.PC.

In its final ruling, the Gauhati High Court sided with the appellant in holding that the 1963 Resolution establishing the CBI is not an executive action that is consistent with the meaning of Article 73 of the Constitution since it was not the product of legislation and expressly violated the rights of state legislatures to make laws and subjects within their domain. The Court stated that the resolution was akin to 'departmental instructions' that could not have the force of law.[12]

Having stricken down the resolution setting up the CBI as unconstitutional, the Court concluded that the CBI is neither a part of the DSPE under the 1946 DSPE Act, nor can it be treated as a 'police force' under the same Act. The central government challenged this decision before the Supreme Court, which stayed the judgment of the High Court. The matter remains pending.

Another controversial issue that has affected the performance of the CBI was the administrative instructions issued in 1969 popularly known as the Single Directive.[13] Among other changes, these instructions limited the power of the CBI to even conduct a preliminary inquiry into allegations of corruption against officers from any civil service of the rank/grade of Joint Secretary and above without prior approval from the government. In 1997, the Supreme Court in *Vineet Narain & Others vs Union of India & Another* struck down the Single Directive.[14] A three-judge bench ruled that the Single Directive was arbitrary and violated the guarantee of equal treatment and equal protection of the law under Article 14 of the Constitution.

In 2003, Parliament restored the Single Directive as a statutory provision. Section 6-A of the DSPE Act required approval of the central government to conduct an inquiry or investigation where the allegations of commission of an offence under the PC Act (1988) relate to employees of the central government at the level of Joint Secretary or above. The Supreme Court once more held this directive invalid and in violation of Article 14 of the Constitution.[15] In response, the government inserted a new Section 17A into the PC Act through an amendment in 2018, prohibiting initiation of an inquiry or investigation by any police officer against a public servant for an act committed in the affairs of a state or the central government. In other words, crimes committed under the PC Act no longer remain 'cognisable' crimes, or crimes for which police can initiate an investigation without written permission from a court. Some insiders have argued that this provision has blunted the power of the CBI, preventing it and other anticorruption agencies from tackling corrupt activities.

While the CBI remains focused on offences covered by both the PC Act of 1947 and the PC Act of 1988, the growing list of offences notified for investigation has given it much a wider role. By 2018, the CBI was authorized to investigate 275 offences under various sections of the Indian Penal Code, as well as 92 offences under other Central Acts and 34 under various State Acts.[16]

National Investigation Agency (NIA)

The response to terrorist attacks in India, which can have interstate or transnational ramifications, has proven especially difficult for the State Police to manage. With perpetrators spanning state or national borders, some terror cases have been entrusted to the CBI at the request of the state government. That bureaucratic delay, however, has impeded many investigations.

For years, security experts, political parties, and even parliamentary committees called for a national-level agency with the ability to investigate terrorism and other threats to internal security without waiting for state-level consent. For instance, the Second Administrative Reforms Commission, in its reports on public order and combating terrorism, also recommended the creation of a federal agency to investigate terrorism.[17] After 174 people died in the ghastly 2008 terror attack in Mumbai—known as 26/11—the government fast-tracked a bill in the Lok Sabha to set up the National Investigation Agency, or NIA. The agency's stated mandate is to investigate and prosecute offences affecting the sovereignty, security, and integrity of India.

The NIA officially came into existence through the NIA Act, passed by Parliament on the last day of 2008. The Act gives the NIA concurrent and overriding jurisdiction over State Police to probe any offence committed under the Unlawful Activities (Prevention) Act (UAPA), SAARC Convention (Suppression of Terrorism) Act, Chapter VI of the Indian Penal Code (offences against the state, including sedition and waging war against India), possession and circulation of counterfeit currency, and other Scheduled Offences. In 2018, the Act was amended to include human trafficking,[18] the manufacture or sale of prohibited arms,[19] offences under the Explosive Substances Act, and cyberterrorism.[20] Significantly, it granted extraterritorial jurisdiction to the NIA, subject to international treaties and domestic laws of the nation(s) concerned. Under section 3(2) of the Act, the NIA is empowered to investigate offences throughout India and exercise all the powers of the police.

Section 6 of the Act makes the NIA the central government's most capable investigation agency. Unlike the CBI, the central government does not require the NIA to seek state-level consent before it investigates any offences in its schedule. This provision has also prompted much controversy, resulting in several court cases over whether the NIA Act violated the constitutionally enshrined principle of federalism and the distribution of powers. In one such petition, *Sadhwi Pragya Singh Thakur v. State of Maharashtra*,[21] the Bombay High Court upheld the validity of the Act.

The court based its reasoning on an earlier Supreme Court decision—*PUCL v. Union of India*[22]—which upheld the validity of the 2002 Prevention of Terrorism Act.[23] Observing that terrorism is a transnational rather than state-specific problem, the Court determined that it would not fit within the ambit of 'public order' under the State List, which is confined to disorders of lesser gravity. In an earlier judgment—*Kartar Singh v. State of Punjab*[24]—the Court held that activities of a more serious nature, which threaten the security and integrity of the country as a whole, relate to the defence of India and thus fall within the ambit of Entry 1 of the Union List. Further, the Court concluded that Parliament had the legislative competence to enact the NIA Act as it could legislate on any matter not covered under the State List.

The latest challenge to the NIA's legitimacy is a petition filed by the State of Chhattisgarh in the Supreme Court. It holds that the NIA Act is '*ultra vires* the Constitution' and 'beyond the legislative competence of the Parliament'. The petition states that the Act takes away the state's power to conduct an investigation through its police, while conferring

'unfettered, discretionary and arbitrary powers' on the central government. It further adds that

> the provisions of the Act leave no room of coordination and pre-
> condition of consent, in any form whatsoever, by the Central govern-
> ment from the State government which clearly repudiates the idea of
> state sovereignty as envisaged under the Constitution of India.

The challengers have also claimed that the provisions of sections 6(4)
and 6(6) of the Act have undermined Entry 2 of List II (State List), which
holds that investigation of matters arising within the territorial jurisdiction of any state are generally investigated by State Police.

As widely reported in the media,[25] diplomatic cables exposed by
WikiLeaks revealed that in 2011 P Chidambaram, who was Home
Minister at the time, told the US Federal Bureau of Investigations
Director Robert Mueller in March 2009 that he was unsure of the NIA's
constitutionality. The Supreme Court's final decision on the validity of the
NIA Act remains pending.

Organizational Structure

For many years following the creation of the CBI, the DSPE had two primary investigation wings: the General Offences Wing, which dealt with
cases of bribery and corruption, and the Economic Offences Wing, which
the central government added in 1964 to deal with violations of fiscal
laws.[26]

Over time, several states requested that the CBI investigate other conventional crimes such as assassinations, kidnappings, crimes committed
by extremists, large-scale banking and insurance frauds, hijackings, as
well as specific sensitive cases like the 1984 Bhopal Gas Tragedy. Since
the early 1980s, constitutional courts have also entrusted cases including
murders, dowry deaths, and rapes to the CBI, based on petitions filed by
the aggrieved parties.

In 1987, the two investigative divisions were renamed the Anti-
Corruption Division and the Special Crimes Division. Later, other cells—
called the Special Investigation Team, the Special Investigation Cell, and

the Special Task Force—were created to investigate blockbuster cases such as the assassination of former Prime Minister Rajiv Gandhi, the 1992 demolition of Babri Masjid in Ayodhya, and the 1993 Mumbai bombings. In 1992, amidst the infamous Harshad Mehta scandal, the Bank Frauds and Securities Cell was created to investigate significant cases of securities fraud and the involvement of banks.

Due to its increased workload—especially given the spike in economic offences that followed the liberalization of India's economy in the early 1990s—the DSPE was reorganized in 1994 into three investigative divisions: the Anti-Corruption Division, the Economic Crimes Division, and the Special Crimes Division.

The Anti-Corruption Division deals with cases of corruption and fraud committed by public servants from any central government departments, central public sector undertakings, and central financial institutions. The Economic Crimes Division handles bank frauds, financial frauds, import–export or foreign exchange violations, and large-scale smuggling of narcotics, antiques, cultural property, and other contraband items. Finally, the Special Crimes Division investigates cases of terrorism, bombings, sensational homicides, kidnappings for ransom, and crimes committed by the mafia or underworld.

In the Supreme Court's 1997 ruling on the *Vineet Narian* case, it made several recommendations regarding the functioning of the CBI, the Central Vigilance Commission (CVC), and the Enforcement Directorate (ED). The CVC is an independent anti-corruption body set up in 1964 to monitor vigilance activities relating to the central government in New Delhi. The ED, in turn, is an economic law enforcement and intelligence agency dating back to the 1950s entrusted with addressing economic crimes in India.

One recommendation was to confer statutory status on the CVC and conferring superintendence power of DSPE to CVC in corruption cases. Another recommendation was to establish a Directorate of Prosecution independent of the CBI Director. Pursuant to the Court's orders, the Legal Division of CBI was reconstituted as the Directorate of Prosecution in July 2001 and was tasked with (i) tendering legal advice in cases and inquiries taken up by CBI for investigation; and (ii) conducting and monitoring prosecution of CBI cases. The CVC Act came into existence only in 2003.

To date, the CBI consists of the following divisions:

1. Anti-Corruption Division	DSPE
2. Economic Offences Division	
3. Special Crimes Division	
4. Policy & International Police Cooperation Division	
5. Administration Division	
6. Directorate of Prosecution	
7. Central Forensic Science Laboratory (Now called Technical, Forensic and Coordination Zone)	

The entire CBI—including the DSPE—is headed by a single director. The director is assisted by three special or additional directors, 20 joint directors (or JDs, some of whom, such as those who lead the policy or administration wings, report directly to the director), 41 deputy inspectors general of police (DIGs), and 129 superintendents of police (SPs). Not all of these officers are part of the DSPE, however. Some are deployed in support units such as the Administrative Division, the Policy Division, or the National Central Bureau (Interpol). Unlike personnel posted to divisions that comprise the DSPE, these officers do not enjoy any police powers and cannot undertake or supervise investigatory work.

As the DSPE's inspector general of police (IGP), the CBI director is responsible for the administration of the organization. The Act also provides a mechanism for the selection and tenure of the CBI director and other senior officers.[27] A DSPE Act amendment grants the director an initial two-year tenure. A subsequent amendment to the Act in December 2021 allows the government to extend the tenure of the CBI director one year at a time in the public interest, up to a total of five years.[28] However, according to the Supreme Court's judgment in *Vineet Narain*, the CVC should have functional control over the CBI, and its director and other senior officers should be chosen via selection panel. Since passage of the 2013 Lokpal and Lokayuktas Act, the director is selected by a committee headed by the prime minister. Control of the DSPE now lies with the central government except for investigations regarding offences under the 1988 PC Act, when superintendence is vested in the CVC. In matters referred to the DSPE by the new Lokpal (an anti-corruption ombudsman) for inquiry or investigation, the Lokpal exercises superintendence.

The branch is the most crucial functioning unit of the DSPE. Cases are investigated by branches, which are headed by SPs or DIGs. Some branches even work under an additional superintendent of police (Addl. SP). Until 2008, there was a uniform supervising hierarchy wherein each branch was headed by an SP, who in turn was overseen by a DIG reporting to a JD. Since 2008, however, this is no longer the case. Based on a report by external consultants, the DSPE's hierarchical supervision structure was amended. Now, branches can be led by Addl. SPs, SPs, or DIGs, who may report directly to a JD. This has resulted in serious anomalies in uniformity and standards of supervision.

The NIA has a similar organizational structure, but superintendence lies with the Ministry of Home Affairs.

Human Resources

Inspectors and deputy superintendents of police (DySPs) handle the majority of investigations. Along with SPs (the first level of supervisory officers), they form the backbone of both organizations. In earlier years, most of these officers were inducted on deputation from State Police. However, increasingly, many are being recruited directly into the rank of sub-inspectors, trained at the CBI Academy, and promoted to the post of inspector after working for four or more years. After putting in 12 or more years of service, they rise to the rank of DySP. For a brief period, officers were recruited directly at the level of DySP, but the process was discontinued and most of the officers continued to be inducted on tenure deputation from State Police and the five Central Armed Police Forces (CAPFs).

One of the most challenging aspects of the CBI/DSPE (as well as the NIA) has been the quality and adequacy of human resources. According to available information, 75 per cent of DIG posts, 34 per cent of SP posts, 23 per cent of Addl. SP/DySP posts, and 36 per cent of inspectors' posts were vacant on 31 December 2019. Similarly, in the NIA, 32 per cent of the sanctioned number of SPs posts are vacant (8 of 25), 40 per cent of crucial Addl. SP/DySP posts are vacant (47 of 79), and 25 per cent of inspector posts remain unfilled.

The situation has not improved for a number of years despite the Supreme Court's direction to fill the vacant posts. Even incentives like additional remuneration have not been able to attract new officers on deputation. State Police officers are reluctant to join the CBI and NIA for several reasons. In order to fill existing vacancies, the CBI and NIA continue to induct a large number of officers from CAPFs who are neither recruited, trained, or equipped to handle complex investigations. Many authorities, including Parliamentary Standing Committees, have called for increasing the captive recruitment of officers at various levels. However, others—including this author—are of the opinion that this would not be an ideal solution. These officers may not have the requisite investigation experience and may lack essential language skills and local knowledge. Further, attempts to directly recruit officers at the level of DySP had to be discontinued after some years—a particularly discouraging sign.

Earlier, CBI officers up to the rank of DIG were recommended by a junior board; other senior officers were selected by a senior board. These boards consisted of the CBI director and other senior officers from the Ministries of Personnel and Home Affairs. The senior board's recommendations were, in turn, approved by the Appointment Committee of the Cabinet.[29]

Indian Police Service (IPS) officers working in the states were cherry-picked to join the CBI based on their integrity, competence, and aptitude for investigation. Only after detailed vetting by the field and intelligence units would the CBI director recommend them for induction. For senior officers, an earlier successful stint in the CBI was the key. Any officer found undeserving or not up to the task could be reverted by the government on recommendation of the director.

A new system of selection was introduced by an amendment to the DSPE Act in 2014. Now, a high-level committee—chaired by the prime minister and including the leader of the opposition in Lok Sabha and the chief justice of India or their representative—selects a panel of IPS officers to be recommended for the director post. A director is then chosen from the panel by the central government and given an initial two-year fixed tenure extendable to a maximum of five years in the public interest. The director can only be removed at the recommendation of the committee that proposed his induction. At the same time, a committee led by the CVC recommends the selection of other officers in the rank of SP or above. The new system stipulates that the director only consult with the selection committee—he is not actually a member. The tenure of these senior officers can be extended or curtailed based on recommendation of the selection committee.

While IPS officers inducted on deputation can climb the ladder according to the IPS' relevant rules for promotion, other CBI officers are promoted based only on seniority and their annual performance. At present, no other method of upward mobility exists, especially for fast-track promotion. A proposal to facilitate expedited promotion to higher ranks—from sub-inspector and inspector to DySP—through a limited departmental examination has been pending for some time. The CBI does not provide any other kind of incentive for meritorious work, except for a limited cash reward at lower levels.

Within the CBI, the director of prosecution heads the Directorate of Prosecution—a nominally separate wing established by order of the Supreme Court. The director is generally an officer taken on deputation from the Ministry of Law and Justice. In addition to other duties, their primary role is to provide legal advice to the CBI director, especially regarding investigations undertaken by the DSPE. The director of prosecution is assisted by a staff of additional legal advisors, deputy legal advisors, senior public prosecutors, public prosecutors, and assistant public prosecutors. They are appointed at the recommendation of the Union Public Service Commission.

By ordering the creation of this separate prosecution wing, the Supreme Court intended to segregate investigations from prosecution to ensure the latter's independence. In reality, however, this has failed. These legal officers not only interact with and advise investigating and supervisory officers but also appear in court as prosecuting officers. These prosecuting officers are not only overworked but often do not match the calibre of defence advocates, leading to a high acquittal rate. Thus, the DSPE and the NIA also engage the services of outside counsel, subject to approval of the Ministry of Law and Justice.

Like the CBI, the NIA also faces an acute crisis of human resources. Unlike the DSPE, however, superintendence of the NIA lies with the central government. Under the 2008 National Investigation Agency (Manner of Constitution) Rules, the government may appoint an officer of or above the rank of additional director general of police to be director of the NIA. There is no separate mechanism for the selection of officers; they too are appointed or inducted by the central government in accordance with the Recruitment Rules. Similar to the CBI, there is a pressing need to induct NIA officers with experience in investigations, preferably from the State Police.

Additionally, there is an urgent need to identify talent within both organizations and those working on deputation, and to provide emerging leaders with the opportunity for fast-track promotion. Based on their academic background and aptitude, officers need to be given advanced training in different domains so that they are equipped to handle complex investigations with little support from experts in the area. The CBI Academy is well equipped to provide such a platform. Experienced investigators, legal experts, forensic accountants, financial analysts, cyber experts, forensic experts, and others could be invited to help train DSPE officers. This training must be supplemented by occasional refresher courses.

Another pressing need is to introduce the concept of "team" investigations to both the CBI and the NIA. As crimes become more complex and criminals more tech savvy, the investigating officers need the support of experts from several specialized domains to help them understand the offences, collect, and analyse evidence, and lead to successful prosecution.

Financial Resources

The entire budget of the DSPE and other divisions of the CBI (except for the Central Forensic Science Laboratory) comes from the government. In financial year (FY) 2020–21, the CBI was allocated just over 8 billion rupees, compared to 7.98 billion rupees the previous year—a nominal increase of 40 million rupees. The budget allocation for the NIA in FY 2019–20 was just over 1.7 billion rupees. The majority of this money goes towards meeting the establishment charges of both organizations.

One important aspect is that the directors of the CBI and the NIA are not free to utilize the funds once they are allocated. Rather, they must obtain government approval for every major expenditure incurred—even within the allocated budget. This has proven to be a major handicap for both organizations, which are unable to put budgetary resources towards priority items.

Performance and Reform

The DSPE has often been accused of inertia in its probes against high-level dignitaries and a lack of professionalism when investigating important cases. In one prominent case—*Vineet Narain*—the Supreme Court ordered significant changes to the selection process of officers, hoping to ensure greater professionalism and independence. Shifting superintendence of investigation in corruption-related cases from the central government to the CVC and establishing the Directorate of Prosecution did not improve the DSPE's credibility. Rather, some argue it has eroded even further. Many important cases—some of which had political overtones, including the Bofors scandal, the Mayawati corruption case, the Mulayam Singh Yadav inquiry, the 2G scam, and the coal block allocation scam—ended with a whimper.

As far as the accountability of officers is concerned, the CBI Crime Investigation Manual (as well as the NIA Crime Investigation Manual) does detail standard operating procedures and supervisory frameworks for closely monitoring investigations and prosecutions at multiple stages. However, over the years, the process has become slack and suffered a serious setback after the uniform supervisory structure was tinkered with. Poor leadership and the induction of senior supervisory officers with no prior DSPE or anticorruption investigation experience has further compounded the problem.

External accountability via the power of superintendence—whether exercised by the CVC or by the central government—remains nothing more than an academic exercise of periodical review. DSPE officers do remain accountable to courts of law; however, on account of inordinate investigation delays, overburdened courts, and delayed prosecutions, the courts have also failed to hold officers accountable in a timely fashion. Further, by the time the lapses in investigation, supervision, or prosecution are noticed, it is often too late to monitor or initiate any meaningful action against officers responsible for failures or omissions. Senior officers remain reluctant to initiate any remedial action, as the process could be cumbersome and unpleasant. Even the constitutional courts, which have occasionally stepped in to monitor investigations, have failed to remedy the problem.

The Supreme Court also had an opportunity to look into the accountability of investigation agencies. In *State of Gujarat v. Kishanbhai*,[30] dated 7 January 2014, it directed that:

> On the culmination of a criminal case in acquittal, the concerned investigating/prosecuting official(s) responsible for such acquittal must necessarily be identified. A finding needs to be recorded in each case, whether the lapse was innocent or blameworthy. Each erring officer must suffer the consequences of his lapse, by appropriate departmental action, whenever called for. Taking into consideration the seriousness of the matter, the concerned official may be withdrawn from investigative responsibilities, permanently or temporarily, depending purely on his culpability. We also feel compelled to require the adoption of some indispensable measures, which may reduce the malady suffered by parties on both sides of criminal litigation. Accordingly we direct the Home Department of every State Government, to formulate a procedure for taking action against all erring investigating/prosecuting officials/officers. All such erring officials/officers identified, as responsible for failure of a prosecution case, on account of sheer negligence or because of culpable lapses, must suffer departmental action. The above mechanism formulated would infuse seriousness in the performance of investigating and prosecuting duties, and would ensure that investigation and prosecution are purposeful and decisive. The instant direction shall also be given effect to within 6 months.

Though these directions were not specifically aimed at the CBI, the NIA, or other investigation agencies, they are equally applicable to them. It is not known whether any institutional arrangement has been put in place in either the CBI or the NIA to implement the Court's recommendations.

These internal and external controls have not worked well, evidenced by the fact that there have been several allegations about the objective functioning of the CBI and the NIA. In addition to rampant criticism about the DSPE succumbing to political pressure, the Supreme Court has also come down heavily on the functioning of the DSPE and the entire

CBI, labelling it a 'caged parrot' rather than an independent, objective investigation agency. The CBI has also been subject to severe criticism from the Indian bureaucracy for prosecuting public servants who enjoyed impeccable reputations before they were prosecuted or made scapegoats without evidence after allegedly unprofessional investigations. The DSPE, along with Courts and the Comptroller and Auditor General of India (CAG), has been accused of both avoiding making difficult decisions as well as being too independent and objective. The banking sector, in particular, has blamed DSPE investigations for tardiness in the loan sanction process, as even bona fide defaults on loan repayments have been subject to investigations for connivance and corruption. Much of this criticism has not been without reason. The standards of investigation and quality of supervision and prosecution have declined over recent years, leading to acquittals in many high-profile cases.

The DSPE, which is required to act as a vanguard in the fight against corruption, has not been able to perform its expected role. It is not adequately equipped in terms of personnel and domain experts to handle the increasing number of complex corruption cases. Its ability to perform has also been blunted by recent amendments to its governing laws, requiring it to seek prior permission to start an inquiry or investigation against a corrupt officer. With states able to withdraw their consent on a whim, the DSPE is hamstrung in its capacity to investigate even public servants of the central government or belonging central public sector units. Limiting their jurisdiction is a serious handicap to the DSPE's efficacy. Another challenge is cases being charge-sheeted after they have been taken over from State Police. After such a long interval, evidence tends to have disappeared by the time the DSPE moves in.

The DSPE has claimed significant conviction rates over the years, but this is mainly on account of smaller, less consequential cases. According to the CBI's 2018 annual report, 68 per cent of cases that went to trial ended in a conviction. However, this statistic could be misleading for a number of reasons: First, it does not take into account the number of individuals who are charge-sheeted and acquitted or discharged. Second, it does not include cases in which a higher court reversed the conviction upon appeal.

The NIA, immediately after its formation, was delegated many of the terrorism cases being investigated by the DSPE and State Police, including the Samjhauta Express attacks (2007), the Ajmer Dargah bombing (2007), the Mecca Masjid blast (2007), and the Malegaon bombings (2008). The investigation and prosecution of these cases, entrusted to the NIA after a long delay, have been subject to much criticism after all the accused in the Samjhauta Express and Mecca Masjid cases were acquitted by the trial court and only two accused were convicted in Ajmer Dargah bombing. The Malegaon case is still pending trial.

Other significant cases entrusted to and investigated by the NIA include the Maoist attack on Sukama district of Chhattisgarh (2013), the Bodh Gaya Temple Complex bombings (2013), the Dilsukhnagar twin blasts (2013), the Burdwan blast case (2014), the Uri attack (2016), the Pathankot Airbase attack (2016), the Jammu and Kashmir terror-funding case (2017), and the Pulwama attack that killed more than 40 Central Reserve Police Force personnel (2019). The Bodh Gaya Temple, Dilsukhnagar, and Burdwan cases have resulted in convictions. The others are either still under investigation or at trial. The first-ever case registered under the extra-territorial jurisdiction vested in the NIA was the 2020 attack on a Sikh gurudwara in Kabul, Afghanistan.

The NIA's history of successful investigations and prosecutions has been rather chequered. Even though it claims that more than 90 per cent of cases charge-sheeted have ended in conviction, the figure is likely misleading. To date, very few cases investigated by the NIA have resulted in a completed trial. And in many cases where convictions have been obtained, appeals filed by the convicted are yet to be heard.

A swirling controversy has embroiled the government of the day, which has questionably invoked provisions of the Unlawful Activities Prevention Act in order to entrust cases to the NIA rather than State Police. These actions have even been questioned by the courts. It is, without doubt, not a healthy practice and may bode poorly for the NIA's enduring credibility.

The unfortunate number of vacancies in various ranks across both the CBI and the NIA presents a serious challenge to the agencies' efficiency and must not be allowed to persist. The problem of vacancies has also spread over to senior ranks of SPs and DIGs in the past few years. This author has been an advocate of a system wherein the central government would finance a certain number of inspectors and DySPs in State Police investigation wings, and the states would be obligated to send an equivalent number of officers to the CBI and the NIA. These officers could revert back to the states after an interval of five or six years, carrying with them valuable investigative experience.

The new system of selection, as detailed previously, was intended to ensure the CBI's autonomy. Unfortunately, the mechanism has not delivered. It has clearly failed to ensure integrity, competence, or autonomy in the organization. Officers of questionable competence and integrity made the grade in the CBI, even at the level of director. Some recent directors inspired little confidence and now are themselves being investigated for corruption. Under their leadership, the CBI lost its direction, earning the dubious moniker of 'caged parrot'.

The internal vigilance system, intended to ensure that corrupt officers were identified and punished, was largely undermined. In certain cases, no action was taken against known rogue officers. The dilution of these time-tested internal checks and balances has led to questionable decisions about prosecutions and resulted in a number of embarrassing acquittals.

The credibility of any investigative organization is built and sustained on the competence of its human resources, the quality of its leadership, and its professionalism. In these areas, the CBI's standards have declined for many years, damaging its credibility. Fixing it will require major structural reforms.

One major hurdle is the new director selection process, especially in light of the recent amendment to the DSPE Act, which empowers the government to extend the director's initial tenure of two years by one year at a time, up to a total tenure of five years. The selection committee is unable to select the right candidate—out of many apparently qualified officers—for director in just an hour-long meeting. At present, members of the committees to select the director and other senior officers largely depend on annual performance appraisal reports and the traditional vetting process. Many officers posted often lack experience supervising investigations and do not possess the necessary qualities of a leader capable of making independent and objective decisions. The net result is poor supervision at the senior level, a steady decline in investigative standards, and slower, less efficient work.

The only way forward is to revamp the induction process. The selection committee chaired by the prime minister should be assisted by independent experts, who may be tasked with screening eligible officers and carrying out detailed background checks to evaluate their integrity and professional competence. The committee could shortlist four or five officers, rank them on merit, and recommend names to the selection committee, which can then interview shortlisted officers before making its choice.

Similarly, the CVC-led committee that selects supervisory officers should be assisted by a body of independent professionals. The expert panel may also consider the inputs of the CBI's internal vigilance unit. The selected senior officers must meet clearly defined standards of professional acumen. Officers who have distinguished themselves during a previous tenure in the CBI should be given preference. An analogous system should be installed to select the director and senior officers of the NIA.

Finally, investigations officers with experience and proven integrity, drawn from different state police forces, must be recruited into the organization, as they were earlier. These officers could revert back to the states, like IPS officers on deputation, after an interval of five to seven years.

Conclusion

No proposal to strengthen the CBI by giving it legal status as a federal investigation agency can succeed, as most states will not be willing to support any constitutional amendment that supersedes their exclusive jurisdiction. The only possible way to ensure the CBI has broad jurisdiction across India is to amend the Constitution of India to include the concept of federal offences and a central investigation agency or agencies in the Union List. These federal offences may include corruption by central government personnel and other public employees, as well as crimes involving internal security and that have interstate or transnational ramifications.

However, in order to ensure the integrity and autonomy of the CBI and the NIA, it is necessary to radically change the way senior officers are selected to ensure that only officers of integrity and proven professionalism are inducted. The directors of the CBI and the NIA must play an integral role on the committees that select senior officers—and they must also be held accountable to ensure high standards and objectivity across investigations.

At present, superintendence of the CBI is exercised by the CVC, Lokpal, and the central government, while the NIA is overseen by the central government and the courts (to whom any investigation agency is ultimately accountable). This multi-pronged approach to oversight has decidedly failed to ensure objective and professional conduct by the agencies. Therefore, there is a clear need to put in place an independent single body—consisting of domain experts, including those drawn from the CVC and Lokpal—to supervise the conduct of the central investigation agencies. This independent body may report to Parliament. To preserve the institutional integrity of the CBI and the NIA, measures must be put in place to strengthen internal checks and balances. Officers must be held accountable for inordinate delays and lapses in investigations or prosecutions. Finally, financial autonomy—apart from the tenure of officers—is essential for the organizations to implement their long-term visions and ultimately achieve their stated objectives.

Notes

1. Under the India and Burma (Emergency Provisions) Act, 1940 enacted on June 27, 1940 by the British Parliament.
2. Under the Emergency powers vested in the Governor General under Section 72 of the Ninth Schedule of the Government of India Act, 1935.
3. Since been restored in November 2019.
4. Since been restored in October 2022.
5. The following divisions were brought into existence: Investigation & Anti-Corruption Division (Delhi Special Police Establishment), Technical Division, Crime Records and Statistics Division (later this function was shifted to National Crime Record Bureau), Research Division (later this function was shifted to Bureau of Police Research & Development), Legal and General Division, and Administration Division.
6. List 1 of the Schedule 7 of the Constitution, known as Union List, entry 8 reads as Central Bureau of Intelligence and Investigation.
7. A.G. Noorani, "A Charter for the CBI," *The Hindu,* August 21, 2013, https://www.thehindu.com/opinion/lead/a-charter-for-the-cbi/article5042518.ece.
8. See Rajya Sabha, "24th Report on Working of Central Bureau of Investigation by Department Related Parliamentary Standing Committee on Personnel, Public Grievances, Law and Justice," March 11, 2008, https://emsnmp.files.wordpress.com/2015/05/working-of-central-bureau-of-investigation-cbi-click-here-open-file2.pdf.

9. *Navendra Kumar vs The Union of India & Ors* on November 6, 2013, W. A. No. 119 OF 2008 in W. P. (C) No. 6877 OF 200, https://ghconline.gov.in/Judgment/WA1192008.pdf.

10. *Navendra Kumar vs The Union of India & Ors.*

11. *Navendra Kumar vs The Union of India & Ors.*

12. *Navendra Kumar vs The Union of India & Ors.*

13. Para 4.7 (3) (i) of the Single Directive, as amended from time to time.

14. "Vineet Narain & Others vs Union of India & Another," 1 SCC 226 (1997).

15. "Dr. Subramanian Swamy vs. Director CBI & Another (Writ Petition (Civil))," No. 38 of 1997, 8 SCC 682 (6 May 2014).

16. Refer "CBI Annual Report, 2018."

17. See Para 4.11 of Eighth Report of Second Administration Reforms Commission, June 2008 on Combatting Terrorism.

18. Section 370 and 371 of Indian Penal Code.

19. Sub-section (1AA) of section 25 of Chapter V of the Arms Act, 1959 (54 of 1959).

20. Section 66F of Chapter XI of the Information Technology Act, 2000 (21 of 2000).

21. Criminal Writ Petition No. 4049 of 2012.

22. "People's Union for Civil Liberties vs Union of India" on December 16, 2003 (Writ Petition (Civil) 389 of 2002).

23. Since repealed.

24. "Kartar Singh vs. State of Punjab" on March 11, 1994 (1994 SCC (3) 569, JT 1994 (2) 423)

25. Nirupama Subramanian, "NIA Pushing Constitutional Limits, Chidambaram Told FBI," *The Hindu*, March 19, 2011, https://www.thehindu.com/news/the-india-cables/NIA-pushing-constitutional-limits-Chidambaram-told-FBI/article14953597.ece.

26. A short-lived Food Offences Wing was also added in 1964 to deal with the inter-state ramifications of food hoarding, black markets, smuggling, and profiteering, before it was merged with the Economic Offences Wing in 1968.

27. Refer to Section 4 of the DSPE Act.

28. Refer to Section 4 B of the DSPE Act.

29. This section draws on Navneet Rajan Wasan, "How to Rebuild the CBI," *Firstpost*, February 2, 2019, https://www.firstpost.com/india/how-to-rebuild-the-cbi-6010871.html.

30. Criminal Appeal No. 1485 of 2008.

Index